THE BELEAGUERED
PRESIDENCY

THE BELEAGUERED
PRESIDENCY

Aaron Wildavsky

Transaction Publishers
New Brunswick (U.S.A.) and London (U.K.)

Library of Congress Catalog Number: 90–46282
ISBN: 0–88738–401–3
Printed in the United States of America

Library of Congress Cataloging-in-Publication Data

Wildavsky, Aaron B.
    The beleaguered presidency / Aaron Wildavsky.
        p. cm.
    Includes bibliographical references and index.
    ISBN 0–88738–401–3
    1. Presidents—United States.   2. Political culture—United
States.   3. United States—Politics and government—1945–
I. Title.
JK511.W54 1991
353.03'13—dc20   90–46282
                                                                                CIP

Contents

Acknowledgments

Samantha Rosen, then a student at the Georgetown University Law Center, helped me in numerous ways. She brought the chapter on presidential succession and disability up to date. She discussed every chapter with me, making suggestions for deletions and additions, many of which I adopted. And she helped me understand what a younger generation wanted to know about the presidency and why. I am grateful for her insightful and enthusiastic contribution.

I owe a debt to the friends with whom I have discussed the presidency over the years—Dave Barber, Fred Greenstein, Nelson Polsby, Austin Ranney, Raymond Wolfinger, and James Young. The revisions, reformulations, and reconsiderations in this volume owe a great deal to their good sense and acute observation.

Students at Oberlin (1958–62), Berkeley (1963–88), and the Georgetown University Law Center (1989–90, on leave as Interdisciplinary Visiting Professor) have asked better questions than I could formulate answers. Over the years, as presidents have become more and more beleaguered, these students have asked for explanations. Why are presidents in trouble? Do they have too much power or too little? How, from day to day, can they appear alternately strong and weak? How come past presidents seem so much smarter than present presidents? The emphasis of this book on answers to such questions—most of what is usually found in a text on presidential power is here, when such information is necessary to help solve a problem—I owe to my students.

If any group of people is more perplexed than students it is their parents, who remember a time when presidents were mostly admired and only sometimes beleaguered, instead of the reverse. Where, they want to know when I talk about the presidency, have all the good presidents gone? *The Beleaguered Presidency* is for them, too.

Introduction

In rereading and reworking these essays, which constitute the second volume of my collected papers, I was struck by their consistent theme: the presidency is in trouble, for criticism was rising and approval declining, while demands were impossible to meet. At first, I thought the problems were inherent in the nature of events. History was giving recent presidents a bum rap. Problems were harder to solve. Constituencies made contradictory demands that could not all be met. Perhaps some of the aberrations of presidential behavior, from Lyndon Johnson in Vietnam to Richard Nixon in Watergate to Jimmy Carter in micromanagement, were due not entirely to their defects but were forced on them by their political environments.

As time passed, however, I began to believe that events cannot force themselves on our consciousness. It is human beings and they alone who are the active organizers of their perceptions, not events or things. Absent force by other human beings, there had to be another explanation. After all, these presidents did many good things, from the opening to China (Nixon) to major (and long overdue) civil rights legislation (Johnson). Why, then, the uniformly negative tone toward them?

Briefly, I was attracted to what were called "new class" explanations. For some reason, a segment of the middle and upper-middle class—information specialists and professionals of various kinds—had set itself up in opposition to established authority. Its interests were self-serving (fame, income, environmental protection against upstarts), all the more insidious for being hidden. Soon, however, this class explanation began to pale. Why people who were generally better off would want to do this was never stated. Why would wordsmiths bite the hand off of which they fed? And why were other people, similarly situated, like me, opposed to their views? Gradually I became interested in explanations in which culture was used as a synonym for a way of life. The question that appealed to me was:

What sort of people, organizing themselves into which ways of life (that is sharing values that justify corresponding sets of social relations), would want to subject people in authority, especially presidents, to ceaseless criticism in order to do what every group must, namely, support its way of life and denigrate others?

Cultural answers to this supremely political question appealed to me because they made sense out of my observation and reading: People who prefer a hierarchical social order might be punitive or secretive, but the last thing they would do is tear down authority. Scratch one. Fatalists do not launch campaigns; it takes too much effort and no reason to believe it will pay off. Fatalists are in the mode of accepting or avoiding, not criticizing, authority. Down two. Hermits who inhabit the contemplative culture are in the business of observing the world, not changing it. Hermits extinguish desire; they do not fan the flames of controversy. Three gone. Individualists might fit the bill because they seek to substitute self-regulation for authority. But these competitive individualists are pro, not anticapitalist; they criticize socialism, not capitalism.

It makes social sense for egalitarians to criticize leadership because they regard followership as a form of subordination (i.e., of inequality). Converted by the civil rights movement into belief in greater equality of condition, training its adherents to spur and spawn other egalitarian movements—women's rights, gay rights, children's rights, animal rights—they attack existing authority as a sign of their opposition to inequality. Put in cultural terms, egalitarians oppose hierarchies because of their coerciveness, and they oppose individualism because it generates inequality.

In our time, the egalitarian attack on authority takes on two characteristic forms: environmental safety (corporate capitalism causes cancer)[1] and governmental immorality (hidden hierarchies).[2] Here, I am concerned with attacks on presidents as the most visible symbol of public authority in the United States.

Of course, not everyone agrees that presidents are under attack. If you feel that a president deserves far more censure than he gets, then he is never criticized enough, no matter how severe the attack. My claim is that the Johnson presidency (1963–1968) ushered in a quantum increase of criticism amplified through the media. This was the time during which press conferences became battle grounds, reporters exposed rather than excused personal misbehavior, the networks started contradicting presidential addresses as soon as they were made, and politicians in general became fair game.

When I say that the presidency has become beleaguered, which the *Random House Thesaurus* defines as "to harass, badger, assail, vex, bombard, besiege, and plague," I intend its primary meaning: under perpetual assault. I do not say and do not mean that the presidency has become less important or that presidents are less powerful than they used to be. Not at all. The continuing increase in the size and scope of the federal government means that its importance to citizens and foreigners has grown. Thus more individuals and groups and nations want presidential support than ever before.

The first chapter, " 'Greatness' Revisited" (with Richard Ellis), applies cultural theory to the behavior of presidents from Washington through Lincoln, with analogies to recent presidents. It clues us in to the importance of how presidents resolve the dilemmas with which they are confronted. The problems of presidents and parties of different cultural persuasions are not at all the same. How to lead when one's party is opposed to leadership is quite different from leading a hierarchical party amidst a largely nonhierarchical people. If our presidents keep failing us, what exactly is the nature of the problem they cannot solve?

Before I became aware of the trends animating this series of essays, I thought presidents did better in foreign, as opposed to domestic, policy. This contention spawned a critical literature that continues to this day. As Duane Oldfield and I argue in our review of the evidence, the 1950s, which provided the backdrop for the "two presidencies" thesis, is a misleading decade. It was literally the calm before the storm. Things have not been the same since, not for the American people or for political activists or for presidents. Closing on a cultural note, we attribute the by-now familiar picture of beleaguered presidents to the growth of political dissensus—opposing views not only on domestic and foreign policy but also on environmental and safety matters and social issues—based on conflict between (largely Democratic) egalitarians and (largely Republican) individualists and hierarchists. or, in common parlance, between economic and social conservatives.

"The Past and Future Presidency" begins to grapple with the phenomena of presidents under constant attack. It seeks to show how cultural conflict over authority is played out in the presidency. The "past" refers to the time when presidents (Roosevelt, Truman, Eisen-hower, Kennedy) appeared to me (and, much more important, to them) to have a chance to do well. The "future" refers to the time we are living through, in which presidents seek to adapt to their slim chances of leaving office with their reputations intact. One such device is to concentrate on a few major policy matters, putting the rest, as the next essay says, on "automatic pilot." A different way of reducing expo-sure is to keep the reins of government in the hands of a small number of presidential friends. (To avoid suspense, I have in mind the Bush administration.) Yet another strategy is to encourage a crisis atmosphere (over the environment, competitiveness, the deficit, AIDS), so as to encourage reliance on presidents who promote policies of prevention. If planet earth is in danger, who but the "prophylactic presidency" could come to the rescue?

Presidential elections also serve as an arena for carrying on cultural conflict. The emergence of a Republican party opposed to govern-ment is explored in "The Party of Government, the Party of Opposi-tion, and the Party of Balance." Criteria were set up in 1980 to deter-mine whether the Reagan administration was a party of opposition. Yes, it turned out to be, but, to anticipate, the Republican Bush ad-ministration is not.

The other side of the presidential coin involves the question of why the Democratic party keeps losing presidential elections. "The Turtle Theory" argues that white Christian working men reacted against egali-tarian efforts to reduce their power while increasing their taxes by voting Republican.

My earliest interest in party change came from studies of national nominating conventions. The last old-style convention took place in 1960, when I studied the Ohio Democratic delegation and discovered the textbook-writers delight, moderate liberals interested in forming a victorious electoral coalition and sharing in the benefits afterwards. Conventions have not stopped changing since.

By 1964 the Republican convention was radically different. Domi-nated by supporters of Barry Goldwater, its delegates were more inter-ested in living up to their conservative (individualist and hierarchical) ideology than in living in the White House.[3] I called them purists because winning office did not come first with them; only later did I realize that I had witnessed the resurgence of cultural politics. This feeling was confirmed by my study of the symbolism surrounding the

1968 Democratic convention.[4] Upset by the beating taken by my political hero, Hubert Humphrey, which gave the election to Richard Nixon, I thought the Democrats had evolved their own purists, a feeling confirmed by their nomination of George McGovern in 1972. I was closer but not yet fully appreciative of the movement into the Democratic party from 1964 on of egalitarian activists. For Republicans and (from 1968 on) for Democrats, cultural activists increasingly dominated the major parties. While most observers figured that the crushing presidential election defeats of McGovern in 1972 and Goldwater in 1964 meant the end of their party factions, these observers confused the party in the mind of the people with the much smaller but more influential cadres of activists. It is the Democratic and Republican losers of 1972 and 1964 respectively that have taken over their parties. Party activists were growing more distant from (a) their voters and (b) each other.[5] It is in the context of ideological dissensus expressing deep cultural conflict that analyses of the Nixon, Reagan, and Bush presidencies should be considered.

Looking back is a lot easier than looking forward. Professor Hindzeit is smarter than the rest of us. "Richard Nixon, President of the United States" is a tongue-in-cheek title meant to disarm his many opponents who thought he had no chance to become president because they thought he shouldn't. I present it exactly as published, to preserve both the correct predictions and the ones that went awry, especially these concerning party spats. At that time I did not understand that rather than splitting apart, the Democratic and Republican parties were actually changing their characters while retaining their names, each becoming what it was before, only more so—the Democrats more egalitarian and the Republicans more individualistic and hierarchical. Perhaps the greatest barrier to contemporary understanding of party politics, and hence policy politics, is that the continuity of names implies a continuity of content. As far as party activists are concerned, the Republican party of Eisenhower and Rockefeller, and the Democratic party of Truman and Humphrey are no more.

My "Sermon on Watergate" is hard on Nixon. I still feel that way. Concerned about the incessant attacks on American authority, (believing it to be imperfect but far superior to the then-existing alternatives) and beginning to understand that there were systemic forces at work, I reacted strongly, not so much to the break-in at the Watergate, aptly termed a third-rate burglary, but to the seemingly endless cover-ups. Watergate decreased the legitimacy of our political institutions. I might add that this chapter is about Watergate, not the Nixon presidency as a whole. Had I attempted such a task, President Nixon would have fared considerably better. Indeed, it may be, as Martin Anderson wrote in an Op-Ed column, that the Nixon foreign policy, with its opening to China and its détente with the Soviet Union, kept the peace long enough for the policy of containment to work.

Written before and published soon after Carter became president, "Jimmy Carter's Theory of Governing" (with Jack Knott) could just as well be read as an epitaph on his administration. Spotting some suggestive remarks in a couple of Carter's speeches, I had Jack Knott, then a graduate student, check out whether the candidate actually was a believer in management science doctrine. I knew that acting out this doctrine, which held that implementation of policy did not require political agreement, was incompatible with presidential leadership in a separation of powers system. Carter did not do brilliantly, in my estimation, but he did a lot better than he was credited with doing, which is to say that the Carter administration was far from the helpless bunch of incompetents it was pictured as being.

The title of chapter 12, "Ronald Reagan as a Political Strategist," is meant as a direct challenge to the common portrayal of him—not to put too fine a point on it—as ignorant and foolish. I have also interpolated into this essay a smaller one, "The Triumph of Ronald Reagan," to present a panoramic portrait of a leader who moved his nation in his desired direction. Where Jimmy Carter envisaged the national government as a hierarchy in which he was the Chief Hierarch, Ronald Reagan thought it was composed of congeries of groups, some sympathetic but most opposed, that his administration would have to win over or override. Since this is the only analysis that credits Reagan with outthinking his opponents, I have added criticism of his operation in the Iran-Contra affair and a critique of my criticism by James David Barber.

With Lyndon Johnson forced to drop out of the presidential race, Richard Nixon impeached, Gerald Ford unable to suceed himself, and Ronald Reagan nearly brought down by the Iran-Contra affair, it seems only natural to follow with a study of presidential succession and disability (with Samantha Rosen). We may need it sooner than we think.

Presidents come and go but the presidency lives on. Proposals for reform of the presidency are both interesting in their own right and reveal how the institution works. Whenever a change is proposed, the originators, in order to defend their ideas, must specify the causal connections between them and the good consequences they believe will flow once their proposals are enacted. Thus the reform process opens a window into diverse conceptions of how our institutions work. The problems of determining presidential succession and overcoming presidential disability challenge our ingenuity, compel us to articulate our basic values, and provide pictures of how knowledgeable people believe our institutions work. Proposals for direct election of the president, by abolishing the electoral college, deserve analysis because they bring out basic beliefs about how our government should be constituted.

"The Human Side of Government," a preface to a book of essays by people in government under a Republican president, many of whom feel hurt because they did not get the support to which they felt their loyalty to Reagan's views entitled them, explains why, under a separation of powers system like ours, presidents cannot be regarded as reservoirs of power. Appointees are expendable, and because they are human, they are hurt. But as Mafia chieftains are reported to say before dispatching those who chose the wrong side, it's not personal, just business. As a former department chair and dean, I tell those who aspire to such positions that as soon as they begin to feel that life is unfair and that their colleagues are ungrateful, it is time to quit. The rewards are all in the next world. The same goes for presidential appointees.

The most difficult president to understand is George Bush. Without apparent ideology (other than a mild conservatism), with no apparent coherence in policy, we are left with a passion for friendship and an ability to lie low. Kerry Mullins and I specify the complaints against Bush—but we also try to make sense of his behavior through a cultural analysis. Once we understand the overriding emphasis President Bush places on process rather than policy, his behavior becomes much more understandable. Sufficient time has elapsed (Bush has been president for two years) for the early view that this experienced and flexible politician would escape being beleaguered to be proven erroneous.

In conclusion, I would like to state my position on recent proposals to limit presidents to a single six-year term. The idea is to prevent presidents from acting politically by preventing them from succeeding themselves. From this the reader may gather that I am not a big fan of the limitations of presidents to two terms: all it does is make presidents lame ducks in their second terms. Taking presidents out of politics, in my estimation, would be like depriving people of oxygen to help them breathe. Though some of us feel some of the time that presidents are too responsive to public pressures, their responsiveness is our guarantee of democracy. If limiting the time a president could spend in office was a good one, we would find presidents performing more effectively in their second term, when they can no longer succeed themselves than in their first. This thesis would be hard to prove with Nixon (Watergate) or Reagan (Iran-Contra). Our task as a free people is to make democracy work, not abandon it. I feel the same about current efforts (fall, 1990) to limit legislative terms.

Notes

1. See Mary Douglas and Aaron Wildavsky, *Risk and Culture* (Berkeley: University of California Press, 1982).
2. Aaron Wildavsky, "The Three Cultures: Explaining Anomalies in the American Welfare State," *Public Interest,* no. 69 (Fall 1982): 45–58.
3. Aaron Wildavsky, "The Goldwater Phenomenon: Purists, Politicians and the Two-Party System," *Review of Politics* 27, no. 3 (July 1965): 386–413.
4. Aaron Wildavsky, "The Meaning of 'Youth' in the Struggle for Control of the Democratic Party," in *Revolt Against the Masses and Other Essays* (New York: Basic Books, 1971), 270–87.
5. See the evidence cited in Nelson W. Polsby and Aaron Wildavsky, *Presidential Elections,* 7th ed. (New York: Charles Scribner's Sons, 1988), 127–42.

1

"Greatness" Revisited: Evaluating the Performance of American Presidents in Terms of Cultural Dilemmas

With Richard Ellis

What is the mark of a "great" president? Will George Bush be inducted into this select class? If not a great, then how about a near-great president? Or will he be remembered as merely average, or worse still, a failure? Does he deserve a ranking higher or lower than Ronald Reagan? Jimmy Carter? Lyndon Johnson? Dwight Eisenhower? Harry Truman? How does his performance compare with that of James Madison, John Tyler, or Andrew Jackson?

Polling a panel of "experts" has become the accepted way of rendering history's judgment of presidential performance. The presidential greatness game began in earnest in 1948, when Arthur Schlesinger asked fifty-five prominent historians to grade our past presidents: A signified Great; B, Near Great; C, Average; D, Below Average; and E, Failure. Believing there to be wisdom in numbers, subsequent surveys have expanded the panel of experts from 571 in 1970 to 953 in 1983.[1]

The practice of evaluating presidential performance by polling historians is a curious one. Characteristically, surveys are conducted to obtain information about the respondent, either in the form of preferences—which candidate or party do you prefer?—or beliefs about the empirical world—how many members are in the House of Representatives? We do not as a rule conduct surveys to gauge the validity of a claim. Why, then, do we do so with respect to presidential performance? The answer is that we lack agreed-upon criteria for making these judgments. If we had accepted criteria, surveys would be superfluous (and subject to corroboration); we would need only to check presidential performance against the established yardsticks.

While these surveys have yielded interesting information about the respondents—Murray and Blessing's poll, for instance, finds that American historians specializing in women's studies hold George Washington in much lower esteem than the sample as a whole—they are not a good tool to evaluate presidential performance. There is no reason to think the mean judgment of 1,000 historians more valid than the estimate of a single scholar specializing in past presidents. Insofar as our aim is to compare the performances of presidents rather than gather information about the pollees, energies should be directed to devising appropriate criteria for evaluating performance.

The original Schlesinger survey completely sidestepped the issue of criteria to be used in appraising presidential performance. The only instructions in the first poll were that "the test in each case is *performance in office*, omitting anything done before or after."[2] How one was to gauge the performance in office was left unspecified. In the absence of such criteria, the finding that president X ranked higher than president Y was difficult to interpret.

In *Presidential Greatness*, Stephen Bailey attempted to remedy this deficiency by identifying criteria by which presidents could be measured. He came up with forty-three yardsticks for measuring presidential greatness: achievement, administrative capacity, appointees, blunders, eloquence, industriousness, scandals, sensitivity, and many more.[3] If the Schlesinger survey suffered from a lack of guidelines as to the unit of comparability, the surfeit of tests devised by Bailey left the reader with a commendably broader view of the many facets of the presidency, but equally helpless. By including everything and excluding nothing, we were no better than before at evaluating presidential performance.

Often the standard of presidential greatness employs measures such as amount of legislation passed, activity in office, or number of objectives pursued. But these criteria create a pronounced bias toward activist presidents, as indicated by Schlesinger's conclusion that the 1962 survey showed that average or mediocre presidents "believed in negative government, in self-subordination to the legislative power."[4] Why should a contemporary activist view—the presidency is best that adds functions to government and/or the presidency—be a standard for scholars?

Though acutely aware of the limitations of presidential ratings as presently conducted, we do not accept the claim that "comparing eminent figures is only a game," or that "each [president] operated within a unique political environment."[5] By taking aim at the easy target of presidential ratings, attention is deflected away from what we contend is a more significant defect—the tendency to wrap each president and his times in a unique cocoon, thereby reducing the study of the presidency to political biography. The result, as James McGregor Burns correctly pointed out two decades ago, is that "We know everything about the Presidents and nothing about the Presidency."[6] It would be both ironic and unfortunate for the most well-known effort to compare presidencies to discredit the laudable, indeed essential, goal of making comparisons among administrations. The presidential greatness game remains popular precisely because it holds up the tantalizing prospect of comparing presidencies. Our aim is to do just that.

Resolving Cultural Dilemmas: A Mark of Greatness

All presidents face cultural dilemmas, albeit of different kinds and intensities. Their ability to.resolve these dilemmas, we believe, provides a criterion for evaluating their performance. Our hypothesis is that presidencies can be evaluated in terms of dilemmas confronted, evaded, created, or overcome. "Great" presidents are those who provide solutions to culturally induced dilemmas.

By political culture we do not mean national customs. Nor are cultures countries. All those residing in America are not, as we use the term, adherents of the same political culture. Rather, we analyze politics from a perspective of cultural dissensus, *i.e.*, the conflict between cultures or ways of life. We posit the existence of three competing political cultures: hierarchical, individualist, and egalitarian.[7] The type of leadership preferred and feared, and the kinds of support given to, and demands made upon, leaders vary according to political culture.

The individualist regime is organized to maximize the scope of individual autonomy and thus minimize the need for authority. Individualist regimes perform delicate balancing acts between having leaders when they want them and getting rid of them when they do not. Ideally, they give up only as much autonomy as the immediate engagement requires. Individualists dread most the leader who overstays his welcome. Adherents of individualist regimes know that from the leader flows the hierarchy, and among its multitudinous ranks are found policemen and tax collectors. Not wanting the one, they choose not to have the other any longer than absolutely necessary. Following Groucho Marx, they believe that any leader strong enough to help them is too strong to be trusted.

Egalitarians are dedicated to diminishing differences among people. Would-be egalitarian leaders are thus in trouble before they start, for authority is a prima-facie instance of inequality. Followership, to egalitarians, implies subordination of one person to another. If they push themselves forward, attempting to lead rather than merely convening or facilitating discussion, leaders will be attacked for attempting to lord it over others. Aspiring leaders must therefore dissemble, at once persuasive about the right course to follow and self-effacing, as if they were not leading at all.

Exercising leadership in a hierarchical regime is much easier. Prospective leaders are expected to lead; authority inheres in position. The regime that guides and constrains them gives consistent advice: leadership is necessary and, therefore, should be supported. Fearing disorder, hierarchies shore up authority in every way they can. While sharing in the credit, leaders are generally absolved from blame. Differences in prestige or privilege that accompany positions of authority in a hierarchy are legitimized by the greater sacrifices required of the superior in the name of the whole. Errors are attributed to the deviance of subordinates. Because they give so much backing to leaders, however, hierarchies fear the charismatic leader who, instead of working through the hierarchy and obeying its notions of reciprocal restraints, substitutes himself for the law, thereby breaking down all previous distinctions.

Cultural theory is not a substitute for historical analysis. The instruments of policy emerge in interaction with historical experience. Believing that government was a source of inequality, for instance, egalitarians in the early republic sought to limit the central government's ability to interfere with the natural equality generated by American conditions. After the rise of corporate capitalism and the depression of the 1930s, by contrast, egalitarians came to believe that the national government was a potential source of greater equality. Historical experience had altered their beliefs about the desirability of government action, but their objective—increased equality—remained the same. Similarly, the Federalist alliance of individualism and hierarchy wanted a more active national government to counter egalitarian tendencies; in the modern era, however, their Republican successors have sought a less interventionist government because of a belief that it would engage in redistributive policies.

America has been characterized by relatively strong individualism, weak hierarchy, and waxing and waning egalitarianism. This means exactly what Alexis de Tocqueville and Louis Hartz and Samuel Huntington have said it does: support for authority is relatively weak in America.[8] With egalitarians rejecting authority, individualists trying to escape from it, and hierarchical forces too weak to impose it, presidents seeking to rely on formal authority alone are in a precarious position. This antiauthority cultural context justifies Richard Neustadt's emphasis on persuasion,[9] for that is what presidents must do when they cannot rely on the authority inherent in their position.

National political parties, like other complex social organizations, are composed of more than one political culture. The Democratic party under Andrew Jackson, for example, constituted an alliance of individualism and egalitarianism. United by its opposition to hierarchy, this coalition was virulently antiauthority. The Jacksonian alliance was kept together by a belief that minimal government intervention in individual lives would increase equality of condition. Despite their shared distrust of hierarchy, however, the individualist alliance with egalitarianism is problematic, for individualists may find egalitarian opposition to inequality constrains their preference for personal gain through risk taking.

Joint rule by individualism and hierarchy, a cultural combination known in current parlance as "the establishment," is an option open to those individualists who find the alliance with egalitarianism undesirable. Individualists get sufficient order to carry on bidding and bargaining, while hierarchy gains the growth and flexibility it might otherwise lack. Despite these mutual benefits, the establishment alliance, too, suffers from disagreements. If individualists find the egalitarian benchmark of equality of conditions constricting, they may also be frustrated by hierarchy's penchant for rules and regulations.

The following examples are drawn from a larger project that applies this cultural analysis to all presidents from Washington through Lincoln. We have focused on early presidents in part because the passions of yesteryear have cooled sufficiently so that these presidencies are more likely to be treated dispassionately. Were we concerned with evaluating the performance of recent presidents, we fear that disagreement with the policies of these presidents would interfere with the purpose of evaluating and comparing presidencies. To those who doubt this proposition, we remind them of the angry reaction that Carter's low ranking in a recent greatness poll drew from Atlanta Mayor Andrew Young, who accused the raters of "insensitive elitism."[10] Speaking ill of John Adams or James Polk, we trust, will not engender the same reaction.

Four Great Presidents:
Washington, Jefferson, Jackson, and Lincoln

We propose two primary categories of cultural dilemmas. The first involves the president with some blend of egalitarian and individualist cultural propensities. All Jeffersonian and Jacksonian presidents labored, with varying degrees of success, to square their own and their followers' antiauthority principles with the exercise of executive authority. The second type is the president of hierarchical cultural propensities. While the precise contours of the dilemma varied with the historical situation and configuration of cultures, all hierarchical presidents struggled, in one form or another, to reconcile their, and their party's, hierarchical cultural preferences with the antihierarchical ethos dominant in the society and polity. This conflict animated the presidencies of George Washington, John Adams, and John Quincy Adams, as well as hamstringing Whig leaders such as Henry Clay and Daniel Webster, who aspired to the presidency. Thomas Jefferson and Andrew Jackson provided solutions to cultural dilemmas of the first type, George Washington and Abraham Lincoln to the second type.

George Washington

President-raters agree that George Washington was a great president. But wherein lies Washington's greatness? Stripping away the myths surrounding "the godlike Washington" has left the basis of his preeminence unclear. If, as Marcus Cunliffe concludes, he was "a good man, not a saint; a competent soldier, not a great one; an honest administrator, not a statesman of genius!" what made him "an exceptional figure?"[11] How can good, competent, and honest—a characterization that well describes Jimmy Carter—add up to a great president?

The deepest fear of an individualist political culture, we have suggested, is the leader who overstays his welcome. Acutely conscious of this fear, Washington continually reassured his countrymen of his desire to step down immediately after he had completed his assigned task. Before assuming command of the Revolutionary armies, he told the Continental Congress that he harbored "no lust for power." In a letter to the governors of the states upon the disbanding of the army, Washington insisted that he had no wish to "share in public business hereafter," longing only for "the shade of retirement."[12] Both as general and as president he repeatedly declared his aversion to the glare of public life and his preference for "the shadow of my own vine and my own fig tree."[13] While Washington's public pronouncements were ideally suited to alleviate the prevalent fears of power, it was his actions—twice retiring from the most powerful office in the land—that brought him the country's highest accolades.

By voluntarily relinquishing power and spurning offers to make his leadership permanent, Washington became the paragon of individualist political leadership. "Commitment to a political culture," Barry Schwartz argues, "showed up in the form of devotion to a man." Washington's self-denying behavior made him a "visible symbol" of individualist values and tendencies.[14] In being good he thus became great. That Washington was revered for leaving office did not, however, guarantee support when he was in office.

As president, Washington's cultural dilemma was that he was a president primarily of hierarchical propensities[15] in a society where individualism was predominant. With severe limits on the substance of power, Washington had to make do with the appearance of power. Painfully aware of the revolutionary bias against central rule, Washington carefully nurtured the new government's reputation. Before announcing federal appointments, for instance, he sought assurances that the nominee would accept in order to avoid the government being embarrassed by a candidate refusing to serve.[16]

Where he could, Washington presided over compromises that would create agreement among disputatious factions that he could neither control nor overawe. Unseemly disagreements among elites, he believed, undermined respect for authority, a proposition confirmed again by public dismay over disagreement about measures for reducing the budget deficit. Washington supported funding of the debt because he was persuaded by his experience under the Articles of Confederation that financial solvency was essential to gaining the respect of foreign governments and the domestic population. Rather than ask whether Hamilton's financial schemes were equitable—as Madison and Jefferson did—Washington asked whether they would contribute to the prestige of the central government.

Washington tried to enhance the government's image of competence and strength by employing federal power where it was not merely adequate to the purpose but overwhelming, as in the Whiskey Rebellion. So anxious were Hamilton and Washington to demonstrate federal authority that the military force they gathered to put down the local rebellion rivaled the total fighting force of the entire Revolutionary army. Beneath the impressive appearance of strength lurked the government's thinly disguised weakness, for the massive military force was not a well-trained national standing army, but rather a disorganized conglomeration of state militias.

It was in the realm of foreign relations that Washington was most successful in avoiding the embarrassments that might discredit central authority. The first president's foreign policy resolved the dilemma of a hierarchical regime in a nonhierarchical context by combining a commitment to a strong central government with an appreciation for the limits of authority in America.

National defense had been a compelling argument for jettisoning the Articles of Confederation in favor a stronger central government.[17] But having ceded the authority they believed necessary to secure the nation from attack, individualists and egalitarians were loathe to further extend its scope. Hoping to minimize the need for authority, Jefferson and his followers were driven constantly to downplay the threat posed by foreign nations. Great Britain, argued William Branch Giles on the House floor, was a dying hierarchy "tottering under the weight of a King, a Court, a nobility, a priesthood, armies, navies, debts, and all the complicated machinery of oppression."[18] The Federalists, in contrast, wishing to promote hierarchical relations domestically, continually played up threats from abroad.

When Citizen Edmond Genet arrived in the United States in the spring of 1793 as a special emissary from the newly proclaimed Republic of France, he was greeted with enthusiastic popular applause. Having declared itself at war with all European monarchies, France hoped that sending Genet to America would promote American support for the cause of "liberty, equality and fraternity." Republicans adopted the French Revolution as akin to their own. "The liberty of the whole earth," gushed Jefferson, hinged on the success of the French armies. Fearing that popular enthusiasm might sweep an unprepared nation into a holy war on behalf of liberty and equality, Washington responded by issuing a Proclamation of Neutrality.[19]

Popular antipathy toward the British was subsequently fanned by news that Britain had seized 250 unsuspecting and unarmed American ships in the West Indies. The Republican press urged retaliation; war seemed imminent. Federalists, though anxious to avoid war with Britain, were nonetheless determined that the nation be adequately prepared for that eventuality. Hamilton and his allies in Congress pressed for increased taxes and strengthened armed forces. While Republicans in Congress were eager to adopt a hard line with respect to commercial restrictions against the British, they still refused to support efforts to strengthen national defense.

Given the opposition's reluctance to support a build-up in national defense, Washington correctly perceived that involvement in European affairs was likely to result in a humiliated national government. Washington's Farewell Address provided a creative solution to this dilemma. It disarmed the Republican opposition by echoing the familiar warning against "entangling alliances." Republicans could see in these words an affirmation of their isolationism. In the Republican view, European struggles were to be avoided because power politics was the road to corruption, executive aggrandizement, and standing armies.

Washington's motivation for warning against becoming embroiled in foreign disputes was radically different. He feared that the new nation, through misfortune or ideological fervor, would be drawn into a war that would thoroughly discredit the new national government. Once the revolutionary "infancy" had passed and the people had gotten over their hostility to standing armies, executive power, central government, taxation, and debt, then and only then, Washington believed, would America be able to throw itself onto the global scales of power and assume a leading position in the world of nations.[20] In the absence of public support for peace-time preparations, Washington avoided committing American military forces to ventures that might expose the weakness beneath the carefully cultivated appearance of strength.

So successful was Washington at substituting the appearance of power for the reality of power that his successor, John Adams, was left with the erroneous impression that the president operated in a hierarchical political system. Where Washington, recognizing that hierarchy was weak in America, carefully nurtured support for authority, Adams assumed that support for authority inhered in position. The president, in Adams's view, had only to announce the correct decision and others would obey. His Solomon-like pronouncement in early 1799 to reopen negotiations with the French, throwing his party into total disarray, reflected his vision of the president as perched atop a hierarchical structure, responsible for keeping the peace by arbitrating between the parts in the name of the whole. Not having consulted anyone prior to announcing his decision, no one had a stake in defending it. Long-time congressional supporters of the president hurled abuse at Adams; cabinet members ran for cover, assuring friends that they had no part in the "insane" action.

Adams's son, John Quincy Adams, was no better at reconciling his own hierarchical dispositions with the antiauthority bias of the political system. His presidency was severely hampered by a refusal to exploit patronage to advance his policy objectives. Believing policy to be agreed upon, and implementation a matter of neutral competence, Adams viewed his subordinates as above or apart from politics. Consequently, he was unwilling to dismiss those whom he considered qualified, even if, as in the case of the postmaster general John McLean, they dispensed patronage to Adams's opponents. It is no coincidence that John Quincy Adams, like John Adams, or, for that matter, Jimmy Carter, lasted only a single term in the presidency. These presidents were hierarchists without a hierarchy, *i.e.*, hierarchically disposed leaders unable or unwilling to make allowances for the antileadership nature of the American political system.

Thomas Jefferson

With Thomas Jefferson's election in 1800, Jeffersonian Republicans (a fusion of egalitarianism and individualism) faced the task of reconciling their deep suspicion of authority with the exercise of executive power. Jefferson's dilemma, as Lance Banning phrases it, was "to govern in accordance with an ideology that taught that power was a monster and governing was wrong."[21] Aware that overt displays of presidential leadership were likely to raise the cry of executive usurpation, Jefferson opted for a covert leadership style. Dumas Malone, Jefferson's biographer, finds his protagonist always making a "conscious effort to avoid all appearances of dictation." The key to Jefferson's political leadership, continues Malone, was that "he did not permit his followers to think of him as a boss at all."[22] He led without appearing to do so, instructed while appearing only to suggest, guiding while seeming to defer.

Jefferson's informal influence was carefully concealed behind a public facade of deference to Congress. In a formal reply to notification of his election, Jefferson vowed to be "guided by the wisdom and patriotism of those to whom it belongs to express the legislative will of the nation [and] . . . give to that will a faithful execution." His first presidential address opened by referring to Congress respectfully as "the great council" of the nation and closed with a pledge to "carry . . . the legislative judgement . . . into faithful execution."[23] Indeed, Jefferson's decision to submit the annual message in writing rather than deliver it in person—a practice that many Republicans viewed as aping the British custom of having the monarch speak to Parliament in person—was calculated to underline executive subordination to the legislative branch. Despite this formal acquiescence to Congress hegemony in policymaking, virtually all important legislation during Jefferson's tenure originated in the executive branch.

While Jefferson's messages politely suggested only the broad outlines of a program, he swiftly followed these up with private communications to legislative leaders specifying the policy in detail. It was not unusual for Jefferson to actually draft the bill himself and then send his draft to influential and sympathetic members of Congress. Jefferson always impressed upon his congressional confidants the value of keeping his leadership of Congress hidden from public view, often asking the member to copy and then burn or return the original.[24]

Jefferson's nightly dinners provided a regular opportunity to build sympathy for himself and his legislative program without appearing to issue commands. The table at these small, informal gatherings was circular, in order to break down hierarchical distinctions and facilitate an air of collegiality. It was the rare dinner guest, notes historian Robert Johnstone, who could "withstand entirely the seductive force of the president's personality."[25]

Jefferson's distaste for public confrontation was expressed by one of his favorite maxims: "Take things always by their smooth handle." Like Dwight Eisenhower, the "hidden-hand" president he so much resembles, Jefferson would not publicly challenge even the most abusive of opponents. When John Randolph recklessly abused and vilified the administration, Jefferson responded, as did Eisenhower to McCarthy, by privately undercutting rather than publicly attacking his adversary.[26]

Jefferson's relations with his department heads displayed the same emphasis on persuasion, conciliation, and discussion that characterized his leadership of the Republican party in Congress. Cabinet members were treated as peers rather than subordinates. "By conversing and reasoning," claimed Jefferson, the Cabinet "scarcely ever failed . . . so to modify each other's ideas, as to produce a unanimous result." In fact, however, as Johnstone makes clear, Jefferson "dominated their collective proceedings and insured his final authority."[27] By leading consensually, the act of leadership—setting the agenda and making decisions—was disguised.

Jefferson's hidden-hand leadership style resolved the dilemma of leadership in an antileadership culture for himself but failed to educate his followers on the need for leadership. Jefferson's successors, Madison and Monroe, who lacked his skill, stature, or luck, were consequently unable to provide much in the way of presidential leadership. Hidden-hand leadership, as Madison soon discovered, was particularly ill-suited to preparing for and fighting a war. With the disastrous setbacks of the War of 1812 fresh in their minds, Madison and then Monroe attempted, with more success than is commonly acknowledged, to modify the dominant cultural coalition in a less virulently antiauthority direction. As the postwar retreat from Jeffersonian orthodoxy accelerated under Madison, Monroe, and particularly John Quincy Adams, however, true believers issued a call for a rededication to original Jeffersonian principles.

Andrew Jackson

The Jacksonian movement was a self-conscious revival of Jeffersonian political culture. Believing the central government created inequalities and suppressed competition, Jacksonians attempted to strictly limit the scope of government activity.[28] The Jacksonian aversion to central authority created the same presidential dilemma—reconciling antiauthority dispositions with the exercise of authority—that the Jeffersonians had had to face.

Jackson's greatness consisted in fusing an energetic chief executive with a limited central government. Presidential activism was justified in the name of limiting the activities of hierarchical institutions, the "Monster Bank," "King Caucus," even government itself. Presidential powers were to be enlisted in the battle to remove the institutional impediments to increased equality. Public participation would be increased by extending the franchise, overthrowing the senatorial caucus system for nominating presidents, and instituting rotation in office. Terminating the privileges conferred by government upon private industry through charters and franchises would permit the unfettered operation of free enterprise and, thereby, promote equality.

Since its founding, the presidency had been regarded with widespread suspicion as the institutional representation of hierarchy. Jefferson, Madison, and Monroe all were troubled by the sense that to act openly would constitute a betrayal of their antiauthority ideals. By demonstrating that the executive could be used to undermine hierarchy, Jackson smashed the link in the popular mind between the presidency and hierarchy. Where Jefferson, for instance, fearing cries of executive "corruption," had carefully masked the removal of Federalists from public office, Jackson trumpeted his removals in full view of the public, elevating the principle of rotation in office to a positive good.[29]

Jackson portrayed the president as mandated by the people to check concentrations of political and economic power. Rather than emboldening hierarchy, he argued, strengthening the presidency would flatten the hierarchy by increasing popular control of those in positions of authority. The concept of the mandated presidency provided an effective cover under which leaders could exercise power while denying they were doing anything more than carrying out the popular will. If the president was mandated to carry out a policy, he could not be exercising personal discretion, and therefore there was no reason to fear "executive usurpation." Jackson insisted that he could hear not only the voice of the people in his elections but their precise words. Jackson publicly construed the 1832 election, for instance, as popular vindication of his bank veto and a mandate to continue his financial policies.[30]

The negative power of the veto, which Jackson employed more frequently than all his predecessors combined and more than any other pre-Civil War president, fit well with the antiauthority Democratic political culture. The veto was exercised in the name of curbing power, checking the wasteful expenditures produced by the corrupting mix of public and private power in the halls of Congress. Since the veto could "only be exercised in a negative sense," Democrats reasoned that it could pose no danger to liberty.[31] Originally designed by the Federalists as a check upon democracy, the executive veto was now portrayed as the people's main weapon in their battle to promote equality by limiting government.

As the most visible concentration of financial and political power within the nation, the national bank provided a compelling symbol around which to unite the two antiauthority cultures. Jackson's veto message was carefully crafted to fuse the individualist concern with economic competition with the egalitarian fear of inequalities. "The rich and powerful," Jackson declared, "too often bend the acts of government to their selfish purposes." Jackson acknowledged that "distinctions in society will always exist under every just government," but when "the laws undertake to add . . . artificial distinctions, to grant titles, gratuities, and exclusive privileges, to make the rich richer and the potent more powerful, the humble members of society—the farmers, mechanics, and laborers—who have neither the time nor the means of securing like favors to themselves, have a right to complain of the injustice of their government."[32] By conferring exclusive privileges on selected institutions, the government thwarted economic competition and opportunity, thereby fostering inequalities. If government would leave individuals alone, there would be an increase not only in liberty but also in equality. The belief that increased economic opportunity would produce greater equality of condition permitted egalitarians to unite with individualists, a fusion of cultures nicely captured by Charles Sellers's label "egalitarian enterprise."[33]

By slaying the Monster bank, however, Andrew Jackson left his Democratic successors without a visible hierarchical target around which to unite individualism and egalitarianism. Had the national bank been retained, for instance, Martin Van Buren could have shifted blame for the depression of 1837 away from Democratic policies and onto the bank. While both individualists and egalitarian Democrats agreed that the hierarchical bank was noxious, they could not agree on what to do after ridding the nation of the Biddle's Bank. Individualists had objected to the powerful central bank because it had regulated the economy, but now hoped to call off the bank war in order to unleash the entrepreneurial energies of the nation. Finding that destruction of the Monster bank was causing a proliferation of banks and increasing speculation, the egalitarian wing of the Democratic party, in contrast, wanted to extend the war to all banks.

James Polk hoped that territorial expansion, like Jackson's bank war, would reunite the Democratic alliance of egalitarianism and individualism. If expansion could promote, as John O'Sullivan rhapsodized, the "universality of freedom and equality,"[34] Young Hickory (as Polk was called) could emulate Jackson's forging of a cultural hybrid, while avoiding Van Buren's fate of being torn between the two political cultures. Unfortunately for Polk, as expansion became entwined with slavery, the egalitarian wing of the Democratic party pulled back from supporting it. To egalitarian Democrats, the slave power was analogous to the money power—both demonstrated that "privilege never restrains its ambition to rule."[35] By alienating the more egalitarian wing, Polk's expansionist policies drained the party of the crusading idealism that had characterized it during the 1830s and early 1840s, giving the party an increasingly southern cast. His most conspicuous failing as a political leader was an inability to grasp that, because of slavery, expansion was creating more problems than it was solving, both for the Democratic party and the nation.

The string of failed cultural solutions, and hence failed presidencies, in the decade prior to the Civil War testifies to the extraordinary impediments to presidential leadership produced by slavery. Franklin Pierce tried to reestablish the Jacksonian coalition of individualism and egalitarianism, but slavery brought to the fore the hitherto submerged tension between majority rule and the property rights of a minority. The optimistic doctrine that liberty and equality were mutually supportive, while able to soften class conflict, could not, in the end, cope with racial conflict. Millard Fillmore hoped to hold together the Whig alliance of individualism and hierarchy, the Whiggery of William Seward and Daniel Webster, by removing slavery from the national agenda through the Compromise of 1850 and elevating national economic development to the forefront of the agenda. But Fillmore's solution reproduced the cultural contradiction within Whiggery—for how could the Whig party laud economic development and celebrate industrial capitalism as the highest stage of civilization without looking upon the South's "peculiar institution" as anything but a blight on the economic potential of the nation? Witnessing the failure of both Pierce and Fillmore to reconstitute their old cultural coalitions, James Buchanan attempted to create a new alliance that would unite the establishment against egalitarian abolitionists. But while individualists were content to protect slave property where it already existed, the issue of the expansion of slavery into the territories forced many individualists to repudiate an establishment alliance with hierarchy.

Abraham Lincoln

A loyal adherent of the Whig party for as long as it had remained in existence, Lincoln resolved its dilemma of basing government on weak hierarchy by (a) operating in wartime where he could invoke the commander-in-chief clause and (b) creating a new cultural combination in which hierarchy was subordinated to individualism.

The Whigs were a cultural alliance, predominantly hierarchical, yet with a strong admixture of individualism. When economic times were hard the paternalism of the party served them well. After all, Jacksonians had offered only "cupping and bleeding" to those hurt by the depression that followed the Panic of 1837.[36] But for the most part, Whiggery appeared too restrictive to a nation eager to exploit the resources of a seemingly boundless continent. Henry Clay, the Whig standard-bearer and Lincoln's political idol, lost all three presidential elections he participated in. The only Whigs successes in presidential contests, William Henry Harrison in 1840 and Zachary Taylor in 1848, had been dependent on submerging party principles and policies in favor of popular military heroes.

Lincoln's political ambition, that "little engine that knew no rest,"[37] was thwarted by his identification with the Whig party. From the sobering experience of Clay's defeats in 1836 and 1844, as well as the victories of the apolitical generals in 1840 and 1848, Lincoln learned that his own personal advancement depended on creating a party that could elevate not only war heroes but an Illinois party politician to the presidential office. Making the Whig party a majority party required subordinating hierarchy to individualism. The central figure in Whiggery's metamorphosis,[38] Lincoln was instrumental in creating a new Republican party in which individualism was tempered but not led by hierarchy. He thus helped to give the majority culture in America—individualism—the dominant place in governing the nation. The Republican amalgam of economic individualism and social hierarchy would dominate American politics for the next half century in the same way that Jefferson's and Jackson's alliance of egalitarianism and individualism had dominated the previous half century.

The Whigs' only popular cause had been the cry of executive usurpation. In the Whig mind, King Andrew signified the degeneration of egalitarianism into the charismatic leader who would replace the law with his personal wishes. Thus Whigs were torn between their hierarchical inclination to support central authority and their fear of the disruptive potential of presidential power. The result, in Whig doctrine, was an anomalous executive, one who stood for authority while not actually exercising it. The chief executive was to enforce the laws of the land, but otherwise was confined within narrowly circumscribed limits—no veto power, no congressional influence. As president, Lincoln had to reconcile Whig doctrine with his will to power, restoration of the Union, and the success of the Republican party.

Were the Whigs faced only with what they considered a degeneration of democracy, a lawless executive pandering to the populace, they might have managed or, at least, survived. To the south, however, Whigs were confronted with something worse, the ultimate degeneration of hierarchical principles in the form of the master-slave relationship. Unable to abide its arbitrariness or to condone upsetting its legal status, they floundered, split not only between northern and southern Whigs but also (and more important) between the apparent necessity of giving up either their individualistic adherence to free labor or their hierarchical attachment to patriarchy. Before Lincoln freed the slaves, he had to free his party from being immobilized by this dilemma—an immoral legality, through acceptance of slavery, or an illegal moralism through its abolition.

A Lincoln presidency outside of the Civil War is inconceivable. The firing on Fort Sumter gave Lincoln the opportunity to avoid his predecessors' fate by reconciling the dilemmas handcuffing his party. The slavery issue, which had shackled the presidency in the previous decade, now served as a means for unleashing presidential power.

Lincoln wrung authority from the commander-in-chief role, the presidential oath to "preserve, protect, and defend the Constitution of the U.S.," as well as the constitutional injunction that the President "shall take Care that the Laws be faithfully executed." "When rebellion or invasion comes," reasoned Lincoln, "the people have, under the Constitution, made the commander in chief of their army and navy ... the man who holds the power and bears the responsibility of ... [deciding] what the public safety requires." Lincoln began the Emancipation Proclamation by invoking "the power vested in me as Commander-in-Chief."[39] On the basis of these formal roles, Lincoln distinguished his decree, which he termed "a fit and necessary war measure," from General John Fremont's declaration of emancipation that Lincoln condemned as "simply 'dictatorship.'"[40]

Support for presidential authority, however, even during war, was far from automatic. Lincoln's behavior as president reflected an acute awareness of the paucity of support for leadership in America. Better than any previous president, Lincoln understood that given the antiauthority cultural context, popular wrath was bound to shower down upon the national government. One of Lincoln's accomplishments was to set up lightning rods that would protect him from bearing the full brunt of popular anger when the Union army suffered reverses. Toward this end, Lincoln skillfully used the old Whig executive doctrine to shield himself from the torrent of abuse. The necessity of exerting leadership in an antileadership system, in our opinion, explains the "peculiar paradox" of Lincoln's presidency first pointed out by David Donald in his seminal essay, "Whig in the White House."[41]

Donald contrasts Lincoln's vigorous extralegal use of executive authority in regard to his war power with his timid, obsequious, virtual nonuse of presidential resources to influence domestic policy. Over a wide range of domestic policies, including the introduction of the first income tax, the creation of a Department of Agriculture, tariffs, banking, and land-grant colleges, Donald contends that Lincoln showed little interest. When his proposed appointees were turned down by the Senate, Lincoln thought it improper to resubmit their names. Donald resolves the paradox of a simultaneously strong and weak chief executive by arguing that Lincoln was unable to "rid himself of the political ideas with which he had been raised."[42]

While not explicitly taking issue with Donald's thesis, G.S. Boritt provides an interpretation of Lincoln's behavior in the White House that undercuts Donald's contention that Lincoln's "political education" explains the paradox of his presidency. Lincoln, points out Boritt, faced a Congress dominated by a Republican party that was in essential agreement with Lincoln's preferred economic policies. Therefore "there was little call for Lincoln to pressure senators and congressmen, to use those 'certain indirect influences on behalf of 'sound' economics." Lincoln did not have to work so hard because Congress was disposed to do much of what he would have liked with regard to tariffs, internal improvements, finance, and homestead legislation. Boritt concludes that "Lincoln thus had the pleasure of signing into law much of the program he had worked for through the better part of his political life," legislation that amounted to what Leonard Curry has called a "blueprint for modern America."[43]

Boritt also shows that Lincoln was much more active in domestic policy than he appeared to Donald as well as to contemporaries. When it came to the establishment of a national banking system, Lincoln did attempt to influence Congress. He sent one of his private secretaries to influence wavering senators, persuaded influential senators to go to bat for him, talked the matter up in the cabinet, and even seems to have cashed in on patronage, all the while exclaiming to New York financiers, "Money, I don't know anything about 'money.'"[44]

That Lincoln was not the enthralled captive of Whig doctrine that Donald portrays is indicated by Lincoln's active involvement on behalf of the Thirteenth Amendment. Jackson-like, Lincoln informed the lame-duck session of Congress that in the recent election "the voice of the people" had been expressed in favor of the proposed amendment. He did not, however, rest content with a firmly worded message urging passage of the amendment. The president employed his considerable powers of persuasion and patronage to enlist conservative Republicans as well as wavering Democratic members to back the amendment.[45]

What about Lincoln's "curious failure" to control his cabinet, which

Donald sees as compelling evidence of the grip the Whig view of the presidency had on Lincoln. This interpretation neglects the tremendous advantages Lincoln reaped by keeping distance between himself and the cabinet. "When Congress showed unhappiness with executive direction," points out Boritt, "the separation between the President and his official family often diverted the legislators to attacking the latter. With the Cabinet absorbing much of the fire, the White House could often escape untouched." Attorney General Edward Bates, for example, took most of the heat from the radicals for Lincoln's decision not to enforce congressional acts confiscating the property of slave owners.[46]

We may be excused for believing that a man possessed of as formidable an intellect as this nation has produced was putting on his publics by his avowals of naiveté or disinterest in matters of banking, finance, and foreign affairs—"you understand these things. I do not," Lincoln told Secretary of the Treasury Salmon Chase.[47] Allowing his cabinet members to think themselves superior gave Lincoln protection against what would otherwise have been a crescendo cry of usurpation. His humble posture, the log-cabin stories, and the like served as a shield against the pervasive antiauthority bias.

From the individualist perspective, Lincoln's greatness consisted in demonstrating that an individualist regime could cope with large-scale crises without a transformation in its cultural identity. Lincoln's example offered hope that individualist regimes were not subject to an "inherent and fatal weakness"; such a regime could be strong enough to maintain its existence in an emergency without permanently altering internal social relations in a hierarchical direction. Temporary emergency leadership in times of total war, they now knew, did not lead inexorably to permanent dictatorship in peacetime.

From the hierarchical standpoint, Lincoln's leadership was equally exemplary, but for very different reasons. In Woodrow Wilson's view, Lincoln's greatness lay in moving America "from a divided, self-interested contractual association to a unified, spiritual, organic state."[48] Lincoln's presidency had also recreated the alliance of a strong government with a strong executive, previously rent asunder by the party battles of the 1830s and 1840s. By elevating the prestige and expanding the prerogatives of the presidential office, Lincoln left a permanent legacy on which future hierarchies would try to build.

Greatness Has Its Limits

If these four presidents were great in that they resolved cultural dilemmas, they were not perfect, for their solutions had limits. Washington's attempt to compensate for the weakness of hierarchy by stressing the appearance of strong leadership was limited because those who did not share the cultural assumptions of hierarchy often found the display of power anywhere from alarming to ridiculous. Washington was caught in a dilemma in which a mode of behavior designed to compensate for authority's weakness often undermined it still further. For instance, while the administration expected that a firm response to the Whiskey Rebellion in western Pennsylvania would increase respect for the central government, Republican leaders found it menacing that the government would arm "against people at their plows." Washington, Jefferson lamented, had been "dazzled by the glittering of crowns and coronets."[49] Far from impressing, the administration's display of might had evoked images of oppressive monarchy. Building up authority without appearing as a George III proved extremely difficult. As Washington became increasingly identified with the hierarchical Federalists during his second term, his reputation was greatly tarnished; it could be mended only through the route it was gained—by once again relinquishing power.

The limits of Jefferson's hidden-hand strategy became apparent in his embargo policy. Rather than publicly defend the need for individuals to suffer restrictions on their freedom, Jefferson presented, in the words of Leonard Levy, "an imperturbable, almost sphinx-like silence to the nation."[50] The embargo produced severe economic deprivation for many segments of the public and therefore required public explanation of the need for individual sacrifice to further a collective goal. But rather than trying to rally the country around him, Jefferson, as Malone comments, "followed the general policy of keeping as much out of sight as possible."[51] A leadership style, which had hitherto served Jefferson so well, ensured that the embargo would be a disaster. Previous Jeffersonian policies, like cutting taxes or the Louisiana Purchase, did not call for individuals to make material sacrifices, nor did people need persuading that a great public good was being furthered. Well-suited to achieve popular goals, Jefferson's covert style of leadership was ill-equipped to manage unpleasant tasks that required the leader to be a public educator.

Andrew Jackson's solution of appealing directly to the people over the head of Congress was well-suited to his negative policy aims. Because he did not have a positive legislative program that required the support of a majority, he could afford to alienate Congress. The national bank had been struck down by presidential veto, the deposits were removed without congressional approval, and the pet bank system was managed through executive fiat. But the limits of Jackson's energetic negativism became apparent when his successor, Martin Van Buren, responding to calls for positive action during the depression that followed the panic of 1837, tried to secure the Independent Treasury proposal that required congressional assent. If Van Buren was to direct the legislative process, he could not afford the provocative vetoes and the angry battles over appointments that had soured Jackson's relations with Congress.[52]

Even Abraham Lincoln's solutions had limitations. By keeping his war aims ambiguous so as to attract the support of all three cultures, Lincoln left his successor, Andrew Johnson, with a lack of guidance as to how to proceed with reconstructing the Union. Moreover, by relying vigorously on his powers as commander in chief and spending money on his own, asking Congress to ratify his actions only after the fact, he made Congress eager to bring the presidency back to its constitutional position as soon as the war ended. One wonders to what extent Johnson's impeachment was a judgment on Lincoln's usurpations. In resolving one set of cultural dilemmas, great presidents may sometimes create insoluble dilemmas for their successors. Presidential greatness is thus intimately related to presidential failure.

Presidential Failure

While presidential greatness (or, more modestly, success) is never guaranteed to any president, there are many presidents who are never in the running. This may be, as we have indicated above, on account of an intractable dilemma bequeathed by a "great" predecessor. Martin Van Buren, for instance, although the most adroit politician of his day, could not hold together individualists and egalitarians in the aftermath of Jackson's destruction of the national bank. The act that helped give Jackson his mantle of greatness—destroying the "money power"—left Van Buren without a hierarchical enemy on which to blame the ensuing financial panic and depression.

Van Buren's fate indicates that being an accomplished politician is insufficient to guarantee success in the White House. While poor politicians have rarely, if ever, been successful presidents, faltering presidencies have often come from the ranks of accomplished politicians—James Madison, James Buchanan, Lyndon Johnson, Richard Nixon, to name a few. If it is not a lack of political acumen that barred the door to greatness for these presidents, what did? The usual response would be to emphasize personal features: Madison's indecisiveness, Buchanan's timidity, or Johnson's self-loathing. Without minimizing the impact of personal characteristics, we remain dissatisfied by explanations that stop here.

A focus on the president's personality fares poorly when failure in the White House comes on the heels of other political successes. Take, for instance, John Quincy Adams, who as diplomat and secretary of state must rank among the greatest this nation has produced, yet as president was a disappointment. Explanations that focus on personality (psychological rigidity, compulsiveness) leave us wondering how such an inflexible, uncompromising man could have been the most successful diplomat of his age. Not Adams's prickly personality, we contend, but his hierarchical propensities best explain why he could succeed so spectacularly in the realm of diplomacy yet be such an ineffective president. The hierarchies' forte, negotiating jurisdictions—who has the right to do what—and adjudicating statuses, while valuable talents for a diplomat, were ill-suited to the president's competitive relationship with Congress and his position as the leader of a political party.

Nor will it do to explain the three failed presidencies prior to the Civil War—Millard Fillmore, Franklin Pierce, and James Buchanan were ranked 24th, 26th, and 27th (out of 29) in the 1948 Schlesinger poll—solely in terms of personal inadequacies. All three were accomplished politicians, particularly Buchanan, who was one of the most politically experienced men ever to occupy the White House. Each offered a credible political solution to the cultural dilemma bequeathed in large part by the expansionist policies of James Polk, rated by the Schlesinger polls as a "Near Great." In the absence of civil war, slavery proved to be an insoluble national problem. Little wonder that Lincoln seemed to welcome the onset of war.

The pattern of prepresidential success followed by presidential failure can also be seen in the public career of James Madison. So successful as a congressional leader and constitution-maker, he is considered by many scholars to be a flop as president. The usual explanation (personal compliancy, a need for affection) cannot explain his bold maneuvering in Congress and at the Constitutional Convention. Madison's difficulties in the presidency, we contend, had more to do with the antiauthority cultural propensities of his followers than with any features of Madison's personality. Where no one is disposed to follow, no one, no matter how psychologically healthy, can lead. When, in the aftermath of the War of 1812, people were more disposed to support authority, Madison performed ably.

Will it do, to take examples closer to home, to explain the troubled presidencies of Lyndon Johnson, Richard Nixon, Jimmy Carter, and (partly) Ronald Reagan solely in terms of their personal shortcomings? Is the historical reading of America as a land particularly favored by providence to be replaced by a new myth of Americans as an unlucky people done in by unworthy presidents? Without denying that there is much to criticize, there is also much that might be praised: Johnson's Great Society, Nixon's opening to China, Carter's Camp David Accords, Reagan's reduction of marginal tax rates. Why, then, do we hear only that these were failed presidencies, as if that is all there was? A hypothesis worth considering is that reports of failed presidencies have risen along with egalitarian movements (civil rights, feminism, environmentalism, children's rights, etc.) because dedication to reducing differences among people leads to rejection of leadership, which is an a priori form of inequality. An alternative hypothesis is that our wonderful people mysteriously keep getting terrible presidents. If you believe that, you will believe anything. Why you might believe that when the rigid right-wing ideologue, Ronald Reagan, was replaced by the flexible, moderate George Bush, the new president would win the respect of the American people.

Notes

1. Arthur M. Schlesinger, Jr., "A Yardstick for Presidents," in *Paths to the Present* (New York: Macmillan, 1949), 93–111; Gary M. Maranell, "The Evaluation of Presidents: An Extension of the Schlesinger Polls," *Journal of American History* (June 1970): 104–13; Robert K. Murray and Tim H. Blessing, "The Presidential Performance Study: A Progress Report," *Journal of American History* (December 1983): 535–55. Other

greatness polls conducted in the past decade include the U.S. Historical Society's 1977 survey of the heads of one hundred history departments (Robert E. DiClerico, *The American President*, [Englewood Cliffs, N.J.: Prentice-Hall, 1979] 332), David L. Potter's 1981 unpublished survey of forty-one historians (Murray and Blessing, "The Presidential Performance Study," 536), and a 1982 survey of forty-nine presidential scholars (Steve Neal, "Our Best and Worst Presidents," Chicago Tribune *Magazine*, January 10, 1982, 8–13, 15, 18).

2. Thomas A. Bailey, *Presidential Greatness: The Image and the Man from George Washington to the Present* (New York: Appleton-Century, 1966), 24. Italics in original.

3. Ibid., 262–66.

4. Arthur M. Schlesinger, Jr., "A Yardstick for Presidents," in *Paths to the Present* (Boston: Houghton Mifflin, 1964), 107.

5. Bailey, *Presidential Greatness*, 34; Curtis Arthur Amlund, "President-Ranking: A Criticism," *Midwest Journal of Political Science* (August 1964): 309–15, quotation on 309.

6. James McGregor Burns, *Presidential Government: The Crucible of Leadership* (New York: Avon, 1965), xi.

7. These categories are adapted from the work of Mary Douglas. See especially *National Symbols: Explorations in Cosmology* (London: Barrie & Rockliff, 1970), and "Cultural Bias," in *In the Active Voice* (London: Routledge & Kegan Paul, 1982). The theory is further elaborated in Mary Douglas and Aaron Wildavsky, *Risk and Culture* (Berkeley: University of California Press, 1982). The most comprehensive statement is in Michael Thompson, Richard Ellis, and Aaron Wildavsky, *Cultural Theory* (Boulder, Colo: Westview Press, 1990).

8. Alexis de Tocqueville, *Democracy in America* (New York: Harper & Row, 1966); Louis Hartz, *The Liberal Tradition in America* (New York: Harcourt Brace, 1955); Samuel P. Huntington, American *Politics: The Promise of Disharmony* (Cambridge: Harvard University Press, 1981).

9. Richard E. Neustadt, *Presidential Power: The Politics of Leadership* (New York: Wiley, 1980).

10. Arthur B. Murphy, "Evaluating the Presidents of the United States," *Presidential Studies Quarterly* (Winter 1984): 117.

11. Marcus Cunliffe, *George Washington: Man and Monument* (Boston: Little, Brown, 1958), 212.

12. Washington to President of Congress, December 20, 1776, in Saul K. Padover, ed., *The Washington Papers* (New York: Grosset & Dunlap, 1955), 100; Circular Letter to the Governors of All the States on Disbanding the Army, June 8, 1783, ibid., 206, 213.

13. See, *e.g.*, letters to Archibald Cary, June 15, 1782; to Robert Stewart,

August 10, 1783; to Lafayette, February 1, 1784; to James Madison, May 20, 1792; to David Humphries, June 12, 1796; to Henry Knox, March 2, 1797; and to Oliver Wolcott, May 15, 1797, ibid., 78, 79, 83, 88, 90, 91, 92, quotation on 83.

14. Barry Schwartz, "George Washington and the Whig Conception of Heroic Leadership," *American Sociological Review* (February 1983): 18–33, quotation on 30.

15. On Washington's adherence to hierarchical Federalism, see David Hackett Fischer, *The Revolution of American Conservatism: The Federalist Party in the Era of Jeffersonian Democracy* (New York: Harper & Row, 1965), 377–79.

16. James R. Perry, "Supreme Court Appointments, 1789–1801: Criteria, Presidential Style, and the Press of Events," *Journal of the Early Republic* (Winter 1986): 371–410, esp. 373, 397.

17. Frederick W. Marks III, "Foreign Affairs: A Winning Issue in the Campaign for Ratification of the United States Constitution," *Political Science Quarterly* (September 1971): 444–69.

18. Drew R. McCoy, T*he Elusive Republic: Political Economy in Jeffersonian America* (Chapel Hill: University of North Carolina Press, 1980), 141.

19. Jefferson to William Short, Jan. 3, 1793, cited in Gilbert Lycan, *Alexander Hamilton & American Foreign Policy: A Design for Greatness* (Norman: University of Oklahoma Press, 1970), 134.

20. Burton Ira Kaufman, "Washington's Farewell Address: A Statement of Empire," in Kaufman, ed., *Washington's Farewell Address: The View from the 20th Century* (Chicago: Quadrangle, 1969), 169–87.

21. Lance Banning, *The Jeffersonian Persuasion: Evolution of a Party Ideology* (Ithaca, N.Y.: Cornell University Press, 1978), 273. See also James Sterling Young, *The Washington Community, 1800–1828* (New York: Harcourt Brace, 1966), esp. 207.

22. Dumas Malone, *Jefferson the President: First Term, 1801–1805* (Boston: Little, Brown, 1970), 112; Dumas Malone, Tho*mas Jefferson as Political Leader* (Berkeley: University of California Press, 1963), 34.

23. Jefferson quoted in Robert M. Johnstone, Jr., *Jefferson and the Presidency: Leadership in the Young Republic* (Ithaca, N.Y.: Cornell University Press, 1978), 128; Malone, *First Term*, 95; Edward S. Corwin, *The President: Office and Powers, 1787–1957* (New York: New York University Press, 1957), 18.

24. Noble E. Cunningham, Jr., *The Process of Government Under Jefferson* (Princeton, N.J.: Princeton University Press, 1978), chap. 9, esp. 188–93.

25. Johnstone, *Jefferson and the Presidency*, 144–48.

26. Fred I. Greenstein, *The Hidden-Hand Presidency: Eisenhower as Leader*

(New York: Basic Books, 1982). On Jefferson's attempts to quietly undercut Randolph, see Dumas Malone, *Jefferson the President: Second Term. 1805–1809* (Boston: Little, Brown, 1974), 108–9, 161–62; and Noble E. Cunningham, Jr., The *Jeffersonian Republicans in Power: Party Operations, 1801–1809* (Chapel Hill: University of North Carolina Press, 1963) 86–88.

27. Johnstone, *Jefferson and the Presidency,* 86, 95–98; Cunningham, *Process of Government,* 60–71, 319–20; Dumas Malone, "Presidential Leadership and National Unity: The Jeffersonian Example," *Journal of Southern History* (February 1969): 16; Jefferson quoted in Leonard D. White, *The Jeffersonians: A Study in Administrative History: 1801–1829* (New York: Free Press, 1951), 80.

28. Richard B. Latner, *The Presidency of Andrew Jackson: White House Politics, 1829–1837* (Athens: University of Georgia Press, 1979), 7–30; Robert V. Remini, *Andrew Jackson and the Course of American Freedom, 1822–1832* (New York: Harper & Row, 1981), 12–155.

29. Jackson, according to Arthur Schlesinger, Jr., "ousted no greater a proportion of officeholders than Jefferson" (*The Age of Jackson,* Boston: Little, Brown, 1945, 47).

30. Latner, *Presidency of Jackson,* 165. See also ibid., 50; Remini, *Jackson and American Freedom,* 323; and Wilfred Binkley, *President and Congress* (New York: Vintage, 1962), 83.

31. John Ashworth, *'Agrarians' and 'Aristocrats': Party Political Ideology in the United States. 1837–1846* (Atlantic Highlands, N.J.: Humanities Press, 1983), 35.

32. Remini, *Jackson and American Freedom,* 367–69.

33. Charles Sellers, Introduction to Sellers, ed., A*ndrew Jackson: A Profile* (New York: Hill & Wang, 1971), xvi. See also Daniel Walker Howe, *The Political Culture of the American Whigs,* (Chicago: University of Chicago Press, 1979), 22.

34. Schlesinger, *Age of Jackson,* 427. O'Sullivan coined the phrase "Manifest Destiny."

35. Eric Foner and John Ashworth, among others, have shown that the wing of the Democratic party that was most hostile to banks, corporations, monopolies, and tariffs was most attracted to the free-soil cause and most likely to defect to the Republican party. See Eric Foner, *Free Soil, Free Labor, Free Men: The Ideology of the Republican Party before the Civil War* (New York: Oxford University Press, 1970), esp. 168–69; John Ashworth, "The Democratic-Republicans before the Civil War: Political Ideology and Economic Change," *Journal of American Studies* (December 1986): 375–90, Kinsley Bingham quoted on 380.

36. Azariah Flagg to Martin Van Buren, April 10, 1837, quoted in Major L.

Wilson, The Presidency of Martin Van Buren (Lawrence: University Press of Kansas, 1984), 143.

37. William H. Herndon cited in Richard Hofstadter, The American Political Tradition (New York: Vintage, 1973), 118.

38. See Howe, Political Culture of Whigs, chap. 11.

39. Arthur M. Schlesinger, Jr., The Imperial Presidency (Boston: Houghton Mifflin, 1973), 60–63.

40. J.G. Randall, Lincoln the President: Springfield to Gettysburg, (vol. 2; New York: Dodd, Mead, 1945), 165–66.

41. David Donald, "Abraham Lincoln: Whig in the White House," in Norman Graebner, ed., The Enduring Lincoln (Urbana: University of Illinois Press, 1959), 47.

42. Ibid, 51–53, 60.

43. G.S. Boritt, Lincoln and the Economics of the American Dream (Memphis: Memphis State University Press, 1978), 196–97; Leonard P. Curry, Blueprint for Modern America: Nonmilitary Legislation of the First Civil War Congress (Nashville: Vanderbilt University Press, 1968).

44. Boritt, Lincoln and the American Dream, 201–3.

45. Ibid, 299; Richard Current, The Lincoln Nobody Knows (New York: Hill & Wang, 1958), 230; Stephen Oates, "Abraham Lincoln: Republican in the White House," in John L. Thomas, ed., Abraham Lincoln and the American Political Tradition (Amherst: University of Massachusetts Press, 1986), 106; J.G. Randall and Richard Current, Lincoln the President: Last Full Measure (New York: Dodd, Mead, 1955), 308–9, Lincoln quoted on 308.

46. Donald, "Whig in the White House," 59; Boritt, Lincoln and the American Dream, 228.

47. Boritt, Lincoln and the American Dream, 199.

48. Michael Paul Rogin, "The King's Two Bodies: Lincoln, Wilson, Nixon, and Presidential Self-Sacrifice," in J. David Greenstone, ed., Public Values and Private Power in American Politics (Chicago: University of Chicago Press, 1982), 80.

49. Jefferson quoted in Dumas Malone, Jefferson and the Ordeal of Liberty (Boston: Little, Brown, 1962), 188; James Thomas Flaxner, George Washington: Anguish and Farewell, 1793–1799 (Boston: Little, Brown, 1969), 191.

50. Leonard W. Levy, Jefferson and Civil Liberties: The Darker Side (Cambridge: Harvard University Press, 1963), 96.

51. Malone, Second Term, 576.

52. James C. Curtis, "In the Shadow of Old Hickory: The Political Travail of Martin Van Buren," Journal of the Early American Republic (Fall 1981: 258–59, 263.

2

The Two Presidencies

The United States has one president, but it has two presidencies;
one presidency is for domestic affairs, and the other is concerned with
defense and foreign policy. Since World War II, presidents have had
much greater success in controlling the nation's defense and foreign
policies than in dominating its domestic policies. Even Lyndon Johnson
has seen his early record of victories in domestic legislation diminish
as his concern with foreign affairs grows.

What powers does the president have to control defense and foreign
policies and so completely overwhelm those who might wish to thwart
him? The president's normal problem with domestic policy is to get
congressional support for the programs he prefers. In foreign affairs,
in contrast, he can almost always get support for policies that he
believes will protect the nation—but his problem is to find a viable
policy.

Whoever they are, whether they begin by caring about foreign policy like Eisenhower and Kennedy or about domestic policies like
Truman and Johnson, presidents soon discover they have more policy
preferences in domestic matters than in foreign policy. The Republican and Democratic parties possess a traditional roster of policies,
which can easily be adopted by a new president; for example, he can
be either for or against Medicare and aid to education. Since existing
domestic policy usually changes in only small steps, presidents find it
relatively simple to make minor adjustments. However, although any
president knows he supports foreign aid and NATO, the world outside

Reprinted from *Trans*-action December 1966. Copyright 1966 by the Community Leadership Project of Washington University, St. Louis.

changes much more rapidly than the nation inside—presidents and their parties have no prior policies on Argentina and the Congo. The world has become a highly intractable place with a whirl of forces we cannot or do not know how to alter.

The Record of Presidential Control

It takes great crises, such as Roosevelt's hundred days in the midst of the depression, or the extraordinary majorities that Barry Goldwater's candidacy willed to Lyndon Johnson, for presidents to succeed in controlling domestic policy. From the end of the 1930s to the present (what may roughly be called the modern era), presidents have often been frustrated in their domestic programs. From 1938, when conservatives regrouped their forces, to the time of his death, Franklin Roosevelt did not get a single piece of significant domestic legislation passed. Truman lost out on most of his intense domestic preferences, except perhaps for housing. Since Eisenhower did not ask for much domestic legislation, he did not meet consistent defeat, yet he failed in his general policy of curtailing governmental commitments. Kennedy, of course, faced great difficulties with domestic legislation.

In the realm of foreign policy, there has not been a single major issue on which presidents, when they were serious and determined, have failed. The list of their victories is impressive: entry into the United Nations, the Marshall Plan, NATO, the Truman Doctrine, the decisions to stay out of Indochina in 1954 and to intervene in Vietnam in the 1960s, aid to Poland and Yugoslavia, the test-ban treaty, and many more. Serious setbacks to the president in controlling foreign policy are extraordinary and unusual.

Table 2.1, compiled from the Congressional Quarterly Service tabulation of presidential initiative and congressional response from 1948 through 1964, shows that presidents have significantly better records in foreign and defense matters than in domestic policies. When refugees and immigration—which Congress considers primarily a domestic concern—are removed from the general foreign policy area, it is clear that presidents prevail about 70 percent of the time in defense and foreign policy, compared with 40 percent in the domestic sphere.

World Events and Presidential Resources

Power in politics is control over governmental decisions. How does the president manage his control of foreign and defense policy? The answer does not reside in the greater constitutional power in foreign affairs that Presidents have possessed since the founding of the Republic. The answer lies in the changes that have taken place since 1945.

TABLE 2.1 Congressional Action on Presidential Proposals from 1948–1964

Policy Area	Congressional % Pass	Action % Fail	Number of Proposals
Domestic policy (natural resources, labor, agriculture, taxes, etc.)	40.2	59.8	2499
Defense policy (defense, disarmament, manpower, misc.)	73.3	26.7	90
Foreign policy	58.5	41.5	655
Immigration, refugees	13.2	86.0	129
Treaties, general foreign relations, State Department, foreign aid	70.8	29.2	445

Source: Congressional Quarterly Service, *Congress and the Nation*, 1945–1964 (Washington, D.C., 1965)

The number of nations with which the United States has diplomatic relations has increased from 53 in 1939 to 113 in 1966. But sheer numbers do not tell enough; the world has also become a much more dangerous place. However remote it may seem at times, our government must always be aware of the possibility of nuclear war.

Yet the mere existence of great powers with effective thermonuclear weapons would not, in and of itself, vastly increase our rate of interaction with most other nations. We see events in Assam or Burundi as important because they are also part of a larger worldwide contest, called the cold war, in which great powers are rivals for the control or support of other nations. Moreover, the reaction against the blatant isolationism of the 1930s has led to a concern with foreign policy that is worldwide in scope. We are interested in what happens everywhere because we see these events as connected with larger interests involving, at the worst, the possibility of ultimate destruction.

Given the overriding fact that the world is dangerous and that small causes are perceived to have potentially great effects in an unstable world, it follows that Presidents must be interested in relatively "small" matters. So they give Azerbaijan or Lebanon or Vietnam huge amounts of their time. Arthur Schlesinger, Jr., wrote of Kennedy that "in the first two months of his administration he probably spent more time on Laos than on anything else." Few failures in domestic policy, presidents soon realize, could have as disastrous consequences as any one of dozens of mistakes in the international arena.

The result is that foreign policy concerns tend to drive out domestic policy. Except for occasional questions of domestic prosperity and for civil rights, foreign affairs have consistently higher priority for presidents. Once, when trying to talk to President Kennedy about natural resources, Secretary of the Interior Stewart Udall remarked, "He's imprisoned by Berlin."

The importance of foreign affairs to presidents is intensified by the increasing speed of events in the international arena. The event and its consequences follow closely on top of one another. The blunder at the Bay of Pigs is swiftly followed by the near catastrophe of the Cuban missile crisis. Presidents can no longer count on passing along their most difficult problems to their successors. They must expect to face the consequences of their actions—or failure to act—while still in office.

Domestic policy making is usually based on experimental adjustments to an existing situation. Only a few decisions, such as those involving large dams, irretrievably commit future generations. Decisions in foreign affairs, however, are often perceived to be irreversible. This is expressed, for example, in the fear of escalation or the various "spiral" or "domino" theories of international conflict.

If decisions are perceived to be both important and irreversible, there is every reason for presidents to devote a great deal of resources to them. Presidents have to be oriented toward the future in the use of their resources. They serve a fixed term in office, and they cannot automatically count on support from the populace, Congress, or the administrative apparatus. They have to be careful, therefore, to husband their resources for pressing future needs. But because the consequences of events in foreign affairs are potentially more grave, faster to manifest themselves, and less easily reversible than in domestic affairs, presidents are more willing to use up their resources.

The Power to Act

Presidents' formal powers to commit resources in foreign affairs and defense are vast. Particularly important is their power as commander in chief to move troops. Faced with situations like the invasion of South Korea or the emplacement of missiles in Cuba, fast action is required. Presidents possess both the formal power to act and the knowledge that elites and the general public expect them to act. Once they have committed American forces, it is difficult for Congress or anyone else to alter the course of events. The Dominican venture is a recent case in point.

Presidential discretion in foreign affairs also makes it difficult (though not impossible) for Congress to restrict their actions. Presidents can use executive agreements instead of treaties, enter into tacit agreements instead of written ones, and otherwise help create de facto situations not easily reversed. Presidents also have far greater ability than anyone else to obtain information on developments abroad through the Departments of State and Defense. The need for secrecy in some aspects of foreign and defense policy further restricts the ability of others to compete with presidents. These things are all well known. What is not so generally appreciated is the growing presidential ability to *use* information to achieve goals.

In the past, presidents were amateurs in military strategy. They could not even get much useful advice outside of the military. As late as the 1930s the number of people outside the military establishment who were professionally engaged in the study of defense policy could be numbered on the fingers. Today there are hundreds of such men. The rise of the defense intellectuals has given the president of the United States enhanced ability to control defense policy. He is no longer dependent on the military for advice. He can choose among defense intellectuals from the research corporations and the academies for alternative sources of advice. He can install these men in his own office. He can play them off against each other or use them to extend spheres of coordination.

Even with these advisers, however, presidents and secretaries of defense might still be too bewildered by the complexity of nuclear situations to take action—unless they had an understanding of the doctrine and concepts of deterrence. But knowledge of doctrine about deterrence has been widely diffused; it can be picked up by any intelligent person who will read books or listen to enough hours of conversation. Whether or not the doctrine is good is a separate question; the point is that civilians can feel they understand what is going on in defense policy. Perhaps the most extraordinary feature of presidential action during the Cuban missile crisis was the degree to which the commander in chief of the armed forces insisted on controlling even the smallest moves. From the positioning of ships to the methods of boarding, to the precise words and actions to be taken by individual soldiers and sailors, the president and his civilian advisers were in control.

Although presidents have rivals for power in foreign affairs, the rivals do not usually succeed. Presidents prevail not only because they may have superior resources but because their potential opponents are weak, divided, or believe that they should not control foreign policy. Let us consider the potential rivals—the general citizenry, special interest groups, the Congress, the military, the so-called military-industrial complex, and the State Department.

Competitors for Control of Policy

The Public

The general public is much more dependent on presidents in foreign affairs than in domestic matters. While many people know about the impact of Social Security and Medicare, few know about politics in Malawi. So it is not surprising that people expect the president to act in foreign affairs, and they reward him with their confidence. Gallup Polls consistently show that presidential popularity rises after he takes action in a crisis—whether the action is disastrous, as in the Bay of Pigs, or successful, as in the Cuban missile crisis. Decisive action, such as the bombing of oil fields near Haiphong, resulted in a sharp (though temporary) increase in Johnson's popularity.

The Vietnam situation illustrates another problem of public opinion in foreign affairs: it is extremely difficult to get operational policy directions from the general public. It took a long time before any sizable public interest in the subject developed. Nothing short of the large-scale involvement of American troops under fire probably could have brought about the current high level of concern. Yet this relatively well developed popular opinion is difficult to interpret. While a majority seems to support President Johnson's policy, it appears that they could easily be persuaded to withdraw from Vietnam if the administration changed its line. Although a sizable majority would support various initiatives to end the war, they would seemingly be appalled if this action led to Communist encroachments elsewhere in Southeast Asia. (See "'The President, the Polls, and Vietnam" by Seymour Martin Lipset, *Trans*-action, September/October 1966.)

Although presidents lead opinion in foreign affairs, they know they will be held accountable for the consequences of their actions. President Johnson has maintained a large commitment in Vietnam. His popularity shoots up now and again in the midst of some imposing action. But the fact that a body of citizens does not like the war comes back to damage his overall popularity. We will support your initiatives, the people seem to say, but we will reserve the right to punish you (or your party) if we do not like the results.

Special Interest Groups

Opinions are easier to gauge in domestic affairs because, for one thing, there is a stable structure of interest groups that covers virtually all matters of concern. The farm, labor, business, conservation, veterans, civil rights, and other interest groups provide cues when a proposed policy affects them. Thus people who identify with these groups may adopt their views. But in foreign policy matters the interest group structure is weak, unstable, and thin rather than dense. In many matters affecting Africa and Asia, for example, it is hard to think of well-known interest groups. While ephemeral groups arise from time to time to support or protest particular policies, they usually disappear when the immediate problem is resolved. In contrast, longer-lasting elite groups like the Foreign Policy Association and Council on Foreign Relations are composed of people of diverse views; refusal to take strong positions on controversial matters is a condition of their continued viability.

The strongest interest groups are probably the ethnic associations whose members have strong ties with a homeland, as in Poland or Cuba, so they are rarely activated simultaneously on any specific issue. They are most effective when most narrowly and intensely focused, as in the fierce pressure from Jews to recognize the state of Israel. But their relatively small numbers limits their significance to presidents in the vastly more important general foreign policy picture—as continued aid to the Arab countries shows. Moreover, some ethnic groups may conflict on significant issues such as American acceptance of the Oder-Neisse line separating Poland from what is now East Germany.

The Congress

Congressmen also exercise power in foreign affairs. Yet they are ordinarily not serious competitors with the president because they follow a self-denying ordinance. They do not think it is their job to determine the nation's defense policies. Lewis A. Dexter's extensive interviews with members of the Senate Armed Services Committee, who might be expected to want a voice in defense policy, reveal that they do not want men like themselves to run the nation's defense establishment. Aside from a few specific conflicts among the armed services, which allow both the possibility and desirability of direct intervention, the Armed Services Committee constitutes a sort of real-estate committee dealing with the regional economic consequences of the location of military facilities.

The congressional appropriations power is potentially a significant resource, but circumstances since the end of World War II have tended to reduce its effectiveness. The appropriations committees and Congress itself might make their will felt by refusing to allot funds unless basic policies were altered. But this has not happened. While Congress makes its traditional small cuts in the military budget, presidents have mostly found themselves warding off congressional attempts to increase specific items still further.

Most of the time, the administration's refusal to spend has not been seriously challenged. However, there have been occasions when individual legislators or committees have been influential. Senator Henry Jackson in his campaign (with the aid of colleagues on the Joint Committee on Atomic Energy) was able to gain acceptance for the Polaris weapons system, and Senator Arthur H. Vandenberg played a part in determining the shape of the Marshall Plan, and so on. The few congressmen who are expert in defense policy act, as Samuel P. Huntington says, largely as lobbyists with the executive branch. It is apparently more fruitful for these congressional experts to use their resources in order to get a hearing from the executive than to work on other congressmen.

When an issue involves the actual use or threat of violence, it takes a great deal to convince congressmen not to follow the President's lead. James Robinson's tabulation of foreign and defense policy issues from the late 1930s to 1961 (Table 2.2) shows dominant influence by Congress in only one case out of seven—the 1954 decision not to intervene with armed force in Indochina. In that instance President Eisenhower deliberately sounded out congressional opinion and, finding it negative, decided not to intervene—against the advice of Admiral Radford, chairman of the Joint Chiefs of Staff. This attempt to abandon responsibility did not succeed, as the years of American involvement demonstrate.

The Military

The outstanding feature of the military's participation in making defense policy is their amazing weakness. Whether the policy decisions involve the size of the armed forces, the choice of weapons systems, the total defense budget, or its division into components, the military have not prevailed. Let us take budgetary decisions as representative of the key choices to be made in defense policy. Since the end of World War II the military has not been able to achieve significant (billion dollar) increases in appropriations by their own efforts. Under Truman and Eisenhower defense budgets were determined by what Huntington calls the remainder method: the two presidents estimated revenues, decided what they could spend on domestic matters, and the remainder was assigned to defense.[1] The usual controversy was between some military and congressional groups supporting much larger expenditures, while the president and his executive allies re-

TABLE 2.2 Congressional Involvement in Foreign and Defense Policy Decisions

Issue	Congressional Involvement (High, Low, None)	Initiator (Congress or Executive)	Predominant Influence (Congress or Executive)	Legislation or Resolution (Yes or No)	Decision Violence at Stake (Yes or No)	Time (Long or Short)
Neutrality Legislation, the 1930s	High	Exec	Cong	Yes	No	Long
Lend-Lease, 1941	High	Exec	Exec	Yes	Yes	Long
Aid to Russia, 1941	Low	Exec	Exec	No	No	Long
Repeal of Chinese Exclusion, 1943	High	Cong	Cong	Yes	No	Long
Fulbright Resolution, 1943	High	Cong	Cong	Yes	No	Long
Building the Atomic Bomb, 1944	Low	Exec	Exec	Yes	Yes	Long
Foreign Services Act of 1946	High	Exec	Exec	Yes	No	Long
Truman Doctrine, 1947	High	Exec	Exec	Yes	No	Long
The Marshall Plan, 1947-48	High	Exec	Exec	Yes	No	Long
Berlin Airlift, 1948	None	Exec	Exec	No	Yes	Long
Vandenberg Resolution, 1948	High	Exec	Cong	Yes	No	Long
North Atlantic Treaty, 1947-49	High	Exec	Exec	Yes	No	Long
Korean Decision, 1950	None	Exec	Exec	No	Yes	Short
Japanese Peace Treaty, 1952	High	Exec	Exec	Yes	No	Long
Bohlen Nomination, 1953	High	Exec	Exec	Yes	No	Long
Indo-China, 1954	High	Exec	Cong	No	Yes	Short
Formosan Resolution, 1955	High	Exec	Exec	Yes	Yes	Long
International Finance Corporation, 1956	Low	Exec	Exec	Yes	No	Long
Foreign Aid, 1957	High	Exec	Exec	Yes	No	Long
Reciprocal Trade Agreements, 1958	High	Exec	Exec	Yes	No	Long
Monroney Resolution, 1958	High	Cong	Cong	Yes	No	Long
Cuban Decision, 1961	Low	Exec	Exec	No	Yes	Long

Source: James A. Robinson, Congress and Foreign Policy-Making (Homewood, Illinois, 1962)

fused. A typical case, involving the desire of the Air Force to increase the number of groups of planes is described by Huntington in *The Common Defense*:

> The FY [fiscal year] 1949 budget provided 48 groups. After the Czech coup, the Administration yielded and backed an Air Force of 55 groups in its spring rearmament program. Congress added additional funds to aid Air Force expansion to 70 groups. The Administration refused to utilize them, however, and in the gathering economy wave of the summer and fall of 1948, the Air Force goal was cut back again to 48 groups. In 1949 the House of Representatives picked up the challenge and appropriated funds for 58 groups. The President impounded the money. In June, 1950, the Air Force had 48 groups.[2]

The great increases in the defense budget were due far more to Stalin and modern technology than to the military. The Korean War resulted in an increase from $12 to $44 billion, and much of the rest followed Sputnik and the huge costs of missile programs. Thus modern technology and international conflict put an end to the one major effort to subordinate foreign affairs to domestic policies through the budget.

It could be argued that the president merely ratifies the decisions made by the military and their allies. If the military and/or Congress were united and insistent on defense policy, it would certainly be difficult for presidents to resist these forces. But it is precisely the disunity of the military that has characterized the entire postwar period. Indeed, the military has not been united on any major matter of defense policy. The apparent unity of the Joint Chiefs of Staff turns out to be illusory. The vast majority of their recommendations appears to be unanimous and is accepted by the secretary of defense and the president. But this facade of unity can only be achieved by methods that vitiate the impact of the recommendations. Genuine disagreements are hidden by vague language that commits no one to anything. Mutually contradictory plans are strung together so everyone appears to get something, but nothing is decided. Since it is impossible to agree on really important matters, all sorts of trivia are brought in to make a record of agreement. While it may be true that, as Admiral Denfield, a former chief of naval operations, said, "On nine-tenths of the matters that come before them, the Joint Chiefs of Staff reach agreement themselves," the vastly more important truth is that "Normally the *only* disputes are on strategic concepts, the size and composition of forces, and budget matters."[3]

Military-Industrial Complex

But what about the fabled military-industrial complex? If the military alone is divided and weak, perhaps the giant industrial firms that are so dependent on defense contracts play a large part in making policy.

First, there is an important distinction between the questions "Who will get a given contract?" and "What will our defense policy be?" It is apparent that different answers may be given to these quite different questions. There are literally tens of thousands of defense contractors. They may compete vigorously for business. In the course of this competition, they may wine and dine military officers, use retired generals, seek intervention by their congressmen, place ads in trade journals, and even contribute to political campaigns. The famous TFX controversy—should General Dynamics or Boeing get the expensive contract?—is a larger-than-life example of the pressures brought to bear in search of lucrative contracts.

But neither the TFX case nor the usual vigorous competition for contracts is involved with the making of substantive defense policy. Vital questions like the size of the defense budget, the choice of strategic programs, massive retaliation versus a countercity strategy, and the like, were far beyond the policy aims of any company. Industrial firms, then, do not control such decisions, nor is there much evidence that they actually try. No doubt a precipitous and drastic rush to disarmament would meet with opposition from industrial firms among other interests. There has never been a time, however, when any significant element in the government considered a disarmament policy to be feasible.

It may appear that industrial firms had no special reason to concern themselves with the government's stance on defense because they agree with the national consensus on resisting communism, maintaining a large defense establishment, and rejecting isolationism. However, this hypothesis about the climate of opinion explains everything and nothing. For every policy that is adopted or rejected can be explained away on the grounds that the cold war climate of opinion dictated what happened. Did the United States fail to intervene with armed force in Vietnam in 1954? That must be because the climate of opinion was against it. Did the United States send troops to Vietnam in the 1960s? That must be because the cold war climate demanded it. If the United States builds more missiles, negotiates a test-ban treaty, intervenes in the Dominican Republic, fails to intervene in a dozen other situations, all these actions fit the hypothesis by definition. The argument is reminiscent of those who defined the Soviet Union as permanently hostile and therefore interpreted increases of Soviet troops as menacing, and decreases of troop strength as equally sinister.

If the growth of the military establishment is not directly equated with increasing military control of defense policy, the extraordinary weakness of the professional soldier still requires explanation. Huntington has written about how major military leaders were seduced in the Truman and Eisenhower years into believing that they should bow to the judgment of civilians that the economy could not stand much larger military expenditures. Once the size of the military pie was accepted as a fixed constraint, the military services were compelled to put their major energies into quarreling with one another over who should get the larger share. Given the natural rivalries of the military and their traditional acceptance of civilian rule, the president and his advisers—who could claim responsibility for the broader picture of reconciling defense and domestic policies—had the upper hand. There are, however, additional explanations to be considered.

The dominant role of the congressional appropriations committee is to be guardian of the treasury. This is manifested in the pride of its members in cutting the president's budget. Thus it was difficult to get this crucial committee to recommend even a few hundred million increase in defense; it was practically impossible to get them to consider the several billion jump that might really have made a difference. A related budgetary matter concerned the planning, programming, and budgeting system introduced by Secretary of Defense McNamara. For if the defense budget contained major categories that crisscrossed the services, only the secretary of defense could put it together. Whatever the other debatable consequences of program budgeting, the major one was to grant power to the secretary and his civilian advisers.

The subordination of the military through program budgeting is just one symptom of a more general weakness of the military. In the past

decade the military has suffered a lack of intellectual skills appropriate
to the nuclear age. For no one has (and no one wants) direct experience with nuclear war. So the usual military talk about being the only
people to have combat experience is not very impressive. Instead, the
imaginative creation of possible future wars—in order to avoid them—
requires people with a high capacity for abstract thought, combined
with the ability to manipulate symbols using quantitative methods.
West Point has not produced many such men.

The State Department

Modern presidents expect the State Department to carry out their
policies. John F. Kennedy felt that State was "in some particular sense
'his' department."[4] If a secretary of state forgets this, as was apparently the case with James Byrnes under Truman, a president may find
another man. But the State Department, especially the Foreign Service, is also a highly professional organization with a life and momentum of its own. If a president does not push hard, he may find his
preferences somehow dissipated in time. Arthur Schlesinger fills his
book on Kennedy with laments about the bureaucratic inertia and re-
calcitrance of the State Department.

Yet Schlesinger's own account suggests that State could not ordinarily resist the president. At one point, he writes of "the President,
himself, increasingly the day-to-day director of American foreign policy." On the next page, we learn that "Kennedy dealt personally with
almost every aspect of policy around the globe. He knew more about
certain areas than the senior officials at State and probably called as
many issues to their attention as they did to his."[5] The president insisted on his way in Laos. He pushed through his policy on the Congo
against strong opposition with the State Department. Had Kennedy
wanted to get a great deal more initiative out of the State Department,
as Schlesinger insists, he could have replaced the secretary of state, a
man who did not command special support in the Democratic party or
in Congress. It may be that Kennedy wanted too strongly to run his
own foreign policy. Dean Rusk may have known far better than Schlesinger that the one thing Kennedy did not want was a man who
might rival him in the field of foreign affairs.

Schlesinger comes closest to the truth when he writes that "the

White House could always win any battle it chose over the [Foreign] Service; but the prestige and proficiency of the Service limited the number of battles any White House would find it profitable to fight." When the President knew what he wanted, he got it. When he was doubtful and perplexed, he sought good advice and frequently did not get that. But there is no evidence that the people on his staff came up with better ideas. The real problem may have been a lack of good ideas anywhere. Kennedy undoubtedly encouraged his staff to prod the State Department. But the President was sufficiently cautious not to push so hard that he got his way when he was not certain what that way should be. In this context Kennedy appears to have played his staff off against elements in the State Department.

The growth of a special White House staff to help presidents in foreign affairs expresses their need for assistance, their refusal to rely completely on the regular executive agencies, and their ability to find competent men. The deployment of this staff must remain a presidential prerogative, however, if its members are to serve presidents and not their opponents. Whenever critics do not like existing foreign and defense policies, they are likely to complain that the White House staff is screening out divergent views from the president's attention. Naturally, the critics recommend introducing many more different viewpoints. If the critics could maneuver the president into counting hands all day ("on the one hand and on the other"), they would make it impossible for him to act. Such a viewpoint is also congenial to those who believe that action rather than inaction is the greatest present danger in foreign policy. But presidents resolutely refuse to become prisoners of their advisers by using them as other people would like. Presidents remain in control of their staff as well as of major foreign policy decisions.

How Complete Is the Control?

Some analysts say that the success of presidents in controlling foreign policy decisions is largely illusory. It is achieved, they say, by anticipating the reactions of others, and eliminating proposals that would run into severe opposition. There is some truth in this objection. In politics, where transactions are based on a high degree of mutual interdependence, what others may do has to be taken into account. But basing presidential success in foreign and defense policy on anticipated reactions suggests a static situation, which does not exist. For if presidents propose only those policies that would get support in Congress, and Congress opposes them only when it knows that it can muster overwhelming strength, there would never be any conflict. Indeed, there might never be any action.

How can anticipated reaction explain the conflict over policies like the Marshall Plan and the test-ban treaty in which severe opposition was overcome only be strenuous efforts? Furthermore, why doesn't anticipated reaction work in domestic affairs? One would have to argue that for some reason, presidential perception of what would be successful is consistently confused on domestic issues and most always accurate on major foreign policy issues. But the role of anticipated reactions should be greater in the more familiar domestic situations, which provide a backlog of experience for forecasting, than in foreign policy, with many novel situations such as the Suez crisis or the Rhodesian affair.

Are there significant historical examples that might refute the thesis of presidential control of foreign policy? Foreign aid may be a case in point. For many years, presidents have struggled to get foreign aid appropriations because of hostility from public and congressional opinion. Yet several billion dollars a year are appropriated regularly despite the evident unpopularity of the program. In the aid programs to Communist countries like Poland and Yugoslavia, the Congress attaches all sorts of restrictions to the aid, but presidents find ways of getting around them.

What about the example of recognition of Communist China ? The sentiment of the country always has been against recognizing Red China or admitting it to the United Nations. But have presidents wanted to recognize Red China and been hamstrung by opposition? The answer, I suggest, is a qualified no. By the time recognition of Red China might have become a serious issue for the Truman administration, the war in Korea effectively precluded its consideration. There is no evidence that President Eisenhower or Secretary Dulles ever thought it wise to recognize Red China or help admit her to the United Nations. The Kennedy administration viewed the matter as not of major importance and, considering the opposition, moved cautiously in suggesting change. Then came the war in Vietnam. If the advantages for foreign policy had been perceived to be much higher, then

Kennedy or Johnson might have proposed changing American policy toward recognition of Red China.

One possible exception, in the case of Red China, however, does not seem sufficient to invalidate the general thesis that presidents do considerably better in getting their way in foreign and defense policy than in domestic policies.

The World Influence

The forces impelling presidents to be concerned with the widest range of foreign and defense policies also affect the ways in which they calculate their power stakes. As Kennedy used to say, "Domestic policy . . . can only defeat us; foreign policy can kill us."

It no longer makes sense for presidents to "play politics" with foreign and defense policies. In the past they might have thought they could gain by prolonged delay or by not acting at all; the problem might disappear or be passed on to their successors. Presidents must now expect to pay the high costs themselves if the world situation deteriorates. The advantages of pursuing a policy that is viable in the world, that will not blow up on presidents or their fellow citizens, far outweigh any temporary political disadvantages accrued in supporting an initially unpopular policy. Compared with domestic affairs, presidents engaged in world politics are immensely more concerned with meeting problems on their own terms. Who supports and opposes a policy, though a matter of considerable interest, does not assume the crucial importance that it does in domestic affairs. The best policy presidents can find is also the best politics.

The fact that there are numerous foreign and defense policy situations competing for a president's attention means that it is worthwhile to organize political activity in order to affect his agenda. For if a president pays more attention to certain problems, he may develop different preferences; he may seek and receive different advice; his new calculations may lead him to devote greater resources to seeking a solution. Interested congressmen may exert influence not by directly determining a presidential decision, but by indirectly making it costly for a president to avoid reconsidering the basis for his action. For example, citizens groups, such as those concerned with a change in China policy, may have an impact simply by keeping their proposals on the public agenda. A president may be compelled to reconsider a problem even though he could not overtly be forced to alter the prevailing policy.

In foreign affairs we may be approaching the stage where knowledge is power. There is a tremendous receptivity to good ideas in Washington. Almost anyone who can present a convincing rationale for dealing with a hard world finds a ready audience. The best way to convince presidents to follow a desired policy is to show that it might work. A man like McNamara thrives because he performs; he comes up with answers he can defend. It is, to be sure, extremely difficult to devise good policies or to predict their consequences accurately. Nor is it easy to convince others that a given policy is superior to other alternatives. But it is the way to influence with presidents. For if they are convinced that the current policy is best, the likelihood of gaining sufficient force to compel a change is quite small. The man who can build better foreign policies will find presidents beating a path to his door.

Notes

1. Samuel P. Huntington, *The Common Defense* (New York: Columbia University Press, 1961), 41.
2. Ibid., 375–76.
3. Ibid., 160.
4. Arthur M. Schlesinger, Jr., *A Thousand Days: John F. Kennedy in the White House* (Boston: Houghton Mifflin, 1965), 425.
5. Ibid., 424–25.

3

The Two Presidencies Thesis Revisited at a Time of Political Dissensus

With Duane Oldfield

The United States has one president, but it has two presidencies; one presidency is for domestic affairs, and the other is concerned with defense and foreign policy. Since World War II, presidents have had much greater success in controlling the nation's defense and foreign policies than in dominating its domestic policies.[1]

Made over twenty years ago, Aaron Wildavsky's claim has led to a seemingly endless debate. Did the "two presidencies" phenomena ever exist? If so, *why* did it exist? Has it now departed from the political scene? If so, why has it gone? And how does one measure such things? In 1966 Wildavsky felt confident in stating that "in the realm of foreign policy there has not been a single major issue on which presidents, when they were serious and determined, have failed."[2] Today such a claim would be hard to sustain. The Iran-Contra scandal, exacerbated by the Reagan administration's frustrating failure to win Congress over to its Central American policies, is a case in point. A reassessment of the two presidencies thesis is thus in order.

Too often discussion of the two presidencies is limited to "success rates." Wildavsky claimed that presidential success—however measured—was more likely in foreign policy, but equally important were

Reprinted from *Society* 26, no. 5 (July/August 1989): 54–59.

the reasons that lay behind this claim. "The Two Presidencies" argued that foreign and domestic policy are shaped in distinct political arenas, marked by quite different political configurations. First, given the international responsibilities assumed by the United States in the aftermath of World War II, foreign policy has come to dominate the president's agenda. The pace of international events is rapid, decisions are irreversible, and success or failure is quickly apparent. Events in obscure corners of the world come to be seen as integral aspects of a global conflict. Presidents, therefore, devote more and more of their resources to foreign policy questions. Second, foreign policy is largely outside the field of partisan conflict. Unlike domestic policy, the president does not inherit a detailed party program. "Presidents and their parties have no prior policies on Argentina and the Congo."[3] Third, for a variety of reasons, the president's competitors in the foreign policy arena are weak. Relatively few interest groups are active; Congress is deferential; the public is uninformed and unable to provide policy direction. An expanded, expert staff allows the president to challenge the entrenched interests of the military and the State Department.

The overall picture is that of a foreign policymaking process insulated from the pluralistic pressures normally associated with American democracy. The battle of interest groups, parties, and bureaucracies fades into the background. What emerges is a rather apolitical, technical realm of presidential problem solving. "In foreign affairs . . . he can almost always get support for policies that he believes will protect the nation—but his problem is to find a viable policy."[4]

This picture of the foreign policy-making process is evidently wrong today. Before we ask what went wrong, however, we turn to a somewhat narrower issue: *are* presidents actually more successful in the foreign policy area? This is a hotly debated question.

Are Presidents More Successful in Foreign Policy?

Presidential success in Congress, perhaps because it is easily quantified, has become the central issue of this ongoing debate. Yet here, quantification has not led to agreement. "The Two Presidencies" applied a relatively simple measure of presidential success—*Congressional Quarterly* "boxscores" on the fate of presidential initiatives. For the period from 1948 to 1964, it was found that whereas only 40.2

percent of domestic policy proposals were approved by Congress, 58.5 percent of foreign policy and 73.3 percent of defense policy proposals were successful.[5] LeLoup and Shull made the same calculations for the 1965–75 period. A gap between domestic and foreign policy success remained, but it was much smaller for the latter period (46 percent domestic versus 50 percent foreign and 61 percent defense).[6]

The boxscore measurements ran into several problems. First, presidential proposals go through many modifications prior to final congressional approval or rejection. How does one determine whether the original proposal has been approved or whether it has been modified out of existence? Doubts about reliability led *Congressional Quarterly* to drop its boxscore tabulations in the mid-1970s. Second, a compilation of *all* initiatives mixes together the crucial and the trivial and may, therefore, be misleading. How important is foreign policy success if much of it comes on such uncontroversial matters as increasing the number of members of the Air Navigation Commission?[7]

Lee Sigelman, therefore, decided to use a more restrictive measure of presidential success. Sigelman looked at votes (on which the president had taken a position) rather than at presidential initiatives. Analysis was limited to *key* votes, as determined by *Congressional Quarterly*.[8] Harvey Zeidenstein built upon Sigelman, examining separately the results in each chamber of Congress.[9] Yet key votes have their problems as well.[10] They are small in number and, thus, shifts on a few close votes can lead to large shifts in the percentage of votes won. Also, it is difficult to tell from aggregate vote totals exactly where support for the president is coming from.

Richard Fleisher and Jon Bond attempted to overcome these problems by looking at a wider array of votes.[11] They examined presidential success on foreign and domestic conflictual roll calls. In addition, they constructed a measure of "important" votes that was broader and less volatile than the "key" vote measure.[12] Finally, the individual voting records of members of various party factions were examined to determine the sources of support for, and opposition to, the president. The analysis of individual voting records followed upon the work of George Edwards III.[13] Rather than measure the percentage of votes won by the president, Edwards looked at the percentage of votes on which each congressman supported the president, broken down by policy area, party, chamber, and region.[14]

What is to be made of these controversies over measurement? Multiple methodologies have led to multiple conclusions. A few themes, however, do emerge.

The Eisenhower administration provides the clearest example of the two presidencies phenomena. Each approach finds significantly greater support for Eisenhower on foreign policy issues. Beyond Eisenhower, confusion reigns. The Kennedy and Johnson administrations do not fit well with the two presidencies thesis. In fact, if we look at aggregate key votes, we find significantly greater support for their *domestic* policies. The Senate, in particular, was likely to object to their foreign policies.

The results for the Nixon and Ford administrations are mixed. Edwards finds slight advantages in foreign policy, Sigelman shows Ford doing better in domestic policy, and Zeidenstein finds opposite patterns in the House and Senate. The Carter presidency is also difficult to interpret. Carter won many foreign policy key votes by very small margins. When one looks at aggregate key votes, as Sigelman and Zeidenstein do, Carter's foreign policy success rate is extremely high. The two presidencies appear to have returned. Yet when individual voting patterns are analyzed by Edwards, little support for the two presidencies thesis is found.

Less complete data is available on the Reagan administration. Edwards finds success rates in foreign and domestic policy to be quite similar for Reagan's first three years. Fleisher and Bond come to a similar conclusion for the 1981–82 period but find that the two presidencies return in 1983–84. After some decisive early victories, Reagan ran into serious difficulties with Congress. In 1987 he became the first President since *Congressional Quarterly* has kept records to win on less than half the votes on which he took a stand. The greatest decline came on domestic issues, and by 1987 the gap between foreign and domestic support characteristic of the two presidencies had reappeared.[15] Leon Halpert's study of House voting patterns for the years 1981–1986 also finds greater support for Reagan on foreign (particularly defense) policy votes.[16] Halpert and *Congressional Quarterly* use measures significantly different from Sigelman and Edwards. Caution must therefore be used in comparisons with earlier periods.

Fleisher and Bond find a somewhat different pattern than the other authors. Like the others, they find the two presidencies to be most pronounced during the Eisenhower administration. Unlike the others, they find it exists for all Republican presidents. They conclude that the phenomena is linked to party and has not significantly diminished over time. These findings, however, are true only of their measure of all conflictual roll calls; on "important" votes, little evidence of the two presidencies is found.[17]

Sources of Support for Foreign Policy

To the extent that the two presidencies do exist, where does greater foreign policy support come from? Foreign policy success is often seen as crucial to a president's image, therefore we might expect members of the president's party to rally around him, particularly on key foreign policy votes. This, however, is not the case. Both Sigelman and Edwards find that the president's party is more likely to support his domestic than his foreign policies. Fleisher and Bond agree that when the two presidencies appear it is the result of greater support from the opposition. This should not, however, be taken as an indicator of true bipartisanship in foreign policy. Edwards finds that only during the Eisenhower administration do opposition members support the president on over 50 percent of foreign policy votes.[18]

The End of Consensus, the Beginnings of Dissensus

These studies cast serious doubts on the conclusions of "The Two Presidencies," outside the period in which they were proposed. Only Eisenhower is clearly more successful in foreign policy. Presidents cannot count upon bipartisan support when they find a "workable" policy. From Richard Nixon's Vietnam policies, to Gerald Ford's attempts to intervene in Angola, to President Reagan's difficulties gaining support for the Contras and SDI, it has become clear that presidential control of foreign policy is not so complete as Wildavsky claimed. (It is important to remember that success in Congress is only one aspect of presidential power. When other aspects are considered, the two presidencies thesis looks considerably stronger, a point to which we shall return later in the essay.)

The controversy over President Reagan's Strategic Defense Initiative provides a useful perspective on these issues. One would expect this to be a technical issue. Will the proposed system be effective in combatting incoming missiles? How much will it cost? How quickly can it be developed? If, as "The Two Presidencies" claims, foreign policy is a realm of technical problem solving, the debate over SDI could be expected to exemplify it.

This is not how the debate has unfolded. Presidential success has not been easy. If the questions involved are technical, we are left to account for the fact that the debate has split neatly along party lines. SDI became a litmus test for candidates of both parties in the 1988 presidential campaign. The executive branch has no monopoly on expertise.[19] The president's arguments for SDI have been subjected to expert criticism from a wide variety of sources. The debate over SDI illustrates the limitations of the analysis presented in "The Two Presidencies."

The most important issue is that of ideological and partisan divisions. Wildavsky uses McNamara as an example of a man who "thrives because he performs; he comes up with answers he defends."[20] Yet the sort of "answers" a McNamara provides can be widely accepted only if participants in policy debates are asking the same questions, accepting a similar framework for interpreting the evidence. Shortly after the publication of "The Two Presidencies," it became clear that McNamara's techniques could not overcome ideological divisions over U.S. policy in Southeast Asia. Nor could the expertise of the Kissinger Commission resolve more recent controversy over Central American policy. Ideological and partisan differences are too intimately involved; different questions are being asked, different evidence cited.

The studies of congressional voting patterns referred to earlier provide strong evidence of partisan divisions in foreign policy. If we look at key foreign policy votes from the Eisenhower through the Carter administrations, we find that a majority of the opposition party supports only Eisenhower more than half the time. Lyndon Johnson is the only other president to receive such support on over 30 percent of key foreign policy votes.[21] Edwards paints a similar picture; after the Eisenhower administration, opposition members' level of support runs below (usually well below) 50 percent for each chamber of Congress in each administration. While post-Eisenhower presidents tend to receive slightly less foreign than domestic support from their own party and slightly greater foreign than domestic support from the opposition, party differences on foreign policy remain very large. Leon Halpert's study of House voting patterns under President Reagan comes to a similar conclusion. "The recent characterization of foreign policy as a field engendering greater partisan based controversy and competition is empirically buttressed by our data . . . when partisanship developed on foreign policy matters during these years it evoked the most intense interparty conflict."[22]

Did the President *ever* have the kind of secure, bipartisan support described in "The Two Presidencies"? George Edwards thinks not. Even under Eisenhower, he argues, foreign policy success had little to do with inherent presidential advantages. Edwards attributes Eisenhower's success to a simple fact: he proposed foreign policies that Democrats agreed with. His internationalist policies drew strong support from northern Democrats who approved of such a course. Northern Democrats were even more supportive of Eisenhower than were Republicans.[23] Conservative southern Democrats, with neither ideological nor party ties to the president provided much lower levels of support. Northern Democrats abandoned Eisenhower on domestic issues, where they disagreed with him, and thus created the differential between foreign and domestic support characteristic of the two presidencies. "Presidents have enjoyed no free ride in the foreign policy realm." Edwards concludes, "They have generally obtained support the old fashioned way: appealing to independent power holders with the substance of policies."[24]

Edwards argues that, in effect, the two presidencies arose briefly because of the chance agreement of opposing parties. Perhaps, however, agreement was rooted more deeply. A different interpretation of Edwards's data is possible, an interpretation that makes more understandable the claims of "The Two Presidencies." Wildavsky argued that presidential control of foreign policy arose from the new world role taken on by the United States in the aftermath of World War II. What we would argue today is that agreement as to the proper understanding of that role was also crucial. This understanding is what broke down in the years after Eisenhower. When basic agreements concerning the direction of foreign policy break down, bipartisan deference to the president is unlikely to survive. Let us look in more detail at the changes that have undermined the two presidencies.

Two Foreign Policies Competing for One Presidency

"The Two Presidencies" is time- and culture-bound. It succeeds in showing that the Eisenhower administration had higher support in foreign and defense matters as compared to domestic policy and in explaining why. It fails in that both the patterns of behavior and the reasons for their maintenance did not exist in the decades before or after the 1950s.[25] In addition to being time-bound, the thesis is also, as we will argue, culturally limited. By that we mean that the shared values that sustained consensus on defense during the 1950s gave way in the late 1960s to different ones with far different results.

The breakdown of a postwar bipartisan policy consensus has been a common theme among foreign policy analysts.[26] Clearly, bipartisanship was never complete. Partisan battles over missile gaps and the loss of China were intense. Wildavsky had little use for the concept of a "cold war consensus." Yet looking back from the perspective of the last twenty years, this consensus appears to have had a bit more reality to it. The breakdown of this consensus, we believe, has profoundly altered the operation of the two presidencies.

Not only is the president more likely to face opposition, the nature of foreign policy conflicts has changed as well. In the 1950s and early 1960s, partisan battles tended to be about performance (or lack thereof) in pursuit of commonly shared objectives, as in the missile gap debate. Recent years have seen more fundamental disagreement concerning the objectives of American foreign policy.

A persuasive account of these changes is provided by Michael Mandelbaum and William Schneider.[27] They argue that, among the general public, an internationalist consensus has given way to two new, and opposed, internationalisms. In the twenty years after World War II, the main division was between internationalists and noninternationalists, those suspicious of an active American role in world affairs. Internationalism was dominant, particularly among the educated public and the elite, who helped shape policy. Vietnam and detente, however, led to serious divisions *within* the internationalist public, and two groups emerged. Liberal internationalists support cooperative endeavors—arms control, giving economic aid to poorer nations, strengthening the United Nations—but put less emphasis on fighting communism. They show little support for the use of force. Conservative internationalists see a much more hostile world environment in which American interests and values must be actively defended. They support a strong military and the use of force in international affairs. Noninternationalists remain from the earlier period. Less educated and less interested in world affairs, this group is suspicious of both cooperative and competitive international commitments.[28] The crucial development, however, is the rise of serious ideological divisions among the active, educated internationalists. For it is with their demands that foreign policymakers must deal.

Mandelbaum and Schneider's data fits into a larger pattern of cultural change affecting both foreign and domestic policy. Whereas during Eisenhower's time in office, defense and domestic issues were on separate ideological dimensions, so that public officials who disagreed on one would frequently agree on the other, later the two spheres of policy became fused along a single ideological dimension. What needs clarification is how and why major issues that were once fairly separate became fused.

In the Eisenhower era, once the old isolationist forces had been defeated, there was widespread agreement on the desirability and efficacy of American national political institutions.[29] There was the slave world, with its captive nations; it was bad and dangerous. There was the free world, with its liberty-loving alliances; it was good. Protecting good against evil was the role of the United States as "the leader of the free world." This "Western" version of the showdown eventually came into question.

The range of national issues in the 1950s was woefully narrow, compared to today. A liberal was a person who believed in a greater role for the federal government in providing social welfare. A conservative wanted less. Social issues, such as prayer in school and abortion rights, were unheard of. Civil rights for blacks was on the agenda, but not prominent. Environmental issues were discrete entities, not a movement. Foreign policy mattered, but it was not debated on principles that divided the parties.

The presidency of John F. Kennedy proved to be the dividing line. Recall that Kennedy ran on the basis of a stronger defense in which, among other things, the alleged missile gap figured prominently. When he told the American people how much he regretted the Bay of Pigs fiasco, President Kennedy said it was so awful that he would never speak of it again. And, remarkably, from the perspective of the 1980s, he got away with it. Not now! Kennedy's relationship with the media was excellent, a phenomenon that used to be commonplace but has not recurred since. While Kennedy may have reduced one barrier in being the first Catholic to become president, he was not a champion of civil rights. His exhortations to the American people involved reaching the heights of technology (the space program) or bearing international burdens, not redressing injustices or inequalities at home. America was good; it had only to extend that goodness outward and onward.

The hostile reaction to the war in Vietnam that began in Kennedy's time and was extended by his successor, Lyndon Johnson, is usually credited with turning many Americans against military intervention abroad and institutions they suspected of deceiving them at home. No doubt the war was a factor. But if the cause was the war, or mainly the war, then we cannot explain what happened afterward. For one thing, there was no national consensus on the war, aside from its inefficacy, or on the American use of force in the international arena. Although there was no new massive use of force, that did not stop the mounting criticism of those in authority—a cascade so constant it has become a natural condition, the opposite, say, to the "end of ideology" thesis of the 1950s.

The split on foreign policy was intensified by increasing division over domestic policy. Merely to list the major movements that began or became prominent from the late 1960s onward—not only civil rights but women's rights, gay rights, children's rights, animal rights, environmentalism, gray power, and more—is to trace the emerging differences.

Of special interest to us is the fact that these issues do not appear at random but are politically clustered. All of these issues belong to the Democrats, in that their party has become the advocate, while the Republicans have become the opponents of using government to protect these rights. Even more striking, foreign and domestic issues line up quite nicely, with the Republicans urging more for defense and less for social welfare and "rights," and Democrats willing to do less for defense and more for rights and welfare.

Here we have it: domestic *and* foreign issues now divide the parties. And there are many more issues—social, civil, "rights, ecological, defense—to divide the parties. American parties are becoming more ideologically distinct. Conservative southern Democrats are moving toward the Republican party, and liberal Republicans are now an endangered species. While diversity still exists in each party, particularly at the mass level, the parties are slowly edging their way toward internal ideological unity. In Congress, despite earlier academics' fears of weakening party ties, partisan voting is on the rise. In

1987, *Congressional Quarterly*'s measure of party unity voting in the House hit its highest level since such measurements began in 1955.[30] Warren Miller and Kent Jennings document growing ideological differences between the parties' convention delegates. Indeed, each party's activists are more united internally and more distant from each other than at any period for which data exists.[31]

Furthermore, division on international issues are coming to reenforce, rather than cut across, domestic ones. In Mandelbaum and Schneider's terms, the Democrats and Republicans have become the parties of, respectively, liberal and conservative internationalism. In the 1950s the division between internationalists and noninternationalists occurred *within* each party. Eisenhower had the more isolationist Taft wing of the party to deal with, and many southern Democrats did not share their northern counterparts' enthusiasm for international commitments. Barry Hughes finds that congressional support for defense spending and foreign aid did not split neatly along party lines in the 1950s and the early 1960s. Northern Democrats, as the more internationalist group, tended to be more supportive, but the pattern was not always clear. In the mid-1960s and early 1970s a significant change on these issues took place when control of the White House changed hands. Northern Democratic support for defense spending and military foreign aid dropped dramatically. Support for economic foreign aid remained high, in keeping with the principles of an emerging liberal internationalism. Republican and southern Democratic support for defense spending and military foreign aid rose dramatically as conservative internationalism emerged among them.[32]

In order to draw implications for the two presidencies thesis from these developments, we must try to specify the dimensions along which contemporary cleavages occur, dimensions which serve to unify the parties against each other so as to wipe out the differences in treatment of foreign and domestic policy that took place during Dwight David Eisenhower's presidency. If we inquire about which values unite the Democratic party of the 1980s, the answer is straightforward—greater equality of condition. The main purpose of the movements of which we spoke earlier is precisely to reduce power differences between black and white, women and men, gay and straight, and so on. It is precisely the influx of feminists and blacks, and the exit of southern Democrats who oppose their views, that has given the activist corps of the Democratic party its special stamp. Indeed, the

Democratic party of the 1950s and 1960s, exemplified by Hubert Humphrey and Henry Jackson, who combined strong welfare with strong defense, is no more (try thinking of current exemplars). The leading candidates for the Democratic nomination in 1988, Jesse Jackson and Michael Dukakis, were well within the mainstream of their party's activists.

The Republican case is equally clear, but a bit more complex because it is two dimensional, corresponding roughly to economic and social conservatism. In the period from the 1930s through the mid-1960s, to provide a brief historical dimension, the United States could correctly be called a capitalist country (compared to most others), but there were few talented defenders of its legitimating values. Perhaps capitalism was too firmly ensconced to require constant overt justification. In any event, in the 1970s and 1980s there arose a considerable cadre of capitalist intellectuals who provided new designs for public policies, from privatization to the flat tax. More animated and self-confident than their predecessors and, backed by the apparatus of modern economics, they constituted the free market, or equal opportunity dimension of Republicanism.

In mentioning modern social movements, we deliberately left out one that informs the contemporary Republican party, the Protestant fundamentalists. Believers in patriarchy and sharing hierarchical values, they sought to maintain social distinctions within family and society. Thus they gave the Republican party a second dimension. To be sure, social and economic conservatives disagree about government efforts to enforce social norms, but they are sufficiently close on a limited economic role for government, including opposition to such measures as affirmative action in hiring and promotion, as well as opposition to international communism, to constitute a viable coalition.

But how, we still have to ask, were the domestic and foreign policy concerns joined through these dimensions? Our hypothesis is that the egalitarians who gravitated to the Democratic party viewed defense as taking away from welfare, therefore inegalitarian. In a corresponding manner, they saw the United States as a First World country beating up on Third World countries, *i.e.,* as engaging in inegalitarian behavior abroad. Liberal internationalist policies were to help address these inequalities and to free up resources for use at home.

Republican social and economic conservatives viewed life in the

United States very differently. To them, American institutions were marvelous except that they weren't pursued as much as they would have liked. Freer markets and stronger adherence to moral norms was what they wanted. At home they wanted less government because the underlying institutions were benign. Abroad they favored a conservative internationalist policy, both to protect democratic capitalism and to project its institutions further, where they would do even more good.

Dissensus Undermines the Two Presidencies

How has the rise of ideological and partisan divisions affected the operation of the two presidencies? Let us take a quick look at the political configuration within which foreign policy was made in the 1950s and early 1960s. An internationalist consensus (a belief in the legitimacy of American institutions and the need to extend them) among northern Democrats and the Eisenhower wing of the Republican party led to a situation in which fundamental disagreement over objectives was rare. Internationalism was particularly strong among political elites. "Responsible" opinion among politicians, academics, and the press held that the United States must be willing to uphold its international obligations even if—as in the case of Korea—this was expensive and unpopular. Elites were held to have a duty to stick together so as to educate the public away from its dangerous tendencies toward isolationism. Internationalism was in the public interest.

In such an environment, Wildavsky's description of the two presidencies had some validity to it. Where fundamental disagreement was not present, Congress was often willing to give the president the benefit of the doubt. The president's advantages in terms of access to information, public stature, and ability to take rapid and decisive action all contributed to congressional deference. The executive branch was seen as the bastion of internationalism, while the Congress was viewed as more likely to support irresponsible parochialism.[33] This, we believe, led to elite support for presidential control of foreign policy. Given the high value placed on presidential leadership, responsible opinion was reluctant to directly attack the president. Although presidents were likely to suffer the consequences if their policies did not succeed, they did have relatively broad discretion to initiate policies they believed necessary.

With the breakdown of consensus, the situation changes. If members of Congress disagree with the basic objectives of a president's foreign policy, deference is much less likely. Expert execution counts for little if the policy is deemed to be fundamentally flawed or immoral, inegalitarian or un-American. Instead of uniting in an attempt to educate the apathetic masses (noninternationalists), elites now appeal to that group as a source of support in their wars against each other. As ideological and partisan divisions have come to reenforce each other, prospects for unity erode further. Or, to put it another way, foreign policy has become more like domestic policy—a realm marked by serious partisan divisions in which the president cannot count on a free ride.

The old system of foreign policymaking was further weakened by a number of additional changes in American political life. The press has grown less deferential in all areas.[34] A more educated and active public is also a more ideological public, so ideologically oriented interest groups have come to play a greater role in the process of presidential nomination. There are also more domestic groups with foreign policy agendas, not only Jews on Israel, but blacks on South Africa, Poles on Poland, and more. All these changes have added to the difficulty of keeping foreign policy isolated from public scrutiny and pressure.

From the viewpoint of the 1950s this looks unusual, but perhaps the 1950s are a poor benchmark. Conflict and shared control of foreign policy are quite normal in the American system, which is to say that we agree with Bert Rockman who writes:

> This relatively rare circumstance [the post-second World War "bipartisan national security consensus"] has since been shrouded in legend as a norm from which America's recent foreign policy-making process has deviated, moving from consensual premises and presidential leadership to conflicting premises and to frequent policy disagreement.

> The institutional supposition behind this traditional concept of a foreign policy based on consensual premises is one of a virtually exclusive presidentialist approach to American national security policy-making, and one thereby removed from the tugs and pulls and parochial pressures of domestic policy-making. . . . The "repluralization" of national security policy-making, of course. is intimately related to the growth of fundamental disagreement about policy course. But the American system of government also provides considerable opportunities for the opposition to influence policy that are unparalleled.[35]

The Two Presidencies: What Remains?

Twenty years ago "The Two Presidencies" exaggerated the degree of presidential control over American foreign policy. Given the changes we have discussed, is anything left of the two presidencies?

First, it is important to point out that partisan and ideological divisions do not affect all areas of foreign policy equally. Many positions do not fit neatly into opposing ideological frameworks (the Arab-Israeli conflict, for example). Or, as in the case of the Persian Gulf, no side feels that it has a viable solution to the problem. In these situations the president may be given more leeway to develop an approach of his own.

Second, the fact that foreign policy has become more like domestic policy does not mean that presidents cannot win; they must simply win differently. After all, presidents have been known to prevail on domestic issues. The new environment favors a plebiscitary presidency; public appeals replace establishment consensus.[36] The president, symbol of the nation and center of media attention, is not without resources in such an environment.

Third, much of the President's power in foreign policy lies outside the measures of success we have focused upon in this essay. Easily measured, success in Congress has been the central concern of the two presidencies literature.[37] Yet the obvious must be stated: The president is commander in chief, and this does matter. There is little Congress can do about a Grenada invasion or, for that matter, a decision to initiate nuclear war. Nor can Congress play the president's diplomatic role. It can express its preferences concerning arms control; it may frustrate the president's plans by refusing to further arm the Nicaraguan Contras; but without presidential action, little positive can be done.

Dissensus: What Is to Be Done?

In the era of blessed consensus now gone, things were better. Or so it is claimed. We would all love consensus—around our own values. President Reagan called for bipartisan support of his Central American policies. Democrats claim all would have been well had he not been so divisive. In other words, consensus consists of the other side giving in. As the parties divide more neatly, over more issues, the temperature of national politics rises. According to the theory of cross-cutting cleavages, when decision makers agree on some issues while disagreeing on others, they have an incentive to moderate their conflict in order to work together when necessary. When the same people take opposing sides over more and more issues, by contrast, each difference tends to deepen mutual hostility. Nowadays there is a lot more than a "dimes worth of difference" between the major political parties. Disagreement of this sort, combined with the separation of powers, can be a recipe for stalemate.[38] Or, as in the case of the Iran-Contra affair, it can lead to something worse. It is frustrating, as Oliver North discovered, to find that the American government is not a finely tuned machine coordinated in pursuit of one's own values. That, however, is not only as the Founding Fathers intended but as most Americans still prefer.

Short of rewriting the Constitution, what can be done? We believe that calls for consensus are likely to fall on deaf ears. The public is more educated and ideological than it used to be, the divisions we discussed earlier are deeply rooted in the party system. Neither side is likely to give in. Yet dissensus is not necessarily a bad thing.[39] It is desirable that foreign policy be openly and frequently debated. Perhaps contacts with more minds from diverse perspectives would have avoided past blunders. Perhaps the inability to find a publicly acceptable rationale for the growing involvement in Vietnam or for giving arms to "moderates" in Iran should have sent up warning signals. Whatever short-run difficulties it causes, public debate is more likely to lead to a policy that can be supported in the long run. On some issues, such as the INF treaty, debate may lead to agreement across party lines. On others, we may, for the moment, have to learn to live with disagreement. Attempting to suppress debate with pleas for consensus and presidential discretion cannot hide the reality of ideological division. Nor does it place much faith in the democratic process.

Notes

1. Aaron Wildavsky, "The Two Presidencies," *Trans*-Action 4 (1966): 7–14, reprinted in Aaron Wildavsky, ed., *Perspective on the Presidency*. (Boston: Little, Brown, 1975), 448.
2. Ibid., 449.
3. Ibid., 448.

4. Ibid., 448.
5. Ibid., 449.
6. Lance T. LeLoup and Steven A. Shull, "Congress versus the Executive: The Two Presidencies Reconsidered," *Social Science Quarterly* 59, no. 4 (1979): 707.
7. Lee Sigelman, "A Reassessment of the Two Presidencies Thesis," *Journal of Politics* 41 (1979): 1198.
8. LeLoup and Shull, "Congress versus the Executive," 704–19.
9. Harvey G. Zeidenstein, "The Two Presidencies Thesis Is Alive and Well and Has Been Living in the U.S. Senate Since 1973," *Presidential Studies Quarterly* 11, no. 4 (1981): 511–25.
10. See the exchange between Sigelman and LeLoup and Shull concerning the relative merits of their approaches. *Journal of Politics* 43 (1981): 563–65.
11. Richard Fleisher and Jon R. Bond, "Are There Two Presidencies? Yes, But Only for Republicans," *Journal of Politics* 50 (1988): 747–67.
12. Fleisher and Bond define conflictual roll calls as votes on which there is less than 80 percent support for the president's position. Their measure of "important" votes includes *Congressional Quarterly* key votes and additional votes determined by a formula based on closeness of the vote and turnout. See ibid., 748–50.
13. George Edwards, "The Two Presidencies: A Reevaluation," *American Politics Quarterly* 14 (1986): 247–63.
14. Edwards also creates separate measures of support on overall voting versus voting on key issues and finds support for the view that inclusion of minor matters tends to inflate success rates. As this occurs in both foreign and domestic policy, however, the impact on measurements of the two presidencies is not great.
15. Janet Hook, "Reagan's Clout in Congress Falls to Record Low," *Congressional Quarterly* 46, no. 3 (1988): 91–100.
16. Leon Halpert, "Presidential Leadership of Congress: Evaluating President Reagan's Success in the House of Representatives, 1981–86," unpublished.
17. We have our doubts concerning "important" votes as they measure them. The formula they use is tied to the closeness of the vote (as well as turnout). It should not be surprising that presidents do not win significantly more extremely close foreign policy votes than extremely close domestic policy votes. The two presidencies argument would suggest, however, that the votes on crucial foreign policy issues would only rarely be extremely close. Thus their important vote measure does not seem to be a fair test of the two presidencies.
18. Edwards, "The Two Presidencies," 253–57.

19. See Aaron Wildavsky, "Administration Without Hierarchy? Bureaucracy Without Authority?" Preface to *Public Administration: State of the Discipline*, Naomi Lynn and Aaron Wildavsky, eds., (Chatham N.J.: Chatham House, 1990), xiii–xix; Aaron Wildavsky, "Ubiquitous Anomie: Public Service in an Era of Ideological Dissensus," *Public Administration Review* 48, no. 4 (July/August 1988), 735–55, on the extent to which rival teams of analysts, layers deep, now exist in virtually all spheres of public policy.

20. Wildavsky, "The Two Presidencies," 461.

21. Sigelman, "Reassessment," 1195–1205.

22. Halpert, "Presidential Leadership," 43–44.

23. Edwards, "The Two Presidencies," 259.

24. Ibid., 262.

25. For a discussion of the 1950s as the "misleading decade," see Aaron Wildavsky, "Resolved, That Individualism and Egalitarianism Be Made Compatible in America: Political Cultural Roots of Exceptionalism," paper presented at a conference on American Exceptionalism at Nuffield College, Oxford, April 14–16, 1988.

26. See, for example, Bert Rockman, "Mobilizing Political Support for U.S. National Security," *Armed Forces & Society* 14, no. 1 (1987): 17–41; and I.M. Destler, Leslie Gelb, and Anthony Lake, *Our Own Worst Enemy* (New York: Simon & Schuster, 1984).

27. Michael Mandelbaum and William Schneider, "The New Internationalisms: Public Opinion and Foreign Policy," In Kenneth Oye, Donald Rothchild, and Robert Lieber, eds., *Eagle Entangled* (New York: Longman, 1979), 40–63.

28. Ibid., 40–41.

29. Gabriel A. Almond and Sidney Verba's The Civic Cultur*e: Political Attitudes and Democracy in Five Nationsl* (Princeton Univ. Press, 1963) is a remarkable demonstration of how citizens felt then.

30. Hook, "Reagan's Clout," 93.

31. Warren Miller and Kent Jennings, *Parties in Transition* (New York: Russell Sage Foundation, 1986).

32. Barry Hughes, *The Domestic Context of American Foreign Policy*, (New York: W.H. Freeman, 1978), esp. chap. 5.

33. This can be seen in studies by Kesselman (1961) and Tiddmarch and Sabatt (1972). Looking at cases in which control of the White House switched hands, these studies attempt to measure how the voting patterns of party members in Congress changed on foreign policy issues. What is interesting from our point of view is that internationalism is assumed to be synonymous with support for the president. Thus when a new president takes office, members of his party are expected to shift to a more

internationalist voting pattern. This holds true for the transitions of 1953 and 1961 but, as our argument might suggest, the expected pattern does not emerge in 1969. See Mark Kesselman, "Presidential Leadership in Foreign Policy," *Midwest Journal of Political Science 5* (1961): 284–89 and Charles M. Tidmarch and Charles M. Sabatt, "Presidential Leadership Change and Foreign Policy Roll-Call Voting in the Senate," *Western Political Quarterly* 25 (1972): 613–25.

34. Destler, Gelb, and Lake, "Our Own Worst Enemy," 139–40.
35. Rockman, "Mobilizing Political Support," 18.
36. See, in particular, Theodore J. Lowi's *The Personal President* (Ithaca, N.Y.: Cornell University Press, 1985), esp. chap. 5, and Sanford Weiner and Aaron Wildavsky, "The Prophylactic Presidency," *The Public Interest*, no. 52 (Summer 1978), 3–19.
37. Exceptions are to be found in Rockman and in Donald Peppers, "The Two Presidencies: Eight Years Later," in Aaron Wildavsky, ed., *Perspectives on the Presidency* (Boston: Little, Brown, 1975).
38. This can be seen in the continual inability to agree to the annual budget, a classical sign of ideological dissensus, as well as division over how to balance the budget. See Aaron Wildavsky, *The New Politics of the Budgetary Process* (Glenview, Ill.: Scott, Foresman/Boston: Little Brown, 1988); and Joseph White and Aaron Wildavsky, *The Deficit and the Public Interest* (Berkeley: University of California Press, 1990).
39. Others disagree. See Destler, Gelb, and Lake, *Our Own Worst Enemy*.

4

The Past and Future Presidency

In the third volume of *The American Commonwealth*, Lord Bryce wrote, "Perhaps no form of Government needs great leaders so much as democracy." Why, then, is it so difficult to find them? The faults of leadership are the everyday staple of conversation. All of us have become aware of what Bryce had in mind in his chapter on "True Faults of American Democracy," when he alluded to "a certain commonness of mind and tone, a want of dignity and elevation in and about the conduct of public affairs, an insensibility to the nobler aspects and finer responsibilities of national life." If leaders have let us down, they have been helped, as Bryce foresaw, by the cynical "apathy among the luxurious classes and fastidious minds, who find themselves of no more account than the ordinary voter, and are disgusted by the superficial vulgarities of public life." But Bryce did not confuse condemnation with criticism. He thought that "the problem of conducting a stable executive in a democratic country is indeed so immensely difficult that anything short of failure deserves to be called a success." Explaining "Why Great Men Are Not Chosen" in the first volume of his classic, Bryce located the defect not only in party politics but in popular passions: "The ordinary American voter does not object to mediocrity."

Ultimately, Bryce was convinced, "republics Live by Virtue"—with a capital V, meaning "the maintenance of a high level of public spirit and justice among the citizens." Note: "among the citizens," not merely among public officials. For how could leaders rise so far above the led; or, stemming from the people, be so superior to them; or held

Reprinted from *The Public Interest,* no. 41 (Fall 1975): 56–76.

accountable, stray so far from popular will? Surely it would be surprising if the vices of politicians stemmed from the virtues of the people. What the people do to their leaders must be at least as important as what the leaders do to them. There are, after all, so many of us and so few of them. Separating the presidency from the people—as if a president owed everything to them and they nothing to him—makes as much sense as removing the people from the government it has instituted.

If the reciprocal relations between political leadership and social expectations could be resolved by exhortation, the problem would long ago have ceased to be serious. If expectations are not being met, it is leaders who are not meeting them, and either lower expectations or higher caliber leadership is required. But both may be out of kilter. Should one or two leaders fail, that may well be their fault. When all fail (Kennedy, Johnson, Nixon), when, moreover, all known replacements are expected to fail, the difficulty is not individual but systemic. It is not the action of one side or the reaction of another but their mutual relationships that are flawed. That the people may reject their presidents is obvious; that presidents might flee from their people is less so. Once presidents discover the embrace of the people is deadly, they may well seek to escape from it. Presidents who tried to exercise powers they did not have might then be replaced by presidents unwilling to exercise the powers they do have. The future of the presidency will be determined not by the presidents alone but by how they behave in response to the environment "we-the-people" create for them. Presidents, we shall learn, can retreat as well as advance.

Presidents Face Contradictory Demands

We shall never learn what needs to be learned about the American political system until we understand not only what the system does to the people, but what the people do to the system. Political institutions are no different from other organizations: to the great question of organizational life—who will bear the costs of change?—the answer, in the public as in the private sphere, is, "someone else, not me." The universal tendency to make life easy for ourselves and to impose difficulties on others applies equally to politicians, and when they find their lives intolerable, no one should be surprised that they react by seeking to lay their burdens on the shoulders of others.

Almost our whole attention as citizens has been devoted to the ways in which politicians have failed to serve the people. Few have asked how politicians manage to live in the world, because it is assumed that they are doing fine and that the problem is to make them behave decently toward us—almost as if politicians lived somehow apart from American life. Yet it would be strange indeed if our politicians were a special breed, uninfluenced by their milieu, springing full-born, like Minerva from the head of Jove, in a world they never made but on which they work their mythical powers.

Politicians are like other animals; indeed their behavior, like our own, can often be analogized to that observed in lower forms of life. Laboratory experiments show that rats who are consistently given contradictory commands become neurotic, if not psychotic. The same phenomenon is readily visible among politicians. Give them incompatible commands, insist that they fulfill contradictory impulses at the same time, and they too will show the classical symptoms—withdrawal, self-mutilation, random activity, and other forms of bizarre behavior unrelated to the ostensible task at hand. An occasional deviant has even been known to lash out at his experimenters, or at least at the apparatus in which he is enmeshed, though he remains quite incapable of understanding why he worked so hard to accomplish so little, or why life is so bitter when it should be so sweet.

We are all, in fact, doing better and feeling worse.[1] Every standard of well-being, from housing to health, shows that every sector of the population, however defined, including all racial, religious, and ethnic groupings, has improved its lot in past decades. Even the twin problems of crime and drugs, areas in which we are vividly conscious of recent deterioration, have been considerably reduced in severity, so far as we are able to judge, since the turn of the century. When heroin was legal, there were proportionately more addicts in the population; when the nation was younger and poorer, there were more criminals, or at least a correspondingly greater degree of crime. Why, then, do so many feel so bad—and why do they continue to feel so bad when, of the two causes reflexively invoked to explain this feeling, the first, the Vietnam war, has come to an end, while the second, racial inequity, has clearly and visibly diminished? I cannot pursue this subject in all its ramifications here. Instead I wish to add another element to the puzzle—the manufacture of incompatible policy demands that impose burdens on government that no government can meet.

The fact that the public demands on government in the various areas of policy are contradictory, in the sense that pursuing one policy inevitably means prohibiting the enactment of another, does not mean that an evil genius has been at work programming the political system for a nervous breakdown. Coordination need not require a coordinator; it can be tacit and informal as well as overt. People coordinate their activities through adherence to a common body of assumptions or through the sharing of a common world view. Quite the same kinds of contradictions can be created by various people in different places making vocal demands that turn out to be mutually opposed. The lack of central direction, in fact, is an advantage because it adds to the general confusion: politicians are given a hard time but they do not know on whom to vent their own frustration. For our purposes, it is not necessary to know whether demands on government are made by those who wish to see it fail, and therefore delight in giving it tasks it cannot manage, or who wish to see it succeed, and take pleasure in asking it to perform feats hitherto unaccomplished. Whether it stems from those who love government too little or from those who love it too much, the results of this pressure are the same: government is asked to perform wonders, but the attainment of one wonder often automatically precludes the possibility of attaining another, or many others.

The incompatibility of policy demands is a manifestation of a more general withdrawal of sovereignty from government in America. The rights of government and of politicians are being systematically whittled down. Public officials and professional politicians can no longer organize their political parties as they please, or hold meetings in closed sessions, or keep their papers secret, or successfully sue others for slandering them—even when they can show the allegations to be false—or make the smallest decisions without being hauled into court to convince judge and attorney they have followed standards of due process, considered every conceivable alternative, consulted all who might possibly be injured, or otherwise abandoned virtually every sense of what it used to mean to rule by enforcing binding regulations. We demand more of government but we trust it less.

Yet the Government, Hence the Presidency, Must Be More Important

The importance of presidents is a function of the scope of government; the more it does, the more important they become. Even if one assumes the worst—a weak president opposed by strong Congressional majorities—the president's support will make it easier for proposals to receive favorable consideration, and his opposition will make it less likely that legislation will be considered at all or be passed over his veto. Limiting presidential importance would require the one thing no one expects: limiting what government does.

What are the consequences of constructing and defining issues so as to pose incompatible demands on decision makers? Both the kinds of policies that we get from government and the kinds of attention paid to the various realms of policy are affected. Within the executive branch a greater emphasis will come to be placed on foreign than on domestic policy because, even given a random occurrence of events, it seems likely that some good can be achieved—for which, moreover, credit may accrue to the president. In domestic matters, on the other hand, presidents have come to see little for which they will be applauded, and much for which they will be condemned.

There are also substantive consequences of having incompatible demands made on government. Why should government continue to administer a welfare system that everyone hates, when one of the few things that can really be done well in Washington is programming a computer to write checks? If guarded with exceptional closeness, such a machine will actually write the checks it is supposed to write and people will actually receive them. In this way government does away with the middle men, the agitators for welfare rights. It may spend more money, but it will reduce the size of the bureaucracy and may actually make it possible for people to realize that the help they are getting has come from the government. Another policy consequence is revenue sharing, a bone thrown to cities and towns with a warning attached that if the bone should taste bad or if indigestion should ensue, they have no one to blame but themselves. Cities are now beginning to understand that they are getting a little money and a lot of trouble. Increasingly, they become the center of demand and lack the capacity to respond. So they respond by spending only on one-shot programs, thus undermining the enterprise–no wonder revenue sharing has been abolished.

Making incompatible demands on government is bound to have an impact on the federal system. When there is no way to garner credit, when everything attempted is clearly slated to fail, an effort will be made by government to rid itself of the source of anxiety, namely, its responsibility for policy. Any time the federal government can trade trouble for money, it will. The consequences, of course, need not all be bad: people with demands to make will find it more worthwhile to approach the cities and states because these will have more to give. But in a federal system in which each level deliberately seeks to pass its worst problems on to the next, in which blaming the other party has become a national pastime, it will become harder than it is already to know who is responsible for not solving our latest set of insoluble problems.

Fairly construed, the government's record on social policy during the last decade has been one of vigorous effort and some noteworthy if nevertheless defective accomplishments. Food stamps do feed the hungry (as well as the hippies). Steps have been taken in numerous areas to meet the needs of those who had previously been neglected. Those who have contended with these confusing times deserve compassion rather than contempt, and even a measure of applause. Yet it is only now, when programs are threatened with reductions, that a chorus of concern arises—and this, from quarters that had previously denounced the nation's social programs as too little, too late, misguided, or even positively harmful. It is, in any event, certain that these programs will die unless those who benefit from them (or who identify with the beneficiaries) come forward with vocal support. The critics of social policy have overplayed their hand; they wanted more and better, instead they are getting less and worse. The Nixon administration eventually came to the conclusion that since no visible credit was forthcoming from the presumptively natural supporters of social programs, it might as well gain whatever benefits it could from the conservatives who opposed them. Like any other institution that wishes to remain solvent, governmental bodies must reestablish their credit when their policies begin to earn a deficit of political support.

Presidents remain preeminent in foreign and defense policy. Formal authority is theirs; informal authority, the expectations as to who will do what, is almost entirely in their domain. There does not have to be a discernible foreign policy but, if there is, presidents are the people who are expected to make it. The exceptions—the Jackson

Amendment on Soviet Jews, restrictions on aid to Cambodia, Vietnam, Turkey, and Nicaragua—prove the rule. They show that presidents are not all-powerful in foreign policy; they do not get all they want when they want it. But these incidents are just what they seem—minor. Congress may anger foreign governments and dismay secretaries of state, it may point to itself as evidence of national disagreement, but it will not succeed in making foreign policy.

The exception may be Nicaragua. Perhaps, with much greater support, the Contras would have done better. We shall never know. But they could not have done better than free elections won by the opposition to the Sandinistas. Today (Spring 1990) the parties vie to see who can gain credit for this outcome. My guess is that the combination of a tough Republican administration and a conciliatory Democratic Congress was the equivalent of the good cop/bad cop routine—more effective together than any single line alone.

I risk belaboring the obvious because, in the backlash of Watergate, it has become all too easy to imagine a weakening of the presidency. Not so. Does anyone imagine fewer groups will be interested in influencing a president's position in their own behalf, or that his actions will matter less to people in the future? The question answers itself. The weakening of the presidency is about as likely as the withering away of the state.

To be important, however, is not necessarily to be popular. Let us conceive of presidential popularity as a vector of two forces: long-term dispositions to support or oppose the institution, and short-run tendencies to approve or disapprove what the occupant of the office is doing. Either way, I believe, the secular trend in popularity will be down.

By far the most significant determination of presidential popularity is the party identification of the population. Since the proportion of people identifying with the major parties has shown a precipitous decline, future presidents are bound to start out with a smaller base comprised of less committed supporters. This tendency will be reinforced by a relative decline of the groups—the less educated and the religious fundamentalist—who have been most disposed to give unwavering support regardless of what a president does or fails to do. Education may not make people wise, but it does make them critical. As the number of critical people in the country increases, criticism of presidents will naturally increase. Thus, future presidents will have to work harder than have past presidents to keep the same level of popularity.

The rise of egalitarian forces, moreover, bodes ill for the presidency. People who believe that leadership is a form of unquality are unlikely to support presidents.

Why have contradictory demands for public policy arisen? And what are the political consequences of trying and failing to satisfy them?

Public Policy and Political Responsibility

There is no consensus on foreign policy; the lessons learned from the past have not proved helpful. The 1930s apparently taught the United States to intervene everywhere, and the 1960s to intervene nowhere. Neither lesson is supportable. Under the spell of Vietnam, the instinctive reaction to foreign policy questions is no. Foreign policy requires faith: Evils must be avoided before their bloody consequences manifest themselves to the doubtful. But there is no faith. As in the parable of the Doubting Thomas, Congressmen would not believe the president concerning the situation in Cambodia until they actually went there, plunged their hands into the wounds of the people, and saw they were red. For presidents the adaptive response will be inaction until it is too late, after which there is no point in doing anything. After all, presidents have suffered from armed action but not yet for inaction.

Reaction to the oil embargo of 1973 and the manyfold increase in oil prices is a portent of things to come. When it came in the midst of an Egyptian and Syrian invasion of Israel, the United Stated did not react at all. Why were the American people not told of the inevitable consequences of the oil price increase, from starvation in poor countries and financial havoc among allies to inflation at home? Because then presidents would have had to do something about it. What would happen if they did? Severe criticism.

Future presidents will allow foreign events to speak for themselves after the fact so they don't have to speak about them beforehand. They may reluctantly give in to popular demands for strong action, but they will not act in anticipation. Followership, not leadership, probably will best describe future presidential foreign policy. I don't think, to use the Reagan Administration as our example, that an abortive episode in Lebanon and the invasion of a tiny island (Grenada) add up to much in the way of armed intervention. And the same is true for the Bush Administration's invasion of Panama. Only the response to Iraqi's invasion of Kuwait has been substantial.

There is not today, nor is there likely to be in the near future, a stable constituency in support of social reform. The legislation proposed by Lyndon Johnson and enacted during the first eighteen months of his presidency wiped out the New Deal agenda and destroyed the historical coalition and the common assumptions that had long helped Americans understand what was happening in the national life. By enacting every piece of social legislation it could lay its hands on, Congress obliterated all the old issues; where once a citizen knew on which side of a given question he stood, now all was confusion.

The passage of the Great Society legislation, in addition, had a devastating effect on many sectors of the federal bureaucracy. The second worst thing that can happen to a person is to strive for a lifetime and fail to get what he wants. The first worst thing is to strive and get what he wants and then discover that it is not good. Think of people who spent, say, twenty years in the Department of Health, Education, and Welfare and its predecessors, trying desperately to secure huge federal appropriations for education. In the mod-1960s they got them; they still have them, but they have discovered that the ground has shifted and that the clientele whose interests they thought they were serving is not the clientele the new policies are aimed at. So they are bewildered.

In the past the clients of the New Deal had been the temporarily depressed but relatively stable lower and middle classes, people who were, on the whole, willing and able to work but who had been restrained by the economic situation; if the economic picture brightened, things improved for them right away. It hardly mattered one way or the other what government did or did not do in their behalf. Now, however, government policy was being designed to deal not with such people but with the severely deprived, those who actually needed not merely an opportunity but continuing, long-term assistance. No previous government had ever attempted to do for this sector of the population—those whom Marx had called the lumpenproletariat—what the American government set out to do. Nobody knew how to go about it, either. In the field of education, for example, no one had the faintest clue as to what amount of "input" would produce the desired result, and so vast amounts of money, and even vaster amounts of enthusiasm, were poured into various programs that ultimately ended in failure and bewilderment. (As it turns out, we have learned that variations in expenditures of almost four to one make little difference in student performance.)

Far from giving up in the face of such complex ignorance, the tendency, instead, was to place the emphasis on those variables that did seem controllable. This led to the concept of community action. If no solutions were available, it was possible to increase the demand for solutions, to create pressure from below that would effect the release of ever-increasing amounts of federal money. But the fact that government was trying to deal with a different clientele and that no one knew how to do it meant that an awful lot of money was invested without accomplishing very much. The escalation of demands, together with the lack of knowledge of solutions, meant a multiplication of programs, each under- or over-financed, each justified by the notion that it was somehow an experiment that would prove something.

Perhaps there is nothing new in all this, but the political consequences have not been seen as clearly as they might be. Welfare today has become a political albatross. In the past, those who paid for welfare may not have liked it, but those who received it, if they did not love it, at least found it preferable to the alternative. Government got credit from those who received and demerits from those who had to pay. Since the poor were more numerous than the wealthy, a political trade-off was effected and things seemed to work out. Today, the taxpayers curse, the recipients tell government where to get off, and the welfare system gets credit from neither group.

That was in the late 1970s. Nowadays "homebusiness" has captured the nation's attention. The situation is the same or worse: lots of criticism but no solution.

The 1930s through the 1950s were easy to understand. The "haves" did not like to pay, and the "have nots" preferred the benefits they received to the alternative. By the late 1960s, however, the poorer beneficiaries had learned from their leaders that they did not benefit, which led the richer providers to add ingratitude to their list of complaints. Then the passion for equality, against which Tocqueville warned, asserted itself to label anything the government was able to accomplish unworthy of achievement. Too little too late, or too much too soon, the result was always the same: a sense of failure. For as long as contradictory demands are made on public policy, governments (and hence presidents) will be unable to get credit for what they do.[2]

People who are involved in revolutions are usually the last to recognize what has been happening all around them. While the War on Poverty was being waged, those fighting the battles understandably lacked the time, energy, or discernment to see anything like the full implications of their actions. Like good soldiers everywhere, they went from skirmish to skirmish, leaving the grand strategy to generals who, as every classic account of warfare tells us, understood less than anyone else. First, as noted, the generals radiated a sense of hope: wonderful things could be done. On this basis many new programs were launched and even more were proposed, to capitalize on the new potential for eliminating poverty. Second, also as noted, they generated a sense of despair: hardly anything seemed to be working. Out of this was born a new determination to overcome obstacles—in the form of new programs. Third, whether one had hoped or despaired, it became almost a reflex action to call on government to justify the hope or overcome the despair. One consistent trend in this concatenation was the proliferation of demands on government from all quarters. Another trend, seldom noticed, was the incompatibility of the demands.

Public housing is a good example of how to make an evident failure out of an apparent success. The nation started with a low-cost shelter program for the stable working poor. Public policy concentrated the available resources in housing projects, so some people could be helped; and resident managers used their discretion to screen out "undesirables," so tenants could live in peace. It was not necessarily the best of worlds for all, but it was at least better for some. All that changed, however, in the 1960s. Screening was condemned as racism and worse: Didn't justice require that the worst-off be given preference? Not long after, public housing was attacked as a failure for all the crime it attracted. The dynamiting of buildings in St. Louis's Pruitt-Igoe Project symbolized, unfairly (but persuasively) the blowup of hopes for public housing.

More medical care for the poor and aged is incompatible with easier access and lower costs for the whole population. By now the poor see doctors about as often as anybody else. This might be considered an accomplishment of Medicare and Medicaid—except that no one wants to accept responsibility for the consequences. Because access increases faster than facilities, the medical system gets crowded; because doctor and patient are motivated to resolve their uncertainties about treatment by using the insurance and subsidies at their disposal, the system gets expensive; because medical care is only moderately related to health, morbidity does not decline and mortality does not decrease in proportion to expenditure. Hence we hear that the system is in crisis because it is overcrowded, too expensive, and doesn't do much to improve aggregate health rates.

The growth of big government, followed by the onslaught of "stagflation" (rising unemployment plus inflation), has led to serious reflection, and not a little alarm, about whether this double trouble is due to defects inherent in democratic government.[3] Politics, it is said, had become promises. Politicians seek to get into office, or maintain themselves there, by promising specific financial benefits to their importunate constituents. If special interests did not exist before, they come into being to take advantage of governmentally guaranteed subsidies. Citizens become owners of a new property in the form of entitlements to funds or services. Because benefits are specific, whereas costs are diffused among millions of taxpayers, resource allocation gives way to resource addition. Since every voter expects an ever-higher living standard, and no one is willing to give up any gain, benefits are piled up on one another until, eventually, the productive base is too narrow to sustain this pyramid of premature pensioners.

Following a policy of too much too soon, as used to be said of dissipated heiresses, government gets overloaded. The larger the number of policies, the more they interact, the less they can be controlled. The more flexibility government requires to juggle competing claims, the less it has, being locked in by past commitment. Unable to match resources and objectives directly, it does so indirectly. Inflation becomes the main instrument of public policy, reducing the value of wage settlements, redistributing income, and giving government temporary room for maneuver as tax receipts surge ahead of spending. Indexing benefits against inflation becomes the name of the game, only to be followed by indexing taxes. Soon enough everyone, by law, is guaranteed everything and no one is sure of anything. The end of ideology in the just-right mixed economy, according to the Goldilocks of the 1950s, gives way to the mixed-up overheated economy of the 1970s, to be followed, we are told, by the end of democracy in the 1990s. Q.E.D. Finis.

How do politicians know that their actions will be efficacious? Better still, exactly *when* do they think they know? Election time is too late to act; a year before may be too early to discern the trends telling them whether inflation or unemployment or whatever will be the major issues. Aside from being uncertain about the consequences of their actions, politicians in turbulent times may not know what ends they should seek. If they end on target, this is more likely to be an inadvertence than an aim.

Are citizens, then, you and me included, boobs manipulated by the beasts in office? If the game is beasts and boobs, democratic government is sure to be the loser. Are we-the-people really so dumb that we do not understand what is happening?

If one asks whether people favor stable prices, full employment, higher incomes, naturally they do. So do we all, including politicians. But, given experience, what do we expect? In a subtle analysis of what constitutes "realism," Alt shows that over time the proportion of people who think some goals are incompatible with others goes up. The proportion of realists in the 1960s was not overwhelming—a third—but it went up. The more people believed full employment was at odds with inflation, the less willing they were to support spending. And as inflation grew worse, the public professed readiness to give up gains to control it.

The evidence is that as people's expectations go unfulfilled, they grow more realistic over time. They do not believe political parties can keep their promises or will manage the economy well. Alt concludes that

> in large measure, then, the story of the mid 1970s is the story of a politics of declining expectations. People attached a great deal of importance to economic problems, people saw clearly the developments that were taking place, and people expected developments in advance and thus were able to discount the impact of the worst of them. However, in unprecedented numbers, people also ceased to expect the election of their party to make them better off, largely because they also ceased to expect it to be able to do very much about what they identified as the principal economic problems of the time. The result of this ... was not a politics of protest, but a politics of quiet disillusion, a politics in which lack of involvement or indifference to organized party politics was the most important feature.[4]

How about democracy? Whatever the disarray, there is no one around to take advantage of it. Comfort may be had in understanding that citizens are reasonably intelligent and adaptive. Discomfort comes from the realization that, if government is widely regarded as ineffective, citizen cooperation, not to say sacrifice, is less likely. Is this a comforting conclusion? That depends on whether you are a pessimist or a catastrophist. One could build on the best, or one could make more contradictory demands.

The demand that the political parties be "democratized" and made more representative is often linked to the demand that the costs of elections be reduced so that the rich will not control the democratic process. As Nelson Polsby has pointed out, it is impossible to do both: democratization in practice means more primaries, more conventions, more meetings—in other words, increased costs.

Or consider employment. There have basically been two objectives in this area of policy: employ the hard-core and create jobs at reasonable costs. It is very expensive to train the hard-core; that is why they are hard-core. It is also very discouraging, because many will not get jobs and many others will not keep them. But in addition, if a government agency has actually been able to show that it created a number of jobs that people filled and stayed in for a while at some kind of reasonable cost (by reasonable cost I mean that it cost less than it would have just to give them the money), it has then been criticized for dealing with people who were too employable. This is known as "creaming," getting jobs for the best of the worst, so that anyone who actually found a job was easy to employ in the first place.

The political ramifications are rising discontent on the part of both those who pay the costs and those who get the benefits. The have-littles are plunged into conflict with the have-nots (the working and lower-middle classes with the poor) because compensatory mechanisms fail to help the one, and do not stretch far enough to reach the other. Observing dissatisfaction on the part of those receiving extra resources, the people who pay are likely to call it ingratitude. Part of the secret of winning, as any football coach knows, lies in arranging an appropriate schedule. Governmental performance depends not only on the ability to solve problems but on selecting problems government knows how to solve.

Examples of incompatibilities could come from almost any area of public policy, but I will content myself with one less obvious example: party reform. "Government," Alfred Marshall wrote, "is the most precious of human possessions; and no care can be too great to be spent on enabling it to do its work in the best way: a chief condition to that end is that it should not be set to work for which it is not specially qualified, under the conditions of time and place." Once government is given not just one or two things it cannot do, but a whole host, the effects will be felt throughout the political system. The nature of political campaigns has also changed. In 1972, instead of defending their record, the leaders of government concentrated on the alleged horrors about to be perpetrated by the opposition—or that had been perpetrated by their own party's past.

If parties cannot make good on the promises of their candidates for office, what can they make good on? Party structure, for one thing; they can promise to organize themselves in a given way, if only because this is something over which they can exercise control. Thus parties, like politicians, move more strongly into the realm of the expressive and the symbolic rather than of substantive policy. The Democratic party can arrange itself in order to contain certain proportions of this or that ethnic group or gender. It can conduct endless meetings, primaries, conventions, all the while gradually shifting the definition of a party from an instrument seeking to govern the nation to an instrument seeking to govern itself. What parties contribute to the nation, then, is not so much candidates attached to a policy as procedures that meet certain norms.

Politicians, too, are shifting emphasis from substantive policy to personal political style. They talk of basic changes in the political process but move into action only when this consists of a form of opposition. They offer adherence to proclaimed moral principle, where they cannot fail, instead of offering innovation in policy, where they cannot succeed. They are often "against" what is happening but see themselves under no obligation to suggest viable alternatives. A sign of the political times is the growing proportion of presidential candidates who come from the United States Senate, for that is the office that combines the longest term and the highest national visibility with the least responsibility. When people are angry they may picket mayors and shout down governors, but they rarely advance on the Senate or its occupants.

Not only the Senate but the House as well is involved in the dilemma of acting responsibly at a time when substantive achievements are hard to come by. The quandary in which congressmen find themselves is illustrated in the controversy over impoundment. It is all too easy to blame the conflict entirely on President Nixon; he had ample discretionary powers under the Anti-Deficiency Act of 1951, but he chose instead to throw down the gauntlet by saying that he might refuse to spend money in appropriations bills even after they were passed over his veto. That bit of arrogance deserves what it got. But underneath the surface clash of personalities lies a deep-seated unwillingness in Congress to accept responsibility for raising the revenues required to support its own spending requests. It is easier to vote for this or that while laying the burden of reduced expenditures, or of finding new revenues, at the door of the president. The growing practice of presidential impoundment may be part of a tacit agreement that Congress will get credit for voting the funds, while the president takes Congress off the hook by refusing to spend. By allowing impoundment to go on for as long as it did and to cover so extensive a range of policies, Congress demonstrated its apparent willingness to see spending cut only if the blame could be placed elsewhere.

The evils besetting our major political parties are supposed to be excessive influence of money and insufficient power of participation. But participation requires more meetings, conferences, primaries; in a word, more money. Told that money is the root of all evil, on the one hand, and required to dig deeper for it to promote participation, on the other, the position of our parties must be as perilous as that of presidents, who are urged simultaneously to limit their own powers and to lead the people.

In the view of these circumstances, the barest extrapolation from current events, it hardly seems likely that the nation will have to worry about a too-powerful presidency, a legislative dictatorship (as President Ford claimed in overzealous campaign rhetoric), judicial tyranny, or any of the other scare slogans of the day. There will be enough blame for everyone.

The "Offensive Retreat"

Future presidents will be preoccupied with operating strategic levers, not with making tactical moves. They will see their power stakes, to use Neustadt's term, in giving away their powers; like everyone else, they will have to choose between what they want to keep and what they must give up. Not so much running the country (that was Nixon's error) but seeing that it is running will be their forte. The cabinet, or at least the inner "super-secretary" cabinet, will undergo a visible revival because presidents will trade a little power for a lot of protection. The more prominent a president's cabinet, the less of a target he becomes. When presidents wanted to keep the credit, they kept their cabinets quiet; but they will welcome cabinet notoriety now that they want to spread the blame.

The "offensive retreat" of the presidency will not be the work of a single president or a particular moment in time. Nor will this movement be unidirectional. Like most things, it will be a product of trial and error, in which backsliding will be as prominent as forward movement. But as presidents discover there is sickness in health and ignorance in education, they will worry more about their own welfare.

Presidents, and the governments for which they stand, are either doing too much or too little. They need either to do a great deal more for the people or a great deal less to them. They must be closer to what is happening or much further away. At present, they are close enough to get the blame but too far away to control the result; for government to be half involved is to be wholly abused. Which way will it move?

One way is nationalization. The federal government would take over all areas of serious interest; there would be a national health service, a national welfare system, and the like. Industry would not be regulated at a remove—but run for real. The blame would go to the top, but so would the power. Presidents would literally be running the country. The danger of overload at the center would be mitigated by mastery of the periphery. Uncle Sam would be everybody's tough Uncle, and it would not be wise to push him around. Before it comes to this, however, presidents will try to move in other directions.

Presidents will seek the fewest levers but those with the most consequential effects. They will be money men, manipulating the supply to citizens through income floors and the supply to business through banks. Taxes will vary with expenditures; if government spends more, taxes will go up, and if it spends less, they will go down, with the upper limit set by constitutional limitation. Income will determine outgo. Regulatory activities and agencies will be severed from all presidential connection; why should presidents get into trouble for fixing the price of milk or determining routes for airlines or setting railroad rates? States and localities will undertake whatever supplementary programs they are willing and able to support.

Presidents will handle systemic crises, not ordinary events. They will be responsible for war and peace abroad and life and death at home, but not much in between. The people will not call on their president when they are in trouble; a president will call on his people when he is in trouble.

The expectations created by the body politic (or by a small but influential part of it), the rewards and punishments it administers, go far to shape the successes and failures of public officials. Anyone who writes or speaks or thinks seriously about public policy has a special obligation to consider what his contribution—even when placed in the context of many others—implies for the ability of government to perform adequately. Otherwise, private vices will become public vices as well (to reverse Mandeville), and government, seeing that the game is rigged, will respond once again by attempting to change the rules.

When the preceding paragraphs were first written I was conscious of incompatible demands on government but was hardly aware of what or who caused them. Now, with the aid of cultural theory, I ask "Who would want to level constant criticism against existing institutions?" Certainly not supporters of hierarchy, who want to maintain the existing order; certainly not individualists, unless they protest against too much regulation. Nor would those attacks come from fatalists. That leaves criticism of institutions to egalitarians, who wish to weaken hierarchical and individualist sources of inequality. Yet egalitarians also want governments, and hence presidents, to do a lot more. No wonder citizens are confused when they hear that presidents are too weak *and* too strong. No wonder, too, that presidents, not knowing which way to go, when not vacillating, are likely to duck.

Notes

1. See my essays, "The Empty-head Blues: Black Rebellion and White Reaction," *Public Interest,* no. 11 (Spring 1968); "The Revolt Against the Masses," in *The Revolt Against the Masses and Other Essays on politics and Public Policy* (New York: Basic Books, 1971); "The Search for the Oppressed," *Freedom at Issue,* no. 16 (November/December 1972).
2. See Dennis Coyle and Aaron Wildavsky "Requisites of Radical Reform

Income Maintenance versus Tax Preferences," *Journal of Policy Analysis and Management* 7, no. 1 (Fall 1987): 1–16. See my "Dispelling America's Gloom: Why Bother?" *The American Enterprise* 1, no. 2 (March/April 1990): 26–31.

3. Taken from a review of James E. Alt, *The Politics of Economic Decline: Economic Management and Political Behavior in Britain Since 1964,* (Cambridge: Cambridge University Press, 1979).
4. Ibid., 270.

5

Putting the Presidency on Automatic Pilot

When American political scientists look for enlightenment, for comparison or contrast with the problems of their own political system, they most often turn to Great Britain, where they can see either the future or the past writ large. If we look at Mrs. Thatcher's government today, we see that on the one hand it is better organized than our own to confront its major external problems; and, on the other, that its government, being so much larger comparatively than our own, is less able to deal with its internal society. British government is a federation of departments. The prime minister has no operating role whatsoever. Her task is to step in when others fail—failures that she can define for herself or leave unexamined. Thus we have the possibility—sometimes realized—of government by exception, with a prime minister who is not a bureaucrat or a manager, who does not have routine, ongoing, everyday responsibilities, but who can focus on what she considers the major problem of her people and her government.

Two variables are interacting here: one is the style of leadership—either managerial a la President Carter or individualist like Prime Minister Thatcher; another is the scope of leadership—many major issues or only a few.

My insight into these matters, I think, has been strengthened by reading some recent books that deal with managing the presidency. All of them agree that managing his own office is the major policy problem of the president. They all say that by expanding the presiden-

Reprinted from *The American Presidency: Principles and Problems*, ed. Kenneth W. Thompson (Washington, D.C.: University Press of America, 1982), 23–33.

tial office, the president does indeed get some modicum of control over outside events, but what he gets even more, as Hugh Heclo tells us in *The American President*, is the capacity of outside constituencies to control his activities. When you have somebody there dealing with minorities and with Congress, they bring the congressional and minority concerns to the president. The result is that the further out the president reaches, the further in other people reach to him.

There was a time when scholars were overoptimistic: the presidential office, being bigger, was also going to get better; it all seemed upward and onward. But today there is a more sophisticated appreciation of the limitations of presidential bureaucracies and a greater interest in whether our president is to be an administrator or a leader.

Telling presidents to cut down their staff, not to get involved with everything, doesn't tell them what to get involved with or how to manage their affairs. Indeed, given the fact that the scope of government, even in the United States, has increased manyfold so that the government of 1961 is utterly unrecognizable in its scope and content from the government of today, presidents cannot wish themselves back to a simpler era. Nor can they, or the country, afford to give up their aspirations for leadership. What then?

If an incoming chief executive wants the best available advice on how to organize his office and his time, *Memorandum for the President*, by Ben Heineman, Jr., and Curt Hessler, is it. No one knows better. Keeping the staff small, avoiding overloading Congress, choosing only a few key measures, husbanding political and personal resources—all the sophisticated advice is there. Thus the reader has the opportunity of asking whether any president can perform the functions required by this scaled-down, less-than-heroic, made-to-fit-human-proportions presidency.

Would anyone want a job in which his first mistake would be his last? Yet this is exactly what Heineman and Hessler imply when they write that "he [the president] must choose quickly and make few mistakes because time has him in a vise." The rule of "one strike and you're out" is a tough one under which to play any game.

Although the authors say they do not underestimate the "surpassing difficulty of this task," they assert that "there is no other way. *His* [the president's] *must be the central organizing intelligence of his administration:* and that requires a vision, a mental strength and a procedural discipline—a political, substantive and managerial sense—that has been all too rare in our chief executives" (emphasis in original). No wonder. Where will Americans find this wonder worker?

The decade-long decline in the power of the presidency, the next president is told as if it were a commonplace (like bad weather or the impetuosity of youth) is due to well-known circumstances: the decline of parties able to organize multiissue, crosscutting coalitions; a Congress that is as fragmented as it is willful; a judiciary that intervenes more often than it implements; a citizenry doubtful that government can help and yet unwilling to do without it; an economy beset by international forces it cannot control, but which can reduce the value of its currency; and economists who cannot figure out why unemployment and inflation rise together or how to bring them down without making either one worse. How organize the presidency to cope with such circumstances?

The basic advice offered is to reduce the size and clarify the jurisdiction of the executive office of the president. Only a few issues (five to ten) are to be identified as of presidential importance; twenty-five to thirty-five are to be mainly departmental, with presidential advice; the rest are to be left to secretaries, with only general guidance. In short, reduce the scope and staff. The advice is certainly superior to the opposite. All the president has to do, according to Wayne Vallis, writing in *The Future Under President Reagan*, is "turn around the vast American government and economy, reducing inflation and unemployment, enhancing productivity, stabilizing the value of the dollar, addressing our energy needs and at the same time remedying rapidly deteriorating foreign and defense policy deficiencies. Above all, President Reagan must restore a sense of optimism about America's future, a sense that America has once again regained its lost vitality." How is the president to do this?

The president is advised, Heineman and Hessler write, to use his "peripheral vision—the subtle, occasionally obscure connections between the disparate spheres of your own domain." This is a plea for political artistry, which is nice if you can get it. The new president is urged to stick to his basic choices but "not in bullheaded fashion"; make orderly retreats, the authors advise, but not too often. *"Think comprehensively,"* they say, *"but act incrementally"* (emphasis in original). Being careful and being bold may be difficult to manage. Presidents should avoid isolation, it appears, but neither should they be overly influenced by the cacophony of discordant signs outside the

Oval Office, for then they would lose consistency. Between hearing they are too political (doing what is feasible instead of preferable) or not political enough (losing so often the presidency is weakened), presidents may wonder how they can win.

Heineman and Hessler present instructive case studies of what not to do (the authors call them "cautionary tales") from the Carter administration. Their most specific conclusion is that presidents

> cannot hope to steer the economy in any precise sense. The most you can do over four years is influence its course and structure in a very general way. To accomplish even this much will require that you carefully choose a manageably small and mutually reinforcing set of general economic objectives and pursue them with relentless consistency, keeping your policies and the political forces at your command clearly in focus over your whole term. If, instead, you become bogged down in detail, or you become diverted by an excessive number of conflicting goals, or you decide to change strategic course in midterm, you will forfeit any prospect of affecting what the economy will look like four years hence.

At times the book does read like a primer on how to avoid Jimmy Carter's errors, a task easier in retrospect than in prospect. Cold comfort! What will we do if we don't have Jimmy to kick around anymore? If the political economy is so unforgiving, no president is likely to prevail.

Understanding the interrelatedness of everything is not the same as understanding how things are related or what can usefully be done about them. What is a president to make of the excellent advise that economic issues "be presented in the context of a four-or-five-year budgetary projection," with the unexceptional comment that he should understand as well that "over the last fifteen years such exercises have often led presidents into a false sense that the future would yield big budget surpluses"? The world is so full of pitfalls that even this good advice leaves a president (with the rest of us) adrift on a sea of uncertainty.

How is a president to get his bearings from advice that is both knowledgeable and contradictory? The knowledge comes from close study of the subject; the contradictions come from mirroring the social reality in which providing positive leadership is coupled with concern over the opposition it encourages. The political system is fragmented; knowledge of public policy is inadequate; government has become unwieldy; no president is likely to do everything well;

and a turbulent external world will continue to punish presidents and everyone else who can be held accountable for disagreeable consequences. If we add in the objections of egalitarian forces among political elites and in the media to people in authority, the chances of going wrong are multiplied.

When we understand that even the reduced scope that better advice suggests—a smaller presidential staff, paying attention only to a smaller number of major issues—is likely to overwhelm any incumbent, then we have underestimated the scope of our problem. Even the sophisticates among us have not understood well enough that the scope of big government is so great that ordinary remedies will not do. What do I suggest? Putting the presidency on automatic pilot.

What I mean by that is not that government should blunder ahead any which way—something that will no doubt happen apart from any advice that I might give—but rather that it consider general policies that subsume particular policies, and that it construct processes that will lead to resolution of conflicts (in ways acceptable to presidents) so that whole hosts of policies are subsumed under more general decisions. Presidents are presumed to continue to try to lead. This leadership role signifies that they must (a) make new decisions and (b) be useful to other political actors by doing things they cannot do— like focusing national attention on critical policy problems and repairing processes and institutions that have broken down. Thus presidents need policies and processes that make most decisions routine and that, by providing general guidance, also surface exceptions that do deserve presidential attention. A tall order. But, perhaps, not so tall as standing end on end all the decisions presidents try to deal with today.

In a word, we can't run the presidency retail anymore. It's got to be wholesale or not at all. Again, general advice is not very useful. Let's get specific. Whether I agree with the particular policy I'm recommending or not—sometimes I do, sometimes I don't—the purpose is not to start an argument about the merits of particular programs. It is what these processes and policies would do to presidential management that is the focus of this chapter, and not whether you're a Republican or a Democrat or whether you would like a bigger or a smaller government.

Let's start with a favorite proposal of mine: spending limits. The idea is that federal government spending would be limited to a fixed amount so that proposal to increase a given program would require either spending cuts elsewhere or new revenues. What this proposal does is fix the relative size of the private and public sectors. If presidents were to seek such spending limits, they could do so at a lower level or at a higher level. So ideology would not necessarily matter here. What I want to focus on is the way in which such a mechanism could wholesale presidential decisions.

First of all, think of the outside world: How do we deal with spending? There is a group of people who are interested in distribution of resources in order to achieve greater equality. If you ask them where we're going to get all this wealth that we're going to distribute, they'll say, "That's not my problem." By linking distribution to production through a spending limit, we're going to increase cooperation in society. Instead of all this nonsense about how corporate boards should set up social services—for which they have no flair—the representatives of poorer people are going to say, "Get off your backsides, go to work, be efficient! If you don't create wealth, we can't distribute it." Coalitions between the heads of black groups and the heads of corporations, let us say, would become much more prevalent than they are today, making the president's task easier.

Within the government you would have increased conflict. Today we do budgeting by addition, never by subtraction. Why should bureau heads fight when they can combine their resources and pass them on in inflation or in taxation to the private sector? Once people in the government know that there is a limit on everyone, all sorts of bargaining will be encouraged. The bureaucrats are going to guard one another because otherwise they'll get swamped. If more for one means less for another, agencies will have to bargain. And since presidents are deemed unpredictable, agencies will want to come to an understanding on their own. The decisions they cannot make are exactly those that need presidential attention.

Obviously, the president prefers his own set of priorities. But, rather than have a much larger budget, or, rather than have to participate in each and every decision, any distribution may be better than having to participate in each individual funding decision. Could it be that how much government does is more important than what it does?

Notice the form of this proposal. By making one very great decision (although presidents could not make it alone), acres and mountains of future decisions would be subsumed.

How about a uniform income tax without exemptions or deductions? Every American I know thinks that somebody else is cheating. Even when you sit around the table and you're talking about where you're going to take a vacation, you say you could go here because you're getting your way paid, or you can make that trip deductible because it's connected to some business purpose. If you talk politics to political scientists anywhere, it's a business purpose, right? Mostly, but not exactly. This is not good for public morality. There's a vast number of accountants and lawyers who could be put to work at honest labor, increasing the national product. So long as government holds more of people's money than they do, their time is much better spent getting it back from the government than in working. If there was a uniform tax, it would not be worthwhile trying to find ways around it. All the loopholes, all the tax expenditures, all the many things that irritate economists and ordinary people alike would be done away with, not because people wouldn't know how—we are very creative in financial matters in this country—but because tax rates would be so low that it wouldn't be worth doing.

For the president, a uniform (or flat) tax would mean that the legitimacy of government in the hearts and minds of the people would increase, which makes governing easier. Instead of a multitude of tax decisions, there would be only one—the rate. With very high rates, there are enormous reasons why exceptions should be made. Everybody has a good reason. There's a whole restaurant industry—the bellboys come from Puerto Rico, the waiters come from Samoa, the owners from the midwest. They also benefit from the three-martini lunch. A uniform tax cuts the policy knot. It makes the president's life easier by reducing the number of constituencies that have their teeth into government. The tax reform of 1986 moves in the direction of realizing the potential of this proposal.

Now I want to discuss several issues in an attempt to show how considerations of presidential time and strategy, in the sense of putting the president on automatic pilot, of wholesaling instead of retailing, would make a difference. (The reader should realize that the paragraphs that follow were written in 1982. My purpose was to illustrate how presidents might make decisions that would influence many other decisions.)

Let's look at Poland. Why do I think Poland should be a presidential issue? Because, if that were to work out well, it would subsume endless other issues. The best conceivable thing that could happen would be that the Solidarity union would thrive, and there would come into being a communist state with a genuine opposition movement. If it were possible, this would mean that the whole Soviet system and its satellites would change. Some people say Soviets act the way they do because the United States encircles them. Naturally, the more countries the Soviets occupy, the closer they get to other countries that might be hostile. This argument is as close to pure logic as you ever get in international relations. My view—and presidents will have their views—is that the Soviets are fearful because the nature of their regime is an obstacle to any source of diversity. If the Soviets learn to live with some diversity, this would mitigate our mutual antagonisms. A change in the Soviet system could reduce defense budgets. If the president is looking for strategic levers, subsuming decisions that bring in their wake many other decisions, Poland is the most important thing that has come along in a long time.

Let's now go to energy and, from a presidential perspective, challenge the conventional way we look at it. The belief today (circa 1982) is that the great American problem is the denial of quantities of petroleum. If enemy forces, whoever they might be, were to seize the Persian Gulf, or if the producing countries would blow themselves up, or do something dreadful, then the United States would be deprived of oil and the Western world would come to a halt. This is said to be intolerable. This doomsday perspective comes from substituting an economic for a political mode of thought. A political mode of thought— and that is the mode that we hire presidents to do with us and for us— would lead to a contrary conclusion. If anything happens in the Persian Gulf to shut off supplies, economically this is temporarily very bad, but politically it's like apple pie. Our allies are going to go down the drain faster than we are; most of them haven't any oil at all so they're going to unite with us. Politically, the president stresses conservation at home; instead of being ignored, however, he is followed because of the evident necessity of sharing the problem.

For a president, prices are more important than quantities. Prices are invisible. Many countries are working for OPEC, which waits until there's a little more increment in productivity and then scoops off the cream. How does a president explain to his own people that they are working harder but are not making more money? How does a president explain the several-percent-a-year inflation? It's an impossible issue. Everybody says the oil companies are doing it; they're domestic monsters. I have often wished that we could improve our nation by beating up on somebody, even if it was an oil company. Alas it won't help. What would?

Lowering the international price of oil would do wonders. It would lower inflation, increase employment, and reduce hostilities between environmentalists and developers. If Americans didn't have to pay such high oil prices, they would not be faced with pushing nuclear energy and coal conversion so hard. One cannot name any problem facing this country—class conflict, regional conflict, racial conflict, environmentalist conflict—that would not be markedly improved by lower oil prices. One can hardly mention any foreign policy problem—getting our allies to invest more in their own defense, for example—that would not markedly be improved by lower prices. So if the president wants to focus on a major policy problem (admittedly, one of great difficulty), stabilizing and then lowering the price of oil brings in its wake an enormously favorable train of consequences.

In the area of foreign policy, the Carter administration, like administrations before it, importuned allies in Japan and Western Europe endlessly to do more for their own defense. Many of them, of course, have their own idea of the good life, *i.e.* that no war be fought, or, if it is, it be fought with nuclear weapons someplace in the mid-Atlantic, with the fallout divided between the United States and the Soviet Union. This is not hard to understand. What is the United States going to do about it? President Reagan, like his predecessors, appears to believe he'll talk nicer, or smoother, or tougher, or in some way will say things that will persuade his allies to behave differently. Maybe. I doubt it. What could he do that would make a difference? Something the United States decided not to do. If it took its troops out of Korea, America would not have to persuade the Japanese to rearm. Americans would not have to worry about whether Japanese generals are talking to their admirals, or the admirals are talking to their bureaucracy, or the party elites are talking to whoever, which are the favorite explanations these days. It's very straightforward. Korea is like a dagger at the heart of Japan. If they're not sure that we're shouldering their burden, they're going to pick it up right away.

No one talks about Iran in terms of presidential time. How many Irans can any administration afford in terms of time? If we are going to spend that time for every fifty Americans, the approximate number of hostages, there isn't going to be enough left for the president to do anything else. The idea that any government would view presidential time as a free good, that the time of top officials could be parcelled out for such a purpose, suggests that the people at the top see themselves either in a purely managerial role, playing the part of the desk officer in some God-forsaken post, or that they don't think their time is valuable at all. Our presidents have to regard themselves as valuable people with some contribution to make to this country. There are important problems that they should concern themselves with, but if they view their time as simply endless, and themselves as third-rate managers in some fourth-rate country, then they will become helpless and the idea of presidential leadership will be hopeless.

No doubt the question of the compatibility of unlimited government and presidential leadership has to be faced. The larger the government, the less any elected official, including the president, is going to be able to control it. But the argument can be turned around as well: the bigger the government, the greater the need for putting the presidency on automatic pilot. If we're going to have big government, it becomes all the more important to wholesale rather than retail policies. If there were a rule, for example, that said that you could not have any new regulation without giving up an old one, necessitating priorities—one of the ways we measure the size of government is by taking a yardstick to the federal register of regulations—such a rule would mean that bureaucrats would have to negotiate among themselves, not over whether rules were desirable, but about which rules were more important. Those questions that cannot be answered through the normal processes are the right ones for presidents. They can then be pretty sure that the problems brought to them because others cannot resolve them are among the more important issues they ought to be addressing.

What happens with all these action-forcing processes is that presidents make one decision instead of many, so that they're then able to deal with exceptions. None of these processes, to be sure, will be perfect. Even if you put a plane on automatic pilot, by the time you get near your destination, you've got to take it off and steer the plane yourself. Naturally, you're going to be in better shape for emergency landings if you've had a more leisurely day.

Even those of us who believe that the presidential staff and office have to be cut down to size have vastly underestimated the scope of the problem. We have to consider whether there are not families of policies that, by putting presidents on automatic pilot, enable them to focus on matters that concern you and me. Thus, two things could happen that haven't happened lately: presidents would have a chance of being effective, and citizens would perceive them to be effective.

Looking back nearly a decade later (1990), I find these suggestions to be better at ferreting out the future than on getting credit for presidents. His version of the flat tax helped Ronald Reagan keep taxes down, while the spending limit/balanced budget amendment (as it is now known) has not progressed; its spirit, however, is embodied in what is called the "pay as you go reform" proposed by Democratic Representative Leon Panetta and already in force in the Senate. Reducing the number of issues with which presidents deal came to full flower in the Reagan administration, but Jimmy Carter's presidency was in the opposite mold. Markets did more about oil prices than did presidents. And we now see the consequences of the Soviet Union's domestic changes in its more pacific foreign policy. Whether American presidents had much to do with these great changes will be a matter of controversy for a long time, perhaps forever.

Note

1.   See Joseph White and Aaron Wildavsky, *The Deficit and the Public Interest* (Berkeley: University of California Press, 1990).

Bibliography

Hugh Heclo. *A Government of Strangers:* Executive Politics in Washington. Washington, D.C.: Brookings Institution, 1977.

Ben Heineman, Jr. and Curt Hessler. *Memorandum for the President: A Strategic Approach to Domestic Affairs in the 1980s.* New York: Random House, 1980.

Wayne Vallis. *The Future Under President Reagan.* Westport, Conn.: Arlington House, 1980.

6

The Prophylactic Presidency

With Sanford Weiner

Most decisions are reactions to what has already happened. When evils are perceived, we attempt to mitigate them. Then our security depends on our capacity to cope with changing circumstances. Suppose, however, that collective confidence wanes, either because of decreasing trust internally or increasing menace from without. The institutions through which people relate may be in such disrepute or the environment perceived as so precarious that the slightest error could ramify throughout the system to cause catastrophe. In this situation we would need to anticipate difficulties from which we could not recover, rather than just reacting to those that can be overcome. Now the evils that do appear are limited, if by nothing else, by our capacity to recognize them. But the nightmares that might occur are potentially limitless. Shall we err by omission, then, taking the chance that avoidable evils might overwhelm us? Or shall we err by exhaustion, using up our resources to anticipate evils that might never happen, in order to forestall those few disasters that might actually do us in?[1]

The vision of a prophylactic presidency has its rationale in preventive planning; it answers these questions by projecting an anticipatory democracy whose purpose is to prevent bad things from happening. Planning is being offered once again as the solution for

Reprinted from *The Public Interest,* no. 52 (Summer 1978): 3–19.

government's inability to prevent the crises of recent years—the deficit, the environment, competitiveness. Proposals inevitably center on the presidency, the only institution that is also a person.

Demands that presidents become planners lead us to unsettled questions about the power and purpose of the presidency itself. We intend to use the concept of planning, then, to illuminate unresolved conflicts about the appropriate functions of the presidency in American life.

The Planners' Vision

What makes planning attractive to its advocates? What is a good plan, and what benefits should it bring about? First, through good planning, future problems should be more readily foreseen in the present. Henry Ford II, for example, told The *New York Times* that recent shortages in the supply of metals and other industrial materials "could have been anticipated if there had been planning."[2] George Meany (who was then the long-time head of the AFL-CIO) is one of many who expect planning to anticipate society-wide crises, even a decade in advance: "We need long-range economic planning and priorities to minimize unforeseen major developments and reduce the degree to which American society has stumbled and fumbled along in the past few years . . . . the United States was not prepared for the urban crisis of the 1960s, which could have been foreseen by sensible long-run economic planning in the 1950s.[3]

But anticipation is only half the effort. Planning also is meant to include control of the future by current action. According to the advocates' manifesto, "planning can spare all of us the sense of helplessness we feel as the economy drifts from crisis to crisis and replace frustration with a sense of hope, with the conviction that we can, in fact, exert some control over our affairs."[4] This control escalates quickly from a point of satisfaction to a matter of duty. Not only is planning "an economic and social necessity," but, for Leonard Woodcock, of the United Auto Workers, "it is a crime to allow millions of workers to lose their jobs because we refuse to plan."[5] For Wassily Leontief, planning unites the themes of anticipation and control; it is the "preventive medicine" that the country should take to "inoculate itself against forever repeating the same miserable mistakes."[6] Thus its champions see planning as essentially prophylactic—a technique to foresee and forestall future evils before they have manifested themselves.

To achieve these aims, moreover, special mechanisms must be established. Planning advocates believe in a technocratic process embodying comprehensive rationality to override the messy, decentralized political institutions that now make decisions. As their manifesto puts it: "We leave so much to chance. Instead of systematically trying to foresee the needs of the nation in years ahead we have dozens of separate uncoordinated agencies making policy." Planning is thus conceived as a direct antidote to politics ("planning could help us look beyond the next election");[7] ultimately, it is supposed to embrace all governmental decisions. To advocates of comprehensive planning, everything becomes relevant: Energy, housing, and transportation are "obvious examples" of policy areas in need of planning. But (the logic is inescapable) "a planning office cannot look at energy alone, transportation alone, housing alone, or at any other sector of the economy in isolation; all these sectors interact." Thus we see that the apocalyptic language of the mid-1970s is not so far from that of the mid-1980s or today.

Robert Dahl has recently described how initiatives for activist reform in America naturally focus on the presidency: "The Presidency became the institutional center from which a majority coalition . . . would be mobilized, organized, and given voice."[8] Advocates of planning contend that their Office of National Economic Planning "must be set up at the center of our economic and political life . . . within the White House." Nor will it be just one more high-level advisory body. Planners envision an office that will dominate all existing institutions, with its director as the president's chief economic advisor, and its six-year plan as the guiding document for the executive branch. The president, through this planning office, would oversee implementation of the six-year plan in all major policy areas throughout the bureaucracy. A felt need for more control over the future has thus led to a call for greater central control in the present, and—inevitably in our system—to demands that the president be responsible for it.

On what basis might a prophylactic presidency emerge in the last decade of the twentieth century? The collapse of communism in the Soviet Union and Eastern Europe in 1989 and 1990 makes central command planning a lot less likely. And the fortuitous existence of divided nations with markedly different economic systems (the two Germany's and the two Korea's) but the same sort of people has led many to decide that capitalism is the superior economic system. In the same way, the disintegration of the Warsaw Pact and the pluralization of the Soviet Union make aggression from that quarter less likely. And no other nation appears willing and able to challenge the United States militarily. Against what danger, then, might a future prophylactic presidency be justified?

Throughout the world the cry of ecological crisis is heard. As the fear of nuclear winter recedes, concern over global warming takes its place. The thinning of the ozone layer in the Antarctic is worrisome to a variety of people. The general idea that mother earth is being assaulted (raped some say) is being bandied about. Local, state, and national regulations are being put in place. International agreements to further this and prevent that are in the process of being written and, to a degree, being enforced. The editors of *Time* and *Newsweek* write that defending the earth is their highest priority. Environmental policies have acquired widespread public support. In brief, the cause may differ but a prophylactic presidency is still possible. Should the AIDS epidemic show signs of spreading, for instance, would-be saviors might arise, and who better to prevent this scourge but the president of the United States?

The Plan in Action

How would this restructured presidency function? And would we like a prophylactic president if we had one? To meet these new demands, the president would have to become our great anticipator—first foreseeing evils hidden in the future, then forestalling them in the present. But carrying out this dual role would require shifts throughout the political system, which are only implicit in the planners' design. If we demand that presidents avoid future evils, we cannot then deny them the power to act on their personal foresight.

This logic rings a faint but still familiar sound. In the era before Vietnam, similar deference to superior presidential foresight was called "bipartisan foreign policy." At that time, the future evil was expected to be Soviet expansion toward world domination, which called for American containment around the world. In such a complex and perilous situation, it was argued, only the chief executive could anticipate the measures needed to forestall future Soviet gains. Domestic differences had to be submerged in favor of presidential judgment on the Marshall Plan, the Truman Doctrine, NATO, SEATO, et cetera.

The analogy is relevant because the full flowering of the planners' vision today would be the domestic equivalent of this coldwar situation. Indeed, as Harvey Sapolsky has pointed out, the key to the notable "success stories" of systematic planning—the Polaris submarine and the Apollo landing—was actually the strength of that cold-war consensus, which made those projects unchallenged national priorities.[9] The impetus behind the new call to swift, centralized action is again the domino theory—now generalized to include the evils of domestic policy. In the past we feared that an unfriendly regime in Laos would bring the inevitable "fall" of Vietnam and Cambodia, which in turn would undermine Thailand, then the Philippines, then even Japan or West Berlin. Our alliances appeared to be a tightly linked, volatile system, in which every action transmitted a cumulative impact, so that if the initial evil were not countered, the international system would explode.

Nowadays, after Vietnam, one may ask who still believes in this sort of system. Why, none other than environmentalists (among others), who see nature's tightly linked but fragile systems threatened with catastrophic consequences if wetlands are dried out, or the ozone layer depleted. When all systems are interrelated, a single mistake opens the door to cumulative evils. So just as in the past, each action in the proposed planning system is inextricably linked to the next. The variety of areas to which such a domestic domino theory might be applied are evident in the numerous calls for impact statements. Inflationary-impact statements may have lapsed with Gerald Ford, but energy, health, research, and safety statements are all on the planners' agenda. Environmental-impact statements are now required for the smallest governmental activities. As we write this, the city of New York is processing a fifty-page environmental report, pursuant to federal regulations, for turning one vacant lot in Flatbush into a playground.[10] (There has even been a proposal that planning, itself, should be subject to planning-impact statements.)

Understanding the impacts in any one of these areas could be effective, but identifying them is essentially a claim for special priority. To include all possible impacts makes for a world of all constants and no variables, with no room for trade-offs, bargaining, or judgment.

Anticipatory Democracy

When all policy areas are subject to interrelated impact statements, we would achieve an anticipatory democracy. Each policy area would then take on the characteristics prominent at the height of the cold war: secrecy, "cooperation" with, or deference to, executive leadership, and an insistence on the moral authority of the president to make (unending) crucial choices. A prophylactic presidency, in fact, could succeed only if it were invested with enormous faith (action in the absence of things seen), for that is what is required to trust a leadership acting to control dangers that cannot yet be observed by the rest of us.

President Carter's energy program, for example, conceived after the OPEC price increases, might be a blueprint for anticipatory democracy. As reconstructed by The *New York Times,* "the plan was conceived in secrecy by technicians," and it "reflected a detached, almost apolitical attitude." The secretary of transportation was not privy to the plans for automobile taxes, and even senior economic officials were in the dark until the last minute. The atmosphere "was one of wartime urgency." Schlesinger and his aides "functioned as if they were a self contained unit and their task as hush-hush as the Manhattan Project."[11]

The program that came out of this process was presented to the public in exactly the same spirit. The key to the plan, noted Richard Rovere, "was to convince the public that a crisis existed or, at least, was imminent, and that a failure to meet it with a 'comprehensive' policy would invite 'national catastrophe.'"[12] It was thus entirely consistent with the overall approach for Carter to summarize the proposal as "the moral equivalent of war."

These hallmarks of the prophylactic presidency—secret and centralized policymaking coupled with demands for urgency and faith — appear (in less virulent form) in several other recent experiences. The decisions about swine-flu vaccine, for example, also took place swiftly and privately. Congress and the country were informed only after President Ford had committed himself to the new vaccine. Then, again in an implied atmosphere of emergency, Congress was bidden to ratify the president's decision before the impending evil arrived. No independent evaluation was asked for or achieved.

As the saccharin decisions made clear, the goal of forestalling future risks has been pursued so actively by Congress that it has been crystallized into law. By statute, the Food and Drug Administration (FDA) must ban each food substance showing any trace of carcinogenic properties in animals. By legislation, a two-step scientific extrapolation is thus frozen into place: first, the assumption that any cancer found in animals will be similarly produced in humans; and second, the assumption that the incidence of cancer produced in a few animals by very high doses (the normal testing procedure) is equivalent to the incidence that might be found if large numbers of animals received normal doses. Such data can be evaluated only within a larger scientific context, in which overall risks can be weighed against benefits. When benefits vary with the individual, as with saccharin, only the individual can properly judge the trade-offs. But the FDA is given no discretion to consider ambiguous (or even contrary) scientific evidence, economic costs in relation to probable benefits, or public opinion. Under the law, a showing of potential carcinogenic danger, no matter how uncertain, produces immediate action. (It took special legislation to exempt saccharin long enough to conduct further studies.)

The ideal prophylactic presidency would receive warnings far in advance, so planning and action would take place calmly in the open, rather than urgently in secrecy. The only difficulty is that omniscience and omnipotence would be required—vast predictive ability and an even greater capacity for control. But this suggests that the notion of the prophylactic presidency is inherently self-contradictory. If we did know what would or would not cause serious problems, we could pinpoint our concerns; the rationale of the prophylactic presidency, however, is precisely that we do not know (and are unlikely to agree about) what will happen, whether government should intervene, and, if so, how. The sense of urgency is thus necessary because it is essential to convince people to act in the absence of compelling evidence.

This pattern might be called the collectivization of risk: Citizens may not choose what dangers they will face. Individual judgment and choice are replaced by governmental action to ward off automatically potential evils before they materialize. Yet if presidents act to avoid every imagined evil, where will their control end . . . or begin?

Four Types of Presidencies

We have presented the prophylactic or preventive presidency as an ideal type, its features purposefully exaggerated to stand out in bold relief. The prophylactic type can also be compared with several other presidential models. The apparent opposite of the preventive presidency is the reactive presidency, which would try to deal with problems after, rather than before, they showed up. (The administration of George Bush fits this model.) Information costs would be lower because the president would be responding to problems instead of trying to anticipate them. Political costs would be mixed: On the one hand, because problems would be apparent, it would be easier to mobilize consent; on the other hand, because the evils would already be experienced, discontent might reduce political support.

Both prevention and reaction, however, only describe presidential decision making—that is, determining which problems are accepted or rejected as worthy of solution. We also need to understand an explicitly political dimension of the presidency focusing on power— the mobilization of consent. The dualism inherent in the office has never been between action and reaction, as if the matter were one of individual vigor; the question, instead, concerns the relative domain of the institution. The political problem is whether the presidency is to remain the one institution that steps in when all others fail to function (as so happened often in recent times), or whether it will be content to perform only its essential functions.

A pluralist presidency operates in a constitutional context (as Richard Neustadt put it so well) of separated institutions sharing powers. The purpose of the office is to perform tasks especially entrusted to the executive, without responsibility for the functioning of other institutions; when there is disagreement, the presidency is not required to coerce the others. The pluralist presidency is only one part of a larger whole, in which interaction (hence the stress on compromise and bargaining) is more important than individuality. All elements of the system, not only the presidency, have legitimate mandates from the people.

California Governor Jerry Brown illustrates this kind of executive in pure form. Brown was the first to apply the norms of both more equality and less consumption to government—hence balanced budgets and salary increases for state employees in absolutely equal (instead of proportional) amounts, to help those worst off economically. A cartoon showing a motorist approaching the California border and gazing at a sign reading "Depress Expectations" captures the prevailing impression that the governor is telling people what they have long known—that government cannot make them happy.

The governor also expressed an idea about proportioning responsibility. Just as government is not properly responsible (i.e., should not be held accountable in public) for the state of society—which has its own inner dynamics—so, too, the governor, as chief executive, is responsible for his own actions (hence Brown's refusal to live in the opulent new mansion), but not those of his legislature. If, after reasonable activity on his part, the legislature refused to share his views on farm labor, Brown would wait until a more propitious moment for agreement. For a time, then, Brown could accept stalemate as proper.

According to James Sterling Young, the theory expressed in *The Federalist* (though no wholly authoritative interpretation can be given) suggests that stalemate was both possible and proper until the president and majorities in the House and Senate were in agreement.[13] Justice might be divine, but transient majorities were not. The framers hoped that time would cool passion, size would dilute it, and institutional invention confound it. In this way, no interest opposed to most men's ideas of justice would last long enough to prevail. About defense, to be sure, the framers were more concerned and gave presidents greater powers, but they stressed that only Congress could declare war or supply the armed forces. To prevent or prepare for war, presidents were made commanders in chief, but the act itself—the power to declare and wage war—was not given to them alone.

Several recent presidents, by contrast, have operated on the assumptions of a different model, in which superior authority, instead of stalemate, characterizes political relationships. This predominant presidency tries to overcome obstructions created by other institutions and assumes the right to step in when they fail to function, on the grounds that the presidential electoral mandate—the only one derived from all the people—has the most legitimacy. The predominant presidency, when thwarted, therefore feels free to go over the heads of other institutions by renewing this mandate, in an attempt to force compliance. Such a situation typically arises because mankind has achieved greater control over its natural and social environment. In practice, this increased power is gained only at some cost, and the new technology presents society with new choices. Quite often the trade-offs are obscure or unrecognized—as with the belief, long held in the West, that appropriate fiscal policy could cure mass unemployment with no real costs (such as inflation, loss of social confidence, and dependence on government) to the political economy. Even when the nature of the trade-off is appreciated, political institutions may be inadequate to resolve the resulting conflict of interests. This is what is meant by "overload" of political institutions.

The naive solution to this problem is simply to increase the amount of power enjoyed by one of the decision-making institutions in the system, so that the president or Cabinet can enforce the particular trade-off chosen. Since government in a democratic system does not and should not have such power in normal circumstances, the authorities are forced to make circumstances appear abnormal—by inventing crises and impending catastrophies to justify an extension of their power.

Of course, the prophylactic presidency is only a model, and an extreme one at that. No one expects the presidency to become prophylactic in all areas all at once. The question is one of proportion and degree. The struggle of a preventive presidency against its pluralist heritage is now in the making. The prophylactic presidency, combining prevention with predominance, would make huge demands for knowledge and power. Knowledge is necessary for anticipation; it takes power to support broad-gauged policies. The demand for knowledge suggests that those who can produce it will be favored. The demand for power means that institutions other than the presidency will be threatened.

What will the fight be over? Money, naturally. The politics of prevention is expensive. The cost of anticipating evils, whether or not they materialize, is enormous. (Biologists tell of organisms that die not so much because of invasion by lethal foreign bodies but because the attack arouses all the defense mechanisms of the organism at once, thereby leading to annihilation by exhaustion.) Ways must be found, therefore, to raise huge sums. By asking who benefits from (as well as who pays for) the prophylactic presidency, we should be better able to predict its future patterns of action.

The Politics of Prevention

The purpose of the prophylactic presidency is to ward off evils, as yet unseen, by spreading the risk around. Who gains from this collectivization of risk?

Seeking to provide protection without visible taxation, the prophylactic presidency is likely to rely heavily on what we might call "market socialism," thereby adding new impetus to an already powerful social trend. Instead of appearing directly in the government budget (to be supported by taxes and borrowing), costs are passed on to consumers indirectly through higher charges to producers. Indeed, costs may even appear as government revenues—taxes on business—that are also ultimately passed on to consumers. When new safety standards are imposed, for example, governmental expenditures (usually just for inspectors) appear relatively small but larger costs are incurred by industry on more equipment, additional safety supervisors, and new tests that become part of production costs. Naturally, the consumer identifies the company rather than government with higher prices. Think of regulations about housing density, insulation, safety features, and the like: Each raises the cost of housing, diffusing it among the population, with only a few inspectors charged up as governmental expenditure. Finally, consider the proposed effluent charges: By placing a tax on pollution, government would try to make it worthwhile for producers to reduce levels of noxious substances without direct regulation. Producers would, in effect, become tax collectors by passing on those charges to private citizens.

Market socialism is the name for this reverse-tax process. Arthur Okun has cited examples of how strong this trend already is:

> Our chance for some net relief from inflation has been reduced by a new wave of legislative actions that add to particular costs and prices. [In addition to higher payroll taxes] ... the minimum wage seems slated to move up from $2.30 to $2.65 next year. The first installment of the wellhead tax on crude oil is scheduled to take effect in 1978. Government farm programs reinstituted acreage cutbacks—deliberately reducing the productivity of our agriculture. Many of these cost-raising measures have some justification. No one of them spells the difference between price stability and rampant inflation But, in combination, they may well add 1.5 percent to the inflation rate by late 1978.
>
> Reliance on such measures is nothing new, but their total magnitude does

set a new record. The Congress may have been tempted to load costs on the budgets of consumers and employers in order to avoid loading more onto the Federal budget. In several of these areas, the President initially advanced proposals that were admirably restrained but then compromised in the face of strong political opposition. (While some of the press welcomes such instances as evidence of the President's education in the ways of Washington, I cannot share the enthusiasm.) Meanwhile, the financial and business community has been so preoccupied with Thursday afternoon reports on M_1 and Federal deficit reestimates that it has missed the big new inflationary game in town.[14]

As a solution, Okun suggests his own form of impact statement:

No net Federal cost-raising. First, the Administration should set a target of zero net cost-raising measures for 1978, and should report quarterly to the American people on the achievement of that target. Any new cost-raising governmental action that imposes higher labor costs on employers or higher prices on consumers would have to be neutralized by a Federal cost-reducing measure—lightening the burden of some regulation or providing a cost-cutting subsidy.[15]

But if we are correct, his advice is unlikely to be taken.

The chief concomitants of market socialism are low visibility, capital intensity, and social selectivity. Consider, first, low visibility; market socialism blurs cause and effect between public and private sectors. Which sector, for instance, is responsible for increased housing costs? Which sector inflates the cost of safety features in manufacturing? Suppose, to make the contrast vivid, government closes down a plant because it is unsafe for workers or neighbors. Everyone can see what is happening. If workers and neighbors prefer existing hazards to threatened unemployment, they might be able to exert their will. Suppose, however, that environmental and safety regulations prevent a projected plant from locating in such a low-income area, shifting it instead to a more affluent suburb. No one would know that the location had been passed over, thus imposing costs on residents who wish employment. It is harder to mobilize support for something that did not take place than for something about to be taken away.

Allied with low visibility is the widespread displacement of costly effects onto unsuspecting (and unconsenting) adults. Take the well-known issue of drug lag: Because of extensive trials and procedures, for levels of safety difficult to prove, some drugs may not be developed at all, while others are produced only after a delay, or come at a higher cost.

Nowadays we know about this syndrome because the friends of AIDS victims succeeded in putting pressure on government to release new drugs much faster, believing it was better to risk being hurt by side-effects than to lose the chance of improved health.

What happens when government seeks to anticipate a wide variety of risks or to mitigate those that do exist? Less money is available for investment to create future jobs, or for current expenditure to support current jobs.

Only if there is a larger domestic product, providing more for everyone—or more for some, but not less for others—can severe social conflict be mitigated. But this would mean putting resources into production, not prevention. Hence, a no-growth ethic fits well with prophylactic politics. To be sure, there could conceivably be "more productivity and more safety." But unless cost and safety complement each other, there is likely to be an inverse relationship. It is at the margin—where experience is beginning to show that large expenditures lead to little improvement—that small increases in safety work against large increases in productivity. The struggle over who should pay for the politics of prevention, therefore, is likely to aggravate conflicts among institutions over who should rule—*i.e.*, over whether a pluralist presidency should become more predominant.

The Federal Stalemate

Demands for the president to become planner in chief call for a radical redistribution of power within the federal system.

Consider, for example, the full implementation of the swine-flu decisions. While the presidentially-proclaimed emergency carried the day with Congress and much of the press, other actors were not so easily swayed. State and local health departments were responsible for the actual inoculations. These institutions have their own resources and constituencies and need not be responsive to the president. As a result, there was extreme variation in local activity and thus in the proportion of the total population reached—ranging from over 70 percent in Wyoming to less than 20 percent in New York City. Massachusetts declined to conduct any mass campaign at all.

Drug companies, the major interest group involved, played a key role. For several months they declined to schedule full-scale vaccine distribution—until Congress accepted the precedent that government, rather than the companies, would be liable for any subsequent damage suits. And the armed forces went their own way, rejecting the vaccine recommended by civilian scientists in favor of a different type (with higher immunity but more side effects).

A fully established prophylactic president engaged in forestalling evil could not have tolerated any of these deviations once an emergency was recognized; he would need French-style prefects in place to carry out orders, not question their value. Nor could interest groups be allowed to trade issues of value in return for cooperation. Negotiations take time, and compromises weaken the consistency of the plan. Most of all, prophylactic presidents would have to make the federal bureaucracy responsive: Who else would follow a path that the president's own troops openly abandoned?

But all those independent actors are worse than mere inconvenient obstacles to presidential rationality and control—they are the heart of the federal system. As Martin Landau has written, the essence of federalism is overlap and redundancy:

> What appears is a truly messy system—one that is anathema to our prevailing conceptions of a viable organization. There is no unity of command, and there are no unequivocal lines of authority. Domains overlap, jurisdictions are confused, and accountability is dispersed. And for each citizen there is, at least, two of everything. . . . Virtually every aspect, every feature, every agency, and every structure of government was duplicated and still redundancy was not exhausted.[16]

The model of social interaction implicit in the planners' vision does not work for the varied intermediary groups that characterize our political system: political parties, Congressional committees, interest groups, states, semiautonomous agencies. None of them is needed if cognitive calculation can provide one best choice, and all stand in the way of the "direct" relationship between a prophylactic president and the people.

The "federal stalemate" will not appeal to those who want or need to improve their position. Intermediary groups are part of power structures; they reproduce relations of equality or of dominance. Their combined functions may be inimical to rational choice (i.e., pluralist stagnation) or what some see as the realization of greater social justice (i.e., greater equality).

The potential political consequences at stake in these competing models can be seen if we consider the extreme case—if our political institutions were indeed reshaped to eliminate duplication and to promote uniformity. First, the executive and the legislature would not need staggered electoral terms, or different constituencies, or, for that matter, separate forms of representation. One set of members could serve all roles, as in the British Parliament, which the new American government would then resemble.

The British parliamentary system, however, has evolved a set of informal norms to diffuse the enormous pressures that a unitary system would otherwise channel to the prime minister at its center. British government is a federation of departments. Individual ministers themselves take responsibility for departmental choices, and the cabinet collectively, not the prime minister, is in charge of major decisions. Strong programmatic parties also serve as an independent focus for policymaking.

A prophylactic presidency, unprotected by British conventions, would face increased pressures toward the center, with fewer buffers than before. For as we have said, no president can assemble the knowledge and power needed to control all future dangers that he would be responsible for thereafter. What if we run short of oil, for example, even after a master energy plan has been implemented? At the same time, all those unruly intermediary groups, which now serve to buffer the expectations directed toward presidents, would be undercut. Such groups would be too strong to be taken over and too weak to share responsibilities that could overwhelm presidents. Hence the planners' model, seeking to impose centralized choice in place of social interaction, would be most likely to disrupt the interaction instead.

The concept of the prophylactic presidency, of course, is intended to push certain trends, now only dimly perceived, to an extreme conclusion, reflecting a lack of confidence in existing social relations. People who trust one another and the institutions through which they interrelate will have enough self-confidence to deal with most difficulties and enough faith to follow leaders in trying to head off a few evils before they occur. When trust declines, confidence declines, and the need for leadership increases.

Notes

1. For further exploration of this theme, see Aaron Wildavsky, *Searching for Safety* (New Brunswick, N.J.: Transaction, 1988).
2. *New York Times,* May 18, 1975.
3. Ibid.
4. This and later quotations from the manifesto are from "The Case for Government Planning," *New York Times,* March 16, 1975.
5. *New York Times,* May 18, 1975.
6. *New York Times,* February 28, 1975.
7. *New York Times,* May 18, 1975.
8. Robert Dahl, "On Removing Certain Impediments to Democracy in the United States," *Political Science Quarterly* 92 (Spring 1977): 6–7.
9. Harvey Sapolsky, "Science Policy," in Nelson W. Polsby and Fred I. Greenstein, eds., *Handbook of Political Science* vol. 6 (Reading, Mass.: Addision Wesley, 1975) 79–110.
10. *New York Times,* June 24, 1977.
11. See "Carter Shaped Energy Plan With Disregard for Politics," *New York Times,* April 24, 1977.
12. Richard Rovere, "Letter from Washington," *New Yorker,* May 9, 1977, 136.
13. This idea is drawn from a lecture by James Sterling Young at the Graduate School of Public Policy, University of California, Berkeley.
14. Arthur Okun, "The Great Stagflation Swamp," *Challenge* (November / December 1977): 11.
15. Ibid., 12.
16. Martin Landau, "Federalism, Redundancy and System Reliability," *Publius* 3 (1973): 188.

7

The Party of Government, the Party of Opposition, and the Party of Balance: An American View of the Consequences of the 1980 Election

The election of 1980 is pregnant with many possibilities. It could be the beginning of a Republican renaissance, but it could just as well be the beginning of the end of the Republican party. It could be the herald of smaller government, we hear, but perhaps it is the siren song of big government, dashing on the rocks of desire for power the naive hope that less could be more. The point is that the importance of an event is not only inherent in it but also in what it becomes. When we ask whether 1980 was a critical election, we are asking about more than just the Reagan administration and its supporters. We are asking what the world will do to them as well as what they will try to do to it.

With a Republican administration in the White House, a slim Republican majority in the Senate, and gains in the House of Representatives, it is easy to imagine the Republican party in the ascendant. Still, as the song says, "It ain't necessarily so." From the early 1930s until 1980, at least, the United States could reasonably be characterized as having a party-and-a-half system. Something like two-thirds of the potential electorate (including so-called independents who lean toward one party or the other) identify themselves as Democrats. Governorships and state legislative majorities are preponderantly of the Democratic party persuasion. The Senate in the past twenty years

Reprinted from *The American Elections of 1980*, ed. Austin Ranney (Washington, D.C.: American Enterprise Institute, 1981), 329–50.

(again until the 1980 election) has been largely Democratic, the House overwhelmingly so. One can gauge the weakness of Republican representation in Congress by observing that until after the election of 1980 it was difficult to imagine any election that would give that party control of the House. Is it a whole party when it is not even a potential majority party?

Just as one swallow does not a summer make, a single election does not restore a party to the position of a constant contender. Only winning the enduring loyalty of a near majority of voters can do that. To begin to do that, the Republican Reagan Administration must be seen to be successful in maintaining peace and securing prosperity. In view of the turbulence of the international economy and the less-than-perfect understanding of the domestic economy, however, no government is able to ensure success in simultaneously reducing inflation and decreasing unemployment. Nor can any government, hawkish or dovish, ensure peace.

As soon as the clamor over the "imperial presidency" of Vietnam and Watergate subsided, the presidency appeared less conquering than conquered, more impotent than potent. The decline of multi-issue coalitions, the rise of single-issue interest groups, the fragmentation of power in Congress and within the executive branch, the concentration on government as a solver of national problems, all these and more have been cited as reasons for the unsatisfactory performance of presidents in recent times. Can it be coincidental, Americans wonder, that presidents fear to run for a second term or are defeated when they do? Is it mere happenstance that the loser of the last three presidential debates—Kennedy versus Nixon (Nixon had been vice-president in the Eisenhower administration), Ford versus Carter, Carter versus Reagan—has been the incumbent? Hard luck? Systemic defect? Unforgiving environment? Whatever the explanation, the proficiency and popularity of presidents does appear problematic.

History remains contingency. Retrodiction (or predicting the past, which we call history) is still superior to prediction. Speaking in the voice of this skeptical spirit, I shall set out certain forms of accounting for measuring the institutional and policy legacy of the 1980 election. If we can never be entirely sure of where we are going, we can at least learn a little about where we have been.

Political parties are usually discussed primarily in terms of formal organization. In this chapter, by contrast, I am going to refer to parties as doctrinal tendencies competing for the allegiance of the American people. Sometimes these doctrines are espoused by formal party organizations, sometimes not; whether they are or not can be discovered only by observation.

My argument is that there are three significantly different ways of looking at how a government ought to be run, three doctrinal parties; each "party" will follow a somewhat different line of policies. The Reagan administration comes in as a "party of opposition," but only its policies will tell us whether it is truly that or just another right-leaning "party of fiscal balance." A particular group of leaders may start out thinking it is one kind of party when in fact it is another. The policies it tries—as well as the success or failure of those policies—depend not only on the group itself but also on conditions external to it. What makes the Reagan administration so interesting is that it is the best bet for a party of opposition we have had in a long time.

Commentators usually criticize Republicans for being *only* the party of opposition. The usual criticism is that all the party does is slow things down a bit. Thus these critics would say, "Don't be just the party of opposition; strike out with something new." In today's terms the argument would be, "Don't be just the party of balance; be something new—a party of opposition to big government."

The Party of Opposition versus the Party of Responsibility

There are three doctrinal parties competing for control in the United States—the parties of government, of opposition, and of balance. The "party of government," as its name implies, is literally for expanding the role of government—more is better. The citizens it seeks to create are employees of, producers for, or beneficiaries of, government. Name the problem—energy, inflation, employment, poverty, pollution—and the party of government has a governmental solution—rationing, price control, entitlements, welfare, regulation. The "party of opposition" is opposed to growing government; it is for increasing the absolute and relative size of the private sector—less is more. The citizens it creates seek limited government. Placed in this crude conceptual vise, parties race for the allegiance of citizens, one party (in our time, Democratic) trying to tie them to government, the other (now, Republican) trying to tear them away.

What and where is the third party? It is the "party of fiscal balance," or just the "party of balance," composed of the deviant wings of the major parties. Though Democrats generally prefer to meet difficulties with increased spending, their wing of balance will, when inflation strikes, decrease spending and increase taxation. Although Republicans prefer to decrease spending, their wing of balance will, when faced with unemployment, increase spending and, with deficits, increase taxation.

The party of balance is not a conservative but a conserving force. It is reactive. It tends to preserve whatever is there. If government is small, it will remain so; but if government is large to begin with, it will end up the same way it started. The difference is that the party of balance will curb what it sees as excess. If government has been growing too rapidly, the party of responsibility will slow it down. If it has been growing too slowly, the party of balance will speed it up. Stability is the name of the game for the party of balance.

To understand the central tendency of the party of balance, one must set it in the context of its main rival in modern times, the party of government, against which it reacts. The politics of the party of government may be expressed in the same word Samuel Gompers used to characterize the demands of trade unions—*more*. The party of government promises more subsidies, more loan guarantees, and more tax expenditures to business; and it promises more entitlements and more indexing of welfare programs against inflation, and more welfare to individuals. Ultimately, it promises success, for its various policies are held together by the desire to guard against failure.

The political appeal of promising more needs no explication here. Benefits appear in the present and costs only in the future. By this time, a majority of Americans receive some sort of stipend (a tax expenditure like housing deductions and loan guarantees for middle-class students counts as much as welfare for poorer people). What we need to explore briefly is how the party of balance relates to these perennial promises.

Two things turn out to be destabilizing: making future promises and failing to honor past ones. More promises are destabilizing because the debt created leads to inflation and the future resources required lead to higher taxes, which lead to less investment. Slow down while there is still time, is the advice. Social stability, however, according to the party of balance, requires that past promises be perpetuated. To do otherwise would cause social unrest, upset expectations, depress morale. The end result is not the same size of government but the larger size inherent in past promises.

Look at the likely financial consequences of a policy of fiscal balance: the rate of spending increase is slowed down and the rate of tax increase is speeded up. The spending slowdown, it must be understood, is not a spending decrease but a pause to enable revenue to catch up, thus bringing the economy into some sort of balance. Spending decreases result in direct deprivation of groups accustomed to receiving largess. Tax increases, by contrast, appear relatively painless: indirect taxes, like those paid by employers on payrolls, and direct taxes, like the "bracket creep" that pushes people into higher categories in an inflationary period, are favorite devices. When a party of balance leaves office (Jimmy Carter's and Gerald Ford's administrations may serve as prototypes), the effective tax take is much higher than when it took office, and so is spending, except that it has not risen as fast as in prior years.

What happens, we may ask, when elections are fought between parties of balance? The question is relevant because most elections in the United States are fought on this basis: the moderate left offers somewhat more spending and the moderate right somewhat less. If the responsible right appears disadvantaged, at least for all offices except the presidency, that may be because promising more has an advantage over promising less, or the people may trust politicians who want government to do marginally more to do just that. The answer to our question, however, lies less in what the parties promise than in what they do: What happens when parties of balance succeed parties of government?

Let us take Lyndon Johnson's time in office as the party of government. In 1968 Johnson was replaced by Nixon, who resigned under threat of impeachment and was succeeded by Ford, who lost to Carter. The period from 1968 to 1980, according to my criteria, was one of the party of balance, first conservative, then liberal. During that time, Republicans were in power for eight out of twelve years. Looking at trends in spending and taxing, one can easily see that both have gone way up. Taxes take a considerably larger proportion of national income and spending a substantially larger proportion of the gross national product (GNP) than in prior decades and this during a period when inflation-adjusted spending on defense, despite the Vietnam war, remained constant. In short, "balance" meant bigger government. What spending would have been had the party of government been in power one can only imagine; it has certainly risen substantially in real dollars and in proportion to the private sector. Evidently the momentum in the programs inherited from the party of government was sufficient to go far, even when the brake was gradually applied.

It is the political legacy of balance, however, that interests us. To the degree that a party of balance is successful, taxes are higher than they were, and expenditures are lower than they would have been. Such a situation constitutes the ultimate opportunity for the party of government, which can promise spending increases without immediate increases in taxes. Since the rate of spending has slowed down but is still going up, the base for building future increases has been enhanced, and since the tax base has been enlarged, the flow of resources has been speeded up. This is how promising more spending without increasing taxes becomes politically palatable.

As things stand, the party of government and the party of responsibility rule. Some countries (Israel is an example) have only parties of government. Others, like Britain, have largely been ruled by parties of responsibility, whatever name they give themselves. The similarities shown by parties in office are due to the fact that there are only modest differences between a party of balance on the left, which allows spending to keep up, and one on the right, which holds spending increases down. Though Prime Minister Thatcher's government is widely believed to be a party of opposition, for instance, it came into office by increasing the value-added tax (comparable to a sales tax) by 15 percent. What would a government of opposition have done? It would have cut the value-added tax, for that alone, like a reduction in the taxes employers pay on wages in the United States, would have lowered prices instead of increasing them. How would the government have made up the loss in revenue? By deeper cuts in public spending and by fewer contributions to state industry. The deficit would have been used to compel cuts in spending, not increases in taxes. How would the government cope with the resulting increase in unemployment? By lower taxes to spur industry. Suppose there is social unrest? Suppose the policy does not work as well or as quickly as desired? Nothing guarantees success. A genuine party of opposition, if it has to lose, wants to lose on the issues that matter to it—the relative sizes of the public and private sectors.

Parties of government and of balance, to be sure, are not oblivious to the signs of the times. What these might be and how they might react we will discuss later. The point here is that these are parties with a social vision to which economic doctrines are subordinate. No doubt they have their priorities among objects of expenditure and types of taxation. No doubt the party of government is more enamored of central control and the party of opposition of market mechanisms. After all, the "owners" of the party of government are the employees and beneficiaries of government, and the party of opposition is made up of the "owners" of the private sector. Whether markets or regulations work in specific instances (policy analysts know that no instrument of policy is good for all purposes) is less important to them than realizing their separate social visions—life under larger or smaller public and private sectors.

Adherents of the parties of opposition and of government, insofar as they believe in their view of the good life, abide by certain precepts and follow certain rules derived from them. When in doubt, what they do depends on these precepts: (1) the size of spending is more important than its purpose (*how much* government does is more important than what it does); and (2) the size of revenue is more important than its composition. For the party of opposition, the rule is that lower taxes and less spending are always desirable, even if the wrong expenditure or tax is cut. The party of opposition takes it where it can get it. For the party of government, the rule is that any tax is a good tax, even if it would prefer another one. Every spending increase is a good one, even if the object is less desirable than another. Once spending and taxing are at higher levels, strengthening this party and weakening its opponents, the party of government may make adjustments to push one program ahead faster than others, thereby coming closer to its spending priorities as well. Similarly, the party of opposition will lower certain tax rates more than others when it can, all the while regarding any tax cut as doubly desirable for the revenues it reduces and the spending cuts it induces.

Whereas a party of opposition considers driving down taxes and spending good in and of itself, a party dedicated to social stability insists that spending and taxing be balanced. This is easier to do by keeping taxes high. Since a party, once in office, always needs money to satisfy demands, the result is that taxes stay up. Thus the next party of government can use the proceeds of restraint—temporarily lower spending increases and permanently higher effective tax rates—to build a bigger government.

Which way will President Reagan's government go? Will there be more citizens independent of government after his time, as befits a party of opposition, or will there be as many or more dependent on it, as would emerge from a party of fiscal balance? To put the matter in policy terms, is there to be a balanced budget at higher or lower levels of spending and taxation? Speaking in terms of social philosophy, one may ask, Is the domestic government to be made smaller because that is desirable or is it to remain larger because to do otherwise would be "simplistic"?

Will we hear less about "waste," and will we hear more about the desirability of providing fewer services? If the answers are yes, then we know the president belongs to the party of opposition. After he leaves government, will President Reagan say, as he did as governor of California, that he reduced the rate of increase in spending? If the answer is yes, then we will know that he stood with the party of balance. By painting a portrait of the kinds of policies a party of opposition would find desirable, we will be better able to offer an accounting of whether and to what extent the Reagan administration fits the picture of a slimmer Uncle Sam or a decaying Dorian Gray.

Adjusting to External Turbulence and Internal Fragmentation

Ours has not been a great time, as President Carter discovered, for the party of responsibility. The party's old constituency has been lost, and a new one has not been created because no one knows enough to manipulate the economy successfully. That is what is meant when officials lament that "fine-tuning" does not work any more. Knowledge of what to do is deficient, partly because a multitude of programs interacting with great frequency overwhelms our understanding. Marginal moves do not work well because the base from which the move is made is itself not understood or is out of control. A multitude of comprehensive changes overloads the political system (Carter's first two years), and a plethora of minor adjustments increases complexity without improving control. Acting precipitously leads to unanticipated consequences, and delay allows presidents to be overwhelmed by the sheer momentum of events. The stability the party of responsibility seeks to achieve turns out to be the indispensable assumption of making its methods work.

The manual for the party of responsibility by Heineman and Hessler urges their president to

> target carefully. Across-the-board approaches—support of proposals to limit spending to a percentage of GNP or to balance the budget under certain conditions—will cause enormous political battles, and if successful (which is doubtful), will then lead to meat-ax cuts that hit desirable as well as undesirable items. At the other extreme, going to the Hill each year with hundreds of little cuts will mean that you may have to fight hundreds of little skirmishes. Better to target on some major issues selectively, make the case on those issues, and try to drive them through. They are likely to result in bigger long-term savings, anyway.[1]

Whether the income-security programs in which lie the largest possible reductions will prove a boon for presidents is doubtful. More to the moment is the emphasis this proposal gives to item-by-item consideration of savings divorced from the context of presidential government. If a president wants to be part of the party of responsibility, moderately modifying what has gone before, the advice may be excellent. But if a president wants to limit government, and if he recognizes that any government, including his own, finds higher spending and taxing easier than the opposite, then imposing limits on his own administration makes sense.

Whether the party of opposition can succeed depends on its ability to create more citizens who wish to be independent of government faster than citizens who are dependent on it. That, in turn, requires (a) the willingness to formulate policies appropriate for a party of opposition, (b) the ability to get support from Congress, and (c) the capacity to implement the resulting programs. All three requisites are, to say the least, problematic. By envisaging the policies a party of opposition might pursue, we shall be better able to appraise its chances.

Policies for a Party of Opposition

How would a party of opposition deal with inflation? By cutting taxes and spending. Which would it do first? Both together; but if there has to be a choice, taxes first. Cutting spending is more difficult because (a) individual programs are popular, (b) legislation may have to be changed, (c) there are so many programs with which to cope, and (d) some potential cuts—such as student loan guarantees and support for the elderly—affect the party's own constituents. Some cuts may be successful, but others may be blocked by a Congress not committed to opposition. The famed "iron triangle" of interest groups, agencies, and congressional committees will reassert itself on individual items. If tax cuts come first (say, a Kemp-Roth bill of 10 percent a year extended to four years, to go them one better, which would thereby cut real rates, not just keep up with inflation and taxes for social security), deficits will undoubtedly grow. Indeed, given a political propensity to cut taxes faster than spending, the initial deficit under President Reagan may be larger than the one he inherited from President Carter. Why does this matter? It matters in that the size of the deficit may be used as a propellant to drive spending down further. Using the failure to cut spending as a rationale for raising effective tax rates belongs to the party of balance, not of opposition.

The usual political wisdom, taken apart from the kind of party for which it is intended, is that spending must be reduced before taxes can be cut. Otherwise, congressmen may claim credit for cutting taxes without being willing to take the blame for reducing spending. For the party of balance this advice is essential. It is the strategy par excellence, since balance in the economy, like stability in society, is of the essence. For the party of opposition, however, the advice may be misplaced. Of course, the cutting of both taxes and spending simultaneously is the best in the best of all possible worlds. Life, however, is not often so neat. Waiting for both may mean waiting forever. Internal bargaining on both may lead to each one's being cut far less than it might be alone. The party of opposition, therefore, takes whichever can come first, using lower taxes to lower spending and vice versa.

Which taxes are lowered and in what order? The party of responsibility wants to lower taxes on capital by rapid depreciation so as to increase productivity. The party of opposition, although it will take any tax cut it can get, places priority on cuts in personal tax rates because increasing take-home pay is both the symbol and the reality of its program—increasing the size of the private sector and trusting the people to spend their own money.

The emphasis on economic growth is also useful in providing a perspective on unemployment. Whereas the party of government wants to put people to work in or for the public sector, the party of opposition wants them to work in the private sector. Without at least modest growth, there will be substantial and sustained unemployment, driving out of office the party of opposition. Its choice, by no means guaranteed to succeed, is to create employment through growth of the private sector. If that fails, the party of opposition has failed in the right way by testing its vision of the good life against reality.

Apart from resisting the temptation to act as the party of balance, which industrial interests may prefer because they do not like uncertainty and do depend on subsidy, the party of opposition must be careful about how it deals with social issues. It is divided between libertarians, for whom almost any restraint on expression is anathema, and hierarchists, who want their traditional norms of family life and social deference respected.[2] As symbolic leader, the president can lend the moralists what they say they want—moral support. He can unite libertarians and hierarchists by removing governmentally sponsored interventions to which they object, such as subsidies for abortions. Going beyond this negative phase to a positive position of attempting to legislate morality, however, will seriously split the party of opposition.

Polls of public opinion show that most people think government spending is too high, but most also favor many programs. Suspicion of inefficiency is strong. The Reagan administration can build support by demonstrating increased effectiveness in the area where it proposes to increase spending, namely defense.

As time goes on, the party of opposition can expect to be swamped with efforts to reinstate spending programs and to modify tax provisions. Efforts to get around spending cuts through loans, entitlements, and tax expenditures will also accelerate. The administration can deal with them either retail, item by item, year by year, or wholesale, setting up schemes to deflect and direct these demands. From the moment of the inaugural, sure of its own strength and thinking, in the words of the budget director, that all that is necessary is "political will,"[3] retailing is the order of the day. Before too long, however, as it gets worn down by fighting simultaneously on so many fronts, the administration will reconsider its position. When it comes to the more profound understanding that, as the party in government, it is part of the problem—tax money is useful to balance budgets, to relieve strains among departments and their clientele, to respond to this or that exigency—the party of opposition may go wholesale so as to project its position.

On the tax side, once rates are down, it may seek a system of uniform flat rates for income taxes—say, 10, 15, 25 percent top—with no exemptions or deductions. The well-nigh universal belief that everyone else is cheating on taxes, legally or otherwise, would diminish, thus increasing the legitimacy of government in the eyes of citizens. The work of accountants and lawyers would decline, thus freeing these professionals for more productive work.

On the spending side, a constitutional amendment to limit spending to the present level plus the increase in national product would take the pressure off the president. Agencies would fight each other—more for one agency means less for another—rather than the president.[4]

Obviously, low uniform income tax rates and spending limits are, if not utopian, at least visionary. I mention them only to show what a party of opposition might do to institutionalize its doctrines.

Though it is not desirable to run through the gamut of domestic programs, it is possible to capture the essence of the problems they pose in two words: subsidy and equality. Business and citizen are subsidized in so many ways, from soup (the expense-account lunch) to nuts (payments to peanut farmers), it is hard to count them. A structure of privilege so laboriously constructed will be difficult to tear down. It will take time. All I wish to say here is that an even-handed approach will make it easier. If farmers are asked to give up or to accept lower price supports in times of plenty, for example, they must also be able to cash in on times of poor yields. Forbidding food exports because they raise prices, and then cutting subsidies when farmers are about to make money is not equitable.

The rationale for most social programs is equality. No redblooded American, certainly no president, is going to deny that. What the party of opposition needs is its own version of equality. It is not against the "social insurance state," ensuring poor people against adversity, provided the sums do not keep growing so that the public sector overwhelms the private one. Equality of opportunity is a must, but equality of result is not. What, then, is to take the place of equality of result?

Equality as variety is one answer. Each individual should be allowed to develop his or her potential in different ways. Variety as equality is like friendship; one does not treat all friends the same. The political form most appropriate for generating variety is federalism.

Whereas Americans once used to glory in the diversity of our federal system, today there is a tendency to condemn it as incoherent.

Were states encouraged to differentiate themselves, by contrast, citizens could choose among different levels of services and of taxation. By stressing variety at the state level, the nation would be able to make better use of interest groups. By turning off the pump of federal funds, the government could divert energies into local channels. By reducing federal revenues, the federal government would leave room for states to step in—if they wished. What would appear as chaos, were it sponsored from the top, would appear as interesting experimentation from below. In this way the party of opposition might make use of, rather than regret, political fragmentation.

The current question, of course, is whether the Republican party under Ronald Reagan will become a party of opposition or a party of balance. Let us look at what we can see in the entrails of our time and apply these readings to the parties of government, balance, and opposition. Then I will attempt an appraisal of the political feasibility of implementing the program of a party of opposition.

The Future

Just as the importance of the 1932 election was determined by 1936 and the elections that followed, the significance of the 1980 election depends on what happens afterward. The most likely result of any election, however, is that things will be much the same afterward as they were before. There are reasons things are the way they are, and these are usually powerful reasons based on more than inertia. Following the path of least resistance, then, the Reagan presidency should look, if not like Carter's, then at least like Ford's. Like most of his predecessors, President Reagan will get some of what he wants (none, needless to say, got all). Spending and taxation will be lower than they would have been, but probably not—in real terms—lower than they are now. Government will grow, but not as fast and not quite in the same direction as before. The party of opposition, in other words, will give way to the party of balance, and the 1980 election will signify continuity rather than change.

A less likely, but not negligible, possibility is that the Reagan administration will be unable to get any of its programs passed. Perhaps circumstances it does not anticipate will lead it into a series of ad hoc responses similar to those that characterized the Carter administration. The election of 1980 would then be notable for giving rise to an even more acute concern over the viability of the American political system.

The least likely eventuality is that a party of opposition will emerge full-blown out of the brow of the Reagan administration. For one thing, it may not have sufficient support in the Congress or the country. The American people may not want a much more limited government than they have now. They may want a better-run government of about the same size or a bit larger. Should that be the case, converting opposition to balance would be in line with popular sentiment, no small matter in a democracy.

For another, a party of opposition is not the same as a single-shot administration. A governing party implies both a coherent doctrine and an ability to compromise among factions. A narrow sect cannot win and maintain office. Its very emphasis on doctrine may split the party of opposition. The intensity of individual concern that leads its adherents to join such a party may make collective action difficult. Advocates of social regulation may clash with opponents of economic regulation. Proponents of increased defense spending may find themselves at odds with those who wish less total spending.

Nevertheless, in my opinion, the attempt to establish and maintain a party of opposition would be neither futile nor hopeless. Futility does not reside in giving the citizenry an opportunity to select or reject a different vision of the role of government, one in which government might be both smaller and more effective. Even rejection of a party of opposition would clarify the course the country will take in the next several decades. A party of opposition is not a hopeless proposition either. Some signs of the times, as we have seen, are favorable. I do not think anyone can say more than that the political feasibility of reducing tax rates is high and of reducing spending overall is moderately good, without necessarily specifying how much they will decline or which taxes or expenditures will decline most.

Keeping its eye on the strategic direction of a party of opposition— any way that taxes and spending decline is desirable compared with the opposite—is essential if the Reagan administration is to make it through the first term and especially the first two years. If it insists that cuts be made in some precise order and magnitude, the administration will be unable to make necessary compromises. If it can keep its cool, giving here, taking there, so long as the direction of the size of government is down, it may be able to retain sufficient coherence and viability to take its case to the people over a series of elections. And, in a democracy, that is all any party can ask.

Like everyone else, the Reagan administration must start from where it (and the country) is. Unlike its opponents, however, the Reagan administration is committed to changing the course of national policy. This task is more difficult because governments in the Western world have been growing larger (absolutely and relative to the private sector) for a good hundred years. The first facts to be faced are that the Republican party has only a small majority in the Senate and is in a substantial minority position in the House of Representatives. Without give-and-take, it cannot get even part of its program through. On what bases should it stand firm or compromise?

A prototypical illustration of the choices that will face the administration is contained in this effort to teach a lesson in politics to the new and naive party of opposition:

> The incoming Office of Management and Budget director, David Stockman, and other administration officials have indicated the food-stamp program would be one of the first places where budget savings will be sought.

> Food-stamp supporters in Congress already are gearing up for battle over the probable blitz on the program, which is to be reauthorized this year as part of a general farm bill.

> The new chairman of the Senate Agriculture Committee, Jesse Helms, R-N.C., long a critic of growing costs of the program, has talked about major reductions in food-stamp spending, ranging as high as 40 percent.

> But Rep. Frederick Richmond, D-N.Y., chairman of the House Agriculture subcommittee that oversees food stamps, warned recently that Reagan, Stockman and Helms are playing with fire.

> He said any efforts to "emasculate" the program would seriously jeopardize urban-suburban legislators' backing of other farm commodity support programs Reagan and Helms are likely to advocate.

> "This Stockman is not very realistic," Richmond said. "He is talking through his hat, overreacting because he is totally inexperienced in the politics of farm legislation.

> "Without a food-stamp program as part of the package, there is no way a general farm bill can pass. I have conveyed that idea to Sen. Helms and he realizes the tobacco supports so important to his state will not go through without food stamps.[5]

The desire of senators from farm states for crop subsidies is held hostage to preservation of the food-stamp program at present levels of funding. Economically, abolition of the entire farm program would be a boon; politically, loss of support from farm-state senators and representatives might be disastrous. Only those who would like nonpolitical polities can ignore such considerations.

Given the good fortune, or the foresight and the acumen, not only to propose but to pass bills that raise economic growth, the clash of interests may be moderated. With the private sector growing faster than the public sector, there can be increases in real personal income and in government spending. This happy set of circumstances is by no means inevitable, less likely, perhaps, than not. But it is by no means impossible or highly unlikely. There is a sufficient prospect for success—defined as giving the electorate an opportunity to vote in or out a potential majority party of opposition—to make it worth pursuing.

In sum, the 1980 election is more likely to be an election to confirm past trends than it is to realign parties or programs. If the election does turn out in retrospect to have been critical—and it is the analytic purpose of this chapter to provide a mechanism of accounting for that purpose—it will be because it began the first stirrings of a fledgling party of opposition. Whether that party can be kept together to fight future elections is being decided now.

The voice of 1980, before the Reagan Republican victory, has greater resonance in 1990. Revenue remains at around $18^{1}/_{2}$ percent of GNP. Federal spending is showing signs of going below 24 percent of GNP. The difference is the deficit, which has become the most effective force against spending in half a century. As expected, Ronald Reagan's party of opposition has given way to George Bush's party of balance. Neither tendency has yet captured the Republican party.

Notes

1. Ben W. Heineman, Jr., and Curtis A. Hessler, *Memorandum for the President* (New York: Random House, 1980).
2. For an excellent article on these two tendencies, see James Q. Wilson, "Reagan and the Republican Revival," *Commentary* 70 (October 1980): 25–32.
3. *Wall Street Journal*, January 9, 1981.

4. Aaron Wildavsky, *How to Limit Government Spending* (Berkely: University of California Press, 1980).

5. Ward Sinclair, "Budget Chief Proposes Food-Stamp Program Cut," *Oakland Tribune,* January 29, 1981.

8

The Turtle Theory, or Why Has the Democratic Party Lost Five Out of the Last Six Presidential Elections, yet Retained Strong Control of the House, Won Majorities in the Senate, and Retained Three-Fifths of State Houses and Most Governorships?

Presidencies are not lost because of personal failings; all leaders have them. Rather, they are due to such a single-minded focus on failure as to overwhelm considerable success. But that is a topic for another time. Here, I shall concentrate on why the Democratic party, which does so well in state, local, and congressional races, has such a hard time winning the presidency.

Focus on the failures of candidates has detracted attention from the two most evident trends in the American presidency: the high proportion of failed presidencies (Johnson, Nixon, Carter), and the inability of the Democratic party to win the presidency. I think the two trends are related in that the aura of failure and Democratic party loss of the presidency are due to the same causes—the rise of egalitarianism.

Before we come to the underlying forces that make it difficult for Democrats to win the presidency, it is necessary to go over the surface explanations offered for the defeats of Michael Dukakis in 1988 and Walter Mondale in 1984. An interesting attribute of these candidate-centered explanations is that different and opposing reasons are given.

133

Same Results but Contradictory Reasons

Recriminations over the 1984 and 1988 presidential elections within the Democratic party have served to focus attention on the alleged inadequacies of their candidates as campaigners.[1] Aside from taking attention away from trends over time that most need to be explained, a brief comparison of the reasons given during the two campaigns reveal their contradictory as well as unsatisfactory character. Walter Mondale, it was said, was dull compared to his flamboyant opponent, Ronald Reagan. The same was said about Michael Dukakis, except, of course, that he could not have been more so than George Bush. Mondale was said to have given too much to the nefarious "special interests," but then Dukakis was accused of giving too little. Dukakis hid his liberalism, while Mondale showed it too much. Had these elections gone the other way, we would no doubt have heard that the voters appreciated Mondale's and Dukakis's calm and steady ways compared to the excitable Reagan and the indistinct Bush.

The one obvious flaw in Dukakis's presentation of self, his lack of experience, especially in foreign policy, was first of all shared by Ronald Reagan, who was also a two-term governor without Washington experience, but inapplicable in any way to Walter Mondale, who nevertheless lost. Faults are attributed to the losers, the point is, because they lost, not because there was anything necessarily wrong with them or with their campaigns.

Negative Campaigning and the Absence of Issues

What about negative campaigning on one side and the ostensible lack of issues on the other? What about Bush's better and Dukakis's worse use of the media? In regard to all three subjects, I shall argue that they reflect systemic rather than personal factors. No doubt Dukakis could have done better, so could all of us at critical junctures in our lives, but we act against a background of forces that have arisen independent of our will and that necessarily influence us more than we are able to influence them.

Whether or not a television commercial about furloughing a convicted murderer who did harm after his release constituted dirty or negative campaigning (we shall come to race later), the meaning of that message has been missed. If one were to take a cross-section of liberal Democratic activists, compared to their Republican counterparts, and ask whether they served on prisoners' rights or victims' rights committees, I do not doubt that the former would have chosen prisoners and the latter victims. Given their egalitarian propensities, Democratic activists are far more likely than Republicans to believe that the system is to blame for crime, not the individual.[2] Consequently, in the midst of a pandemic of crime, arguably the worst deprivation most Americans face, the Democratic party soft-pedals the issue, treating it often as a code word for racism. No one, to be sure, wants or supports crime. But one's public stance toward it also matters. In this respect, it is not Dukakis who let down the Democratic party, but rather the Democratic party that dragged him down. Living among his fellow liberals, he did not understand that most people want their president to empathize with *their* fears.

When it is said, and reiterated, that there were no issues in the 1988 presidential campaign, my thoughts go back to my parents. They were fervent New Deal Roosevelt Democrats. Their reason was fear of anti-Semitism (as a boy of nine, my father had been beaten in a pogrom in the Ukraine, after which he spent nine months in the hospital). They were particularly fond of Eleanor Roosevelt, who appeared to attend every wedding, *bris* (the circumcision ceremony), and bar mitzvah in Brooklyn. To them, she meant a friend in power, hence protection against future indignities. So they voted for her husband. Was that wrong of them? Were their feelings of safety not issues in the same acceptable way that the minimum wage or the deficit was? I object to some people telling other people their feelings are unworthy. If voters feel safer with George Bush, that is a pretty important consideration in a choice of leaders.

My second reaction to the charge of "no issues" is that the real blame belongs to Ronald Reagan, who took the words out of the mouths of campaigners. The pundits are so used to denigrating Reagan, or so it seems to me, that they fail to see that his was the commanding (albeit less visible) presence during the campaign. For one thing, Reagan's nuclear weapons reduction policy, from the INF treaty to the START negotiations, took the peace issue away from the Democrats. By out-radicaling the Democrats on disarmament, Reagan forced them into silence. They had to either out-radical him, which would have made them extreme in a manner to which he was not vulnerable, or call him soft on communism, which was absurd, and which they did not believe. So they chose silence. Although Bush probably agreed with those who wanted large reductions in Soviet forces in Europe as a prerequisite for nuclear negotiations, he went along. The reason that foreign policy was little debated in the campaign was not that it was a nonissue but, on the contrary, that President Reagan had forced an implicit agreement on its major outlines that neither of his possible successors was willing to oppose.

Domestic policy was dominated by the deficit. When Ronald Reagan pushed through the 23 percent cut in income taxes, and led the way to tax reform (which reduced marginal tax rates from the 70 percent he inherited to a top of 33 percent) and refused to abandon these policies in the light of large deficits, he again rendered both presidential candidates speechless. Departing from the antideficit stand of the Republican moderates who favored stability above all, the price of Bush's support from his party's more individualistic faction was his public pledge against an increase in taxes. No doubt a "no new tax" pledge garnered votes apart from conservative individualists. Fearful he would change his mind, however, they insisted on a public commitment. "Read my lips" is not a bad line for someone who has to accept a position he would rather not defend out loud.

And what could Dukakis do? Recalling the criticism vented upon Walter Mondale for saying what virtually everyone in his party believed, namely, that substantial tax increases were essential to reduce the deficit and run the government, Dukakis said essentially that he would decide when he became president. Nothing stopped him or his party in its platform from saying what they believed. Again, the dog that didn't bark, the refusal to commit to tax increases, was the clue. The issue was there all right but, courtesy of Ronald Reagan, it had been decided more against than for tax hikes.

When I say that systemic forces were at work, I do not mean to denigrate anyone's personal influence but rather to observe that, insofar as the rival presidential candidates were concerned, they faced social issues—laws specifying tax cuts, sizeable deficits, the INF treaty, the START negotiations, a distribution of public opinion either in favor of these things or unwilling to alter them—they could not ignore. It was their adjustment to these facts, more than their personalities or their talents or their campaign staffs, I contend, that made an election so full of portent seem so issueless.

Media Influence and Media Bias

The questions of media influence and media bias withstand easy answers because the forces at work operate in conflicting directions. Research has produced some starting points. After early doubts, it now seems clear that media (especially television) influence is considerable; favorable and unfavorable comments help and hurt presidents and presidential candidates alike, forming public perceptions of what is most important and how the politicians involved perform.[3] Here, as well as elsewhere, as we shall see, there are limits to media influence. (I refer to the elite media, the major newspapers, the *New York Times,* the *Washington Post,* the *Los Angeles Times*; the major networks; and *Newsweek* and *Time.*) If the media help shape perceptions of the state of the nation, which no one can see directly, only individuals are experts on how they are doing. When, as in 1988, citizens are informed they are in trouble, they may choose their personal experience of lower inflation and higher employment as the better guide.

Media bias is contested. A good place to start is with the constants. If we ask who makes up the media elite, the answer is easy: politically they are overwhelmingly liberal Democrats; culturally they are egalitarians. When one asks whether these known occupational biases translate into biased reporting, there is no scholarly agreement. Hence, I give my opinion that biases do exist and do, as one might expect, flow in an ideological direction but that, nonetheless, under certain conditions, such as those prevailing in 1988, there are countervailing forces at work stemming from the media's existence as in institution. In short, there exist both biases and limits to the influence exercised by those biases. Let me explain by example.

Why, I ask, were the hostages held by Iran in the news prominently and incessantly day and night, yet the hostages held in Lebanon since 1986 have gotten very little coverage. It cannot be human interest and tragedy, because that is the same in both instances. Indeed, the Lebanese captives have been held longer. My hypothesis is that the media converged on this coverage because it served to discredit the government, this being part of the egalitarian rejection of authority. True to experience, a foreign crisis sharply increased public support for the president. But as the news focus continued while the hostages remained in captivity, Carter's popularity plummeted. Why, then, the change? The diminution of coverage occurred after the Iran-Contra episode in which President Reagan was pilloried (rightly, I believe) for exchanging arms for hostages. Quickly, the media converged on the view, damaging to the president, that it was wrong to make concessions to terrorists as a reward for releasing hostages. Afterward, I observed that the hostages received much less publicity. Since their captivity could no longer be used to attack the president, the media having ruled out every mode of gaining their release as illegitimate, there was no point in keeping the hostages before the public eye. (There was, to be sure, no conspiracy, only a coming together of like-minded people hostile to authority.)

The lesson I draw from these events is that on matters the media make highly visible, they can go one way or another, but not both ways at once. An important limitation on media influence is generated by the need to maintain minimal consistency in the midst of an audience it has taught one thing and that might be expected to react negatively to a diametrical change of course.

A simpler episode, equally instructive, occurred when Republican presidential candidate George Bush did less well than rival Bob Dole in the Iowa primary. Subsequently, the media was full of damaging comments about Bush's inadequacies and ineptitudes. When Bush did well in the New Hampshire primary, however, the significance of his victory was amplified because the media had previously lessened expectations.

From such events we learn about another limit on media influence: If the effort to run down a public figure fails to defeat him, quite ordinary conduct may thereafter make him appear superior. It could even be that the reason Michael Dukakis stated in his acceptance speech that the election contest was not about ideology but about competence was because the media had taught him that his opponent was a wimp, so much of a nothing it was not necessary to change tactics. All Bush had to do after his initial media treatment was to put two literate sentences together and he appeared to be a savant. And when he did all right, as in the debates, he appeared to be at least a super-wimp, a candidate above the ordinary. Again, we see that putting candidates down can rebound if, by contrast, it makes them seem superior.

While presidents and candidates manifesting egalitarian tendencies should do better in the media than those who are socially hierarchical or economically conservative, there is actually an opposing tendency. Antiauthority bias works in all directions. It is easy to forget that Geraldine Ferraro, as well as Dan Quayle, was savaged.

A pronounced feature of the media coverage of the 1988 election was its concentration on the mechanics—who is winning and how close are the candidates. Its preoccupation with making the campaign appear competitive (the "horse-race" theme) led to a focus on campaign tactics. Often there was less interest in the substance of what was being said than whether a given move was successful in narrowing the gap between the candidates.

Along with the usual discussion of candidate and party positions, therefore, came another theme about the success or failure of campaign tactics. When these policy and tactical themes work against each other, as they did in 1988, with the Democratic candidate being favored on policy by the major media while the Republican candidate was favored on tactics, media biases effectively cancel themselves out. Should a time come when the media's biases toward candidates who are egalitarian and tactically successful reinforce one another, a Republican loss could well become a rout.

It will be useful to give charges of unfair tactics their usual, pre-1988 definition: a negative campaign is one in which the wrong candidate loses. I do not mean to deny the use of smear tactics. The point is that the media get interested in these personal insults only when their favorites get hurt. Discovering to their surprise—given Dukakis's early lead in the polls and their denigration of Bush—that the wrong man was winning, the major media independently hit upon a strategy that would maintain its reputation for nonpartisanship. By charging Bush with "negative campaigning," the media hoped to help Dukakis while avoiding the taint of pushing a candidate of its own. But it was too late.

In order for media policy bias to be effective, in sum, it has to be (a) disguised and (b) unidirectional. This may not be an easy combination to manage. Blatant partisanship would be counterproductive, and biases going in opposite directions are self-canceling.

Republican presidential victories, taken together with Democratic success in congressional (especially the House of Representatives) elections, has provided a puzzle that no one yet has been able to unravel. Nor will I, entirely. But enough progress can be made to make the attempt worthwhile.

Does Size of Constituency Matter?

The path to understanding, I am convinced, lies in better specification of what it is that we are trying to explain. What accounts for the seemingly unshakable grip Democrats have on the House, their small preponderance, occasionally reversed, in the Senate, and their frequent large losses of the presidency? Why is it that the larger the size of the constituency, the better the Republicans and the worse the Democrats do? When Elmer Schattsneider wrote in *The Semi-Sovereign People* that expanding the constituency altered the outcome, he thought that would favor the worse off, not the better off. Gerrymandering, we know, due to Democratic party preponderance in state legislatures, favors its candidates to the extent that Republicans must win 52 to 53 percent of the vote to break even. It is also true that parties and candidates have a greater ability to fit the fancies of the electorate the farther down they go. There can be no movement of boundaries in senatorial or presidential elections. Given the huge advantage of incumbency nowadays, the mere fact that the Democratic party had an earlier advantage may carry over to our time.

Without pretending to offer anything definitive, it could be that voters are looking for different things. Presidents play more of a symbolic role. It may, therefore, seem right to look to presidents for symbolic identification—Is he one of us? Does she exemplify our values?—while looking to Congress to serve material interests. At the same time, incumbent representatives may be better able to gear their presentation of self to local perceptions than can senators or presidents with much longer and usually more diverse constituencies.

Another reason Democrats might do better locally is that their activists, being more interested in public office (not so strange for the party of government), make better candidates. Keeping the government out of things is not likely to be as strong a motive for public service as getting it to do things for which one can gain credit.

The visibility of the candidates is greater the more national the contest. Hence voters may be able to better distinguish the candidates' policy positions from each other and from their own personal preferences. Were the ascending issue-clarity-argument correct—it appears plausible on the surface—one implication would be that voters are by and large closer to the Republican than to the Democratic party on national issues. If this is so, however, why would conservative voters keep returning liberal legislators?

Whether the well-known incumbency effect—well over 98 percent of the representatives and most senators who run for reelection succeed themselves—is due to name recognition, constituency service, or free franking (mailing) privileges, incumbents win. Neither party seems to be advantaged there, except that there are more Democrats to begin with. It is still easier (though by no means easy) to defeat incumbent senators. Why?

Do Voters Intend to Split Control?

A host of commentators have suggested that Americans are so enamored of the separation of powers that they deliberately vote for one party for president and another for Congress. While there is evidence that voters approve of split government, there is none I am aware of suggesting they target their votes to achieve this deliberately. Aside from the lack of evidence to support such intentions, the separation of powers theory fails to explain why it is the Republicans who win the presidency and the Democrats who usually control the Congress.

Byron Shafer has an answer to that. Voters, he hypothesizes, have come to look to the presidency for national defense, and for cultural (or social) policies, such as prayer, abortion, crime, and patriotism, and to Congress for welfare programs.[4] This fits the facts. What is lacking, so far, is evidence of, and explanation for, this bifurcated vision.

Nonetheless, if we look at the gross outlines of public opinion, we do get an interesting clue. Majority opinion favors liberal social welfare programs, a strong defense (though how much spending that requires varies with time), and takes a conservative line on social programs (crime, prayer, patriotism, and the like). Such a political vision should be familiar; it was held by the mainstream of the Democratic party from the 1930s through the mid-1960s, sometimes referred to as the party of Harry Truman, Hubert Humphrey, and Henry Jackson. But it does not exist anymore. Nowadays activists in the Democratic party are preponderantly egalitarian. Their continuity is with welfare programs; their discontinuity is with opposition to defense as inegalitarian, *i.e.*, taking from social welfare, disaffection with capitalism (seen as increasing instead of diminishing group differences in resources), and their support of state-sanctioned positive discrimination to increase equality of results.

Can this sea change in the Democratic party have led to the loss of the presidency? The most salient electoral facts are that while black people have become more Democratic, Jews have maintained their liberalism, and women are pretty evenly split, though moving in a Democratic direction, and white, nonretired, Christian men have been voting overwhelmingly Republican in presidential elections. They account for almost all the differences between the parties. Why, then, have these white working men become so Republican in presidential but not congressional elections? And, why does being married—exit polls in 1984 and 1988 give a 9 percent Republican edge to married over single men and 10 to 12 percent for married over single women[5]— impel voters in a conservative direction? A sociocultural explanation is indicated.

The Revolt of the Turtles

A tale from India tells of how the world rests upon a huge elephant. Upon being asked who holds the elephant up, an Indian man responds that the elephant stands on an even bigger turtle. And who, the questioning continues, holds up the turtle? "Why," the response goes, "it's turtles all the way down." My theory is that the Democratic party has lost five out of the last six presidential elections by a large margin because it made the white working male into the turtle of American political life.

Had the Democrats asked nine-tenths of the working population to help support the other tenth, the more fortunate majority holding up the less fortunate minority, this activity might be considered a matter of honor and compassion. But that is not at all the way it is put.

What role does the Democratic party at its presidential nominating conventions, we may ask, ascribe to its turtles? They are to support more deserving people. Since everyone else had apparently been "locked out" of the political system, they became the residual category who were "locked in," the broad shoulders on which to hold up the rest of the population. They alone were not underprivileged.

The Democratic party expanded the category of the deprived so that it included a good two-thirds of the population. Begin with women, who constitute some 52 percent of the population. Add racial and ethnic minorities, who comprise around one-fifth of the total. Put in the elderly, who make up another fifth. Of course, there is double counting. Cutting back the proportion of seniors and minorities by more than half, however, still leaves at least two-thirds of the population defined as deprived. Yet we have not considered poor people, the physically and mentally handicapped, and numerous others for whom a plausible case of having less and needing more could be made.

To the question of who should pay to provide for this elephantiasis of the deprived, the Democrats give the same answer, "Turtles all the way down." The categories that make up the Democratic party's vision of the deprived are urged to protest that they have not gotten their due. They are told to organize, to mobilize, to make demands. In sum, the deprived have interests it is their duty to declare so that others can meet their obligations.

Turtles, however, had obligations but not, it seems, interests. The usual scenario reiterated during the election campaign called for a turtle to say why he would vote Republican. Democrats then met the answer—"Because I'll be better off."—with the rejoinder—"That's selfish!" I heard this routine several times on public radio and talk shows.

Egalitarian dominance among Democratic activists was made evident as they defined virtually all creatures (except turtles) as endangered. They overreached. Their shared vision of an America peopled by fatalists blinded them to the danger of losing the only significant category of voters who were not to be favored.

Eventually, even turtles get tired. Because the revolt of the turtles did not occur on a particular date, like the storming of the Bastille or the Declaration of Independence, but took place in hearts and minds over the last two decades, it has gone unnoticed. Now the election returns make it evident. Unless it wishes to expand this revolt, therefore, the Democratic party will have to confine the categories of the deprived to the poor or to racial minorities or to some manageable proportion of the population, so that a broader band of turtles can bear the weight.

The lesson is not that the Democratic party has to put up with candidates who lose, but that its candidates have to put up with a party that delegitimizes the nation's second largest constituency— white, working, Christian males. Unless the Democratic party allows the voice of the turtle to be heard once again in the land, one might extrapolate, its next presidential election is also likely to be a loss.

Turning the Turtle

Turtles have hard shells but soft underbellies. A harsh way of putting our turtles' response is to turn it upside down: it is not these white men who feel put upon but those who wish to continue their past practice of putting down black folk (or minorities in general, or add women to all of the above). Seeing blacks and minorities and women so prominent in the Democratic party, this proposed explanation goes, white men have voted Republican in order to retain their past dominance. Nothing complicated about the election, in other words, only simple racism, sexism, and, for good measure, homophobia. The insecurity of masculinity in the face of feminine demands for equality, long a staple of egalitarian thought, merely receives a new form of expression as a generalized "ism"—race, gender, sex, age, *et cetera*.

But is it true? They are male, they are white, they are Christian, they are working, and they do vote Republican in presidential elections. But that by itself, presumably, does not make them racist, nor would it explain why many of the very same people are voting Democratic in congressional races.

The publicity accorded Jesse Jackson and the evident necessity Dukakis faced in coming to terms with him, all in the full glare of television coverage, might have surfaced latent racism. But not necessarily. Paul Sniderman and his colleagues, using experiments as part of survey methods, have shown that attitudes toward black people vary, policies aimed at helping blacks being supported when they are seen to be meritorious by the same criteria applied to whites. Were this proposition to hold up, the turtle theory—white working men feel discriminated against by Democrats—and not the turnover turtle theory—Republicanism as code word for racism—would be validated.

Some substantial proportion of white working men favor welfare programs but do not believe they should be the only ones to sacrifice for them. They might well favor economic redistribution and believe that too much was being spent on defense without opposing prayer in schools. As believers in equality of opportunity, these white working men are opposed to discrimination but in favor of merit-based procedures for employment and promotion. Hence, when they see minorities who work hard discriminated against they object. But these white working men are not prone to blame the system for what they perceive as individual shortcomings. Observing the Democratic party as it presents itself at national conventions, presidential campaigns, and other visible events, our turtles feel rejected by the national Democratic party. It is not of them or for them.

The turtle theory suggests that if only poor people were singled out for special consideration (thus covering many blacks and women and elderly but not by category) public reaction, especially white working male reaction, would be quite different. This would also explain the great success of the Democrats (namely Dukakis in 1988) when they stress "populist" themes.

Marriage, Religion, Race, Poverty, and Other Forms of Socialization

If I am correct in believing that the Republican party provides a haven for those working men unwittingly rejected by the Democratic party, why do these self-same citizens vote Democratic at the congressional levels? The answer, I think, is that the immense publicity at the national level, together with the inability to differentiate appeals to various constituents, makes citizens acutely aware of the relation of the national parties to their conception of self. At the local congressional level, by contrast, they are either less informed about their congressman's policy preferences or less concerned about them (otherwise they'd want to find out more about it).

What is it, we may ask, that those people who voted most heavily Democratic in 1988 might have in common? This list includes African-Americans, Mexican-Americans, Jews, very poor people, single women (especially), and also single men. Again, my answer is that they share a belief in egalitarianism.

It is fairly evident that very poor people and radical minorities would like redistributive governmental policies. But what about Jews who are neither poor nor colored? Obviously, a special explanation is required for the continued high level of Jewish liberalism. I believe that historical experience in being discriminated against has led not only to identification with the underdog, which is standard, but has also been transmuted into fierce resistance to distinctiveness, to being singled out. If we think of conservative Republicans as being concerned with the maintenance of social and economic distinctions, and of liberal Democrats as wishing to diminish distinctions (or levels or ranks) among people, most Jews worry about being too much rather than too little exposed. (The orthodox, by the way, who live by the 613 *mitzvot*, or commandments, are much more hierarchical and therefore, Republican.) Thus even the support for Israel evidenced by fundamentalist Christians worries Jews, who consequently become more liberal.[6]

And what is it about marriage that increases Republican voting in presidential elections? Perhaps, as the old saw has it, marriage increases a person's sense of responsibility. But this is too much like rephrasing the question. My hunch is that the institution of marriage has a conservatizing effect, especially when there are children, because it increases the sense of social differentiation as a source of stability among the people involved. From a study of women we learn that the more they favor the traditional family—wife at home with children—the more Republican they are.[7] They well may identify with the husband, viewing their vote more as furthering the family unit than they did when single; the wife becomes a turtle by marriage. The husband has not only to consider others by virtue of being a family man but, acknowledged "head of family" or not, he is likely to approve of role differentiation.

Alternative Explanations

I have left for last the most obvious and quite possibly the two most accurate explanations of recent Republican presidential victories, namely, favorable economic conditions and the political transformation of the South. Each time a Republican wins, he has been in office during good times or taken over in bad times. For all we know, voters might figure that if a Democratic Congress and a Republican president go with prosperity, they might as well keep the status quo. Nor is it easy for the Democratic party to win presidential elections when it starts by losing all or most of the South. The reasons for this change are fairly well-known. One, which Nelson Polsby attributes to air conditioning, is that numerous Republicans moved to the South as part of its economic growth. At the same time, or perhaps earlier, many black people who generally vote Democratic moved out of the South (though there is now a bit of movement back). In addition to this shift of populations, there has been a lot of conversion on the part of conservation Democrats to the Republican party. The result is that the Democratic candidate has to win most of the rest of the states, a difficult task. Still, I would maintain that the South has become Republican in presidential years not because the Democratic party became economically liberal (which it already was) but rather because it became culturally egalitarian.

Is the Democratic Party Likely to Become Less Egalitarian?

Democrats are often advised to be more centrist, speak positively about defense, talk less about social issues, and perhaps wave the flag a bit more. I doubt whether this advice, whether stemming from turtles or other political animals, is likely to be taken.

The mainstream of the Democratic party, I believe, is now more firmly egalitarian (a) than it has been in the past and (b) than the Republicans are hierarchical or individualistic. The best studies we have, by Warren Miller and Kent Jennings, cover party activists who became delegates to national conventions from 1976 to 1984 (supplemented by various polls in 1988) and reveal that while Republicans are strongly economically individualistic and socially conservative, Democrats are even more egalitarian. Under these circumstances, considering that Democratic officeholders are largely chosen from their party's activists, it is unlikely they will agree to give up their policy preferences in order for their party to gain national office. It is not that they settle on these preferences at random; rather, they choose to expand the ranks of the deprived and to question the righteousness of existing institutions because these policies are part and parcel of a world view dedicated to securing justice by diminishing differences among people. Representative Barney Frank of Massachusetts, himself a liberal Democrat, has publicly asked his party to say things that are no longer fashionable among them, like capitalism is better than other economic systems; I believe he will fail because many Democratic activists do not believe these things.

While Republicans are still the more socially homogeneous party, the division between their individualists and hierarchists are greater than those found among Democratic activists. In any event, were nominating conventions left to their old devices in which state conventions were decisive, the results today would likely mimic those in Michigan in 1988, where party activists were dominant, thus leading to victory by Jesse Jackson for the Democrats and Pat Robertson for the Republicans, because they mobilized more fervent followers than the other candidates. A concession Jackson won at the Democratic convention was a substantial reduction in the number of "superdelegates"—the governors, state legislators, and congressmen recently reintroduced into the convention process. Another concession reduced the proportion of votes a candidate needed to qualify for delegates and did away with "winner-take-all" primaries. This rule change will encourage factionalism by making it worthwhile for candidates to stay in the race longer so as to amass a larger force of delegates. More factions and fewer coalitions, I am afraid, are in store for us.

A Democrat Could Become President; Party Strife Is Just Beginning

I do not believe that Democratic party prospects for winning the presidency are hopeless, just poor. A bad economy, a disgraced president, one or both could defeat a Republican candidate. So might an attractive Democratic candidate, especially one less liberal-egalitarian than his party. Such a candidate might win nomination through the primary system even if most party activists were opposed. The crucial elections would then be the next two when the egalitarian agenda was enacted into law. Whatever happens, the rise of radical egalitarianism and the decline of the alliance between individualists and egalitarians that made the United States exceptional argues for rough political weather ahead. As struggles over foreign policy decline and take on new forms, the great struggle between the forces of equal opportunity versus those of equal results will intensify.

Notes

1. For fun as well as enlightenment, see the *New Republic's* "Quadrennial Recriminations" issue, December 5, 1988 .
2. See Sidney Verba and Gary R. Orren, *Equality in America: The View from the Top* (Cambridge: Harvard University Press, 1985), who state that whereas 50 percent of Democratic activists believed that the system rather than the individual causes poverty, only 12 percent of Republican activists agreed.
3. See my "Where Bias and Influence Meet," *Public Interest,* no. 91 (Spring 1988): pp. 94-98, a review of Shanto Iyengar and Donald R. Kinder, *News That Matters: Television and American Opinion* (Chicago: University of Chicago Press, 1987) .

4. Byron E. Shafer, "The Notion of an Electoral Order: The Structure of Electoral Politics at the Accession of George Bush," in *The End of Realignment?*, ed. Byron F. Shafer, chap 3 (Madison: University of Wisconsin Press, forthcoming).

5. Seymour Martin Lipset, "A Reaffirming Election: 1988," *International Journal of Public Opinion Research* 1, no. 1: (Winter 1989).

6. How does one conceive of affirmative action? Is this a measure that puts Jews together with other Americans so they see it as a form of positive discrimination? Or does it single out high achievers for negative discrimination? Needless to say, this is a disturbing issue for Jewish liberals.

7. Evans, Witt, "What the Republicans Have Learned About Women," *Public Opinion* 4 (October/November 1985): 49.

9

Richard Nixon,
President of the United States

One man sniffs the air of American politics and detects a significant change in the prevailing winds. Another man notices only some
turbulence that is bound to be smoothed out as the traditional flow of
party politics reasserts itself. Most of us feel that something is happening, but we do not know exactly what. Will the presidential election be decided by the normal criteria—the amount of party support
and the candidates' popularity? Will the next government undertake
radical changes in foreign and domestic policies? Will this election be
a harbinger of fundamental alterations in the American party system?

If we want to know whether we have some understanding of the
future, we shall have to risk making predictions now, for one test of
knowledge is prediction (anyone can see how an election turns out
and then propose an ad hoc explanation that appears to fit the facts).
The best way to know if we have a grip on the future is to say what it
will be. By allowing the election itself to pass judgment on the theories that underlie our predictions, we will be better able to determine
whether we have any insight into current trends in American political
life and be in a stronger position to speculate about the future shape of
the American party system.

I predict that 1968 will witness a Republican sweep throughout the
nation. The Republican party will gain a substantial majority in the
House of Representatives. As for the Senate, although present Democratic majorities make the loss of Democratic control unlikely, Republicans will improve their position there as well. Any Republican

Reprinted from _Trans-action_ 5, no. 10 (October, 1968): 8–15.

presidential nominee will win the presidential election. In Richard Nixon's case, however, his relative lack of personal popularity means that in most states he will run behind the congressional Republican. (For those who cannot contemplate the prospect that their old antagonist might become chief executive, I suggest this simple procedure: Every day, when you wake up in the morning, just say, "Richard Nixon, President of the United States." This may help avoid culture shock in November.)

The (Democratic) Party Rejection Theory

The theory underlying these predictions is deceptively simple. People are unhappy about the Vietnam war. They are much more unhappy about racial conflicts and violence at home. To manifest their displeasure, people will take the Democratic party, which is in, and throw it out, and take the Republican party, which is out, and put it in. This instinctive and convulsive changing of the guard need not be caused by a popular belief that the candidate or leaders of one party are better than another. All that is necessary is widespread dissatisfaction and a consequent desire to give a new team a chance.

The Vietnam war has divided and embittered the Democratic party. A large percentage of its activists, intellectuals, and students are opposed to the policies of the Democratic administration and to Hubert Humphrey, who has been identified with it. While these people will not vote for Nixon, they will not campaign for the Democratic candidate and thus will not perform their usual function of stimulating the turnout in a Democratic direction. Indeed, in some states the anti-Vietnam-war Democrats may end up supporting a fourth-party candidate.

The dissatisfaction of Democratic activists will work changes in the present voting preferences of those who identify themselves with the Democratic party. There is unlikely to be a rapprochement between the young, white, middle-class activists supporting Senator McCarthy and the backers of Hubert Humphrey. McCarthy people are fierce in their opposition to the Vietnam war. Their hostility to Lyndon Johnson knows no bounds. They want to make Vice-President Humphrey suffer for "selling out the cause of peace" through his loyal support of the president. In talk and in print, Humphrey will be derided, castigated, and blasphemed. These feelings against the vice-president will be aggravated by charges that the Democratic convention is rigged and that Senator McCarthy's supporters have been shabbily treated. [This article was written during the second week in July, before either convention. Editor's Note.] The anti-Johnson buzzing in the ears of these party activists will prevent them from hearing Humphrey's views on foreign policy, which are similar to their own. The one thing they might hear—an angry rejection of Johnson and his Vietnam policy—will not come from the vice-president. The crescendo of disapproval of Hubert Humphrey by a large portion of the elite of his own party will become deafening after the national convention has exacerbated deep-seated resentments.

Some white Democrats (especially those in blue-collar occupations) may defect from their party on racial grounds. These are the people who directly feel pressure from Negroes. They believe it is their neighborhoods that are in danger, their jobs that are threatened, and their safety that is being undermined. These white Democrats find it difficult to accept compensatory measures designed to help Negroes.

The major beneficiary of this racial protest may be Governor Wallace. Should a big Wallace vote throw the election into the House of Representatives, however, the large Republican majorities predicted by the Democratic Party Rejection Theory would still make Nixon president.

Nor is there any reason to believe that the Democratic party's loss of whites will be made up—in critical states—by an increase in black votes. Many Negroes have not been happy with the policies of the Johnson administration. In the absence of Senator Robert F. Kennedy, the one Democratic leader who commanded their loyalty, Negroes are likely to turn out in lower percentages, thus hurting Democratic chances.

I will try to be precise in specifying the causal mechanisms that will lead to a Republican victory.

- As the summer goes on and the campaign builds up in the fall, there are bound to be racial rebellions. Working-class and lower-middle-class Democrats, together with white independents, will react to fresh evidence of racial violence by defecting to a Republican party perceived to be stronger on the issue of law and order—or by supporting Governor Wallace.
- The Vietnam issue is tearing the Democratic party apart. The hatred

many activists have for Lyndon Johnson (and by extension for Humphrey) will sharply reduce the normal polarization effect through which Democrats would have intensified their loyalty during the campaign. The polarization phenomenon depends upon a reinforcement of one's views by hearing friends, neighbors, and elites support the party and belittle the opposition.

The hostility of Democratic activists to their presidential candidate will be expressed in many ways. For one, the talk among activists will be highly derogatory to Humphrey. The chain of personal communications will reach large portions of Democrats now supporting Senator McCarthy. Then too, these word-of-mouth blasts at Humphrey will be reinforced and amplified through the communications media. The alienated Democratic activists, though not a large percentage of party voters, occupy strategic positions. They include reporters, news broadcasters, writers for the literate "monthlies," and liberal political magazines. The bad impression of Humphrey these publicists leave with their listeners and readers will prevent party support among Democrats from reaching its usual peak.

As of this writing, these predictions of republican victory are not supported by evidence from the polls, although I expect the results to change so as to confirm the Democratic Party Rejection Theory. According to Gallup, Democrats have the support of 58 percent of the voters in the Congressional elections. Both Humphrey and McCarthy appear to be leading Nixon in the presidential contest. A different theory, stressing traditional party support, would explain these findings.

The (Democratic) Party Support Theory

According to the Party Support Theory, the strongest tie between a man and his vote is his party identification. That is, most of the time people vote for the candidate of their party. Therefore, if an election is decided on the basis of existing party loyalty, the Democrats will win because they have many more supporters than the Republicans do. The large Democratic majority of 58 percent projected for 1968 Congressional elections is just what one would expect if party identification were the only consideration in the election. For what good reason, it might be asked, should there be this normal party vote in what otherwise seems to be an abnormal political year?

One answer: Neither Nixon nor Humphrey appears to excite any great interest in the electorate. Thus, there will be no swing away from one party or toward another because of the popularity of one candidate or the unpopularity of another. When President Johnson removed himself from the presidential race, he deprived the Republicans of an opportunity to center their campaign on a rejection of him. The fact that he will not run also makes it more difficult to mount a campaign centered on opposition to the party in office.

No doubt there is widespread dissatisfaction about the Vietnam war. But according to the Party Support Theory, the war will not push voters in any single direction. Some people would like the United States to get out of Vietnam immediately. Others would like the United States to escalate the war even further and then get out. Still others are confused. Since there is unlikely to be a great difference between the candidates on the issue of Vietnam, it will not be possible for the voters to choose on the basis of this issue, even if they know in which direction they wish to move. The candidates of both major parties will promise to bring the war to an end, and voters will have to decide who is better able to do this under the most satisfactory conditions. Under these conditions, the Republican party will not be able to gain enough votes on the Vietnam issue to overcome the normal Democratic lead in the electorate.

The position of both parties on racial conflict is also likely to be similar. They will come out for law and order. They will call for measures to deal with poverty. While some voters may find the Democrats too favorable to Negroes, they would not find the Republican candidate sufficiently unfavorable to justify a switch in party vote. It is far more likely that these republicans would take the opportunity to vote for George Wallace. The polls have shown, however, that Wallace takes two votes from the Republicans for every one he gets from the Democrats. Hence the antiblack vote would do more harm to the Republicans than to the Democrats.

If the voters are divided along party lines now, the proponents of the Democratic Party Support Theory would argue, these differences will be even more pronounced at election time. All of the forces agitating the nation's political life will cancel one another out. Beset by doubt, overwhelmed by confusion, American voters will reaffirm their traditional party positions.

Governing the Nation: Nixon

Whether one chooses to project current polls predicting a Democratic victory, or whether, like myself, one expects future change leading to a Republican triumph, is determined as much by intuition as by science. No one has to remind an American living in 1968 of the contingent nature of political events. What is certain is that the next president of the United States will face grave difficulties in governing the nation. Since I have predicted a Republican victory, let's begin with the dilemmas facing Richard Nixon.

Predicting the Nixon administration's foreign policy is relatively easy because internal political forces will produce substantially the same results, no matter who is elected. It is difficult to imagine any resident maintaining 500,000 troops in Vietnam through the 1970 Congressional election. To do so would lead his party to a crashing defeat. To maintain much more than the air force and navy presence in Vietnam past the 1972 presidential election would be an admission that Nixon's term in office has been a failure. While the American people may not agree on what to do about Vietnam, they are in overwhelming agreement that we should get out. The only difference is that doves wish we had gotten out yesterday and the hawks want to force the enemy into submission tomorrow. Virtually everyone is agreed that the Vietnam war must be ended or vastly diminished.

Each major-party candidate will say that he is the better man to bring the war to an end, and he will know that he must make good on that promise. Senator McCarthy might try to arrange a speedy withdrawal, but he would discover that the lives of millions depend on his negotiating an agreement for their safety. Vice-President Humphrey can be expected to attempt a gradual withdrawal of American troops over a period of four years. Richard Nixon might once have liked to maintain the American commitment over a longer period, but now he recognizes that he cannot. The election of one or another of these men, therefore, will lead to similar patterns of slow withdrawal.

Nixon will, however, enjoy greater flexibility in pursuing a new Vietnam policy than his Democratic opponent. McCarthy has centered his campaign on the Vietnam issue. He would be dreadfully embarrassed by any inability to show immediate results in obtaining the withdrawal of American armed forces. Humphrey is bound by the necessity of placating the furious opposition to the war within his own party. He must call for an immediate cessation of bombing North Vietnam and show actual withdrawal of troops within a few months. Nixon is in the best position because he is broadly acceptable to Republican activists who have never been as strongly opposed to the Vietnam war as their Democratic counterparts. As president, Nixon could afford to wait longer and bargain for more acceptable conditions of American withdrawal.

The party unity that Nixon has labored so hard to bring about is his strongest resource, and yet it might turn out to be his gravest weakness. A unified base of support in the country will surely help Nixon govern. The great question is whether he will have to pay too high a price to his most conservative supporters on domestic policies.

Disaster would follow if the Republican party interpreted its victory as a mandate for racial repression and an abandonment of welfare policies. Then it could no longer hope to recapture the allegiance of part of the Negro population, the only major new group from which it could hope to gain long-lasting support. A Republican government would not be prepared to cope with the vast conflicts its policies unleashed. The combination of racial and class conflicts would be too much for it and might even threaten the survival of our political system. There are radical revolutionaries who count on just this kind of development to leave the people no alternative but a basic transformation of social life (before the rise of Hitler, Communists called this policy "The worse, the better").

Yet there is another course of action that is compatible with traditional Republican views and that holds out much greater promise of free political life. A Republican president and a majority of Republican congressmen could look upon the election as a mandate to try conservative solutions to major social problems. Instead of a welfare-state apparatus directed from Washington, they could come out for decentralization of authority, with large block grants going to cities, states, and neighborhood governments—in which Negroes would play a dominant part in the areas where they predominate. Instead of a guaranteed annual wage, Republicans could insist on vast job programs, with the idea of providing work at good wages for every American. The old virtues about which so much is heard—hard work, local control, citizen participation—could be made the foundation of promising new policies. The nation has a large stake in which alternative the Republican activists choose.

Governing the Nation: Humphrey

The overwhelming problem faced by Hubert Humphrey is not winning the election, however insuperable the odds, but governing the country should he happen to win. To lose may merely turn out to be allowing Nixon to suffer. But to win, and to be unable to lead the country, would be the worst thing that could happen.

The danger is that Hubert Humphrey would take Lyndon Johnson's place as a beleaguered president, unable to travel among his people, a prisoner in Washington without a loyal core of followers in his party, in Congress, or in the bureaucracy. We know that racial conflict has deep roots in our society and will not soon be mitigated. No president, however determined or well-intentioned, will be able to prevent racial rebellions. Though Humphrey will try to bring the Vietnam war to an end, that process is bound to take several years. He will not be able to satisfy people who want a fast end to hostilities. Nor will there be an immediate release of the vast funds tied up in the war, funds that might be used to make a massive attack on racial and urban problems.

Humphrey might face a Republican House of Representatives dedicated to thwarting him at every turn. Even the best he could hope for, a small Democratic majority in the House, would leave control with the conservative coalition. The frustrations of the first two Kennedy years, during which the late president was unable to get most of his program enacted, would be repeated under much more dangerous and disadvantageous circumstances. In the first two or three years of his administration, therefore, Humphrey would be unable to achieve the miracles necessary to win a reservoir of good will. On the contrary, his term in office would probably begin amidst a sullen and angry popular mood. For undertaking the same good policies that would have given Kennedy credit, Humphrey would be abused.

It is important to understand that the nation faces a crisis of legitimacy surrounding its political institutions and leaders. Many blacks who have been treated badly in this country say they are no longer certain they wish to think of themselves as Americans, giving allegiance to national political symbols, institutions, and officials. White opponents of the Vietnam war feel that the president, by escalating the war, has betrayed his promise to limit the conflict. An unsettling series of events—the Kennedy assassinations, Johnson's decision not to run, Rockefeller's refusal to enter the primaries when he still had a chance—has deprived many political activists of both symbols of hope and targets of hostility. Instead of blaming fate, they tend to turn against existing political institutions and Hubert Humphrey, the man who epitomizes their frustrations.

It is critically important that the next president not only do good but get credit for it. If he is constantly under bitter attack, he will not be able to mobilize the resources to create and carry out wise policies. Yet Humphrey may find that history has placed him in a position that will thwart his most noble impulses. That is why his stress on winning the nomination, instead of gaining the support of McCarthy's people for governing the country, seems misplaced. Humphrey has not taken the actions—extreme generosity in allocating delegates to McCarthy's supporters, granting them a preponderant voice in writing the platform, entering into sustained discussions—that would improve his chances of electoral victory and give him a fighting chance to govern effectively.

Only gross miscalculation and grave error could have led Humphrey to denounce McCarthy supporters as brown shirts and suggest they are already determined to set up a fourth party. Humphrey is not supposed to be a political prognosticator but a presidential statesman. His task is not to make it impossible for McCarthy supporters to turn to him but to leave every door open to everyone who could go with him during, and especially after, the presidential campaign; his task is to govern. Perhaps the best parallel is Abraham Lincoln's good sense and forbearance in accommodating leaders of hostile party factions in his administration. He gave away cabinet positions and offered vice-presidential posts to keep his party and nation together. We also face internal rebellion; our unity is threatened. Humphrey should do no less than Lincoln did.

Humphrey's suggestion that Edward Kennedy would be welcome as vice-president may have been a proper symbolic gesture to a tragic family, but it evidences a deplorable insensitivity to the need of obtaining widespread reconciliation. Dissent within the Democratic party is rooted in disagreement over foreign policy, not over whether there should be deference to the Kennedy family. A vice-presidential candidate known to have been opposed to the Vietnam war, like Senator McGovern, together with a platform dedicated to that end, are essential first steps toward healing the party's wounds. McCarthy supporters require acknowledgment that their crusade has merit; they need guarantees that their views and their men will help determine the nation's foreign policy; above all, they require evidence that their leader and his views will be respected. It is unlikely that McCarthy would respond to even such overtures by warmly endorsing Humphrey and the Democratic party. But if he made clear his intention to remain with the party, most of his supporters would follow his lead. If McCarthy's wishes are given special consideration during the presidential term, persuading him to give the party a chance to perform, Humphrey will have gained immeasurably in authority to govern. If Humphrey's presidency were to become "hell on wheels," we cannot forget that his personal tragedy would also be a national disaster.

The Future of the American Party System

Preoccupied with the coming election and its immediate impact upon national policy, we lose sight of the long-term implications of this contest for the presidency. The outcome of the 1968 election may be of critical importance in determining the shape of the future party system and the content of American political life.

Though we are in the habit of talking about the American two-party system, it might be more accurate to say that there is at present a party-and-three-quarters system. By the usual tests of party identification, the Democrats command the support of approximately 46 percent of the voting population, whereas the Republicans are down to about 27 percent. This is a gap so huge that it would not require much for the Republican party to go below the minimum voter allegiance required for effective opposition in national elections. [Only now (circa 1990) have the parties evened out in party identification. A.W.]

The dilemma of the Republican party may be seen by posing the basic question about its disastrous defeat in 1964: Why did the party nominate a man who was disliked by most Republicans and despised by an overwhelming number of Democrats? The major clue was discovered by Herbert McClosky, who found that Republican party activists were immensely more conservative than ordinary Republican voters. In the absence of a moderate candidate commanding widespread public support in primaries, the convention delegates, who represent Republican party activists, just nominated a man like themselves.

The Republican party may be on the verge of a downward spiral in which the tension between party activists and general voters leads to ever-decreasing support.[1] Let us suppose that in 1972 and 1976 the Republicans nominate candidates who represent the conservative activists and not the more moderate voters. Finding the Republican party with a candidate they cannot support, large numbers of voters begin to move to the Democrats. As the Republican party becomes smaller, its activists make up a larger percentage of the whole. Hence they continue to nominate candidates who are extremely popular with the hard-core conservatives but are less and less able to attract popular support. The spiral continues as the Democratic party grows larger and the Republican party grows smaller. The inevitable result would be the conversion of the Republican party into a small sect concerned with maintaining its ideological purity, but not with winning elections. Nor would this outcome necessarily be advantageous for the Democratic party, which would become so large that it would lose whatever cohesion it now has and would most probably disintegrate into warring factions.

The future stability of the Republican party requires that it be able to win with a candidate who is clearly identified with its traditions. The 1968 election presents the party with an extraordinary opportunity to capitalize upon the unpopularity of the Johnson administration. If a real republican like Nixon cannot win under present favorable circumstances, there would not appear to be much hope for the Republican party as it is now constituted.

A defeat for Nixon would split apart the Republican party. Its most conservative elements would conclude that since they cannot win through compromising their position, they might as well form a new party and stand up for what they believe. The possibility of an amalgamation with Governor Wallace's followers would not be entirely out of the question. (Seymour M. Lipset has observed that frustration at losing an election they expected to win in 1948, after decades out of office, led some Republican leaders to give support to Joe McCarthy.) Conservative Republicans might find their body infected by a racist virus. As for Republican liberals and moderates, to understand what they might do, we must first consider the situation in the Democratic party.

A defeat for Hubert Humphrey would leave the Democratic party without a national leader in office. The strategy of the dissident Democrats, therefore, would be to defeat their party in hopes of picking up the pieces after the election. Then it would be possible for the dissidents to take over the party from the inside. The fourth-party movement designed to defeat Hubert Humphrey would dissolve after the election in order to carry on its struggle within the Democratic party.

Our future sight is dim, but is does appear that emergence of a Republican president holds out the best hope for the maintenance of the two-party system. Republicans would unite behind Nixon to enjoy the fruits of office, while Democrats would fight for the right to use the old party name. Both parties (though this prediction is more like prayer than prophecy) would shift somewhat to the left. Republicans would become more reconciled and responsive to conditions of modern political life, and Democrats would be more consistently dedicated to political innovation.

If Humphrey were to win the election, however, the Republican party might break up in despair, and the Democratic party might split because of the dissidents' anger at winning with a "tainted" candidate. The most conservative Republicans, as noted, might join the Wallace forces to create a new rightist Republican party, while the more radical McCarthy supporters might unite with some of the New Left activists to form a party of their own. Liberal Republicans would then have no alternative but to join the Democrats, the one remaining moderate party.

This three-party system—moderates and radicals of the left and right—would likely prove unstable. As Michael Leiserson has suggested, the right-wing party might find itself increasingly regarded as irrelevant to the times. In response, the center and left would unite, and the system would finally change itself into a two-party system defined along radical-versus-gradualist lines. The fulcrum of political life would have shifted dramatically to the left.

Another possibility is that the leftist party would somehow discredit itself, leaving the electoral field effectively to the moderate and right-wing parties. Political life would have moved sharply to the right.

My guess is that a three-party system would lead to perpetual rule by an oversized moderate majority as the right and left parties become too extreme to command public confidence. The alienation of radical right and left parties that could never hope to govern would become serious national problems. The majority party would be torn between its need for unity to prevent the extremes from winning and its desire to break up into more cohesive blocs. We would indeed be in a time of trouble.

After speculation upon speculation, the mind boggles at proceeding so much further than the eye can see. What is clear is that the 1968 election will affect our national political life far after the issues, personalities, and perhaps even the political parties involved have disappeared from our consciousness.

Note

1. In social-science terminology, this downward spiral is called an "unstable equilibrium." Imagine that a husband and wife are in bed, covered with an electric blanket. Unknown to either of them, the electric controls have become switched. He is too warm and moves the indicator to a colder temperature. She is too cold and moves her indicator to a warmer temperature. The colder he gets, the warmer she becomes; the warmer she feels, the colder he gets. Carried to its ultimate conclusion, this unstable equilibrium could burn him to a crisp and freeze her into a block of ice.

10

System Is to Politics as Morality Is to Man: A Sermon on Watergate and the Nixon Presidency

President Nixon has done more to discredit our political institutions than any other person, group, or social movement in this century. All those bodies on all those lines by all those protestors all this past decade do not amount to a pinhead compared to what President Nixon has done all by himself in a year. He was elected to uphold America's institutions; instead he has torn them down.

It is, as usual, the self-inflicted wounds that hurt the most. Why have we Americans done this to ourselves or (what amounts to the same thing) allowed our elected president to do it to us? What should we learn from it? What should we do about it?

The problem of the presidency is not legality but legitimacy. The important question is not whether the president has committed crimes but whether he retains the right to rule. It is not individual misdeeds but institutional faults that should be our concern. Our safety lies not in individual morality but in systemic virtue. We are in trouble not only because one man has let us down but because we raised him up too high.

Now the nation has to live with the question of whether its Congress should impeach and convict a president whom it can no longer trust. I shall return to this question in the end. Here it is enough to say that these events raise fundamental questions about the presidency and the political system: the behavior of presidents, how they are

Reprinted from *Perspectives on the Presidency* (Boston: Little, Brown, 1975), 1–21.

viewed by the people, their interactions with other elites, their management of their own office, and the extent of their powers.

No government is immune to the aberrations of individuals, and especially not at the top. The test of good government, as of good administration or good research, is not the absence of error but the ability to correct errors when they occur. How well have American institutions passed this test in recent months? Have the checks checked and the balances balanced in the American system?

A free press and an independent judiciary have served us well. Segments of the bureaucracy have done their part. The role of Congress in Watergate is a familiar one: to ventilate, publicize, embarrass, expose. Proceeding in its usual crabwise fashion, Congress uncovered the tapes and a lot more.

Nor has the voice of the people been ineffective. The "fire storm" the president's men spoke of immediately after the firing of Special Prosecutor Cox and the resignation of Attorney General Richardson was created by tens of thousands of small fires—signal fires. Without central direction, with virtually no organization, hundreds of thousands of people made their will known. And because we all felt the same way, no one doubted the genuineness of the response. If we could not trust the president, he had to go.

Not all our institutions have performed well. The most notable exception is the nation's major political parties. If party leaders may be excused for not stopping Watergate before it got started, they must surely be faulted for not halting the cover-up once it was uncovered. The remarkable feature of this whole complex of events we call Watergate is the president's persistence in the pattern of secret . . . forced revelation . . . new secret . . . new forced revelation—ad nauseam. Had there been party leaders (congressmen, national committee people, governors, state chairmen, city "bosses") with power in their own jurisdictions, they could have descended on the president en masse and said they would denounce him if he did not do the right thing. They, at least, had to be told the truth so they could judge the truth to tell. But this scenario did not occur. Why not?

The nation lacks party leaders because its parties are weak. The same weakness that allows a Barry Goldwater or a George McGovern—candidates without substantial popular support either in the country or among the voters who identify with their own party— to take the nomination for president also makes party leaders ineffective in bringing pressure to bear on their president. When the House was run by strong party leaders, for example, presidents like Theodore Roosevelt and William Howard Taft had to negotiate with them almost as if they were foreign potentates. At a time when the nation most needs the restraint on office holders exercised by organizations with an interest in the repute of their party that goes beyond the term of any incumbent, it can no longer call on them. The price of making parties too weak to do harm turns out to be rendering party leaders too useless to do good.

How about the presidency? Is it not defective? No doubt. But it is difficult to separate the faults of a specific occupant from the failures of the institution. No president before Nixon, so far as we know, has simultaneously been involved in so many scandals or had so many of his advisers indicted and convicted.

Some presidents may have alienated some national elites some of the time, but only Nixon has alienated all of them, most of the time: the House on expenditures, the Senate on foreign policy, the Republican party on his reelection campaign, the courts on executive privilege, labor on wage controls, the bureaucracy on following channels, and business on campaign contributions. Unlike most American politicians, Nixon has not played his part within a larger system. He has not seen himself as part of government but apart from it.

Look at the question of personal disclosure, which is one of mutual confidence. Let us, for the moment, not consider how the president and his men tried to deal with his enemies—that fortunately comic and discombobulated series of nonevents—but instead let us examine how they treated those who had once been their friends. Allowing Patrick Gray, former FBI Director, to "twist slowly in the wind" when he was in trouble before a congressional committee (a phrase supplied by former presidential counsel John Erlichman when he was still in power) tells us more than we wish to know. Again, think of Professor Charles Wright, an eminent conservative constitutional lawyer from the University of Texas, who went to serve the president because they both agreed about the problem of executive privilege. Think of Wright, under presidential orders, eventually promising the court to make full disclosure of the tapes and hearing from his secretary (who had heard it on the radio) that all the tapes weren't there. Imagine how Professor Wright, or anyone of us who wished to serve a president, would have had to behave to protect his or her integrity. The conversation would have to go something like this:

The President: Charlie, I want you to make full disclosure of the tapes.
Charlie: Can I see them?
The President: What do you wanna see 'em for, Charlie?
Charlie: So I know they're there.
The President: Charlie, I just told you they're there.
Charlie: Can I listen to them?
The President: What do you wanna listen to 'em for, Charlie?
Charlie: So I'll know that there are no gaps.
The President: Why would there be gaps, Charlie?

No human relationship can survive questioning the honesty and intent behind any and every sentence.

Look at the tapes as trust. Contrast the failure of Mr. Nixon's compromise on the tapes with the success of Elliot Richardson's compromise in regard to Vice-President Agnew's resignation. Richardson emphasized from the beginning the problem of legitimacy: the nation must not be confronted with the possible ascension to office of a president whose claim on the people was questionable. The important thing for the nation was that this vice-president be excluded from the succession. Having established the guiding principle, it then became a matter of prudence to arrange for a resignation in a way that would do the nation the least damage, even at the possible sacrifice of some measure of deserved punishment. The president's compromise—You can know more about what I did, but not all and not with any certainty and only indirectly—was a compromise of the very trust that makes adjustments of competing interests and conflicting values possible in a diverse society.

Confusing problems of policy with those of legitimacy has, from the very beginning, been a major defect of the Nixon administration. The problem of policy is how to find a course of action that will meet various needs and demands. The problem of legitimacy is quite different. It is to maintain the right to govern, that is, to be trusted to make future decisions. Failure to understand and act on these distinctions has been harmful before, for instance, hampering the government's approach to ending the Vietnam war. Policy required that some efficacious way be found to end the war; legitimacy, however, demanded that the path to ending the war not contain detours that would cause additional doubts about the government's credibility.

Consider the decision to move American forces en masse into Cambodia. Suppose, for the sake of argument, that it was a good military choice and did indeed have the effect of reducing pressure on American forces in nearby areas in South Vietnam. Unless the government believed that this invasion would end the war, considerations of legitimacy required that it not undertake the action. For the Cambodian venture reawakened the then-dormant peace movement and faced the government with the choice between exposing its military actions and answering the inevitable questions about its activities with less than full candor. Instead of viewing the war as a matter of military and foreign policy alone, by the time of the Nixon presidency it had to be looked at primarily as involving the confidence of Americans in their political institutions.

In the spring of 1973 it had become apparent that the president was operating under a Gaullist or plebiscitary conception of the presidency. Nixon was no longer playing politics; persuasion was giving way to command. Instead of bargaining with major elites—in Congress, the bureaucracy, the courts, and his own party—the president was constantly appealing over their heads to the people. Separation of powers was being replaced by unity of command. The president claimed virtually unlimited rights of executive privilege. And he reserved the right not to spend even after Congress passed bills over his veto. The White House stood almost as an anti-government at odds with legislators, bureaucrats, judges, newspapermen, union leaders, and ultimately even businessmen (many of whom, we were later to learn, had been pressured into campaign contributions), so that it seemed that there was nothing left to uphold the presidency except that Man in the White House and an undifferentiated mass of citizens.

Take the milk deal. Whatever the actual circumstances surrounding the administration decision to raise milk prices, the fact that the milk dealers wrote the president a letter promising contributions in return for favors, without occasioning a presidential reprimand, signified moral collapse. Consider the president's tax returns. There is no need to ask whether the president acted within the law; his insensitivity to his position as exemplar is sufficiently damning.

What we have now is an object lesson in the operational meaning of legitimacy. To be considered legitimate, governments must act (and must be seen to act) according to those norms most highly valued in their societies. To some observers it may appear that these norms are a sham because they are not always (and sometimes not often) followed. The hypocrisy that surrounds them is testimony to their power, however, for if people did not care about them there would be no reason to pretend. Is legality hypocrisy? Not after what President Nixon has just been through.

But legality is the least of it. The chief crime with which the president is charged is our inability to trust him, a serious, perhaps the most serious, public offense with which a political leader can be charged, but an offense that is not necessarily contemplated within the constitutional definition of high crimes and misdemeanors.

The Constitution, it must be admitted, is not very specific. The essential phrases—"Treason, Bribery, or other high Crimes and Misdemeanors"—are not terribly precise. Plainly "high Crimes and Misdemeanors" cover more than ordinary criminal acts, but it is not so plain what these acts encompass. Alexander Hamilton was certainly right in Number 65 of *The Federalist Papers* when he said that cases of impeachment "can never be tied down by such strict rules [as apply to regular criminal statutes] either in the delineation of the offense . . . or in the construction of it."

A way around (though not out of) the dilemma is to say that the decision is entirely political, so that "high Crimes and Misdemeanors" become whatever a majority in the House decides is sufficient to impeach and two-thirds in the Senate conclude is appropriate to convict. As pure description one can hardly fault this approach, but as prescription it lacks a great deal. For one thing, it lacks principle and is therefore certain to lack appeal. The people may wish their president tried and convicted but not, I think, lynched. For another, "political" is as slippery as "high Crimes" or "Misdemeanors."

Political can mean partisan: Will Democrats or Republicans benefit or gain the most at the next congressional and presidential elections if the president is impeached and convicted or if he remains in office? Trendy wisdom has it that Democrats have most to gain by allowing a disgraced and disabled president to remain so that his stigma will extend to the rest of his party.

Political can mean constitutional: Is a president guilty not so much of abuses of power against individuals but of encroachments on the powers of other branches of government? This is presumably the sense in which the phrase "high Crimes" was used in England at the time it was imported into our Constitution—failure to render proper accounting to duly constituted authorities or attempting to take over spheres of action that belong to them. If crimes and misdemeanors are "high," that is because they contemplate abuses of power that only presidents can commit. But the Constitution does not interpret itself. The glittering generalities that make it famous for facilitating changes are, for the same reason, the cause of endless controversy. It is not easy to find principles that would cut down Richard Nixon but leave other presidents (whether they be the favorites of recent memory or the darlings of our future imaginings) still standing. All presidents are accused of abuse of power. All could be accused of invading congressional prerogatives or misleading the public or refusing to divulge requested information or having appointed someone who got into legal trouble or whatever.

Political can mean legitimate: Has a president acted so as to be deprived of the right to govern? Has his behavior caused the political system to fall into disrepute so that its capacity to claim allegiance for future decisions is seriously impaired? There is no law against lack of legitimacy. But what Congress has ultimately to decide is exactly that—not whether a president is popular or right but whether he can continue to be accepted as president.

At the opposite pole on impeachment are the strict constructionists; presidents can be impeached, they contend, only if they violate specific criminal statutes. A high crime to them is the same as a low crime, except that it is more serious. But how serious is serious enough? Should a president be impeached for an indictable offense (such as tax fraud) not directly connected with the office of president? Is failure to act—for example, by reporting attempts by others to obstruct justice—as serious as participating in the questionable activity? Is conspiracy to perform an illegal act (a questionable doctrine if applied to political dissenters) as bad as actually doing it? Do a series of actions, no one of which is necessarily serious enough to warrant impeachment or conviction, possess sufficient cumulative force to warrant disestablishing a president? Sticking to the law can only be the beginning, not the end, of our dilemma.

Yet the strict constructionists have an important point: Unless impeachment is tied to specific criminal acts on the part of a president, there is bound to be doubt about the motives behind his dismissal. Impeachment, we must never forget, involves altering (if not reversing) the verdict of the people in the last presidential election. No one else but the people's choice is being thrown out of office, albeit ceremoniously. Deep disquiet is bound to arise if the people's verdict is cast aside for light and transient reasons or, worse still, for partisan or personal motives.

With President Kennedy shot while in office, and President Johnson shot down, as it were—deterred in his bid for a second term by protests—the possibility that a third president in a row might be removed from the political scene by some force other than the voters directly must be a cause for disquiet. It might make Republicans doubt the virtue of peaceful change. The defects of living with a suspect president for the next three years might be overwhelmed by the prospects of divisions over his dismissal for the following three hundred. The Irish are still paying violent interest on political debts incurred hundreds of years ago.

Worry about creating an unfortunate precedent is understandable but unnecessary. If a president is impeached for a single act, one might worry about whether repetition of it in the future might cause difficulty. But the probability of all or most of these acts occurring in another presidency is (one may still hope) remote. Should future presidents be involved in so many questionable activities, should so many of their advisers be corrupt, should they mislead us on so many occasions, they should also go.

The bad precedents that might be set by removing Nixon from office must be weighed against the consequences of allowing a president with his record to remain. A choice among evils is all this unhappy affair permits.

An individual action is a regrettable lapse; a seemingly endless series constitutes a massive moral collapse. This moral collapse, this never-ending assault on our credulity, this newly learned anticipation, never yet disappointed, of worse yet to come, as revelation of deceit after deceit piles up constitutes the absence of "a decent respect for the opinions of mankind" and the presence of "a long train of abuses" such as are spoken of in the Declaration of Independence.

What is wrong with having a president whose legitimacy is in doubt? It can be argued that the nation could do quite well for a few years with a president reduced in stature. Perhaps we have had too many laws, too many directives, too many initiatives this past decade.

Yet a hampered presidency is unlikely to provide the desired relief. However diminished his moral authority may be, the president still shares powers with the other branches of government. His veto, given the expected divisions in Congress, may still prove efficacious and his initiatives, along a wide range of public policies, will still be sought by innumerable groups in society. The government is too big, its actions too important, its ramifications too wide for a president to do a vanishing act on the job. He can never be a nobody. It is his continuing importance in office, no matter what any of us may think, that raises anew the urgent inquiries about his legitimacy.

In times of crises abroad—and these happen frequently—it is essential that the nation be able to place its trust in the president as commander in chief of the armed forces. But suppose responses to crises are perceived only as diversionary tactics in domestic policy. Illegitimacy is when a president issues a worldwide nuclear alert and everyone suspects him of trying to cover up some misdeed at home.

If legitimacy is the main consideration in determining whether to impeach a president, it must also be the prime consideration in how impeachment is carried out. It is not enough for a president to be impeached and convicted by Congress; he must also be impeached and convicted by the citizenry. The worst thing that could happen is not failure to impeach or convict but an ensuing bitter dispute over whether the right thing had been done. Better late (or not at all) than sorry.

From the standpoint of enhancing widespread acceptance of the results, the procedures followed thus far by the House Committee on the Judiciary cannot be faulted. By slow and deliberate action, they are painstakingly building a case for the legitimacy of whatever action they decide to take. As they go along, members are able to assess sentiment in the country. This is not pandering to public opinion, or an abdication of responsibility, but an essential (perhaps the most essential) aspect of their task. For carrying public opinion is an integral part of doing the right thing.

The opinion with which Congress ought to be concerned, however, is not just out there waiting to be discovered but is influenced by what Congress does. Recent polls suggest that the people are about evenly divided on impeachment, with Democrats largely in favor and Republicans wavering. But substantial majorities would prefer or accept resignation. They are not yet ready, apparently, to move the president out, but they are prepared to see him pushed. The given problems, then, are to bring Republicans along with the rest and to convert passive acceptance into active rejection. The censure of Senator Joseph McCarthy by the Senate, a censure that effectively ended his influence, is instructive on both counts. McCarthy was not formally censured for the worst things he did—unwarranted accusations of Communist sympathies, ruining of careers, disruption of government—but for disobeying the lawful summons of a congressional committee, because this was the charge on which maximal agreement among senators could be achieved. In this way sufficient Republican support was achieved to avoid the stigma of partisan choice on a moral issue. And while public opinion was by no means strongly in favor of censure at the beginning of the proceedings, it swung behind the senatorial decision.

It might be useful to ask whether the presidency will be weakened by the actual (or near) impeachment and conviction of a president. I think not. For one thing, the lowering of expectations may make life easier for future presidents. For another, efforts to formally restrict presidential powers or to curb abuses may have precisely the opposite effect. Such has been the case with the War Powers Act, which, in order to limit unauthorized wars, gives presidents legal sanction to start them for sixty days.

Is it an impeachable offense for a president so to act as to become unbelievable? I think it is, if he wishes to remain president. If the problem is one of proving corrupt acts, then lack of credibility, however pervasive, is insufficient either for indictment or conviction. But if the problem is one of legitimacy, of being accorded the right to govern by critical elites and suspicious citizens, then a president who is universally deemed untrustworthy must go.

An illegitimate president need not mean an illegitimate presidency. Abuses of power by one president do not necessarily mean that the presidency is too powerful. If there is anything we should have learned it is that the safety of the nation depends on the functioning of the political system as a whole. That is the real meaning of checks and balances. In American government cooperation is convenient but conflict is essential. The best safeguard against the abuse of power is not individual but systemic: strengthening each and every institutional component so that it may interact ever more vigorously with the others.

The perennial quarrel between the press and the president inadvertently points up an aspect of their relationship that is more important than whether one institution gets along with the other; like everyone else in America, the press is fascinated by the presidency. If its exaltation of him has declined, its fixation on him has not. And in this regard the press has merely mirrored the people. Being a liberal society, it is not surprising that we in America developed a liberal theory of the presidency. All power to the presidency? We never went quite that far. What is good for the presidency is good for the country? We came close to that. The people wanted a New Deal, and a president gave it to them. They wanted egalitarian social legislation, and, on the whole, presidents were disposed to give it to them. They wanted more, and presidents could promise more. They wanted novelty, and presidents provided it—new frontiers, great societies, fair deals, crusades . . . .

By comparison, Congress appeared confused, courts seemed mired in precedent, and bureaucracies tangled in red tape. Checks turned into obstructions, and balances became dead weights. The separation of powers looked like an eighteenth-century anachronism in a twentieth-century world. In short, we were concerned with results and unconcerned with institutions. The idea that the presidency was implicated in a system of checks and balances, that the safety of the nation lay not in individual virtue but in institutional arrangements, though given lip service, was in fact given short shrift.

The Bureaucratization of the Executive Branch

The organization of the executive office under Nixon continues an ever-growing trend toward bureaucratization, a reaction, in turn, to the perceived failure of the presidential office to influence public policy in ways that will redound to its credit. President Kennedy's and President Johnson's staffs sought to lay the blame for bad public policy on the regular bureaucracy, all the while becoming more bureaucratic themselves. For bureaucratization is a way of seeking shelter from a stormy world.

The presidential office has, as everybody can now see, become a bureaucracy in the same sense that Max Weber defined the term: it has grown greatly in size and is characterized by specialization, division of labor, chain of command, and hierarchy. At the same time, it criticizes, castigates, and blames the regular federal bureaucracy and attempts to circumvent it and intervene directly in the political process at lower and lower levels. From the perhaps three secretaries that Franklin Roosevelt inherited, the executive bureaucracy has risen to several thousand. There are (or recently were) two specialized organizations for dealing with the media, one to handle daily press relations and the other concerned with various promotional ventures. There is a specialized bureaucracy for dealing with foreign policy, begun when John F. Kennedy appointed McGeorge Bundy to the White House; Henry Kissinger's shop, the National Security Council, now boasts a staff of about one hundred. There is a domestic council to deal with policy at home, started by Richard Nixon. And there is also the congressional liaison machinery instituted by President Eisenhower. Since 1965 the growth of the executive office of the president has been geometric. The largest increases of all occurred in Nixon's first term, but he was merely accelerating a trend, not initiating it.

Because President Nixon, especially at the start of his second term, apparently set out to alienate every national elite—the press, Congress, the Republican National Committee—the fact that he had long been attacking his own federal bureaucracy has escaped notice. Such incidents abound, however. At ceremonies establishing the special Action Office for Drug Abuse Control, for example, "the President told an audience of 150 legislators and officials that 'heads would roll' if 'petty bureaucrats' obstruct the efforts of the office's director, Dr. Jerome H. Jaffe . . . . The President said that above all the law he just signed put into the hands of Dr. Jaffe full authority to 'knock heads together' and prevent 'empire building' by any one of the many agencies concerned" (*New York Times*, March 22, 1972). President Nixon also "informed a group of western editors in Portland that he had told Secretary Morton 'we should take a look at the whole bureaucracy with regard to the handling of Indian affairs and shake it up good.' The President blamed the bureaucracy for Indian problems, saying that 'the bureaucracy feeds on itself, defends itself, and fights for the status quo. And does very little, in my opinion, for progress in the field'" (*New York Times*, September 29, 1971).

Here too, Nixon was not so much initiating as continuing a trend. Much the same hostility to the bureaucracy had been manifested by his immediate predecessors. Accounts of staff men under Johnson and Kennedy frequently reveal a sense of indignation, if not outrage, at the very idea of the separation of powers; federalism is anathema to agents of the executive branch. Who are all those people out there thwarting us? they all but ask. Who do they think they are in the Congress and the state capitals? Strongest of all is the condemnation of the bureaucracy. The White House staff has great ideas, marvelous impulses, beautiful feelings, and these are suppressed, oppressed, crushed by the bureaucratic mind.

Why is it that the president, on the one hand, seeks to bureaucratize his own office, while on the other he holds the bureaucracy to blame for all his ills? In the end we return to our beginnings. Presidents have been impelled to attempt stabilization of their own office and desta-bilization of the regular bureaucracy because of radical changes in public policy demands. The structure of domestic political issues is now such that no government, and hence no president, can get the credit for what is done. Like all the other actors in this drama, the president and his men head for cover in the White House stockade and shoot at others more vulnerable than themselves.

It would appear amazing, in retrospect, that we thought about the presidency as if it were uncaused, as if the things that affected and afflicted us as citizens had no impact on the men who occupy public office. How long did we expect attacks on the man and the institution to go on before there was a response? Nixon's counter-attack, it now appears, may have threatened our liberties. Did the growing popular-ity of the idea that illegality was permissible for a good cause have no impact on the men surrounding the president? Did this political peril have nothing to do with the demands we make on our presidents but only with their designs on us? John Kennedy struggled mightily with a sense of failure before he was assassinated. Lyndon Johnson was forced to deny himself the chance for reelection. One or two more experiences like these and someone may think it is more than coinci-dence.

Cabinets: From Weak to Nonexistent

No matter how bad things are, a wise man must once have said, they can always get worse. That presidents may seek to overcome legislative opposition is understandable, especially when Congress is controlled by the other party. Why Presidents should attempt to run the government against the bureaucracy, against even their own politi-cal appointees, is not so obvious. When Richard Fenno first published his classic study, *The President's Cabinet*, in 1959, it appeared that this body was at its lowest ebb. Its lack of a collective interest in decisions made by others and its dependence on the president rather than on cabinet colleagues meant that it had never really been strong in the history of American politics. Under Presidents Kennedy, Johnson, and Nixon, however, the cabinet appeared not merely weak but virtually nonexistent. Its former low ebb seems, in retrospect, almost to have been its high tide.

What happened? In the old days presidents mistrusted cabinets because they were not entirely free in choosing its members. They had, in effect, to "give away" appointments to important party factions outside the government and to powerful congressmen inside. The decline of the party in American political life, however, has meant that recent presidents have not been beholden to it to the extent that their campaigns for office are run, as was Nixon's, outside the national committees. The increasing diffusion of power within Congress has also meant that there are correspondingly fewer powerful leaders to which presidents have to cater in making appointments. Yet their increased freedom in selecting cabinet members apparently has not led presidents to confer greater trust on their appointees. Why not?

Secretaries of the great departments must serve more than one master. They are necessarily beholden to Congress for appropriations and for substantive legislation. They are expected to speak for the major interests entrusted to their care as well as for the president. They need cooperation from the bureaucracy that surrounds them, and they may have to make accommodations to get that support. A secretary of agriculture who is vastly unpopular with the farmers, a secretary of the interior who is hated by conservationists, and all secretaries whose employees undermine their efforts, cannot be of much use to the chief executive. Nevertheless, presidents (and especially their personal staffs) appear to behave as if there were something wrong when cabinet members do what comes naturally to men in their positions. Who, then, do presidents trust?

No one can doubt that personal presidential advisers have gained over official cabinet appointees. Important clues to this shift in power are found in the many quotes from White House staffers in Thomas Cronin's article, "'Everybody Believes in Democracy Until He Gets to the White House . . . .'"[1] Listen carefully to the inner voice of these complaints. These members of the White House staff, spanning several administrations and including both major parties, are frustrated.

They have wonderful ideas, apparently, only to see them sabotaged in the bureaucratic labyrinth. To the White House staff, the separation of powers appears anathema. How dare those bureaucrats get in the way! The idea that the departments might owe something to Congress or that there is more to policy than what the president and his men want flickers only occasionally across their minds. It is as if the presidency were the government. Separation of powers has no place in this scheme of things. The president's men do not see themselves so much as part of a larger system but as the system itself.

Alternatively, going to the other extreme, consider the image of a beleaguered outpost in the White House with all the insignia of office but without the ability to command troops in the provinces. As Arthur Schlesinger, Jr., put it when reflecting on his experiences as an adviser to President Kennedy in *A Thousand Days*, "Wherever we have gone wrong . . . has been because we have not had sufficient confidence in the New Frontier approach to impose it on the government. Every important mistake has been the consequence of excessive deference to the permanent government."[2] Small wonder, then, that other presidents in later times interpreted discontent with their policies or their behavior not as evidence of the intractability of the policy problems or of the unsuitability of their own approach but as another effort by the "permanent government" (readily expanded to include the "establishment press") to frustrate the designs of the people's true government.

As one observed the procession of bright young men apologizing for their misdeeds before the Senate Watergate Committee, men who seemed to derive their sole source of warmth, comfort, and guidance from the dazzling illumination of the Sun King in the White House, it came as some relief to discover that some men—heretofore characterized as petty, narrow, selfish bureaucrats, like J. Edgar Hoover, director of the FBI—had refused to be corrupted. Unlike the faceless men who seemed to lack moral reference to family, country, or God, our myopic parochial bureaucrats knew they had to consider interests other than those of the temporary incumbent of the White House. They had organizations to think about and people in them whose good opinion they valued. The point is not that all bureaucracies (or all bureaucrats, perish the thought) are wonderful, but that they do provide semiindependent centers of power that not only cause our frustration but also are an essential part of the balances that guard our liberties. Had

Hoover agreed to take on the domestic surveillance activities suggested by Nixon, the "Plumbers Unit" in the White House need not have been formed and amateurism would have been replaced by professionalism—to the benefit of the president but to the detriment of the people.

How could these events have transpired? As the roster of indictments at the top levels of the White House staff roll on, few would quarrel with the notion that there was something wrong with the advisory apparatus to the president. Nor did it take these events only to prompt questioning of presidential management. The Vietnam War had led to concern over whether the structure of presidential advice might not be responsible for this decade-long series of calamities. Alexander George advocates multiple advocacy.[3] If the problem seems to be that presidents are listening to only one kind of advice, then the solution appears to be building in a variety of perspectives. I.M. Destler, in his critique, wonders whether this will do any good if presidents are not disposed to pay attention.[4] You can lead a president to advice, so it seems, but you can hardly make him take it.

The problem of advice, according to Richard Johnson, is one of tradeoffs. There are a variety of presidential management strategies, but whatever style is adopted has costs as well as benefits. The formalistic approach may be orderly, but it is also slow; the competitive approach brings in more viewpoints at the expense of increased friction and fatigue; the collegial approach may lead to more consistent policies at the risk of creating a group spirit against all outsiders. Since all these strategies must be used to some extent—all presidents need order, loyalty, and variety in advice—the trick is to get a viable balance among them, taking into consideration the needs of the times and the personality of the president. Of course, if one is absolutely certain that the nation should not use force, surrounding presidents with opposing opinions makes sense.

The Flight of the Presidency

Perhaps the most interesting events of our time are those that have not occurred—the failure of demagogues, parties, or mass movements to take advantage of the national disarray. Maybe the country is in better shape than we think, or they (whoever "they" are) are waiting for things to get still worse. In any event, it now appears that the

United States will have to get out of its predicaments with the same ordinary, everyday, homespun political institutions with which it got into them. How will its future leaders (preeminently its presidents) appraise the political context in which they find themselves? For leadership is not a unilateral imposition but a mutual relationship, in which it is as important to know whether and wither people are willing to be led as why and where their leaders propose to take them.

When you bite the hand that feeds you, it moves out of range. That is the significance of the near-geometric increase in the size of the executive office from Truman's to Nixon's time. Originally a response to the growth of government, it has become a means of insulating presidents from the shocks of a society with which they can no longer cope.

As government tried to intervene both more extensively and more intensively in the lives of citizens, the executive office, in order to monitor these events, became a parallel bureaucracy. The larger it grew and the more programs it tried to cover, however, the more the executive office inadvertently but inevitably became further removed from the lives of the people who were being affected by these new operations. Then the inevitable became desirable and the inadvertent became functional; for as presidents discovered that domestic programs paid no dividends—see Nixon's comment in the Watergate tapes about the futility of building more outhouses in Peoria—insulation from the people didn't seem such a bad idea.

In the first months of Richard Nixon's second term, when his administration was at full strength and he was attempting to chart a new course, he tried both to reorganize radically the federal bureaucracy and to alter drastically his own relations to it. In part, the idea was old—rationalize the bureaucracy by creating a smaller number of bigger departments, thus cutting down on the large number of people previously entitled to report directly to the president. Part of it was new—creating a small number of supersecretaries who would have jurisdiction over several departments, thus forming, in effect, an inner cabinet. Part of it was peculiarly Nixonian—drastically reducing demands on his time and attention. Part of it, I believe, is likely to be permanent—adapting to the increasing scope and complexity of government by focusing presidential energy on a few broadly defined areas of policy. Everyone knows that presidents have to deal with war and peace and with domestic prosperity. There will continue to be, *de*

facto if not de jure, a person the president relies on for advice princi-
pally in foreign and defense policy and another on whom he relies for
economic management. The demands on presidents for response to
other domestic needs vary with the times, so there will undoubtedly
be two or three other superadvisers, called by whatever names or
holding whatever titles, to deal with race relations or energy or the
environment or whatever else seems most urgent. Response to ever-
increasing complexity will continue to be ever-greater simplicity. This
is the rationale behind wholesaling instead of retailing domestic policies, behind revenue sharing instead of endless numbers of categorical
grants, behind proposals for family assistance and negative income
taxes instead of a multiplicity of welfare policies, behind a transfer to
state and local governments of as much responsibility (though not
necessarily as much money) as they can absorb.

Future presidents will be preoccupied more with operating strategic
levers than with making tactical moves. They will see their power
stakes, to use Neustadt's term, in giving away their powers; like everyone else, they will have to choose between what they have to keep
and what they must give up. Not so much running the country (that
was Nixon's error) but seeing that it is running will be their forte.
Advisers will still need to help prepare the president's program, but
its components will be smaller in number and broader in scope. In one
respect, however, the existential presidential situation will be the same:
he will, simultaneously, have too much power for the safety of the
country and not enough to solve the nation's problems.

Although it is convenient now to forget this, from the mid-1960s
onward, national leaders of government have been subject to a crescendo of attack and even personal abuse. They have been shouted
down, mobbed, and vilified in public. It was not possible for men like
President Johnson and Vice-President Humphrey to speak where they
wished in safety, or to travel where they wished without fear. Not
merely their conduct as individuals, but the political system of which
they were a part, has been condemned as vicious, immoral, and de-
praved. This, after all, was the justification offered for the stealing of
government documents—that the government from which they were
taken had no right to be doing what it was doing, that it was not
legitimate. The rationale offered for faking and publishing government documents was the same as that offered by the Watergate con-

spirators: national interest, a higher law than that applying to ordinary citizens.

Watergate emerged, in my opinion, out of an environment in which people who identified with government sought to delegitimate the opposition just as they believed the opposition had sought to delegitimate government. Presumably no one, in their view, had a right to beat President Nixon in 1972, so they sought to get Senator Muskie out of the race. They broke into Watergate ostensibly to find evidence that the Democrats were being financed by Cuban (Communist) money, as if to say that their own illegality was permissible because the Democrats were not then a legitimate American political party. The blame, to be sure, is not the same. Those who stole the Pentagon papers were not entrusted with the care of government, and the Watergate conspirators were. But they cohere in the same syndrome; the one is a reaction to the other, each party rationalizing its exceptional behavior on the grounds of its enemy's illegitimacy.

Watergate is a curious scandal by American standards in that it is not concerned with money; nor is it, like a British scandal, concerned with sex. By contrast, it resembles a French scandal, one in which small groups of conspirators make and execute their clandestine plans in the service of ideologies held by no more than 1 or 2 percent of the population. Watergate may thus represent another step in the "Frenchification" of American political life begun in the mid-1960s, a mode of politics in which apparently inexplicable behavior is found to derive from attachment to ideologies of which the vast majority of the citizenry knows little and cares less.

The French analogy gains strength in light of the entire pattern of President Nixon's conduct before Watergate. Seemingly disparate occurrences fall into place once we understand that Nixon had adopted a plebiscitary view of the presidency, a view that has echoes in the American past but none in the contemporary Western world except in the presidency of Charles de Gaulle and his successors in France. From this perspective, the position of Nixon's attorney general on executive privilege, with its suggestion that the presidency exists wholly apart from other institutions, becomes more explicable. So does Nixon's march on the media. For if the presidency is not part of a separation of powers with Congress but of a unity of power with the people, then its survival is critically dependent on direct access to them. His victory at the polls in 1972 seems to have inspired in him the conviction that as the embodiment of the national will he should brook no opposition from Congress. Even the Republican party could not share in his triumph—it neither ran his campaign nor got any of its leaders appointed to high positions—lest it become another unwanted intermediary between the president and the people; the Republican National Committee owes its spotless reputation on Watergate to having been kept out of (or away from) the presidential branch of government. It was his plebiscitary view of the presidency that led Nixon to attempt to run a foreign and defense policy without the Senate, a budget policy without the House, and domestic-security policy without the courts.

Unlike the celebrated Professor Hindzeit, Peter Sperlich, in his essay on Richard Neustadt's *Presidential Power*, can claim foresight.[5] Neustadt, he says, downgrades emotional ties because he "offers no advice to the President about creating and sustaining a proper ideological climate among his associates." Feeling that Neustadt's notion of command was unnecessarily restricted to giving direct orders, Sperlich holds that "Neustadt does not consider the possibility that a person might accept influence and will do what is requested of him because he has come to identify with the individual who makes the request. Not included among Neustadt's many prescriptions, then, is that a President, within the limits set by other criteria, should select his associates on the basis of personal loyalty and identification, and that he should attempt to create feelings of subjective identification in those in whose selection he had no voice." Otherwise, presidents would spend all their time bargaining. [No doubt Sperlich anticipated the Bush presidency.] No one can say today that Nixon's personal staff showed too little loyalty (if perjury and illegal entry are the appropriate indications of affection). Undoubtedly Neustadt did not feel it necessary to fill his book with Boy Scout maxims—be honest, be good, (as well as) be prepared. But if loyalty can be corrupted it also cannot be done without.

War Power Acts and Other Misfortunes

The legal profession has the right aphorism: hard cases make bad law. Congress has, after the fact, passed the War Powers Act to restrict presidents in the future. In my opinion the gesture was futile and possibly dangerous. Basically, the act provides that within sixty days of the commencement of hostilities, the president must receive positive congressional approval or it all grinds to a halt. Would it have stopped Vietnam? That is doubtful because of the spirit prevailing at the time of the Gulf of Tonkin Resolution. Will it enable presidents to respond when necessary and restrain them when essential? Such judgments, I fear, are more readily made in retrospect than in prospect. My concern is that the War Powers Act can be converted too easily into a permanent Gulf of Tonkin Resolution, bestowing legislative benediction in advance on presidential actions, by which time Congress has little choice left. The lesser defect lies in trying to anticipate the specific configuration of events by general statutory principles. The greater defect lies in trying to frame general principles on the basis of the most recent horrible event. The greatest defect lies in treating a systemic problem, whose resolution depends on the interaction of numerous parts in a dynamic environment, as if it were a defect in a single component operating in a static situation.

History shows, to be sure, that constitutions are often written against the last usurper—the United States Constitution against the Articles of Confederation, the Fifth French Republic against the Fourth and the Third, Bonn against Weimar, the United Nations contra the League of Nations. So, too, do generals frequently end up preparing for the last war. But this is not quite so bad as aiming living constitutional provisions at dead targets. The nation has not been well served by the Twenty-second Amendment, better known as the Anti-third Term (read anti-Franklin Roosevelt) Amendment, which guarantees that if the people ever find a president worth keeping in office, they will have prohibited themselves from doing so. In the guise of denying power to Presidents, it has, in fact, been denied to the people. Were it not for the two-term limitation, moreover, we would be spared the current nonsense of proposing a single six-year term. The proposal seems to assume that the safety of the country is guaranteed, not by the checks and balances of vigorous institutions, but by taking an electoral check away from the president. After all, as far as we know, Nixon did behave somewhat better in his first term, perhaps because he was concerned about reelection. In any event, putting a man in office who never has to run again doesn't guarantee he won't be interested in his successor, and it may make him much less interested in what anybody thinks—a very peculiar doctrine for a democratic country! Why popular control over presidents would be increased by taking them out of the electoral arena after they assume office must remain a mystery. Next thing we know someone will think up an amendment disqualifying the president's friends from running to succeed him, should he turn out to have some small interest in securing an approved successor. Does Nixon deserve to have an amendment named after him?

Disenchantment with President Nixon has led to serious discussion of adopting a parliamentary form of government in the United States. Had the top man been part of a collegial body, the argument goes, he would have been forced to tell them what was going on and they would have refused to go along. Prime ministers, it is supposed, cannot hide from their cabinets. If they do, they can be deposed at once without going through months of revelations culminating in more months of hearings on impeachment. And, so far as it goes, this argument is probably correct. A prime minister who had been disgraced would probably be removed by his colleagues. But there is more (much, much more) to it than that.

What I think we have seen, basically, are exercises in foolishness. Yet I see one cheerful prospect. I have noticed that the words of the Founding Fathers are once again in fashion, and that the words of our Constitution are not a way of putting down unfortunate minorities, but have achieved a renewed nobility.

It requires an electorate that will put in office either a majority party or a compatible coalition, and it requires political parties that will vigorously control their membership in the legislature. Cabinets are steering committees of the legislature chosen from either a majority party or a coalition. Parliamentary government thus depends on sufficient agreement within the population to produce this kind of result, and sufficient cohesion within the majority party or coalition to carry all-important votes. Yet none of the contemporary parliamentary regimes with which America is sometimes compared (whether among Western European countries or in Japan) has the good-old-American combination of racial, religious, ethnic, regional, and class differences. Nor is there reason to believe that the legislative parties in Congress, which have been moving to decentralize their structure (less power to committee chairmen and rules committees), would be amenable to strict party discipline. For a parliamentary system would not require nearly so great a change in the executive—foreign and defense policy, economic management, and national crises still should engage its attention—as in the legislature, which would have to undergo radical structural change. Independent bases of power in constituencies would give way to central direction. Closed party meetings (not open party primaries) would choose congressmen. The executive would control the legislature. Frequent dissolutions of parliament, followed by national elections, would not be a sign of legislative strength but a source of governmental weakness. The Third and Fourth French Republics, in which governments rose and fell with bewildering rapidity and disastrous consequence, also operated under a parliamentary form. Parliamentary government is basically party government. Emasculating Congress is a funny way to curb the virility of presidents. Why a country that won't do anything to strengthen its political parties, that spends all its time thinking of ways to weaken them, would ever contemplate adopting a parliamentary regime, I cannot imagine.

A certain way of limiting the amount of damage a single president can do is to divide his job among several people. The replacement of a single president, as some suggest, by a plural executive certainly would achieve its purpose: the power of any one executive to do harm would be severely limited—almost to the same extent as the capacity to help. If this plural executive follows the norm of reciprocity—you let me do what I want in my area and you can do what you want in yours—it is hard to understand how the temptation to abuse power would be less than it had been before. At least now we know whom to blame. If the plural executive has to get together on everything, it will be difficult to secure agreement on anything. No evil will be allowed and no good will be permitted. Those who think that the growing burden on presidents would be relieved by dividing up the job miss the whole point: coordination costs more than decision; since most important issues overlap with others, it will take much longer to agree than would be saved by splitting the job.

Trust in a president is based not only on trust in a person, but also on trust in the office as part of a larger political system that guides and constrains its incumbent. The framers of our Constitution intended that their overarching structure should restrain each participant through the mutual interaction of the parts. Ordinary citizens now see that in that restraint lies their safety. For President Nixon personally, the genie is out of the bottle; trust in him is gone (or severely diminished) and no one knows how to get it back. But the potential for trust in the system remains. So long as he (or any president) is seen as part of the system, subject to its checks and balances, citizens retain hope and show calm.

Resignation versus Impeachment

It was said that insisting on impeachment instead of resignation was unnecessarily harsh. This conclusion I find morally obtuse. The behavior that led to the former president's resignation was not done in a moment of passion or in a fit of pique. He deliberately kept this nation in a state of turmoil month after month, one year to the next, knowing all the time the truth he was withholding. For that we owe him nothing. There was no reason to let go of him until he let go of us. Experience should have taught us that Nixon gave up information only under duress. The important thing was to compel the president to release the nation from the grip of this episode by telling what there was to know. As things stand, the reasons for the break-in to the Watergate and the surrounding circumstances have not yet been clarified, and this episode cannot be put to rest until that is done. The former president should fulfill his last duty to the nation.

The pardon was preposterous. Ford confused his role as president in a political system with his personal capacity as priest in a family of friends. Only priests can offer absolution—Thou shalt now and forever more be spotless—the ecclesiastical equivalent of a full, free and absolute pardon. President Ford was wrong in both his value and factual premises: the former president did not deserve pardon and it was highly unlikely that a quick pardon would bring the public passion over these events to an early end. For the pardon could not resolve doubts about what had happened and, what is worse, immeasurably worse, created doubts about President Ford's possible complicity in these events. Had he deliberately decided to punish the nation for allowing him to become president, Gerald Ford could not have done worse.

As a boy I had the feeling that history was something that happened "then" and not during my time. No one who has lived through the last two years in the United States (if one missed the news for a few hours there was a good chance that something awful but fascinating had occurred) could possibly feel that way. Now, after the Nixon pardon, history has somehow been left behind and myth has begun: Once there was a common man who suddenly became president in an oval room with seven doors. One was marked wisdom, another power, and so on, until the seventh door was reached. It had a sign that read "Connection with Watergate, invariably fatal, do not enter!" Before he could enter the six doors of service, he went through the seventh door of dismay and discovered he had locked himself out. And he never could get back in.

Where would the nation be if Nixon had been impeached and convicted, or even if he had resigned and not been pardoned? The matter would be in the courts, where almost everyone was prepared to let it be. No doubt a year or so might have had to elapse before a jury could be impaneled, and even more time pass before a trial could be started. This would not have been bad; it would have allowed President Ford to get started without being tainted by Watergate. If Nixon told what he knew, and, at last, did his duty to his country, then President Ford, assuming Nixon was convicted of some crime, would still have been in a position to grant a pardon.

If one were to search for a good omen among the bad signs of the times (I come from a family in which every disaster was interpreted as a harbinger of good fortune), the resignation and pardon might be seen as messages warning against dependence on leaders. The voice of Ezekiel—"Son of man, trust not in man"—has a contemporary echo. If only Nixon went, the hope was, a leader would arise among us. Apparently not. Maybe someone is trying to tell us something. The virtues of a democracy must ultimately be tested, not in the leadership of its great men, but in the enduring power of its great institutions.

About the aftermath of Watergate three things can be said: (1) it has imposed sanctions so great there will be no repetition in our time; (2) once again (soon enough), we will want a strong, action-oriented president to override obstructive courts and dilatory and divided Congresses; and (3) the countless lessons of Watergate will tell us more about the people drawing from them than about the situations to which they supposedly refer. Pluralists will find celebration in the diversity that presumably saved us, and antipluralists, of the elitism that almost did us in. Dispersion of power within Congress will be seen as a weakness that allowed presidential power to grow and as a strength against its further encroachment. Reaction to Watergate is less an index of moral virtue than a political Rorschach test. We will see in these events what is in us, for we are all captives of our time—after, just as much as before, Watergate.

Notes

1. Thomas E. Cronin, "'Everybody Believes in Democracy Until He Gets to the White House . . . ': An Examination of White House–Departmental Relations," Law and Contemporary Problems 35, no. 3 (Summer 1970): 573–625.
2. Arthur M. Schlesinger, Jr., A Thousand Days: John F. Kennedy in the White House (Boston: Houghton Mifflin, 1965), 683.
3. Alexander L. George, "The Case for Multiple Advocacy in Making Foreign Policy," American Political Science Review 66, no. 3 (September 1972):
4. I.M. Destler, Comment: "Multiple Advocacy: Some 'Limits and Costs,'" American Political Science Review 66, no. 3 (September 1972): 791–95.
5. Peter W. Sperlich, "Bargaining and Overload: An Essay on Presidential Power," in Aaron Wildavsky, ed., Perspectives on the Presidency (Boston: Little, Brown, 1975), 406–30.

11

Jimmy Carter's Theory
of Governing

With Jack Knott

"Seek simplicity and distrust it."
— Alfred North Whitehead

If President Carter didn't believe what he said or act on his beliefs, there would be little reason to study his words as predictors of his deeds. Yet, as we shall show, he does care about his beliefs and he does act on them. Why, then, if Carter is a believer, has it been so difficult for observers to determine what he believes or what he will try to do in office? Because we have all been looking in the wrong place. President Carter does change his views on substantive policies, such as tax reform, medical care, and busing. He is not an ideologue of policy, but changes his mind, like most of us, as the times and conditions change.

Our hypothesis is that Carter's basic beliefs are about procedures for making policy—procedures about which he speaks with passion, determination, and consistency. His concern is less with particular goals than with the need for goals, less with the content of policies than with their ideal form—simplicity, uniformity, predictability, hierarchy, and comprehensiveness.

Therefore, if there is a danger for President Carter, it is not that he

Reprinted from *Wilson Quarterly* (Winter 1977): 49–67.

will support unpopular *policies,* but that he will persevere with inappropriate *procedures.* The question is whether he views his procedural criteria merely as rough guidelines for formulating public policy or as immutable principles of good government. If they are hypotheses about governing—subject to refinement or abandonment in the face of contrary evidence—there is no reason for alarm; but if he does not allow his theories of governing to be refuted by experience, we are all in for hard times.

Of all the Democratic presidential candidates in the primaries, Jimmy Carter was criticized the most for his alleged vagueness on policy. Some people saw him as a fiscal conservative who would cut government spending; others wondered about his plans for costly social programs. Actually, his campaign staff put out numerous papers outlining his proposals on issues ranging from busing to abortion to welfare.[1] The problem was not so much that he did not say specific things about issues but that he placed greater emphasis on methods, procedures, and instruments for making policy than on the content of policy itself.

The response of Stuart Eizenstat, Carter's chief "issues" adviser, to a question about what issues would dominate the campaign will serve as an illustration. Eizenstat grouped the issues into three types: one centered on the present lack of long-range federal planning; a second emphasized openness; a third dealt with government reorganization.[2] With all three, the emphasis was not on policy outcomes but on administrative instruments. (Long-range planning, like openness and reorganization, is not a policy but an instrument used to produce policies.)

Carter on Procedures

In contrast to the other candidates, Jimmy Carter made numerous statements during the campaign and during his term as Governor of Georgia (1971–75) in which he explicitly emphasized principles of procedure for making public policy. Although we are aware of the possibility that these statements are in part rhetoric, his ideas do comprise a coherent philosophy, with recurrent and identifiable themes about how government ought to work; and we shall show that he put them into practice as governor of Georgia.

In his own words, a major purpose of reorganizing the federal government is to "make it simple." He favors "drastic simplification of the tax structure";[3] "simple, workable, housing policies";[4] "simplification of the laws and regulations to substitute education for paper shuffling grantsmanship";[5] "simplification of the purposes of the military" and a "fighting force that is simply organized."[6] Rather than the "bewildering complexity" we now have, he intends to create a "simplified system of welfare."[7] His praise goes out to the state and local governments that have devised "simple organizational structures."[8]

How does he intend to simplify? When Carter became governor of Georgia, he reduced the number of agencies from 300 down to 22. He has proposed a similar nine-tenths reduction in the number of units at the federal level—from the present 1,900 down to around 200.[9] His rationale seems to be a general one: the fewer the agencies, the better.

Another way to simplify administrative structure, according to Eizenstat, is "to make sure that duplicating functions are not performed by one agency and that, in fact, we don't have a situation whereby duplicating programs are being administered by more than one agency."[10] Carter has repeatedly stated that one of the purposes of his proposal to introduce "zero-base budgeting" (as he did in Georgia) is "eliminating duplication and overlapping of functions."[11] In restructuring the defense establishment, Carter would like to "remove the overlapping functions and singly address the Defense Department toward the capability to fight."[12]

The Uniform Approach to Policy

A third way President Carter intends to simplify policy is through uniformity. He plans to reform the welfare system by providing a uniform national cash payment, varying only according to cost of living.[13] He intends to standardize the tax structure by eliminating loopholes, thus treating all income the same.[14] To create uniformity, Carter would grant a direct subsidy for new housing.[15] He would also standardize medical treatment—"We now have a wide disparity of length of stay in hospitals, a wide disparity of charges for the same services, a wide difference in the chances of one undergoing an operation"—and make criminal justice uniform by "eliminat[ing] much of the discretion that is now exercised by judges and probation officers in determining the length of sentences."[16]

"There's just no predictability now about government policy," Carter has complained, "no way to tell what we're going to do next in the area of housing, transportation, environmental quality, or energy."[17] He believes in "long-range planning so that government, business, labor, and other entities in our society can work together if they agree with the goals established. But at least it would be predictable."[18] And: "The major hamstring of housing development is the unpredictability of the Federal policies."[19] In agriculture, the greatest need is a "coherent, predictable and stable government policy relating to farming and the production of food and fiber."[20] In foreign affairs, other nations are "hungry for a more predictable and mutually advantageous relationship with our country."[21] Unpredictability led Carter to condemn Henry Kissinger's policy of no permanent friends and no permanent enemies with these words: "I would . . . let our own positions be predictable."[22]

Shared Goals Make Predictable Policies

If only we agree on long-range goals, according to Carter, then we can work together and make our policies predictable. The format of his thinking follows: long-range planning entails the explicit delineation of goals; once goals are known (and agreed upon), policies become predictable. This predictability reduces conflict and increases cooperation.

His theory of conflict explains how Carter would expect to deal with a recalcitrant cabinet: "The best mechanism to minimize this problem is the establishment of long-range goals or purposes of the government and a mutual commitment to these goals by different Cabinet members." By getting early agreement, "I can't imagine a basic strategic difference developing between myself and one of my Cabinet members if the understanding were that we worked toward the long-range goals."[23] When asked how he would resolve differences with the Congress on foreign policy, his response was: "I hope that my normal, careful, methodical, scientific or planning approach to longer-range policies . . . would serve to remove those disharmonies long before they reach the stage of actual implementation."[24]

A major Carter campaign criticism of President Ford was that he "allowed the nation to drift without a goal or purpose."[25] By contrast, when Carter became governor of Georgia, his administration attempted to identify long-range goals: "During the first months of my term, we had 51 public meetings around the state, attended by thousands of Georgians, to formulate specific long-range goals in every realm of public life. We spelled out in writing what we hoped to accomplish at the end of two, five, or even 20 years."[26] Only if government has clearly defined goals, Carter believes, will people be prepared to "make personal sacrifices." One of his favorite quotes from the New Testament is, "If the trumpet give an uncertain sound, who shall prepare himself for the battle?"[27] But suppose others prefer to march to their own music? How would Carter contend with conflict?

If openness is not a form of godliness for President Carter, it must come close. He has proposed an "all-inclusive 'sunshine law' . . . [whereby] meetings of federal boards, commissions, and regulatory agencies must be opened to the public, along with those of congressional committees."[28]

Carter's espousal of openness is connected in his own mind with direct access to the people. Just as he favors giving the people open access to governmental decision making, he plans, as president, to speak directly to them. He values openness "to let the public know what we are doing and to restore the concept in the Congress that their constituents are also my constituents. I have just as much right and responsibility to reach the people for support as a member of Congress does."[29] He has also said that he plans to restore Franklin D. Roosevelt's "fireside chat," accept "special responsibility to by-pass the big shots," and to act, as it were, as the people's lobbyist.[30] Should his policies be thwarted by special interests, Carter says he will go to the people. At times, Carter identifies himself *as* the people. In reviewing his experience with consumer legislation in Georgia, he said: "The special interest groups prevailed on about half of it. I prevailed— rather the Georgia people prevailed—on the other half."[31]

What is consistent in these proposals is Carter's opposition to the intermediate groups—lobbyists who stand between government and citizen or a palace guard who stands between a president and the cabinet. They fracture his conception of comprehensive policymaking.

President Carter prefers to make changes comprehensively rather than "timidly or incrementally." As he has put it:

> Most of the controversial issues that are not routinely well-addressed can only respond to a comprehensive approach. Incremental efforts to make

basic changes are often foredoomed to failure because the special interest groups can benefit from the status quo, can focus their attention on the increments that most affect themselves, and the general public can't be made either interested or aware.[32]

The same theory guides his efforts on government reorganization:

The most difficult thing is to reorganize incrementally. If you do it one tiny little phase at a time, then all those who see their influence threatened will combine their efforts in a sort of secretive way. They come out of the rat holes and they'll concentrate on undoing what you're trying to do. But if you can have a bold enough, comprehensive enough proposal to rally the interest and support of the general electorate, then you can overcome that special interest type lobbying pressure.[33]

In a word, "the comprehensive approach is inherently necessary to make controversial decisions."[34]

Changing everything at once, then, is part of Carter's political theory: comprehensive change enables one both to identify the public interest by considering the merits of opposing claims and to serve that interest by requiring opponents to fight on every front simultaneously, thus diluting their forces while concentrating one's own. The bigger the change, the greater the public attention—and the more likely it becomes that the public interest will prevail over private interests.

A central ingredient in Carter's comprehensive reforms is their inclusiveness. A characteristic Carter phrase is "a complete assessment of tax reform in a comprehensive way." He wants to "establish comprehensive proposals on transportation and energy and agriculture."[35] He favors a "comprehensive nation-wide mandatory health-insurance program" and a "drastic reorganization of the health care services in the U.S."[36] Although we could go on, one more example from foreign affairs must serve: since "the old international institutions no longer suffice," Carter feels that "the time has come for a new architectural effort."[37]

Since special interests—"those who prefer to work in the dark, or those whose private fiefdoms are threatened"—care only about themselves, they prevent inclusive decision making.[38] To avoid this pitfall, Carter wants to restructure the federal bureaucracy, the health system, the welfare system, the tax system, the criminal-justice system, and international institutions.

According to Carter, the comprehensive approach offers a final, decisive solution to problems. On the basis of his experience with government reorganization in Georgia, he has become a leading advocate of what is called the one-step process.[39] In the Middle East, he wants to devise an "overall settlement rather than resuming Mr. Kissinger's step-by-step approach."[40] He contends that with Soviet cooperation, we can achieve "the ultimate solution" there.[41] He aims at achieving an "ultimate and final and complete resolution of New York City's problems, fiscally."[42]

Predictable, Uniform, Simple

Who can object to making governmental policy predictable so that people know what to expect? Predictability is preferable, but is it possible? To be more precise, is predictability for one agency (and its clients) compatible with predictability for others? Is predictability consistent with uniformity, another managerial quality that President Carter seeks? One could get broad agreement, for instance, on the desirability of smoothing out the economic cycle by maintaining a steady, low level of unemployment.

A major instrument used to accomplish this objective is varying the level of government spending. Immediately it becomes evident that predictability in employment (assuming that it could be achieved) is mutually exclusive with predictability in expenditure policy. Similarly, predictability for recipients of governmental subsidies means that all who meet the qualifying conditions receive the guaranteed sum. However, predictability for governmental expenditures (and, quite possibly, for taxpayers) requires fixed dollar limits, not open-ended entitlements. Yet if there are limits, potential beneficiaries cannot know in advance how much they will receive. Since all policy results cannot be predictable, decisions about whose life will be predictable and whose won't are political as well as administrative.

The same is true for uniformity and simplicity. Uniformity on one criterion—say, population—means diversity on other criteria, such as wealth or race or geography. Imagine that President Carter wishes to make good his promise to subsidize the arts, an intention we would like to see realized. Will money be allocated by population (which favors urban density), by area (which favors rural folk), by need (which favors those who are doing the least), or by past performance (which means that those who have will get more)? A uniform policy means that all these differences cannot simultaneously be taken into account.

Comprehensiveness, in the sense of fundamental and inclusive change, often contradicts predictability and simplicity. Fundamental changes, precisely because they are far-reaching, are unlikely to be predictable. That is how the cost of the food-stamp program grew from an expected few hundred million dollars to more than $8 billion; it is also how indexing Social Security against inflation had the unanticipated consequence of (among other things) threatening to bankrupt the system. Thus, acting inclusively, so as to consider all (or almost all) factors impinging on a particular problem at a specific time, is, by its very nature, opposed to predictability, which requires that programs established in the past not be undone in the near future. But zero-base budgeting, the epitome of comprehensiveness, requires reexamination of all major programs every year, the very opposite of predictability.

With Slices for All, How Large a Pie?

Uniformity also lives uneasily with comprehensiveness. Programs that are both uniform and comprehensive may be too expensive. For example, if public housing must be provided everywhere on the same basis or not at all, there may be no public housing. Similarly, a desire to have a uniform level of benefits across all welfare programs for all eligible citizens might lead to a choice between much higher taxes or much lower benefits. "Cashing out" all benefits from food stamps to Medicaid and Medicare might add up to so large a sum that it would not be voted by Congress. Hence, the choice might be between a variety of disparate programs or much lower levels of benefits. Upgrading all eligibles to the highest level of benefits will increase costs, and downgrading all to the lowest level will increase anger. Thus uniformity may come at too high a price in suffering or in opposition.

A word should be said about the relationship between uniformity and individuality. We do not always equate fairness with being treated like everybody else; we would, on occasion, like to be treated as individuals. To be uniform, regulations must place people into large and homogeneous categories. Every effort to take account of special characteristics in the population leads to its further sub-division and to additional provisions in the regulations. It is this effort to treat people in terms of their individual characteristics that leads to the proliferation of rules and regulations.

President Carter's desire for uniformity has led him to advocate a single principle of organization whereby administrative agencies are formed on the basis of function or purpose.[43] He would have all activities involving education or health or welfare or crime, to mention but a few, in the same large organization. As a general rule, one can confidently say that no single principle or criterion is good for every purpose. Suppose that reducing dependency on welfare is a major purpose of the Carter administration. Would this mean that education for employment, rehabilitation in prisons, improvement of health, mitigation of alcoholism, and Lord knows what else should go under welfare?

The New Look: Top-Light and Bottom-Heavy

Carter's strain toward simplicity has led him to advocate reorganization of the federal government. Leaving aside campaign rhetoric about 1,900 federal agencies (a sum that equates the tiny and trivial with the huge and important), reducing the number of agencies at the top of the hierarchy necessarily increases the number at the bottom. If there were only 10 big departments, each could have 190 subunits, and if there were 10 at each level, an issue would have to go through 19 bureaus before it was decided. The president might find this simpler because fewer people would be reporting directly to him. But he also might discover that finding out what is going on is more difficult. The existence of gigantic departments makes it difficult for anyone— Congress, secretaries, interest groups, citizens—to see inside. Conflicts between different departments about overlapping responsibilities, and conflicts revealing important differences are submerged under a single departmental view.

One of the few things that can be said about organization in general is the very thing President Carter denies—namely, that a considerable amount of redundancy (yes, overlap and duplication) must be built into any enterprise.[44] When we want to make sure an activity is accomplished, as in our lunar missions, we build in alternative mechanisms for doing the same thing so that one can take over when the other (or others) fail. Efficiency, the principle of least effort, must be coupled with reliability, the probability that a given act will be performed. A naive notion of efficiency, for example, would suggest that the elderly and the infirm be provided with either a visiting service or an office to which they can come or call. The more one wishes to assure that services to the elderly are actually delivered, however, the more one will invest in multiple methods. Of course, there must be a limit to redundancy; but if we ever actually succeeded in eliminating all overlap and duplication, most things would work only once, and some things not at all. It is ironic that in the public sector, administrative reforms often aim at monopoly or concentration of power, while reforms in the private sector often aim at competition or dispersion of power.[45] Our constitutional mechanisms for coping with abuse of power, the separation of powers, and checks and balances are, after all, forms of redundancy. The House and Senate and presidency overlap in jurisdiction and duplicate functions. That is why they quarrel and why we have been safe.

Carter's criteria cannot guide choice. Their proverbial character—look before you leap, but he who hesitates is lost—becomes apparent when they are paired with equally desirable criteria: the elimination of overlap and duplication detracts from reliability; predictability must go with adaptability; uniformity is worthy but so is recognition of individual differences. President Carter's criteria for decision making, we conclude, are individually contradictory and mutually incompatible.

Zero-Base Budgeting

The practical embodiment of Jimmy Carter's administrative theory is zero-base budgeting. Here, if anywhere, we can learn what it would mean for him to practice what he preaches. Imagine trying to decide whether to buy a tie or a kerchief. A simple task, one might think. Suppose, however, that organizational rules mandate comprehensiveness; we are required to alter our entire wardrobe as a unit. If everything must be rearranged when one item is altered, the probability is low that we will do anything. Being caught between revolution (change in everything) and resignation (change in nothing) has little to recommend it. Yet this is what a zero-base, start-from-scratch, comprehensive approach requires. If one could actually start from scratch each year, the only zero part of the budget would be its predictability, for zero-base budgeting is a-historical. The past, as reflected in the budgetary base (common expectations as to amounts and types of funding), is explicitly rejected. Everything at every period is subject to searching scrutiny. As a result, calculations become unmanageable. Figuring out how everything relates to everything else or, worse still, how other things would look if most things were changed, defeats every best effort. Consequently, attempts to apply intelligence to programs about which something can and needs to be done are defeated by mounds of paper. The trivial drowns out the important because if everything must be examined, nothing can receive special attention. What did Carter do?

According to the originator of zero-base budgeting, the Governor concentrated his time on "reviewing policy questions, major increases and decreases in existing programs, new programs and capital expenditure, and a few specific packages and rankings where there appeared to be problems."[46] In other words, he devoted his time and talent to increases and decreases from the previous year and a few problem areas, just as his predecessors had done.

How Well Did It Work in Georgia?

Interviews with participants in zero-base budgeting in Georgia (aside from showing that 85 percent thought no shifts in spending had been made and the other 15 percent thought shifts had occurred but were unable to recall any) reveal that, when fiscal conditions changed in 1974 and 1975, Carter asked for entirely new budget submissions.[47] Why? The departmental budget analysts in Georgia explained that their priority rankings changed under different funding levels. But the point is that a budgetary process must be able to accommodate change; if it has to be altered every time funding levels change, then zero-base budgeting is really a cover term for unknown and unspecified future procedures.

The main product of zero-base budgeting is, literally, a list of objectives. Rarely, however, do resources remain beyond the first few. The experience of the various federal commissions on national priorities, for instance, is that there is no point in listing 846 or even 79 national objectives, because almost all the money is gone after the first few are taken care of. If you allow us one or two national budget priorities—say Social Security supported entirely from general revenues—you can skip the others because there won't be anything left to support them. Carter knows this. But he would argue that zero-base budgeting requires agencies to supply alternatives. Unless agencies are rewarded for reducing the size of their programs, however, they will manipulate their priorities, placing politically sensitive and otherwise essential items at the bottom, so as to force superiors to increase their income. This might explain why Carter did not lower the zero-base cutoff point to include lower priority items when there was an increase in funds, or raise this point when there was a decrease in funds.[48]

On balance, the people who conducted the interviews feel that the zero-base system has benefited Georgia's administration because it increased information about, and participation in, the budgetary process. However, these increases might just as well have resulted from the introduction of *any* novel procedure that centers attention on the budget. The investigators also believe that as the participants gain more experience, shortcomings will be overcome. Perhaps; it is always possible to believe that more of the same will lead to improvement.

Measuring "Success" in the Carter Era

The overwhelming emphasis that President Carter places on procedural instruments could leave his administration vulnerable to massive displacement of goals; that is, it could result in having success defined, at least within his administration, by degree of governmental effort rather than by degree of social accomplishment. To use prisons as an example, the amount agencies spend, the number of new programs they initiate, and the uniformity of their procedures could replace increase in rehabilitation or reduction in crime as measures of success. That is how agencies succeed in making the variables they can control—*i.e.*, their own efforts and procedures—the criteria against which they are measured.

By putting the emphasis on agreement about objectives, as Carter does, critical problems of how to relate people and activities so that citizens get good results tend to be subsumed under generalities about the desirability of having objectives. If public agencies must have objectives, they prefer a greater rather than a lesser number, so that the consequences of their activities are likely to fit under one of them. Moreover, the objectives of public agencies tend to be multiple and conflicting because different people want different things. Consequently, the objective of limiting the costs of medical care can (and does) coexist with the opposing objective of increasing the quantity and quality of such care. Reconciling these differences is not made easier by telling bureaucrats that their strategic behavior—staking out multiple objectives so they can always claim they have achieved something—has become sanctified as a virtue.

Why, if our views have any credence, has Carter come to hold untenable beliefs about procedures for making policy? Perhaps they were inculcated at Annapolis; but one could just as well argue that he chose to go there because he wanted an instrumental approach to decision making. No doubt his father's influence was important ("My daddy . . . was a meticulous planner like me."),[49] but this could have become mere compulsiveness instead of a well-developed pattern of thought and work. No candidate since Herbert Hoover, the Great Engineer,[50] would have thought it important to talk to the public about so arcane a subject as zero-base budgeting, going so far as to include it in his five-minute television spots last year. Perhaps these views make sense to Carter under the circumstances within which he has operated in the years since he has become a public figure.

Let us remove the burden from Carter and place it where it belongs, on ourselves, by asking why a highly intelligent political executive might interpret his experiences so as to reinforce his belief in an instrumental-cum-technological view of public policymaking. Why, to us, does Carter seem to know worse rather than to know better?

At the outset we can dispose of the cynical view that Carter's ideas on procedures are purely political—that favoring efficiency, opposing the "bureaucratic mess" in Washington, promising more service at less cost are simply noncontroversial positions that project a useful image of a candidate as an effective manager.[51] Reorganization not only suggests rationality, it is also a useful cover for gaining control over positions and agencies that would increase the proposer's power (such as Carter's proposal that the president appoint the chairman of the Federal Reserve Board).[52] Coordination is often a synonym for coercion. To all this we reply, "Yes, but. . ." Yes, politicians are (and ought to be) political, but Carter pursues his procedural proposals above and beyond the call of duty or interest—and he acts on them. No one who has read his gubernatorial messages or observed the consistency and tenacity with which he personally pursued zero-base budgeting, reorganization, and all the rest can doubt his commitment. Carter cares and Carter acts. Why, then, does he persevere with unsuitable procedures for public policymaking?

Why Is Carter a Good Executive?

Carter knows himself well enough to believe that he would avoid many pitfalls of his procedures by applying himself to Washington's problems with energy, intelligence, and a demand for excellence.[53] We agree. In fact, we think it is these attributes—and not his procedural principles—that have brought him whatever success he has enjoyed as an executive. (Other life forms experience a phenomenon called "adverse selection," in which general success is mistakenly attributed to specific attributes that are then wrongly selected as worthy of propagation.)

Yet if Carter is mistaken in his procedural approach, as we think he is, he may be on solid ground in an area that we have not covered— the area of public confidence. He recognizes (and has emphasized) that citizens have a right to understand their government if they are being asked to support it; simplicity and predictability of governmental activity could help in achieving that support. If citizens are to regard government as fair and equitable, their perception that services uniformly treat like people alike might well give them that impression. Carter's concern for how government looks to the people might motivate him to prefer procedures to improve that appearance.

A concern for appearances as a prerequisite for obtaining support to undertake action apparently animates Carter's behavior in other areas as well. His three election campaigns (for the state legislature, for governor, and for president) may be fairly characterized, we believe, as socially conservative, whereas his actions in office have thus far been politically progressive. He takes care to identify himself with the social stance of the electorate so that citizens will feel he is one of them—even if all of them will not be able to agree with programs to distribute income or services in favor of the disadvantaged. As governor of Georgia, his need to keep close to the electorate limited his financial aspirations for state spending; he did not spend new monies for the rural poor, for the mentally handicapped, for prisoners, for those who had the least. After Watergate, no one should look down upon efforts to improve the appearance as well as the performance of government.

But what happens if appearance goes one way and performance the other? Suppose, in other words, that the demands of public policymaking are at odds with the appearance of order and neatness. Objectives are often multiple and conflicting; varied interest groups formulate and reformulate their goals and alliances; there is no single organizing principle good for all times and purposes, nor a single locus of authority in a federal political system. Symmetry, simplicity, uniformity—hence understandability and predictability—may not be achievable if we also want a welfare state and pluralistic policies. How much confusion and complexity is *built in* the things we want government to do and the ways a democratic society insists on doing them? The Carter administration will enable us to put this hypothesis to the test.

We are concerned that President Carter will pursue procedures regardless of their efficacy, and that he will regard opposition to his procedural prescriptions as, if not exactly the work of the devil, at least irrational, a product of ignorance and special interests, not subject to the usual rules of evidence. The comprehensive, scientific approach, which is supposed to work to promote harmony, has as a basic assumption the lack of conflict. If agreement does not result from openness, if seeming support for long-range goals breaks down under short-range pressures, will President Carter be able to tolerate the frustration?

His own recipe for controlling conflict is to make it boil over; comprehensive change, in his view, forces opposing interests into public debate where presidents can confront and overcome them. But how often can this be done? Agitating some of the interests some of the time is not the same as upsetting most of them most of the time. Interests are people, lots of people who depend on government, the very same people to whom Carter must appeal for support. If he can space his appeals out so that he is not fighting on every front at once, he may have a chance; but if he has to fight simultaneously on many fronts, he (and the nation with him) may be in for a difficult time.

"He-the-People"

If he does not get his way, President Carter has promised to go directly to the people. He wishes both to incorporate and transcend group interests. Incorporation works by including virtually all groups in the initial stages of policy formation. Through co-optation, he hopes to commit them to support his programs (or at least not to oppose them vigorously). Transcendence works by investing hierarchy with morality. In order to reflect the people's will, the best way to organize government is to make it democratic at the bottom and centralized at the top.[54] The president, then, as chief hierarch and ultimate definer of the public interest, leaps over group interests through direct contact with the populace. President Carter would rather interpret the inchoate desires of the mass of people than bargain over who gets what the government offers. Nor will he content himself with being the mediator of contending interests, merely keeping the score and announcing the winners. Group interests breed divisiveness, while the public interest breeds unity. Instead, "he-the-people" will interpret their victory.

President Carter's theory of governing suggests opportunities for leadership, but also obstacles to success. To reorganize the executive branch, he will have to overcome the clienteles it serves and the representatives they elect. To put through major reforms, he will need financial support from a Congress accustomed to making its own budget. Should his initiatives falter, private interests may appear to have triumphed over the public interest. According to his own philosophy, he will be compelled to appeal to the people to protect his programs. But in the end, even the people may prove ungrateful; for if they fail the president, it will appear that they have given in to their private interests instead of standing up for their public duties.

The most worrisome aspect of Jimmy Carter's theory of public policymaking is his assumption that discussion will lead to agreement on long-term objectives, which will assure support for present programs. Carter's views on conflict could survive only if past objectives determined future administration. This view of policy politics is untenable because the price of agreement is likely to be vagueness and because administration involves altering ends by changing means. When specific acts require a choice between how much inflation versus how much employment, or how much preservation of natural resources versus how much consumption, it becomes evident that agreement in general need not mean (and has often not meant) agreement in particular. Since conditions change, the agreements that Carter negotiates in time of plenty may have to be renegotiated in times of austerity. Administration of programs would be of little interest if it did not involve continuous redefinition of objectives.

Jimmy Carter as President

What, then, is Jimmy Carter likely to do as president? Contingency may overwhelm concern. Another huge oil price increase, a resurgence of inflation, or a military involvement may do more to shape what a president will do than his own initial ideas worked out under much different circumstances. Personality may prevail over policy. From listening to his policy pronouncements, who would have predicted Franklin D. Roosevelt's eagerness to abandon the deflationary, low-spending policies he advocated during his first presidential campaign? Confronted with crises, policies frequently pass away, but long-learned modes of problem solving often remain. FDR's administration was characterized by eclecticism. He had a willingness to try and a readiness to abandon programs, an incorrigible optimism as well as a love of conflict, even when (or precisely because) it led to contradictions that gave him room to maneuver. These operative administrative theories proved more permanent indicators of his behavior than his past policies. So, too, we think, Jimmy Carter's theory of governing will better indicate his behavior in office than what he says about substantive issues.

Like most Americans, we voted for Carter and worried about him at the same time. Contrary to our fears, there is evidence that Carter can (and does) learn from experience. On busing, for example (we are not passing judgment on the correctness of his stand but rather on his way of thinking about the problem), Carter realized that wealthy parents often avoid the policy by sending their children to private schools or by moving their family out of the area. Despite good intentions, it is mostly the black children who get bused and pay the price. The policy did not achieve the immediate objective of school integration or the more distant objective of better school performance. Carter's proposal has been to substitute a voluntary program for the mandatory one. He places emphasis upon changing the school system from within by getting black persons in administrative and teaching jobs.[55]

Another area in which his policy indicates a positive response to past unsuccessful attempts is his handling of racial and civil disturbances. As governor of Georgia, he discovered that the normal, massive presence of state troopers during civil disorders not only served to aggravate the situation but used up enormous police resources. So he set up biracial community civil-disorder units composed of three persons dressed in civilian clothes. After the disorder, the units were replaced by permanent local committees.[56] When Carter tried to influence the choice of legislative leaders in Georgia, he learned that this caused more trouble than it was worth and vowed not to do it with Congress. Many more examples exist. The question is whether Carter will apply the same standards to procedures, including procedures for handling conflict, as he does to policies.

Read this as a cautionary tale for President Carter and his supporters. There is, after all, no reason to believe that former President Ford followed better procedures or even that he paid much attention to procedures at all. Because Carter is explicit about his own philosophy, because he cares about procedures, we have been able to be critical. But people who care are also more likely to perform. If they care too much, however, they might substitute rigidity for right action. Having been forewarned, perhaps Carter will be forewarned to search for weaknesses in his strengths.

Notes

1. "Jimmy Carter Presidential Campaign Issues Reference Book," July 24, 1976. Cited hereafter as "Issues Reference Book."
2. "Issues: Clearer and More Detailed," *National Journal Reports,* July 24, 1976, 1028.
3. "Head-to-Head on the Issues," *U.S. News & World Report,* September 13, 1976, 21.
4. "Issues Reference Book," 20.
5. "Issues Reference Book," 13.
6. "Interview on the Issues—What Carter Believes, "*U.S. News & World Report*, May 24, 1976, 19; and "Issues Reference Book," 30.
7. "Issues Reference Book," 13.
8. Jimmy Carter, *Why Not the Best?* (Nashville: Broadman Press, 1975), 147.
9. "Jimmy Carter: Not Just Peanuts," *Time*, March 8, 1976, 19.
10. Stated by Stuart Eisenstat, Carter's policy adviser, in *National Journal Reports*, July 24, 1976, 1029.
11. *New York Times*, April 2, 1976 and *U.S. News & World Report*, May 24, 1976, 19.
12. "The View from the Top of the Carter Campaign," *National Journal Reports*, July 17, 1976, 1002.
13. *U.S. News & World Report,* May 24, 1976, 23; and James P. Gannon,

"The Activist: Carter, Despite Image of Outsider Favors Do-More Government," *Wall Street Journal*, April 2, 1976.

14. "What Carter Would Do as President," *U.S. News & World Report*, July 26, 1976, 18.
15. "Issues Reference Book," 20.
16. *U.S. News & World Report*, May 24, 1976, 23; and July 26, 1976, 18.
17. *U.S. News & World Report*, May 24, 1976, 18.
18. "Jimmy Carter on Economics: Populist Georgia Style," *Business Week*, May 3, 1976, 66.
19. "Excerpts from an Interview with Jimmy Carter," *New York Times*, March 31, 1976.
20. "Issues Reference Book," 15.
21. "Carter: Seeking Clearer Goals," *Time*, May 10, 1976, 24.
22. *U.S. News & World Report*, May 24, 1976, 19.
23. *National Journal Reports*, July 17, 1976, 997.
24. Excerpts from the interview with Carter on his concepts in foreign policy," *New York Times*, July 7, 1976.
25. "Carter Says Ford Fails to Check Nation's 'Drift.'" *New York Times*, August 18, 1976.
26. Carter, *Why Not the Best?*, 114.
27. Jimmy Carter, National Press Club, Announcement Speech for Democratic Presidential Nomination, December 12, 1974.
28. "Issues Reference Book," 14; and Albert R. Hunt, "Carter and Business," *Wall Street Journal*, August 12, 1976, 15.
29. *U.S. News & World Report*, September 13, 1976, 20.
30. "Carter Tells Film Stars about Poverty in the South," *New York Times*, August 24, 1976.
31. *National Journal Reports*, July 17, 1976, 998.
32. Ibid., 999.
33. "State Structural Reforms," *National Journal Reports*, April 5, 1975, 506.
34. *National Journal Reports*, July 17, 1976, 999.
35. *U.S. News & World Report*, September 13, 1976, 21.
36. *Wall Street Journal*, April 2, 1976, 23.
37. Eleanor Randolf, "Carter Hits 'Lone Ranger' Foreign Policy of Kissinger," *Chicago Tribune*, June 24, 1976.
38. Carter announcement speech, December 12, 1974.
39. *National Journal Reports*, April 5, 1975, 506.
40. *U.S. News & World Report*, July 26, 1976, 18.
41. "Where Jimmy Carter Stands on Foreign Policy," *Chicago Tribune*, May 8, 1976.

42. "Excerpts from an Interview with Jimmy Carter," *New York Times*, March 31, 1976.

43. This principle has had a long history, having been proposed in 1911 by the President's Commission on Economy and Efficiency: "Only by grouping services according to their character can substantial progress be made in eliminating duplication." Quoted in Peri E. Arnold, "Executive Reorganization and the Origins of the Managerial Presidency," *Polity*, vol. 13, no. 4 (Summer 1981), 568–99.

44. Martin Landau, "Redundancy, Rationality, and the Problem of Duplication and Overlap," *Public Administration Review*, 29, no. 4, (July/August 1969): 346–58.

45. Lewis Dexter has emphasized that modern Western society has followed the route of competition, not monopoly, as a means to clarify issues and procedures. He cites the example that U.S. antitrust laws are "deliberately designed to impose redundancy and duplication on industry." See Lewis Anthony Dexter, "The Advantages of Some Duplication and Ambiguity in Senate Committee Jurisdictions," Temporary Select Committee of United States Senate on Committee Jurisdiction, September 1976.

46. Peter Phyrr, *Zero-Base Budgeting: A Practical Management Tool for Evaluating Expenses* (New York: Wiley, 1973), 97. Quoted in Aaron Wildavsky, *Budgeting: A Comparative Theory of Budgetary Processes* (Boston: Little; Brown, 1975), 295.

47. George S. Nimier and Roger H. Hermanson, "A Look at Zero-Base Budgeting—The Georgia Experience," *Atlanta Economic Review* (July/August 1976): 5–12. In 1974 there was an increase in available funds, and in 1975 a decrease.

48. Ibid.

49. Quoted in Bruce Mazlish and Edwin Diamond, "Thrice Born: A Psychohistory of Jimmy Carter's Rebirth," *New York*, Vol. 9, no. 35, August 30, 1976, 32.

50. Hoover was an unrelenting champion of organization by "major purpose under single-headed responsibility" as a means for making agencies easier to manage and more efficient. See Peri E. Arnold, "Executive Reorganization." Securing broad reorganization authority subject to Congressional veto is also the approach Carter took in Georgia and hopes to repeat in Washington. See *U.S. News and World Report*, July 26, 1976, 17.

51. Although Carter, like any good engineer, knows it is not possible to maximize simultaneously on more than one dimension, his language sometimes suggests the opposite: "I assure you that my primary concern will be providing the maximum amount of services for the least cost." State of Georgia, Governor's Reorganization Message, March 1, 1971.

52. The Reorganization Act in Georgia, for instance, removed an entire administrative level, leaving those positions open to appointment by the governor. See T. M. Simpson III, "Georgia State Administration: Jimmy Carter's Contribution," paper delivered at the annual meeting of the Southern Political Science Association, Atlanta, Georgia, November 1–3, 1973.

53. Carter's qualities as an executive are evoked in the instructions he gave to members of the study group involved in making recommendations for reorganization in Georgia: "Studies of this nature are a full-time job. You cannot drop by to chat with a department head for a few minutes and then go back and write a report. If that were all that is required, I would do the study myself during the next two months. Somebody has to get out in the field and find out what is really happening and why. That is not a part-time job; it means spending eight hours a day working with the state employees and another four or five hours that night analyzing what was learned. It means writing and rewriting the report so that each point is clearly and concisely stated, backed by adequate detail, able to stand up to any question and practical for implementation." State of Georgia, Governor's Reorganization Message, March 1, 1971.

54. In New York City, Mayor John Lindsay "rationalized" the city administration by consolidating and eliminating all intermediate structures, thus forming the "Office of Collective Bargaining." It soon became the sole target of public-employee union demands, thereby greatly strengthening the union's position. In Jack Douglas's apt description, the rationalization "swept away all the hedgerows behind which he [Lindsay] could have hidden." See Jack D. Douglas, "Urban Politics and Public Employee Unions," in *Public Employee Unions: A Study of the Crisis in Public Sector Labor Relations,* Institute for Contemporary Studies, San Francisco, 1976, 103.

55. "Issues Reference Book," 21.

56. Ibid.

12

Reagan as a Political Strategist

Until the 1980s not a single postwar president redirected both domestic and foreign policy while gaining reelection and keeping his party united. Harry Truman established the post-World War II pattern of American internationalism that continues to this day. But he did not get very far with his domestic agenda. Dwight Eisenhower was a maintainer, not an innovator; he brought the Republican party into the postwar consensus—internationalism abroad, acceptance of welfare programs at home—while maintaining domestic tranquility. Alas, what John Kennedy would have achieved must remain a matter of speculation. Lyndon Johnson significantly altered American domestic policy toward a greater role for government, while his policy toward Vietnam split the nation. Richard Nixon's presidency, before it was stopped short by Watergate, was noteworthy for the establishment of a new relationship with China. By all accounts, Gerald Ford ran his part of the government well, but failed the test of reelection. Although frustrated in his overtures toward the Soviet Union and damaged by stagflation, Jimmy Carter can count a variety of small but worthy accomplishments.

Ronald Reagan has accomplished all of the above. Despite continuous efforts to belie his achievements, Reagan remains the most creative president of recent times and, with Franklin Roosevelt, one of the two most influential of the modern era.

When I speak of politicians as strategists, I mean (1) that they have

This chapter combines "President Reagan as a Political Strategist," from *Elections in America,* ed. Kay Lehman Schlozman (Boston: Allen & Unwin, 1987), 221–38; and "The Triumph of Ronald Reagan" from *The National Interest,* no. 13 (Winter 1988/89): 3–9.

a vision, a broad sense of direction toward which they wish the nation to move; and (2) that they use effective and creative (nonobvious) means in pursuing these ends. Nothing is implied about the desirability of the directions chosen, for then politicians could be strategists only by being in accord with the preferences of the analyst. But I do mean to rule out nondemocratic means and ends, for one of the major tasks of a strategist is to work by persuasion rather than coercion. The more a politician alters prevailing policies and expectations concerning behavior while moving events in the desired direction, that movement and direction being compatible with democratic norms, the better the strategist.

There is a difference between being fact smart and being strategy smart. Jimmy Carter was fact smart. Unfortunately for him,[1] but fortunately for Ronald Reagan, the presidency does not depend on memory for facts. The short-answer theory of the presidency—that president is best who would score highest on a short-answer test—leaves a lot to be desired.

President Reagan's disinterest in, and misstatement of, facts about many aspects of public policy have led some observers to characterize him as dumb.[2] His flouting of the conventional wisdom on such issues as deficits has led others to dismiss him as obtuse. The fact that he keeps besting them deeply discomforts his policy opponents. Even then, they seek explanations outside of Ronald Reagan's strategic abilities. They denigrate the public, to whose low mentality the boob in the White House appeals. Or they upgrade his communication skills, damning with faint praise by suggesting he possesses some ineffable essence that exudes persuasiveness. Amiability as a substitute for understanding is the farthest his critics will go in allotting their limited supply of credit. The thesis of this chapter, by contrast, is that President Reagan is a superb political strategist.

Before Reagan, everyone acted as if it were necessary to reduce spending before cutting taxes. By shattering this conventional wisdom with two interconnected master strokes—across-the-board tax cuts followed by tax reform—Reagan has done more for capitalism than any president since FDR, possibly since Grover Cleveland. Instead of the then-prevailing capital formation approach, which led business to compete with liberals for tax preferences, thereby delegitimizing the tax system, he chose to level the playing field, relying on competition rather than subsidy. Republicans have thus become much more of a free-enterprise party. For their part, Democrats have been compelled to give up two of the great instruments of government intervention—debt and preferences—leaving them only with regulations to impose costs on the private sector. Nor will it be easy for future Democratic administrations to rely on regulation in the face of severe foreign competition.

Getting the Democrats to Support Republican Issues

The extraordinary character of the 1984 presidential campaign provides ample evidence of the profound effect that Ronald Reagan has had on national political debate. His steadfast support of across-the-board tax cuts in the face of immense pressure from established opinion led his Democratic party opponent, Walter Mondale, to make the achievement of a balanced budget into a positive moral virtue. Thus a Republican issue that, given its diffuse nature, never served that party well, became the mainstay of Democratic speeches and advertisements. At one stroke the Democratic party denied its traditional (and mostly successful) recourse to spending to create employment; it also obligated itself to keep the revenues it could raise from new taxes to reduce the deficit. The presidential campaign reduced the Democratic party issue—fairness—to a price tag of $30 billion, the additional sums Mondale would have spent on social welfare. If this 3 percent of total spending was all fairness amounted to, the remaining 97 percent was thereby blessed as "fair." Even if he had lost the election, Ronald Reagan would have won the battle over future domestic policy.

If Mondale was so smart and Reagan so dumb, why did the Democrats campaign on Republican issues? Surely the sanctity of the Constitution—due to President Reagan's support of constitutional amendments on budget limits, abortion, and prayer—and budget balance are not the issues the party of government intervention would choose to present itself. Virtually nothing was heard from the Democratic party about social welfare. Hardly a peep sounded in regard to a massive jobs program. That undoubtedly was the president's fault, for he shifted the entire debate in an economically conservative direction.

Domestic Policy Leadership

Denigration of the president has led Democrats to underestimate his policy guidance. For Ronald Reagan has integrated public policy with political support so as to provide creative policy leadership.

Reagan is the first president since Herbert Hoover (although, considering his activist temperament, Calvin Coolidge might be better) to favor limited government at home. Pursuing his aim of restricting the reach and reducing the resources available to the federal government, Reagan helped cut income taxes across the board dramatically, reducing the highest bracket from 70 to under 35 percent. His acceptance of historically high deficits, in an effort to use resource scarcity to depress domestic spending still further, is eloquent testimony to his single-minded devotion to decreasing the size of the domestic government compared to the size of the economy.

Rumor has it that the president is so dumb that he cannot understand complex tax questions. Presumably that is why we hear little or nothing about raising taxes but a great deal about cutting spending. Shaping the congressional agenda so that the major debate is whether defense or domestic programs should be cut the most, even though this is not entirely to the president's liking, represents a substantial strategic success.

Ronald Reagan has succeeded in coordinating domestic policy. Every official in Washington is aware of what the president wants: less. When there are conflicts, the goal of reducing the size of government wins out.

Even when the president's ostensible aim is not achieved, his adherence to priorities provides a sense of direction. Reagan's initiative on restructuring the federal system, for instance, failed for a number of reasons, including his unwillingness to come up with the cash to cover the transition. Nevertheless, the budget cuts have had a similar effect. For, as Richard Nathan's studies of the responses show, a number of state governments have elected to fill in the spending gap.[3] Perforce, state governments are exercising greater responsibility.

Emphasis on individual policies underestimates the accomplishments of the first Reagan administration. There may, for instance, be less deregulation than you or I or, indeed, the president would wish. Consideration of such matters, important as they are, however, does not begin to exhaust the moral influence of the president's devotion to more limited government. For there is an extensive and persuasive (yet unrecorded) influence on individual behavior that weans people from dependence on government. My favorite overheard conversation, in Berkeley no less, goes like this: "It would be a great idea to do such and such. Wonderful. Let's get a government grant. Yeah. Oh, well, with Reagan around that's impossible. Do you suppose we could sell the service and do this ourselves?" Although the uncoordinated efforts of millions of people moving to take care of themselves are not heard at a single time and place (so they are not recorded as events), they add up to a transformation of expectations, and, therefore, of practice in a self-reliant direction.

The sheer strategic brilliance of getting the opposing candidate to adopt your major theme of limited government through a born-again commitment to budget balance, while using the current imbalance as the only effective ceiling on spending the nation has known for a half century, has blinded Democrats to the policy genius of Ronald Reagan. He may not be that great a communicator, since Democrats have missed how badly he has outmaneuvered them, but he has provided both policy leadership and a political strategy to go with t.

The Do-Good Game

Democrats believe in using other people's money to support causes they deem desirable. "Doing good" requires at least a modest increment of resources over the prior year; this way, almost everyone gets a little and a few receive a lot. "Tax and spend," as the slogan went, adding only "elect and elect," was in truth their motto. Ronald Reagan has changed all that. It is not so much that he led the drive for tax cuts (although he did) but that he prevented the substantial tax increases necessary to play the do-good game—you support my good cause and I'll support yours, as long as no one has to take less.

What about the deficit? It is true that the deficit has replaced the butler as the universal fall guy, responsible for whatever ails us. Evidence and logic are harder to come by. Insofar as the deficit keeps the size of spending lower than it otherwise would have been, a reasonable case can be made that it is better for the economy than the alternative. We could, to be sure, bring about a depression in order to avoid a deficit, through cold-turkey budget balance, a project not much more convincing than bombing villages in order to save them.

Before Reagan, the federal government's tax take was approximately 19 percent of gross national product. Now it is just about the same. How can this be, with big marginal cuts in income tax rates? The built-in tax increases passed on by earlier governments—Social

Security above all, but also bracket creep and "windfall" energy taxes—have kept the overall federal tax rate constant. Had nothing changed, the tax take would have risen to about 23 percent, the 4 percent difference making up most of the entire deficit. It could be argued, to be sure, that Democrats could not have gotten away with such a substantial increase in the tax take, but I believe that without a visible increase in the income tax, they would have done (or, more precisely, failed to undo) exactly that. The crucial clue here is the dog that didn't bark; the missing factor for the Democrats is the tax increases that would have gone into effect automatically, which they did not get to spend.

President Reagan has appropriated tax cuts (his good cause) that would otherwise have been available to Democrats for their favorite causes. With one blow, the president wiped out a decade of incremental increases in spending the Democrats would have used to smooth their way. These "it might have beens" are the saddest words as far as the mainline, liberal, left-of-center Democrats (the bulk of the party activists) are concerned.

Look at the deficit as a political strategy. Democrats need to justify a modest deficit either as a fiscal stimulant or as a response to pressing social problems. In the past, Republicans simply rejected deficits, proposing lower spending and higher taxes to fill the gap. To the extent that they follow Reagan's strategy, however, Republicans now prefer to keep marginal tax rates low, and hence economic incentives strong. They follow their president in arguing that if taxes are increased, "they [the liberals] will only spend it." Every time it looks like the Democrats might lower the deficit sufficiently to do good as they see it, Reaganite Republicans will counter with tax cuts so that taxpayers can do good as they see it. Indeed, instead of knee-jerk budget balancing, the Republican party of the future may view a declining deficit as an invitation to cut taxes still further.

Indeed, *if* (it is a big supposition) Ronald Reagan's successor is a Republican who continues to starve liberal Democrats of revenue, the Democratic party may well self-destruct. The reason Democrats have so little to say (observe the vigor of conservative versus liberal publications) is that they literally do not have the money to say it with. Allow them their spending increments and, *voila!* they would have plenty to talk about. In short, it is not a nonexistent decline in intellectual capacities but the lack of food for thought—namely, the money to spend on good causes—that makes modern Democrats appear dumb. Obviously, Reagan's successor, Republican George Bush, is not a Reaganite. (We need look no further than the trouble the Republicans during Bush's presidency have had over abortion, to notice the difference.)

Keeping the Party Together

Ronald Reagan enjoys unparalleled supremacy within the Republican party because he is a perfect exemplar of its two main tendencies: social conservatism and what used to be called economic liberalism (i.e., reliance on free markets). To retain this position he must lend support to both wings of his party. But not, I hasten to add, at the same time. For if the two wings have to decide whether government should restrict individual choice, they would soon be at each other's collective throats. So far the president has managed to sidestep this conflict. One way has been to separate the two wings in time. Social issues have been stressed at election time and economic issues in between. Another way has been to separate the combatants in space. This separation may be accomplished through local option or by shifting the arena via proposals for constitutional amendments. Had the president not papered over the potential cracks in his party coalition, there would not then have been talk about the possibility of party realignment.

The election policy equation (as suggested by Alex Mintz) may be written as

$$revenue + deficit = defense + domestic\ expenditure$$

The candidates filled in the policy equation in assymetrical ways:

	revenue	deficit		defense	domestic expenditure
Mondale	+	−	=	−	+
Reagan	−	−	=	+	−

In the past, as the party of responsible finance, Republicans would try to cut spending and deficits; generally they were successful at neither. Under Reagan they have abandoned the tasks at which they failed in the past, in favor of others that are easier to accomplish.

Because the president has set booby traps for them, Democrats will have to propose straight, out-and-out tax increases. The first "trap" was the passage of tax indexing, which, until now, has resulted in higher revenues without higher tax rates as inflation pushed taxpayers into higher brackets. The second trap is in the flat (more accurately, a broad-based, low-rate income) tax. Of course, if rates are to be lowered, tax preferences must be reduced. The point is that with far fewer preferences, each increase in tax rates will be far more visible. After all, since the promise of tax reform is to reduce rates, it will be even more difficult than in the past to raise them. Given that rates cannot be raised, moreover, the only way to increase revenues is by cutting preferences. By joining preference cuts to rate cuts, the tax reform limits the reduction of preferences as a revenue-raising technique. Thus Ronald Reagan has deprived Democrats of their previously most-potent instruments of public policy. Democrats, therefore, will have to make the argument implicit in their party's preferences: Higher progressive taxes are necessary in order to support social programs. Since most of the people have most of the money, tax increases will have to cover the broad middle masses. That, as Republicans have discovered, is not necessarily the most popular path. As long as Republicans stick to the Reagan path of cutting taxes across the board, moreover, they will keep the question as whether to tax and not who (rich or poor or middle) to tax.

The President as Intervenor of Last Resort

Ronald Reagan has not only altered trends in public policy, he has also transformed the role of president. Indeed, his alteration of the presidential role may be Reagan's most significant contribution. Until Reagan's time, it had been assumed that the breadth of presidential decision making would expand with the scope of government. The invention of presidential machinery to reach into other institutions (congressional liaison; mass media; officials for contact with mayors, governors, and racial, ethnic, and religious groups) had resulted in making the concerns of external institutions part of those in the White House. But Reagan has changed roles and confounded expectations by reinterpreting leadership not to mean what it meant before. Instead of the presidency being the institution of "first resort," stepping in to solve problems—real and alleged—as soon as (perhaps sooner than) they manifested themselves, in Reagan's time the presidency has become the institution of "last resort," entering the fray only when others abdicated. And not always then.

There are, of course, other things the president would like than smaller domestic government, but these are secondary, not primary. Thus the president is not nearly as conflicted about the use of his personal resources because his priorities are clear. The contrast with the mobilization regime of President Kennedy or the restless opportunism of President Nixon or the harmonization of government actors under President Ford or the managerial style of President Carter, all of whom had long lists of priorities even if they altered them frequently, could hardly be greater. It may be that steering in a single important direction, so as to get part of the way, will become more attractive than steering in different (Richard Nixon) or too many (John Kennedy or Jimmy Carter) directions or just emphasizing implementation (Gerald Ford) of existing programs.

Among the many criticisms raised about President Reagan, there is one especially relevant to him as a strategist: He is allegedly run by his staff. My observations are different. From his days as governor of California onward, Ronald Reagan, following his own understanding of how he might best use his talents, has deliberately structured his staff so that he would (a) make the critical choices and (b) save his time.

There is evidence on Reagan's use of staff. In a book that can be described either as generally critical (because of the president's lapses) or disparagingly admiring (because of his undoubted successes), Laurence Barrett reveals that the president is quite capable of reining in his staff. Here, for instance, is an adviser who reported that the president not only rejected advice that three large tax reductions in a row might be too much, but insisted that his preferences be respected.

> You look at all the stories being published about backing and filling and they give the impression that Reagan wag changing back and forth. That's wrong. The people around him were changing, or some of us were. We were having doubts, and the news coverage reflected that. Reagan hardly moved at all. At one meeting Reagan got a little impatient with us. He said, "Listen, you guys are talking to each other and no one is asking me what I think. I'm sticking with it."[4]

It deserves to be emphasized that the president resisted not merely advice from his own staff, including an ever-insistent David Stockman, but also from most of the nation's vocal economists and business spokesmen. Without these cuts, I might add, there would have been no distinctiveness to the president's program and no real reason for electing him rather than any other person.

I am reminded of the insightful discussion of the pluses and minuses of removing a subordinate, which takes place in James Gould Cozzens's fine novel (set in the air force), *Guard of Honor*. The man has many shortcomings, but these are known. His associates have learned how to take them into account. A new man might well be more talented, but his hidden defects would, for a time, remain unknown, and his colleagues would have to invest time and effort in discovering them.

In exactly this sense, President Reagan has an investment in his staff. His reluctance to fire is based on his investment in them, as well as a realization that everyone makes mistakes. When they arranged among themselves to swap places, James Baker going to the Treasury and Donald Regan to the White House, the president swiftly ratified their choice. Is this passive behavior? Or is this a wise realization that weeks of search were unlikely to provide a chief of staff who was necessarily better and about whom he would certainly have known a good deal less?

Has the Iran-Contra affair, widely portrayed as the result of a passive, disengaged president, altered my judgment of Reagan as an active president?[5]

President Reagan was not misled by his advisers. He is the politician; he is the one, above all others, who should have anticipated the near-universal revulsion to sending arms to Iran. "Iranamok" is an act of commission by a president who was continually interested in what was happening and asked far more questions about the hostage situation than might have been expected. It was not that the policy was good but its execution flawed, as the President said, but that using arms shipments to penetrate Iran was a bad idea from the beginning. Bad policy makes bad politics; indeed, bad politics is part of bad policy. Being critical makes it all the more important to criticize presidential behavior for the right reasons.

President Reagan's fall from grace is not a result of inattention but of overreaction. My guess is that with two years to go, he tried too hard to control events. The Danilov affair (where the planes carrying the American reporter out of Russia and a Soviet spy out of the United States nearly passed each other) cost Reagan dearly in credibility when he denied there was a swap.

To the end, the administration did not recognize the loss of public confidence it suffered during the Danilov affair when, even as the American reporter and the Soviet spy virtually passed each other in the air, top U.S. officials insisted there was no swap. The saddest part is that there was no need to do anything. Nothing. Out of pique, the Soviets had stumbled into a losing game. With an American reporter in jail on flimsy (really nonexistent) charges, no matter what the reporter confessed to under duress, Gorbachev could not have conducted his "I am a reasonable man" campaign in Europe. The Soviets had to cough up the American in their own interest, sooner rather than later. Our president should not have been involved in such a low-level matter, nor our secretary of state. After all, as capitalists, we are not supposed to pay for what other people must give us for nothing, and the Soviets would have had to release the American reporter in order to continue their "peace offensive" in Europe.

And what better illustration of the unfortunate consequences of precipitousness than the conversion of the move toward Iran into an arms deal. Had the administration waited a year, it could have utilized the imbroglio in the Persian Gulf to develop a different Iranian policy. The president's real fault in this episode was his inability to anticipate the reaction of his own people. And so he suffered. The escort service in the Persian Gulf must stand as the least cost-effective policy in recent history.

Even Central American policy, which is an issue of presidential stature, suffered from overeagerness. Was it necessary for the president to show he could reach a bipartisan accord on Nicaragua, only to be outflanked by the five-nation agreement, so that he had to spend more time reassuring his supporters than he did in negotiating with the Speaker? What these and similar events have in common with the Iran-Contra affair is that they were unnecessary.

Anyone who doubts that President Reagan has suffered from premature policymaking should try a little mental experiment: had the president (as his critics charged) gone to sleep on these matters after the 1986 midterm elections, he would have been the most popular second-term president in recent history. Alas, the old, perhaps even more than the young, are in danger of becoming victims of their own impatience.

Fusing Personal Style and Policy Preferences

Changes in the role of the presidency and in the expectations surrounding it help explain one of the mysteries about President Reagan's
public standing. Following upon a series of discredited or unpopular
presidencies (how they will look in retrospect is another matter), President Reagan is seemingly immune to the vicissitudes of fortune. He
makes errors of fact with apparent impunity. Failing policies (e.g.,
Lebanon) leave him outwardly untouched. Even the Iran-Contra affair
has not prevented him from leading, as his arms-control agreement
shows. The pall that hung over Nixon's or Carter's last year stub-
bornly refuses, despite what critics consider substantial provocation,
to settle on him. Why?

Attention has been focused on the president's personal constitution
(a charm that makes him difficult to hate) rather than on the changes
he has wrought in the institutional constitution. Although Reagan reads
a prepared speech well, one would have thought the first presidential
debate of 1984 and numerous press conferences, with their hesitations
and misstatements, disposed of him as a "great communicator." The
emphasis on this inexplicable skill, however, does obscure the need to
talk about the substance of what he does and how he does it, that is,
his strategic capacity.

I think personality and role work together; indeed, the fit is so close
(limited government propounded by a man who likes to work limited
hours) that it has deflected attention from the radical change in practices. A president such as Jimmy Carter, who expects to have enacted
a series of substantial changes in policy based on his personal study of
them, naturally reinforces expectations that he will do as advertised.
A president who preaches self-reliance to the citizenry does not have
to work as hard or know as much about public policies the government should not have, or to provide help for people who should look
after themselves. Role and responsibility are related.

Presidents not only make policies, policies make presidents. Ronald
Reagan has arisen as a political force in response to policies promul-
gated by the Democratic party. His strategic creativity (apart from
appropriating Democratic symbols such as Franklin Roosevelt and
Harry Truman) lies in crafting responses to take advantage of Democratic weaknesses.

When the Federalists struggled with the Antifederalists over whether the Constitution would replace the Articles of Confederation, Alexander Hamilton and James Madison turned the tide of opinion by reversing the direction of the political argument. Localism, which had been seen as the source of Republican virtue, became parochialism, a source of special interests. The national government, then regarded as corrupting public virtue by introducing artificial inequality into public life, became the source of disinterested wisdom. Whether or not Ronald Reagan has realigned the electorate, he has reversed the arguments by which political action is justified; he has succeeded in taking the tag of "special interests" away from "the plutocrats" and pinning it onto the Democrats.

An intuitive understanding of the variety of views in American political life, and how to transcend them, is a rare gift. In one area, at least—tax reform—I think Ronald Reagan has this gift. Since it would be out of place here to give my reasons for believing that the heart of American exceptionalism lies in the belief that liberty and equality are (or can be made to be) compatible,[6] let us just take this for an assumption. The recent history of tax reform, meaning essentially a broader-based income tax with fewer and smaller tax preferences, is full of ups and downs. After Ronald Reagan made it a major feature of his second term (not that others, like Senator Bill Bradley [D-N.J.] and Representative Richard Gephardt [D-Mo.], had not pushed the idea to little avail before), he worked hard to make it popular, but with mixed success. Every time the president and tax reform were counted out, however, he and it have bounced back. Why?

The three major American political cultures—individualism, egalitarianism, and hierarchy—are rendered compatible in one piece of legislation. People of low income pay either no taxes or lower taxes. Some businesses pay more but the individuals in them pay much lower marginal rates, and the reduction of tax preferences is promoted as increasing incentives. All the while, higher deductions for children reduce somewhat the cost of larger families. Observe that the president defends the reform on the grounds it is fair, will spur economic incentives, and is good for the family. These terms are contemporary code words for greater equality of condition (fairness), greater equality of opportunity (incentives), and greater hierarchical order (the family). Obviously, Reagan saw something in this issue others did not see.

The fact that such a radical change passed, whereas it had previously been considered near hopeless or even utopian, speaks to the president's willingness to go out on a limb for an apparent loser that he felt would eventually gain support. And the fact that tax reform makes it difficult to raise income tax rates in the near future, thereby holding down spending, will not, from Reagan's point of view, hurt either.

No leader is perfect, and Ronald Reagan is no exception. Anyone can think of problems that remain unresolved. The decisive movement of blacks into the Democratic party, for instance, is not only bad for democracy, it is also a barrier to the potential emergence of a Republican majority able to capture the presidency as well as both houses of Congress. Should Mexican Americans also become overwhelmingly Democrat, the Republicans might forever remain a minority party. It may be that there is an undercurrent of Republican support among blacks and Mexican Americans based on individualism and family values. If so, not enough has been done to make manifest the administration's identification with these people, even if it cannot accede to those among them who view larger government as the main solution to existing problems.

By showing that the presidency can still be a powerful office, Ronald Reagan may have strengthened more than his own office. In a poll of academics who specialize in the presidency, the *National Journal* noted that these observers gave Reagan credit for "his success in . . . reviving trust and confidence in an institution that in the post-Vietnam era had been perceived as being unworkable."[7] As Seymour Lipset points out, "It is ironic that the President's successes . . . have greatly increased faith in governmental institutions, while they have done little to reduce the high level of distrust of private power."[8] Irony, like unanticipated consequences, is the stuff of life. Strategic success may be a double-edged accomplishment.

But I think not. The president's vision is made up of social conservatism as well as economic liberalism (i.e., limited government). He believes in institutions, and he believes they should be effective in doing the jobs his political philosophy deems appropriate for them.

Foreign Policy

In regard to foreign and defense policy, the president initially provided only partial leadership. He wants more for defense, but more for *what* remains unclear. Instead of being guided by a single, overarching framework, he is faced with innumerable smaller decisions that, like Lebanon, often turn out badly. Instead of managing internal conflict, as he does domestically because he knows what he wants, the president lacks a doctrine from which he can give guidance.

The United States had scant support for its foreign policy: European opinion was aghast; American opinion was skeptical. It takes a vast effort to get tiny sums for Central America. The opinion that the United States was the aggressor remained widespread among its elites. The gap between rhetoric and action—two minor interventions in Grenada and Lebanon amid the continual need to deny bellicosity— bothered friend and foe alike.

In sum, the consent necessary to maintain foreign and defense policy had not been secured. Should a time of trouble arise, therefore, no one can say whether even the most modest use of force would be sustainable, nor the least adverse consequence supportable. Among all the contenders for the Democratic party nomination for president in 1984 for instance, there is not one who agreed on the desirability of using force except under conditions—no serious Soviet objection, completely containable consequences, high moral stature of allies—that cannot be met. Yet the forces in society these candidates represent (for the Democrats are still the majority party) will remain in Congress and in the country when the election is over. Nor does one have to go to Democrats to find opposition to foreign military involvements. The conditions laid out by former Secretary of Defense Caspar Weinberger—massive public support, overwhelming superiority, absolution in advance for defeat, an open-ended commitment to do whatever it takes—are no less impossible. Leaving behind a legacy of opposition to foreign and defense policies in a democratic nation cannot be regarded as a success.

When he came into office, Ronald Reagan had long since decided to break with the prevailing doctrine of enhanced governmental intervention by trying to implement a rival doctrine of free-market economics. In regard to defense and foreign policy, however, he did not challenge the direction of existing policies. The United States remained the democratic pillar of a bipolar world in which containment of communism was its major responsibility. Thus the United States remained the decision maker of first resort, undertaking to act first, whether or not its allies went along. The president was faced with a continuing stream of decisions concerning intervention, without substantial support either from his own people or his nation's allies. The choices were ambiguous; the results, tenuous; the willingness of elites and citizens to support drawn-out endeavors, dubious.

There is a blatant mismatch between public support and the missions assigned to the armed forces. The task of the Reagan administration, therefore, is to reduce the disparity by increasing domestic support and decreasing the need for it.

"Star Wars" as a Political Strategy

The president has begun to meet one of the requirements of leadership in the international arena: forging a connection between defense and foreign policy.

By far the greatest influence on the 1988 presidential campaign, largely unheard and unseen but all-powerful, was the presence of Ronald Reagan. When people ask why the campaign said so little about issues, the startling answer is that their president had preempted virtually all the issue space there was.

President Reagan's INF treaty and his negotiation on the START treaty to cut the number of nuclear missiles in half—both charting a direction toward much smaller nuclear forces—determined the lukewarm character of the discussion of foreign and defense policy. Without INF and START, policies impossible to imagine without Ronald Reagan, the entire tone and content of the defense debate (such as it was) would have been different. The Democrats lost the peace-disarmament, we-can-negotiate-with-the-Soviets issue because the president made space-based antiballistic missiles, the Strategic Defense Initiative (SDI), part of the negotiating package. Democratic nominee Michael Dukakis was forced to pledge at least to continue research. Because the Democrats feel the need to differentiate themselves somewhat on defense, they came out for more and better conventional weapons (Dukakis in the tank); and because Republican nominee George Bush supported Reaganism, plus a bit more for conventional defense, there was no argument.

This did not mean, as often alleged, that there were "no issues," but rather that President Reagan compelled both sides to follow his policies. There were substantial policy differences between the candidates and the major parties. Whether the domestic and defense governments should be larger or smaller, how far affirmative action should be pushed, the degree of environmental and economic regulation, the extent to which property rights should be protected or subordinated to social concerns—answers to all these questions turned on the 1988 election. So, too, did the critical issue of judicial appointments. Through the domestic and defense changes he has instituted, however, Ronald Reagan made the election campaign a referendum on his policies— policies from which his own party dared not openly depart and against which the opposing party dared not openly dissent. That is why the discussion of issues appeared muted, even as the future policy direction of the nation was actually at stake.

Why Reykjavik Was Right

The contempt hurled at President Reagan over the principles nearly agreed to at Reykjavik reveal the intellectual and political bankruptcy of his critics. The fact that he showed less than a perfect mastery of the technical aspects of weapon systems at the negotiations, for example, was made much of by "experts" who possess nothing but such knowledge. They pride themselves on their mastery of facts about types of missiles—facts that every spear-carrier knows—but are quite unable to distinguish between such mundane and easily available knowledge and the rare and precious ability to set a new and better agenda for world politics. One cannot but feel that much of the violent reaction to Reykjavik had no more substantial basis than the extreme pique felt by arms control intellectuals at not being consulted in advance. That was Ronald Reagan's real sin in Iceland. For what, after all, was wrong with Reykjavik except that it lacked the imprimatur of the foreign policy establishment?

Before turning to this question, we should recognize that it has a certain familiar aura about it; déjà vu all over again, as the great Lawrence Berra has it. Didn't we hear the same thing when SDI was first proposed? Why would the Soviet Union give up anything to stop or delay so ludicrous a project? Wasn't sending a few bombs over Libya bound to be futile, indeed counterproductive, and set off a new wave of terror? How many in the arms control community thought that a tougher stance toward the Soviet Union would result in a softer response?

The chief objection voiced against the Reykjavik policy, strangely enough (seeing that the objection is nonnuclear), was that the president did not require substantial reductions of conventional forces in Europe, as well as the cuts in nuclear weapons. If the principle was accepted that either everything has to be solved simultaneously or nothing should be tried, to be sure, nothing would happen—which was the point. A policy of linkage was reasserted in full knowledge that it had not succeeded in the past and was unlikely to do so in this instance. None of the critics, so far as I could tell, asked what the effect of "all-or-nothing equals nothing" would be on public opinion in both the United States and Europe. Would this opinion feel betrayed, finding once again that their leaders were opposed to moves toward what they thought of as peace? If this linkage had prevailed, the consequences would have included a resurgence of the peace movement in Europe, and a presidential election in 1988 revolving around the issue of reductions of nuclear forces—with the Democratic party emboldened to seek larger reductions in defense spending and the Republican party cast in the role of supporting "war" (i.e., adequate defense). There would have been issues in 1988 all right, but not the kind helpful for the defense of the nation.

Did President Reagan delegitimate nuclear deterrence by calling for the elimination of nuclear weapons, as some charged? If one doesn't like the destination, it is certainly convenient to call it catastrophic. But what could elimination mean? The president, as usual, was pointing the way. It could mean the elimination of first-strike capability on both sides; or that with SDI such weapons would eventually be useless; or that one day these weapons might physically cease to exist. But other presidents and congresses would decide that. In my opinion, our children are more likely to be around to debate the question if we proceed toward a Reykjavik-like policy. (Eliminating nuclear deterrence, by the way, is impossible. Even if such weapons are no longer in supply, nothing could stop them from being made again. In that sense, nuclear is forever.)

An instructive example of the political problem of maintaining support for defense was the policy, begun in the administration of President Carter and continued by President Reagan, of countering the placement of Soviet SS-20 intermediate range missiles in Europe with American Pershings. The rationale offered for this step was that if and when the Soviets removed their missiles, we would remove ours. The logic of the situation—our Pershings reach Moscow, while their SS-20s cannot reach Washington—suggested that the Soviets would ultimately remove their missiles. On the domestic scene in the West, however, skepticism was expressed that this was simply another ploy to justify placing more nuclear weapons in Europe. But the NATO policy was successful. Immediately, the critical thrust was reversed and a campaign was launched to keep the Pershings where they were, the argument now being that the Pershings constituted a more effective deterrent than other nuclear weapons in Europe and were needed to reduce Soviet superiority of various kinds. Whatever the merits of this proposal in itself, had it prevailed, the delegitimating effect on public opinion would have been devastating: "They" only want to increase, never decrease, nuclear weapons. Fortunately, wisdom prevailed and the United States settled for victory not only in substance but in principle: threat of force should counter threat, so as to reduce rather than increase the level of hostility.

Although the Soviets say they wish to reduce the costs of military spending in order to improve their economy, they have not yet acted in a way consistent with these declarations. Nuclear weapons cost little compared to conventional forces, yet the bloated size of their conventional armed forces and the associated weapons have not been reduced. The reason, given *sotto voce,* is that the military insists on maintenance of forces; therefore, change will take time. That explanation will soon wear thin. The next administration promises to address this issue. In the meantime, the INF treaty and the START negotiations cannot help but highlight the anomaly [this was written before the collapse of communism in Eastern Europe] of millions of troops and tanks East and West, while there is absolutely no threat of invasion and nuclear forces are being reduced. In this way as well, indirectly as well as directly, the Reagan administration's foreign and defense policies are reducing the threat to its allies as well as to the United States itself.

Would, in fact, the Reykjavik policy, beginning with the INF and the proposed START agreements, have increased the likelihood of the Soviet Union launching a conventional attack on Western Europe? Now there is an absurdity. First of all, even with a 50 percent reduction in long-range nuclear delivery systems, there are still a lot of weapons of diverse kinds, enough to give us about as much protection (i.e., a second-strike or strike-back capability) as we have now. By the time nuclear weapons reduction gets to very low numbers, the world situation will have changed in many ways, including the size, destructiveness, and configuration of nonnuclear weapons. Thus there will be time to deal with conventional forces in Europe.

It is said that the proposed START agreement would increase the ratio of Soviet nuclear missiles to American targets in the Soviets' favor. Numerically true, I would say, but substantively false. There are too many weapons with too much variety for this slight change to affect deterrence. When and if there are further massive reductions, such a disparity would be impermissible. Today the point is merely alarmist. If START moves us in the right direction, combining credible defense with sustained public support, it remains the right way to go.

A Bad President or an Evil Empire?

Nowadays people do not ask what they can do for presidents but to them. It is, therefore, not surprising that President Reagan receives so few apologies when he turns out to have gotten things right. I refer not merely to everyday small-change hostilities, but to the crucial matter of the president's foreign policy toward the Soviet Union.

Because we cannot distinguish among numerous possible causes, no one can say with certainty whether the Reagan administration's foreign policy affected the occurrence or the timing or the change in Soviet internal affairs that goes under the names of *glasnost* and *perestroika*. Nor, more broadly, can anyone say whether containment, the staple of American policy for over forty years, had something to do with the Soviet change. Had Soviet foreign policy been more successful, the need for internal change might have been less apparent. In any event, my task here is to appraise the president's approach to the Soviet Union.

Let us begin with his calling the Soviet Union, as he considered it then, an "evil empire." President Reagan took a lot of heat for that. Either it was not true, or it was too true and therefore unsayable. Such an appellation supposedly would anger the Soviets so much that no further relations with them, except the most formal, would be possible. Wrong again, as is now obvious. What I wish to raise here is the possibility, given the well-known (and proven) Soviet sensitivity to Western opinion, that this uncharacteristically bold, direct, and most undiplomatic statement actually influenced events within the Soviet Union. Perhaps attribution of internal Soviet convolutions to moral failure and condemnation will strike some people as odd. The semi-comical explanation, given out by the Soviets themselves and repeated back to them by our experts, is that it all has to do with poor economic performance. No doubt inability to grow economically, as well as to meet ordinary expectations for quality of goods, is an important consideration. But if you think you are doing right, you might redouble your efforts or blame the West, anything and everything except what the Soviet leadership has in fact done: call into question their history, their leadership, their institutions. How else explain their refrain, iterated and reiterated by Gorbachev himself, about coming to understand how and why the Soviet Union engaged in the abominable (indeed, in some cases and by their own account, surely "evil") practices they now condemn under the abuses of leadership? They know there is only one possible answer—their system is to blame. That is not only what outsiders but what their own experience and their training in Marxist doctrine tell them: structure determines function. The true explanation of what is occurring in the Soviet Union is what it has wrongly been alleged is happening in the West: a legitimation crisis reaching ultimately to the right to rule.

The Soviet Union is not performing much worse now than when Brezhnev was in power. Then, the Soviets could still try to get what they needed by threat abroad, while maintaining the party's privileges at home. That the current ruling faction sought to alter this pattern is due to more than worry over economic failure. For if delegitimation is successful, it will have created a more diverse and critical public that is unlikely to permit as many or as serious foreign military adventures. Is it too fanciful to suggest that an outspoken moral rejection of the Soviet system and a confident affirmation of democratic capitalism by an American president may have helped the Soviets face up to their inability to justify dictatorial communism?

American foreign policy has unfolded exactly as Reagan said it would. At the outset, the president said he would help build up the defense establishment; later, having given the Soviets greater reason to cooperate, he would seek mutually advantageous agreements—oversimplified, naturally, but that is what policy guidance from the top is about. Details fail to inspire or provide a sense of direction; concentration on them involves interference at an inappropriate level and is likely to dampen the initiative of those who have to make creative adaptations to as yet unforeseen (and unforeseeable) events.

Probably, the president was lucky in being in office in the midst of a Soviet legitimation crisis. Just possibly, he helped the Gorbachev faction argue that a determined opponent necessitated faster and further-reaching change.

There is more to defense policy than quantity; there is also quality. Did a policy of "more" produce the best possible mix of weapons? We don't know yet. Did raising budget authority so fast in Reagan's first term lead to the usual "peaks and valleys" defense spending? Yes. If the peaks were not so high, would any knowledgeable person be able to assure Secretary of Defense Caspar Weinberger that the valleys would not have been correspondingly lower during the administration's second term? No.

Why is there no acknowledgment that the amateurs—Secretary of State George Shultz, the National Security Council staff, and their "cowboy president"—won the day? It is the invasion of Grenada, not the less-than-wonderful military performance that accompanied it, that matters (though we should work to correct the latter). For similar reasons, it is not the aim of the few bombs tossed Qaddafi's way but the fact that it was done at all that calmed public jitters and restored public confidence in international travel. European governments looked down their noses at the amateurish American (the two words have become synonyms in their vocabulary) use of force, whether it was intercepting terrorists in the sky or safeguarding the passage of oil tankers in the Persian Gulf. Why is it always sophisticated to do nothing or to placate one's opponents?

The testing ground for the European versus the American approach to Soviet-style systems is East Germany, which has received immensely favorable treatment from its Western counterpart. Presumably, if subsidizing socialist regimes alters their behavior, that should show up in East Germany. It does not. Instead, the East Germans lead the opposition to change within the Soviet bloc.

Challenging "Finders Keepers"

The Reagan doctrine is difficult to separate from overblown rhetoric. The effort to help indigenous forces against Leninist regimes is not unique. What else was President Carter doing in Afghanistan? Comments as to the futility of such endeavors have an important grain of truth in them: it is very difficult for *anyone* to intervene successfully in another people's problems, as numerous American and Soviet misadventures testify. Difficult, however, does not mean impossible, especially when there is something indigenous to work with, as in Afghanistan or Angola. Even the halting and minimal support given the Nicaraguan Contras may have led to more democratization than there otherwise would have been, and restricted the scope of Sandinista repression. It has also served to remind the Soviets of the high economic cost of foreign adventures.

Without claiming too much for the administration, the potential contribution of the Reagan doctrine to the lessening of international hostilities has been missed. Under the old rules—what Leninists get, Leninists keep—a look at the long-term was bound to be depressing. If Leninist regimes could not be overthrown, their expansion was only a matter of time. But if there is a checkered pattern—win some, lose some—a more relaxed attitude toward developments in remote places becomes possible. Expanded choice is an important advantage for a government trying to persuade a pacific people to support national defense, support that has been weak not only in recent times but throughout most of American history. Implementation of the Reagan doctrine, while moderately successful in its own right, has helped persuade Moscow that trouble for the United States does not necessarily mean gains for the Soviet Union, thus lessening the need for further American intervention. The mood of fatalism that had heretofore gripped American foreign policy has now been lifted.

One of the president's strengths is his unwillingness to intervene in all but the most important matters. The minor debacles that plagued the Reagan administration in its second term were due to an understandable but harmful desire to make memorable choices before they were ripe for decision. It is not inattention, as Reagan's critics charge, but hyperactivity that led to so many premature, and therefore poor, judgments.

A Meteoric Leader in an Antileadership System

What has Reagan wrought, in sum, that justifies the sobriquet "strategist"? He has devised appropriate means for keeping his party together. He has provided policy guidance (with the exception noted) to coordinate the farflung efforts of his administration. He has integrated his personality with his policy positions and his administrative style.

He has altered expectations, at least in domestic policy, from government as the intervenor of first resort to intervenor of last resort so as to suit his policy preferences. No other postwar president redirected both domestic and foreign policy in his desired direction while gaining reelection and keeping his party united.

In critical areas of policy, the president has shaped the congressional agenda to his liking. Although he cannot control outcomes, not being all-powerful, he has been able to keep items such as income tax increases off the agenda, and to keep those he wants discussed, such as cuts in domestic spending, at the forefront of concern. He has exposed the weaknesses of his opponents; the deficit has deprived them of the opportunity to keep supporting their constituencies. Indeed, he has, so to speak, converted them to a Republican-doctrine budget balance, which will make their political lives much more difficult. Nor was this easy. Confronted with the necessity of giving up not only his tax cuts but all that this implied in terms of his vision of limited domestic government, and incurring large deficits in view of his party's historical opposition to them, Ronald Reagan chose limited government. Reagan has also begun to enunciate a rationale for a defense-led, low-level, nuclear weapons policy that combines domestic support with protection of the nation. Yet, to his critics, this is not enough.

A good part of the objections to Reagan's style comes from those who think that presidents should have many more preferences and should intervene far more directly to achieve them. They must wish someone else was president because their advice would be suitable only for a different person. This is the essence, I take it, of James D. Barber's characterization of Reagan as a "passive-positive" president, that is, someone who is upbeat but reactive rather than proactive. I think not. The difference in appraisal really boils down to whether having many preferences, and therefore, priorities, will get presidents further in advancing their objectives than having very few. In today's political context, where the call for the exertion of leadership is followed immediately by efforts to tear it down, the risk of having a big agenda is big stultification. I see no reason to tie Ronald Reagan to a mode of behavior that has not worked for his immediate predecessors.

Whether by accident or design, Ronald Reagan's political style fits well with the opportunities and constraints offered by the American national political system in the 1980s. The constraints are not only structural—the separation of powers, checks and balances, federalism—which usually operate to restrict what chief executives can do on their own. Hierarchy, the expectation that authority inheres in formal position, has historically been weak in America. Nor are these constraints entirely political, his Republican party being a large minority in the Senate (where Reaganite conservatives are but one faction), and a distinct minority in the House of Representatives. All this means is that the president has to bargain. Nothing new here.

On top of his party's minority status, the president faces a political milieu both desirous and distrusting of leadership. Were this not so, it would be difficult to explain the series of failed presidents who preceded him. When we look at the social movements that have risen as presidents have fallen, with but two interconnected exceptions—the antiabortionists and Protestant fundamentalists such as the Moral Majority—they are devoted to greater equality of condition. The civil rights movement, the women's movement, gay rights, children's rights, gray power, and more, are avowedly devoted to diminishing differences among groups of people. The point here is that authority is a form of inequality, for it would allow some people to decide for others. Viewing the presidency as part and parcel of American social life, it is not so surprising that it has been buffeted (the higher the rank, the stronger the winds) by fierce political storms.

Were these critical currents directed against individual officeholders, they might more easily be withstood. But they are not. It is the political system itself, not a policy or a politician or a party, that is held to blame or, to use the current code, that is deemed unfair. System blame has grown to epidemic proportions. When groups of leaders were asked by Sidney Verba and Gary Orren whether poverty in America was the fault of the poor or the system, for instance, 86 percent of black leaders, 76 percent of feminists, 68 percent of Democrats, 50 percent of media, and 44 percent of intellectuals blamed the system.[9] No wonder Democratic as well as Republican presidents have been held in disrepute!

Presidents are elected for fixed terms and given large constitutional and legislative responsibilities. They cannot appear only at ceremonial occasions, following the national consensus on policies where it exists and returning to obscurity when conflict threatens.

What, then, are our poor presidents to do when the same people who urge government to do much more, simultaneously blame the system that has to do it? Efforts to provide across-the-board guidance on a panoply of problems fail, a la Jimmy Carter, because they become the simultaneous focus of criticism by those who believe the government has taken on too much and those who believe it has not done enough, because the system from which decisions stem is fatally flawed. Similarly, it is not partisan bias that afflicts the media but the disposition to system blame that leads its practitioners to excoriate politicians. The severe reaction to the Iran-Contra episode has only strengthened my conviction that the presidency is situated within an antileadership system. President John F. Kennedy, for instance, after taking responsibility for the Bay of Pigs, was able to shut off all efforts to make him talk about it in public.

There is still time for us to appreciate a great president—not the perfect president of our faulty imaginations, but a human president whose achievements override his errors by a large margin. Compared to the momentous positive changes in policy the president has brought about, the Iran-Contra affair and the debacle in Panama fade into deserved insignificance.

It could be that future governments will raise taxes substantially while increasing or maintaining nuclear arsenals. Then Reagan's influence will have proven short-lived. But if, as I suspect, there will be no majorities for substantial tax increases and no public support for rejecting Reykjavik, Ronald Reagan will have set the policy direction of the United States government well into the next century. Not bad for a "do-nothing" president.

Nevertheless, amid the continuous casting of blame, the demand for presidential leadership continues unabated. Whether the subject is deficits, Social Security, disarmament, trade, tax reform, immigration, or whatever, there is no substitute for the president. Hence presidents are tempted into action, only to discover that whatever they do is somehow not what they were supposed to have done.

Enter Ronald Reagan. By undertaking a very few major initiatives, with widespread consequences, he is seen as a positive leader. By reserving his imprimatur for only those matters he considers most vital, he makes an infrequent target. By disclaiming intimate factual knowledge of specifics, he reduces the expectation that the president is responsible for whatever is disliked. And when the complaints that the president has provided insufficient leadership rise to a crescendo, he may notice, along with us observers, that the demand to do more in the future does not decline (indeed, it may well be enhanced) just because he has refused to rise to the bait before.

Were the United States a country in which authority inhered in position, presidents could emulate Jimmy Carter by emitting constant calls for action. But it is not; and they should not. While no one can look back from a future that is yet to unfold, so we cannot yet know how successful President Reagan will be in changing the vision of America through the long-term alteration of ideas, but he is providing about as much direction as the existing American antileadership system can support. For what he does not attempt, as well as for what he does, President Reagan is the appropriate leader for his time.

Notes

1. See Jack Knott and Aaron Wildavsky, "Jimmy Carter's Theory of Governing," *Wilson Quarterly (*Winter 1977): 49–67.
2. President Abraham Lincoln, often viewed as a paradigm of seriousness, allocated his time predominantly to war and union. A lot got left out. In a distinguished series of essays on Lincoln, David Donald observes:

   Less than any other major American President did Lincoln control or even influence the Congress. Noting that many of the Civil War congressman were his seniors and humbly declaring "that many of you have more experience than I, in the conduct of public affairs," Lincoln bowed not merely to the will but to the caprice of the legislators. . . . The President had remarkably little connection with the legislation passed during the Civil War. He proposed few specific law, to Congress: his bill for compensated emancipation is notably exceptional. He exerted little influence in securing the adoption of bills that were introduced. In some of the most significant legislation enacted during his administration Lincoln showed little interest. The laws providing for the construction of a Pacific railroad, for the creation of the Department of Agriculture, for the importation of "contract laborers" from Europe, for the tariff protection of American manufacturers, and for the establishment of land-grant colleges had little connection with Lincoln aside from his formal approval of them. That approval was usually granted without hesitation. Less than any other important American President did Lincoln use his veto power. . . . Lincoln was also ineffectual in controlling the executive departments of the government. He and his cabinet never formed a unified administration. (David Donald, *Lincoln Reconsidered: Essays on the Civil War Era* [New York: Random House, 1956], 191–93.)
3. Richard P. Nathan and Fred C. Doolittle, "The Untold Story of Reagan's

'New Federalism,'" *Public Interest,* no. 77 (Fall 1984): 96–105.

4. Laurence I. Barrett, *Gambling with History: Ronald Reagan in the White House* (New York: Penguin, 1984), 133.

5. See Aaron Wildavsky, "What the Hell Is Going On? Reagan, Iran, and the Presidency," (with a reply by James David Barber), *American Spectator* 20, no. 4 (April 1987): 14–18.

6. See Aaron Wildavsky, "The Three Cultures: Explaining Anomalies in the American Welfare State," *Public Interest,* no. 69 (Fall 1982): 45–58; "Industrial Policies in American Political Cultures," in Claude E. Barfield and William A. Schambra, eds., *The Politics of Industrial Policy* (Washington, D.C.: American Enterprise Institute, 1986), 15–32; and "The Party of Government, the Party of Opposition, and the Party of Balance: An American View of the Consequences of the 1980 Election," in Austin Ranney, ed., *The American Elections of 1980* (Washington, D.C.: American Enterprise Institute, 1981), 329–50.

7. Dom Bonafede, "Presidential Scholars Expect History to Treat the Reagan Presidency Kindly," *National Journal* 17, no. 14 (April 6, 1985): 743–47.

8. Seymour Martin Lipset, "The Confidence Gap: Down but Not Out" (typescript, April 1985).

9. Sidney Verba and Gary R. Orren, *Equality in America: The View from the Top* (Cambridge: Harvard University Press, 1985), 74.

13

What the Hell Is Going On?
Reagan, Iran, and the Presidency

(With a Reply by James David Barber)

In our local paper I read that the president is easily led. Insofar as we know, the secretaries of state and defense were opposed to the Iranian venture, while the attorney general and the director of intelligence were in favor. At a minimum, the president had to choose among advisers. When David Stockman tried to get the president to raise taxes, the director of the budget failed over and over again. Indeed, when the economists of the nation were lined up insisting that the president abandon his most important policy, he consistently and persistently refused. Over a wide range of issues, I think the accusation does not stand up.

Is the president, as you and so many others say, "disengaged"? I just wrote a lengthy chapter about the major tax reform recently passed. The same charge surfaced there. But it was utterly false. Without Reagan, there is no reform. If he lifts a pinky, it is a non-starter. If he fails to campaign for it, or to give support in Congress, it dies. True, he does not deal with "details," having Richard Darman and James Baker to do that for him, but at every strategic step, without which there would be no reform—insisting on revenue neutrality, trading

This exchange, prompted by op-ed pieces by Professor Barber, was originally published in the fall of 1986 in *American Spectator* 20, no. 4 (April 1987): 14–17.

higher effective taxes on business for lower individual rates—Ronald Reagan was the creative force.

Is there, then, more than one Reagan? Probably. The president is famous for paring his agenda down to the essentials. In a system loaded against leadership, I think Reagan is right. In any event, presidents who have acted otherwise have not, by and large, fared too well.

We are told repeatedly that there is something terribly wrong with the chief-of-staff system in the White House. Are we to conclude from this accusation that the problem is that everything has to go through a single person? Or are we to conclude that the chief of staff is not strong enough, because this matter apparently did not go through him? As all students of the subject know, but are strangely reluctant to say now in regard to Iran, there is no ideal mode of organization that fits all people or presidents, or that guarantees good results or the avoidance of basic errors in all situations. Were we to take a more dispassionate view, difficult as that appears to be, we would say that presidents should choose advisory systems that both suit their own needs and that will give them better results in most instances. Should we say that an advisory system that falls down badly in one case is to be scrapped even though it served this president well in a larger number of cases? Building on success—eight years as governor, six years as president—the president evidently had confidence not only in what he was doing but in the advisory system that was helping him do it. What critics must show is that this system is flawed generally and not merely that it fell down in a particular instance. But even here, sticking strictly to Iran for the moment, critics cannot show even that much. Surely the dissenters did not lack weight within the administration. So what went wrong?

Why might a president feel it desirable to override his secretaries of state and defense? Either the president had failed to override them before, to his regret, or, more likely, he had done so before, when horrible consequences were predicted, only to discover that things turned out all right. Perhaps the invasion of Grenada, the bombing of Libya, and the Strategic Defense Initiative fit that mold. The reaction to SDI tells us something else that is well to keep in mind; those who ridiculed it (and Ronald Reagan who gave it life) have had to recognize it has had far greater value than they, in their sense of superiority, ever imagined. So if it is true that the president saw value in the Iranian venture that turned out to be illusory, it is also true that his critics have been similarly mistaken and arguably on matters of much greater magnitude.

How did the president and his National Security Council (NSC) staff get sucked ever deeper into this morass? Easy! It happens all the time, and not only to presidents. The objectives one has in mind are both long- and short-range, general and concrete. How often have students of policy observed that the long-range and general (Iran after Khomeini) often give way to the short-range and specific (the hostages)? Aphorisms abound: "The measurable drive out the more important but impalpable."

The incremental illusion is also common. Which of us has not discovered himself swearing he would put only so much effort or money or trust into a venture, only to go further and further on the grounds—sometimes valid, usually not—that doing a bit more would bring home the grand prize?

I do not say this to absolve the president. He is a professional politician and public official responsible for his actions. My point, rather, is that the errors in regard to Iran are not extraordinary, revealing of exceptional incapacity, but of the garden variety by which the high and mighty, as well as the rest of us, are brought low.

It is said that we had a Teflon president who either mesmerized the public with nonsense syllables or was apparently so charming that nothing could stick to him. Now we know better. A reasonable conclusion would be that when the president speaks sense to the people, they go along with him, and when he appears to speak nonsense, whether this is about the Daniloff swap or the Iranian swap of arms for hostages, the people reject what they are being told. The flip side of the coin is that the president was apparently making sense to the people before, but I hear very little about this. I am pleased to confirm that our people have a reasonable sense of discrimination.

The failure in Iran is political. The president undertook an action that, when it became known, would be rejected by the vast majority of citizenry as well as by political elites. By me too. And for this political failure there has been substantial political punishment. The Iran policy has been reversed, the NSC has been reorganized, and the president's popularity has plummeted. Since the president lives by his deep intuition of the American public, it is not inappropriate that he should suffer when this insight leaves him. But I do not think you make a case that the president's personality or organizational apparatus is fatally flawed. Indeed, one could imagine, reading your columns and those of many other people, that the ideal president, the one who knew everything about most things and was a great detail man, was none other than the nationally beloved Jimmy Carter.

You write that Reagan is obviously not a man in charge, "in the face of his own revelations that he did not know what his National Security Council was up to regarding the most sensitive area of his entire foreign policy." This is overheated; moreover, it appears to be wrong. What would you say of our relations with the Soviet Union or with NATO nations or with Japan if Iran is "the most sensitive area"? You write further that "major military moves were undertaken without even the obviously appropriate deliberations." On the contrary, the evidence we have reveals that the internal deliberations were appropriate and that all the major players had their opportunity to say their piece. The NSC was involved, and the military significance of the arms shipments was small. While I am not among those who think readily of moderates in the Iranian administration, a dispassionate observer would point out that the Israelis, who are known for hardheaded thinking, and who are certainly in touch with the minute facts regarding these matters, thought this a good idea. Therefore, I believe that the charge of triviality and nonsensicalness does not carry weight. Indeed, this episode has all the hallmarks of classical planning. What the president thought he was doing was not allowing events to take their course, not allowing the market of international relations to dictate what would happen, and not merely reacting to events. Rather, believing he would save the nation much greater difficulty should the Iranian regime collapse and communist elements take over, the president wished to anticipate this danger by taking preemptive action. Must he always be right? Do we say this is bad judgment and pass on to the next matter, or do we go on, as you do, to claim a fatal flaw?

You mention Reykjavik as an example of "chaos at the top." I don't agree. I think of it as "creative ferment," potentially the most creative of the Reagan administration. After all, we did not have lightweights there; the best our government has to offer, Paul Nitze, was there, along with other knowledgeable and talented individuals. Since I think that near-zero nuclear disarmament holds out the best hope for us, I cannot join you in rejecting the president's instincts to at least try to do the most helpful thing as compared with the paltry prospects for traditional arms control measures. Senator Nunn's crit-

icism is mind-boggling. Apparently we left our European allies out on
a limb by giving them only twelve years to create sufficient conventional force. If there must be agreement on everything before agreement on anything can be reached, I leave you to assess the prospects.

You speak of "wild risk taking by Reagan executives." There is, in
fact, no evidence of this, at least none that you or others have provided. On the contrary, the history of the Reagan administration thus
far is one of extraordinary caution, the sole exceptions being Grenada
(which I approved) and Lebanon (which I didn't). Did you even think
when Ronald Reagan became president that you would be in the
seventh year of his presidency and have only these two minor military
ventures to report?

You gloss over the profound differences between the Reagan administration and the Democratic Congress on what our foreign policy
ought to be. When there is such agreement, as in regard to the Philippines, then you do find them working together. But when there is utter
dissensus, as in Central America, one finds quite the opposite. Indeed,
what you are actually urging, given the disposition of opinion in
Congress, is that the president not do what congressmen dislike, which
would give him no foreign policy at all. Do you teach your students
that presidents and Congresses agree on who has the power to do
what? Scholarship suggests not only perennial disagreement about the
division of power but also that conflict over who is constitutionally
empowered to act is part and parcel of disputes over what kind of
action should be undertaken. Far from failing to perform its representative functions, Congresses may well have exceeded them by tying a
president's hands in so many ways that they create additional incentives not to have themselves informed.

Evidently, the degree of trust necessary to make the intelligence
committees work has been damaged, if not lost. Whether this trust
had previously eroded, I do not know. But when informing others
becomes the equivalent of being unable to undertake a policy, the
stage for distrust is already set.

I agree with your other article, "Human Rights Violations Continue
to Spread Throughout the World." But I do not agree with your apocalyptic statements about the decline of Mother Nature, at least not in
the developed countries, which do a lot better job at taking care of
their patrimony than the others. Nor do I think that the odds of nuclear
war have greatly increased from what they have been for a very long

time. It is true that the United States, like so many other nations, finds itself in the midst of vast economic change that it neither fully comprehends nor can quite figure out how to cope with. But why do you want to lay this on Ronald Reagan? Or is he responsible for AIDS too?

At the moment, the economy is doing fairly well, and aircraft accidents are at an all-time low. Yet I keep hearing portents of disaster. If things go badly, as with Iran, then bad times are here. But if they go well, doom is around the corner. It seems to me that you are setting up the president so he cannot possibly come out well.

The demand for total harmony between words and deeds is understandable, but it will not withstand the slightest serious scrutiny. Did Congress agree in advance to Roosevelt's destroyer deal or was that not, in fact—or could it not have been interpreted to be—a violation of the Neutrality Act? Or would he never send our boys to war? Looking at early American presidents from Washington through Lincoln, Washington felt he had to appear to act much more forcefully than he actually could; Jefferson had to pretend to be doing nothing while doing a great deal; and Lincoln left virtually the entire panoply of domestic economic policy, including vast and far-reaching measures such as the first introduction of an income tax, entirely to Congress, refusing to get involved in the slightest way. None of them had an easy time with Congress on foreign policy.

I have said nothing about the diversion of funds because sufficient facts are not yet known. Evidently we cannot countenance illegality. Especially not in the White House. Why, then, is this operation located there? Obviously, the more such operations are located outside the executive office, especially the inner sanctum of the White House, the easier it is for the president to disavow, so self-protection is clearly not uppermost in the president's mind. One possible reason is that there were now so many restrictions that would not have applied in earlier times, that the operation could not have been run elsewhere. Like you, I think this was a strong sign it ought not to have been done. But I remind you that in the past, the president had triumphed by going against his main advisers. I will wait further information before making up my mind on the president's part, if any, direct or indirect, in the funds transfer.

Should Reagan have known about the diversion of funds to the Contras? Presumably, presidents are not expected to know about everything—in fact, most things—going on in government. How about the White House? There are hundreds of top people working there, so how could (and, I would add, why should) a president know what they are doing in fulfilling an agreed purpose, subject to a presidential finding? Surely the time spent in surveillance of associates, aside from its denigration of their loyalty, would be a waste of presidential time. How much less likely, then, would an unauthorized action, such as fund diversion, come to presidential attention? I read that Zbig Brzezinski, as NSC head, read over forms describing what the fifty or so people reporting to him were doing every day. Yet if an action were left out, how would he have known? Of course, one can trivialize the matter by saying that presidents should know about all illegal actions. But how and, more important, at what cost?

A major reason we have security leaks, I think, is that we classify far too many things and require clearances for far too many people. The result is that surveillance is inevitably diffused. How much worse it would be for chief executives to follow their people around (or have them followed). Or should the president have tapped their phones?

It used to be that good executives were those who gave their subordinates the freedom to make mistakes, who encouraged them to make creative improvisations, subject only to general guidelines. Certainly these are the conditions under which you and I would like to work. Subordinates who require detailed supervision are not worth having. Why, then, do we hear that the White House should be full of people constantly reporting to the chief, looking back to see who is gaining on them? Such a system would stultify every White House, not merely that of the incumbent president.

There is nothing wrong with (and much to be said in favor of) delegation, so long as it works. If it breaks down, however, is one better off shoring it up or engaging in detailed supervision? As an observer of a wide range of policies, I think that broad delegation does work for this president most of the time, and that is all one can ask of any procedure. But why would the president give so much leeway to a mere lieutenant colonel? Because this is America, where strict adherence to hierarchy is not the norm, we escape the sclerosis that affects gerontocracies.

There is an awful lot of absolutist talk going around, as if people were purely good or evil, or actions were either all of one thing or all of another. The president thought of arms for hostages as a partial retreat from a policy that otherwise stood in force. Indeed, the administration could presumably have undertaken large-scale weapons shipments, and that would not have been the same as the amount of arms that were actually sent. If a little is the same as a lot, we lose an important sense of discrimination. Similarly, if any violation is the same as the grossest violation, I cannot think of any president, or of any human being, who could make the grade.

The president thought he was acting in the national interest. Others may not know, but you as a scholar do know, how often presidents, even our greatest (Jefferson and Lincoln come immediately to mind) disavowed adherence to strict cannons of legality in order to preserve the essence of liberty. The latest *This Constitution* cites Jefferson's justification for condoning serious extralegal action undertaken to curtail Aaron Burr's activities: "To lose our country by scrupulous adherence to written law would be to lose the law itself with life, liberty, and property . . . thus absurdly sacrificing the ends to the means." Of course, Jefferson may well have been mistaken, as I think President Reagan was this time. But as my mind searches for parallels, I am less inclined to be censorious.

Why would anyone want to pay attention to commentators like us? Presumably, we bring a knowledge in depth, calling on the experience of previous presidencies. Yet that is exactly what is missing, or we would be spared all this nonsense (and narcissism) about how we are uniquely put upon, as if presidents have never acted on their own, or as if the only parallel was with Richard Nixon. Alternatively, commentators could provide analysis in breadth comparing the Iran-Contra affair with other contemporary instances of executive power. This is not done, I fear, because it would show that this is a teapot in a tempest. Whatever happened to the Greenpeace affair in which a life was taken? Is it likely the French premier and president did not know? The French operatives have left New Zealand for a mess of potage or, more accurately, a piece of the lamb import quota. Can the current premier of Israel, when he was head of its Mosad, not have known of the killing of a terrorist? Oh, well, these countries may like intrigue more than we do. And what of the Belgrano affair, in which a boatload of Argentinians was shot out of the water and responsibility was never quite be determined? Or the stories about the efforts of M5 to destabilize the Wilson Labour government? Now there is a serious matter; yet it cannot quite make it past a weekend in the British media. Our mythical analyst would undoubtedly advise that there are indeed problems with secret services that we cannot do without but that are incompatible with democratic life. This analyst, however, would observe that these other democratic nations are proleadership systems, prone to explain away rather than condemn and to make allowances for the demands of office, whereas the support for leadership in these United States is wafer-thin. While this analysis does not excuse, it does make explicable the self-flagellation for what, in a comparative or historical sense, so far as we know now, is pretty small potatoes.

You and I are fact-mongers; while we claim to know that the context in which we put them is all-important, people like us have an unfortunate tendency to look down on others who do not know so many essentially trivial facts and who like to get their information orally rather than in written form. It is easy, and I think mistaken, to disparage people whose form of intelligence differs from ours. In sum, I still don't think that the short-answer theory of the presidency—he who scores highest is best—is the right one.

The other day on the radio, I heard a local congresswoman, Barbara Boxer, say that Congress must act to assure that no illegality ever occurs again in the White House. One way to do this would be to strip the White House of all the accretions it has developed in past decades. Need I remind you, as a student of the presidency, that most of these units have been put there at the insistence of Congress, including, as I recall, the NSC? What have liberals (who think of themselves as the party of positive government) to gain by weakening what our colleague Nelson Polsby has called the "presidential branch"? Soon enough, calls for presidential action will be heard. And who will there be to respond? The antithird-term amendment already creates unnecessary pressure to speed up action so as to shoehorn events into the last years. The only way to assure that an institution will do no harm is to render it powerless. Hamstringing our common heritage, the presidency, is not, I think, a worthy legacy.

American hostages obviously create problems for our people and politicians—from Korea to Vietnam to Daniloff in the U.S.S.R. to Iran. If they are really prisoners of undeclared wars, why does the media keep building up their importance? Surely this visibility, as President Carter discovered, highlights the impotence of the administration. If the government is then not allowed to do what is required to get them back—ransom them or invade the offending nation or take hostages of our own—why are their families given so much publicity, thus suggesting action ought to be taken? Though no one intends to do so, the result is to condemn presidents either for weakness or recklessness (poor Jimmy Carter got it both ways). When one reads in the cartoons that the president is either lying or ignorant, the effect is the same: whatever we find out, he is damned.

Did the president ship arms to Iran to free hostages or to intervene in its internal affairs? Since it must be one or the other, we are told, he is deceiving us whichever way he chooses to explain his behavior. In the normal course of events, we speak of motives invariably being mixed; we also know that they are retrospectively rationalized to suit our future behavior. Yet here we persist in setting up a procrustean category—at once too short and too long—so the president is condemned whichever one he chooses. I am impressed, as you can tell, with how many things we used to believe about administration, the presidency, foreign policy, human behavior, and more that we go against when presidents we dislike on wholly other grounds are involved.

You say that the people and the press have been too easy on this president's grievous faults. False charge, I reply. The only difference between now and then, unless one is utterly insensitive to barrage after barrage of criticism, is that this time the charges stuck. As usual, the implications run two ways: the charges were unbelievable before but not in this instance. What should be done?

The policies have been reversed, the NSC reformed, a high political price exacted. What more? The congressional mantra—we've always done it this way—does not move me. Between the president's review panel, the special prosecutor, and Congress, a joint committee would have been more than enough. Endless hearings have begun to fray everyone's nerves; they are a lousy way to get information; and the public interest in getting the facts could well be served by three rather than four investigations. But there may yet be worse to come.

Watergate in its time was properly regarded as an aberration. Another effort to impeach or to force a president to resign, thus reversing the result of the election without recourse to the people, would create a crisis of legitimacy. Conservatives would conclude that they could not rely on the ballot box to elect and keep the people's choice in the

White House. We should not exchange a small temporary problem for a large permanent one.

Evidently, it is easier to say what should not be done—make this case a capital crime—than to say what should be done. Absent something splendid to do beyond what has been done, with each cure far worse than the disease, we have our negative clue: adopt the policy version of the Hippocratic oath: Do no harm. "Iranamuck" should not become a historical designation for how we made a bad situation much worse.

What should President Reagan do? He has taken full responsibility without admitting that the Iran policy was wrong. My policy design was good, he keeps saying, but its execution was flawed. This will not do. Suppose we were to devise a plan to make the Soviet Union forever peaceful; alas, the only hitch would be that this would require destroying its population. Would we say, then, that the policy objective was great but its implementation left something to be desired? No, ends cannot be separated from the means required to accomplish them. Hence the policy, the means and ends taken together, is wrong.

I would like to join in the great American sweepstakes over what the president should tell the people that would get him off the hook once and for all. One thing and nothing. I say "nothing" partly because he has done and said most of what can be done and said, partly because anything he says will be interpreted unfavorably by some, and partly because he cannot be conclusive about the Contra affair. How does one prove a negative? Observation of contested cases reveals that neutral observers of the same incident often give conflicting accounts. If the president says he did not approve or know of the diversion of funds to the Contras, and someone else says he did, how will we be the wiser? Yet I still think the president should say what the American people believe, knowing also that they believe him to be human (i.e., flawed), wanting to serve his country, yet capable of error.

An apologetic (cringing, Uriah Heepish) president would hardly be believable or followable in the future. The people I know don't like to be taken for fools. Why, they want to know, did the president say one thing about hostages (no deal) and do another? The president has to admit that, although he didn't start out to make a swap, he understands that is what his administration ended up doing and looking to the public like it was doing. The president does not have to apologize for being human; he has only to reaffirm his identification with the rest of us Americans by acknowledging that we-the-people had good reason to feel there was a hostage swap, even as he felt there wasn't. If this sounds like Alphonse and Gaston—a president and a people groping toward mutual understanding—or Abbott and Costello—Whose misunderstanding came first?—that is exactly what gives this episode its farce-like appearance.

Opinion polls not only reveal a decline in support for the president but a corresponding loss in esteem for the media. Is the messenger being blamed for the bad news? Perhaps. A more powerful explanation, I suspect, is that denigration of one major national institution exacts a price by a loss of trust in others. The most powerful explanation for the public lashing out in two directions simultaneously is that people feel they have been let down twice, once by their president trading with the enemy, and again by the media taking so much pleasure in it. At long last, many in the media appear to be saying, everything we have been trying to tell you dim-witted, slow-learning boobus Americanus all along—your president is an idiot—is now confirmed. As you revile him, praise us, for we knew it all along. And will you, my friend, justly famed as a student of political psychology, looking in the mirror, deny the element of pleasure, even glee, at Reagan's fall from grace? You (plural) are trying to have it both ways; we-the-media did not hit Ronald Reagan hard enough early enough and we told you so.

I think the people are sending a dual message: Don't do it again, Mr. President, and Ms. and Mr. Media, don't report it again and again and again. The president has taken the pledge, but others who should, have not.

James David Barber Replies

Dear Aaron:

I'm glad to get your commentary about the Reagan/Iran business. It feels like a pretty speedy expression of thoughts you have been mulling for some time, so it may be some of our differences are merely literary angle problems, as when I call the Middle East "the most sensitive area" of Reagan's foreign policy and you think I mean most important. I try to use language fairly precisely, so I have no trouble at all pledging allegiance to many of your statements, such as that "there is no ideal mode of organization that fits all people or presidents or that guarantees good results or the avoidance of basic errors in all situations," and that presidents should not get lost in detail and that a short agenda is a good presidential idea, and that we need a strong president (provided he's good) and that other presidents have bent the law and that there is more to knowledge than facts, et cetera. Those and similar statements are commonsensical thoughts worth stating again, because people tend to forget them in the hurly-burly of the current daily revelations. Now that the Reagan tide has turned, it is your turn to lean against it, as I have been leaning from the start. But I don't think you will find in my blatherings statements anything that contradicts any of that.

Other problems are fascinatingly empirical. I do look forward to what you will write about tax reform. To me, what was appropriate, given the result of tax cuts, was not tax reform but tax rise, for which tax reform turned out to be a convenient substitute. But if it is the case that Reagan was genuinely engaged in it, even if he did not, as you say, deal with the details, that is going to be a very interesting story, particularly if your facts show him directing the show in person.

In many other places, the question really is simply a matter of evidence. I think I have been through every significant Reagan biography and have tried to keep up with the journalism on him. But as you suggest, there are still lots of gaps in the whole Reagan story, particularly Iranscam. I will be very surprised, however, if your views on the following are ever confirmed by evidence:

— that "the invasion of Grenada, the bombing of Libya, and the Strategic Defense Initiative" are "things [that] turned out all right." The first two did not turn out all right for the dead and maimed, and the third has put the arms race in space, despite the great majority of experts who do not ridicule it, but find it too dangerous for them to make money off of;

— similarly, that "the military significance of the arms shipments was small" would not seem so to the Iraqis;

— that Reykjavik was no example of "chaos at the top," despite what George Shultz had to say about it at first, Don Regan after his spin succeeded, and even Henry Kissinger—but the question is what actually happened there, not some theoretical judgment;

— that "the history of the Reagan Administration thus far is one of extraordinary caution, the sole exceptions being Grenada . . . and

Lebanon." Two hundred forty-one dead boys in Lebanon is quite an Rexception, but it seems to me that to characterize this administration as otherwise one of "extraordinary caution" one would have to deal with quite a range of stories from Stockman on supply-side chaos, through the Falklands and Bitburg, and much else, not to mention the scores of directly and radically counterfactual statements Reagan has pronounced—with serious demeanor—on matters of high significance (and sensitivity).

When you say that "at the moment, the economy is doing fairly well," I suppose you mean that we don't have a depression going yet, or some such; but is the economy doing well with those twin deficits?

To say that Iranscam is "a small temporary problem" seems to me already run over by the facts. (Trivial Pursuit: the Hippocratic oath does not say do no harm.)

The point is that a number of your judgments on this business lean hard against the empirical observations of most others, before and after the revelations, and thus would depend on startling new discoveries—sure to make the front page of the New York Times—about the operations of Reagan's regime.

Then there are matters in which theoretical concerns are laced with the factual ones.

Is Reagan "easily led"? You make accurately the point that he has received lots of competing advice and thus "at a minimum, the president has to choose among advisers." Correct. But my theory is that the passive/positive is most likely to go along with those he is closest to—physically—day by day. As his wife and many others have said, he does not like conflict up close. Like Taft and Harding, he is more dependent than any other president on his inner circle. Tentatively, I think the switch from the early flock of California richies, who moved into the Watergate to shape him along, to the next bunch—the pragmatists, Baker, Meese, Darman, Deaver, who helped him con Congress through the tax cuts, and on to Regan's monopoly of communication—those shifts in close advisers help to explain shifts in presidential policy. In any case, the theory is not that he collapses before every Tom, Dick, and Harry who walks into the Oval Office, but that he is comparatively much more attuned than other presidents to maintaining harmony with those he sees day by day, including the missus.

You're right that there is no one ideal staff system—I agree (and have so written). This is a mistake of the sociologically inclined political scientists who think they can organize character out of the presidency. Lots of luck. But for this president to turn over the office to Regan (in my vision of it) is dangerous, especially, interestingly, because Regan is, in a different way, as lacking in substantive conviction as Reagan is—a managerial analogue to the directable actor looking for a script. The few who slipped by Regan (e.g., Ollie North) seem (only that) to have had quite an impact on Reagan. I agree with Alex George that multiple advocacy is a good idea, and with Janis that groupthink is a danger. But none of that is solvable by restructuring alone. It depends on a president who is curious and realistic, neither of which this one is.

You have interesting comments on why the Teflon fell off at just this point. There are many examples of him speaking nonsense long before this, so I can't see the plausibility of the explanation that the people are just noticing he is starting that. Except this way: Presidents are given enormous benefits of the doubt. Nixon's offenses were brought out in the summer of 1972, to very little effect. Johnson's Tonkin fakery got exposed long before Congress turned against him. You are right that Reagan has been subject to criticism all along, his lies and fantasies repeatedly noted in the press and, indeed, in bound books of his misstatements. That point I think is symbolized best in *The Emperor's New Clothes*, in which right up until the little guy blows the whistle, all the king's men pretend they can't see his nudeness through his imaginary robes. Then, in a paradigmatic shift of focus, suddenly everybody notices—and remembers that he was stark naked before, too.

As for the punishment angle—whether Reagan has been substantially punished ("suffered enough")—that's a dimension I don't get into. Let St. Peter judge this "Man of God," as Larry Speakes calls him. I'm not into rating presidents as humans but as presidents. It is only in that sense that his personality is "fatally flawed," as you put it. I got that into print on his inauguration day in the *Washington Post* and in a long chapter in *PC III* in 1985 (*The Presidential Character*, 3d ed., Prentice-Hall, 1985). That Reagan is professionally responsible for the Contra war, supporting the Chilean torturers, bucking up Botha, and so on, is true. It is judgments about those responsibilities that lead to the conclusion that he should not have been president, not judgments about his personal morals. Unlike Stockman, I did not go to theology school, so I am humble when it comes to deciding how long Ulysses S. Grant should spend in purgatory.

I think you trivialize the Iran thing too much. The president came on loud and clear to the nation and, even more important, to the world: no deals with terrorists. He was urging the Europeans to unify around a strong policy, a hard change from what they had been doing, arguing that only if we all stick together in stonewalling ransom demands can we beat back the kidnappers. Stand firm, he said. Meanwhile, he was doing the opposite. It is that kind of lying, not the interesting deviations you describe from previous presidents, that fundamentally undercut the trust on which effective political leadership depends. When a President vigorously advocates a thrust of policy opposite to what he is actually pursuing, he rips up trust. (Compare Johnson in 1964, Nixon in 1968, etc.) You're right that none of us can achieve "total harmony between words and deed," but most of us blunder along with the words and deeds pointing in roughly the same direction. When a president makes war while pumping peace, describes his compassion while supporting butchers, trumpets a war on drugs while cutting the budget for it, advocates a balanced budget while knocking it farther off its balance than ever before—that kind of disharmony is what erodes trust both domestically and worldwide.

It's hard for me to believe you think the president should not or need not have known about the diversion of funds to the Contras. Maybe I've got your message wrong. Because it wasn't much money? Because competent people were taking care of it? Wasn't aid to the Contras on your list of the major controversies between the president and Congress, and an issue the polls showed had the public against him? Carter did get too immersed in detail. But I cannot imagine any other president, except possibly Harding, who would not have wanted to know that new millions were being switched into that fight.

On Congress's role in recovery, I'm thinking more and more that we need to move toward closer White House-Congress cooperative policymaking, to get past the dangers of isolated presidents going bananas. I'm not sure that's the way to go and would welcome more thoughts of yours on it. As above, structure won't do the job.

What I learn again from all this is the profound necessity of choosing the right president in the first place. Running for president and being president are now separate ball games in which the rules, the tests, the challenges are fundamentally different. Presidential candidates get better and better at playing to the press's professional obsession with novelty and immediacy. It's always what's next, not what is. Journalists claim not to want to be psychologists as they go about psychologizing every day. The problem is partly facts, but more using the sense they should get from observing the actualities of characters in the presidency to assess characters who want to get in there.

At a bigger philosophical level, I think you and other political scientists should take a long and serious look at what you mean by "success" in politics. For most of Reagan's time, a good number of political scientists who found his policies substantively cruel and idiotic nevertheless lauded his success in getting them through. I don't buy that. Neither did Socrates.

Well, enough said. This critic of Reagan, who has been such through all those years when political science conferences one after another puffed him up, this one is not laughing. This one is not out with "I told you so." This one is seriously concerned that the government of the United States fails to work effectively for peace and justice and liberty out there in the real world, and that the quality of discourse has degenerated as far as it has.

14

Presidential Succession and Disability: Policy Analysis for Unique Cases

With Samantha Rosen

The constitutional amendment on presidential succession and disability raises in extreme form the problem of recommending policy for unique cases. These special policies have the following outstanding characteristics:

1. The proposed solutions must work every time.
2. There is little historical experience upon which to base generalizations about future probabilities.
3. Behavioral science does not contain relevant propositions that could facilitate reasonable prediction of the outcomes of different sets of events under varying conditions.
4. The usual way around this kind of difficulty—the application of rules of thumb, like the incremental method, which depend on repeated adjustments of feedback—is not applicable because
   (a) it is so difficult to get the relevant experience, and
   (b) there is not enough time. The "error" of "trial and error" must not happen.

These problem characteristics mean that the one certainty is that

Reprinted from *The Presidency,* ed., Aaron Wildavsky (Boston: Little, Brown, 1969), 777–95. Revised with the aid of Samantha Rosen, a law student at the Georgetown University Law Center.

uniquely favorable solutions cannot be obtained. The existing state of human knowledge means that the problems are insoluble. But there are reasons to believe that no action at all may be worse than any of several alternatives, however unsatisfactory they appear. So how do we proceed? It is possible to clarify the most relevant criteria and to apply them, with some generalizations from political science, to different alternatives. This form of analysis allows us to reject the worst; we can then choose among better, although necessarily imperfect, alternatives.

Application of the relevant criteria to presidential succession will show that the Twenty-fifth Amendment represents a reasonable alternative that neither wholly meets nor completely violates the crucial criteria. In the case of presidential disability, however, the constitutional provisions are a parody of what must be avoided: a prolonged struggle over who has the right to be president. The problem cannot be solved in advance. We must rely on the presumed virtues of our political stratum to work out solutions for problems as they arise.

In our analyses it will be necessary to consider the relationship of presidents to their important publics; for the choice of a successor or a person to act as president during periods of disability depends on the probable reactions of the major publics that, in their mutual interaction, make up the larger patterns we call the presidency. In determining whether a successor might come from a particular institution, moreover, we are required to appraise that institution from a presidential perspective. Although existing knowledge is not adequate, we must attempt to specify the causal connections between different successors and their likely behavior in the presidential office. Consideration of reform thus compels us to summarize a substantial part of our knowledge about the presidency.

Great problems of public policy exert an independent force upon the societies that encounter them. Once a problem is recognized, public energies may be mobilized to find solutions, and scholarly talents may be directed toward historical inquiries in order to determine how the problem emerged. Thus, a great problem of public policy may itself be a source of energy; once its characteristics are determined many new problems arise and numerous old ones become more urgent. Such is the case with the problem of presidential succession and disability. This perennial problem of the American political structure would hardly concern us so much were it not for the specter of nuclear war. The faster events move—witness the extraordinary breakup of Soviet-style communism and the reimposition of harsh central command in China—the more interested we become in maintaining presidential continuity.

The tragic death of President Kennedy, and recognition of the possibility that Vice-President Johnson might have been shot at the same time, has made us aware of the dangers that might face us if we failed to make adequate provision for presidential succession. That is why we have added the Twenty-fifth Amendment to the Constitution. Two basic questions must still be answered: Who should be next in line if the vice-president is unavailable? How far should the line of succession be lengthened to guard against the possibility of a nuclear attack killing all those on call?

History

In trying to answer these questions, we may ask what history has to tell us. There has never been a need to go beyond the vice-president to fill the presidency, although one or the other office has been vacant for approximately 40 percent of the time since the beginning of the Republic. The first succession act was passed in 1792, when the Senate was dominated by supporters of Alexander Hamilton and the House by friends of Secretary of State Thomas Jefferson. The Senate passed a bill putting the president pro tempore of that body next in line, but the House amended it be placing the secretary of state first in line. A compromise was finally reached by putting the Speaker of the House second in line behind the president pro tempore of the Senate who, if a vacancy occurred during the first two years and seven months of a presidential term, would serve until a special presidential election was held. On November 25, 1885, Vice-President Thomas Hendricks died, ten days before the first session of the next Congress. A major impetus to change the line of succession was provided by the fact that Grover Cleveland was a Democrat, while the new president pro tempore was a Republican. The Act of 1886 placed succession among Cabinet positions in the following order: the secretary of state, the secretary of the treasury, the secretary of war, the attorney general, the postmaster general, the secretary of the navy, and the secretary of the interior. After Vice-President Truman became president in 1945, there were those who thought that his secretary of state, Edward R.

Stettinus, was not of presidential caliber, and that House Speaker Sam Rayburn would be better. President Truman, who appeared to accept the argument that the Act of 1886 was "undemocratic," waited until the Republicans gained a majority in the House of Representatives and proposed that the succession act be changed to put the Speaker—then Republican Joseph W. Martin—first in line and the president pro tempore of the Senate next.

The Presidential Succession Act passed in 1947 provides a line of succession first through Congress—the Speaker and the president pro tempore—and then through the cabinet in the order of the 1886 act, with the addition of the secretaries of agriculture, commerce, and labor. In case a Speaker or president pro tempore was not constitutionally qualified to be president by reason of age (a president must be at least thirty-five years old) or foreign birth, the next qualified person in line would assume the office until a Speaker or president pro tempore who was qualified was elected. The act also said that these officials must resign their existing positions when they act as president. This is essentially the succession plan we have today. Because of the circumstances following Kennedy's death and Johnson's succession—a Speaker in his seventies and a president pro tempore in his eighties—questions have inevitably been raised about the suitability of a plan that would permit them to assume the presidency.

What history has to teach us, it appears, is that succession acts have been influenced by somebody's dislike of a particular person or a person of a particular party being next in line to succeed to the presidency. An examination of the problem that avoids considerations of personality or immediate partisan advantage would seem to be in order. Let us begin by developing a set of criteria with which to evaluate the many complicated proposals for dealing with presidential succession. Then we can apply these criteria to the major proposals that have been advanced, with special attention to the victorious alternative embodied in the Twenty-fifth Amendment.

Criteria

Any method for determining presidential succession must be established with absolute *certainty*. There must never be any doubt about precisely which person—whether occupying a particular position or chosen in a specified way—is next in line to assume the presidency. Nor must there be any doubt about the new president's term of office or his right to exercise presidential powers. Untold mischief would result if there were two or more claimants for the office, or if there was no one with an undisputed right to occupy it. Who, then, could speak for the United States in foreign affairs or rally the nation to meet domestic emergencies? Worse still would be the internal upheaval resulting from the bitter disputes of rival claimants and their supporters. To argue about what the president should do is a normal part of politics in a democracy; to argue over which person should be doing what a president has the right to do is an invitation to civil war.

In addition to being certain, presidential succession should be *immediate*. Only a few minutes or at most a few hours should elapse between the demise of one president and the accession of another, as was fortunately the case when Johnson succeeded Kennedy. In a nuclear era, we cannot afford to be without a president. In many ways, we are better off with any one responsible person than with no one in the presidential office, even if that person were inferior to others who might have been chosen.

One reason for insisting that any plan for succession be certain and immediate is that these features help the new president gain acceptance as the legitimate occupant of the White House. When a political system is called "legitimate," the vast majority of people—especially those active in politics—believe that elected and appointed officers have real authority to issue commands within their respective spheres of competence, with the expectation that these will be obeyed as right and proper. Severe policy conflicts are then less likely to overturn the regime. When the legitimacy of a political system is threatened, as was the case in Weimar Germany and Fourth Republic France, even minor political controversies are dangerous because they raise the question not only of "how much shall each interest receive" but also of "whether this form of government shall survive."

If the person who succeeds to the presidency is to be considered legitimate, the plan for determining who it will be should be as stable as possible so that it can gather force from longevity and tradition. Stability is a desirable standard because it gives the greatest assurance that the plan will be known by the largest number of citizens. Taught in the schools and disseminated by the media of information upon suitable occasions, the plan can become part of the political lore that

Americans are expected to know as part of their basic education. Changing the plan every few years could only result in confusion and lack of widespread understanding of the procedures in operation at that time. It would then be much easier for someone to challenge the existing plan and to suggest that since the procedures had been changed so often there was nothing sacrosanct in abiding by them. Stability does not mean that the present arrangement be kept forever, although it does mean that we should try to keep any new plan for as long as possible.

The gravest danger to stability comes from the efforts of those who would tailor a succession act to fit the particular individual they would like to help or hinder, in case the need should arise. While it is not feasible to designate a particular individual by name for succession, it is possible to block a current officeholder, in case he or she is not thought suitable, or to place another current officeholder next in the line of succession. Following such practices would lead to continual changes in the succession act as those who occupied various institutional positions fell in and out of favor. Since no one can guarantee that all of us will always approve of the person designated as the immediate successor, wisdom would appear to require that we make the best long-range arrangement that we can. The futile hope that we can always get the person we would most prefer has to be weighed against creating instability.

The third criterion for determining presidential succession is *continuity*. Whoever succeeds to the presidency should serve until the next regularly scheduled election. A president who is in office for only a short period of time, and who must soon give way to another person, can hardly be expected to act with confidence, vigor, and dispatch. At best, he could undertake holding actions because he could not commit the executive branch to any policy that lasted beyond a few months. Weakness, indecision, futility, even challenges of the right of a temporary occupant to act like a president would be the most likely consequence of failing to allow a successor to serve until the end of the established presidential term. It follows, therefore, that any proposal that permits the presidency to be occupied by alternating individuals is to be rejected.

If we are to meet the criteria discussed thus far, the procedures embodied in a succession plan also must be as *simple* as possible. Simplicity is urged as a criterion because it helps ensure certainty, immediacy, and legitimacy. The more complex the plan, the more time is likely to be involved, the more doubt is likely to arise about who is next in line, and the more opportunities are created for something to go wrong. If people are puzzled over what procedures are to be followed, the way is left open for demagogues to claim that the result is not legitimate. If the occupant of the presidency is not determined beforehand, delay and intrigue may be added to confusion. Hence, we should eliminate any proposals concerning succession that involve more than a few simple steps or that involve lengthy deliberations or consultations.

The transfer of power to a new president should be as *tranquil* as possible.[1] The political life of the country should not be upset by shocks or disruptions in this delicate period, for the death of a president is inevitably traumatic. The nation mourns the loss of the man whose office signifies its unity, capability and hope. More than we realize, presidents provide important guidelines from which we take our bearings in a complicated world. By knowing about them and their customary modes of operation, the world is made somewhat more predictable. Regardless of whether we support their specific policies, their loss creates a void. There is no need, therefore, to add to the disquiet by public contests or controversies, by campaigns or contests that may unleash pent-up emotions.

Any person who succeeds to the presidency should *belong to the same political party* as the former president. The party system is an essential element of democratic government in the United States, so succession proposals should try to strengthen rather than weaken our parties.

That the person who succeeds to the presidency should be capable of exercising the highest office in the land is an evident but elusive criterion. It is difficult to say precisely what combination of characteristics is most desirable in a president. Certain qualities—tenacity, firmness, courage—are so personal that it is impossible to tell whether any person will have them when needed. Such qualities, moreover, may be differently perceived as stubbornness and roughness. Assessments of attributes like intelligence, knowledge, and skill can be discounted, according to one's own political preferences. Would a liberal prefer a highly intelligent but extremely conservative person to a moderately intelligent but extremely liberal one? The president's actions depend on values and preferences as well as personal capacities. We can, of course, do our best to appraise the appropriateness of successors, who would be drawn from various institutions such as Congress, the cabinet, or the Supreme Court. We can say, perhaps, that a successor should have some experience in American politics so that he will have been socialized in acceptable modes of political conduct. It would also be desirable for a potential successor to know something about current developments of special presidential responsibility, especially in foreign affairs.

Proposals for handling presidential succession are designed to see that we always have a president who functions with the full powers of the office. There would seem to be little point in adopting proposals at the cost of weakening the presidency or of diluting the quality of the vice-president, who is most likely to take over if something happens to the president. Any plan that would weaken the presidency or deprecate the worth of the vice-presidency should be turned down. It is difficult, of course, to find any proposal that is costless.

Our ideal presidential succession, then, would be certain, immediate, and widely regarded as legitimate. The succession plan would be simple and stable. It would lead to the choice of good presidents from the former president's party, who would maintain continuity in office. The president would be able to exercise the full powers of the Oval Office, a successor would be ready to take over if a disability occurred, and the strength of the presidency would remain unimpaired.

Succession

Proposals for dealing with presidential succession proceed in one of two directions. They either specify that the holders of certain institutional positions (such as cabinet positions) should succeed to the presidency, or they describe a procedure (such as a special election) through which a successor would be chose. Let us consider the arguments for and against the occupants of institutional positions providing a line of succession and then consider various other procedures for finding a successor.

One proposal, following the act of 1886, suggests that the secretary of state, followed by other cabinet members, should assume the presidency after the vice-president if a vacancy occurs. This plan, supposedly, would keep the presidency moving in the same general direction, especially in the vital field of foreign affairs, because the secretary of state is assumed to share the president's preferences and usually belongs to the president's political party as well. Moreover, secretaries of state have often been men of considerable stature, who are likely to be qualified for the presidency anyway because of their knowledge and breadth of vision. And the secretary has the additional advantage of being instantaneously ready to assume the presidency.

Perhaps the most serious objection to the secretary of state is that he is not an elected official and thus might suffer from a lack of legitimacy. In a time of crisis, some people might challenge his right to occupy the presidency. Nor is it necessarily the case that the secretary of state will be wise. The growing importance of foreign policy will lead some presidents to wish to act as their own policymaker. They may be wary, therefore, of appointing an individual with an independent national standing or following who might challenge them or make it costly to fire them. Such considerations may have played a part in John F. Kennedy's decision to appoint the little-known and deferential Dean Rusk over the well-known and assertive Adlai Stevenson, who could count on his own support in the Democratic party. It is not even certain that a secretary of state would follow the foreign policy of the president he succeeded.

The network of associations that envelopes cabinet members, centered around the major interests they serve, gives them a narrower view and pulls them apart from a president who must juggle and balance many concerns at once. Although the proposition that cabinet members are the president's "natural enemies" may be exaggerated, there is no reason to expect them to agree fully on matters of departmental policy, let alone the broad range of foreign and domestic issues.

In order to avoid some of the difficulties associated with the choice of the secretary of state and still keep succession within the executive branch, it has been proposed that national conventions nominate, and the voting citizenry elect, two vice-presidents. In case two vacancies occurred in the presidential office, the second vice-president would take over. This scheme has the advantage of placing succession in the hands of an elected official of the same political party who could be kept continuously informed of important developments, who could take over immediately, and whose legitimacy could not be questioned. The major question here is whether this scheme might not create

additional difficulties that would be greater than its presumed benefits.

There is, first of all, the problem of getting an outstanding person to
accept a position as second vice-president. This official would not
have the few formal duties of the first vice-president and he would
know that in the course of American history a second vice-president
has not been required to assume the presidency. And should a first
vice-president look forward to the chance of running for the presidency at some future time, he would know that he had a probable rival next to him, thus further reducing the incentive for the ambitious
to take the job. Debasing the value of the vice-presidency in order to
meet the more remote contingency that the two successors might be
required hardly seems advisable.

The introduction of a second vice-president would also lead to what
might be called the "politics of polygamy." In polygamous societies,
the relationship between the first and second wives is not always
noted for light and harmony. Since the president has the discretion to
determine what vice-presidents will or will not do beyond the usual
tedium of presiding over the Senate, vice-presidents such as Richard
Nixon and Lyndon Johnson have had to fight to get important assignments. The potentiality of conflict, favoritism, and intrigue would be
multiplied with two vice-presidents looking for work, perhaps by en-
croaching on the secretary of state or other highly placed officials. We
know that Vice-President John Nance Garner was not averse to suggesting means of overturning the "administration" program to congressional opponents of Franklin Roosevelt's policies. How much
greater, then, would be the temptation of mischief with one or even
two disgruntled vice-presidents looking for an outlet for their talents
and energies. Having a second vice-president without a real job would
introduce such strain—conflict between the president and vice-president and their staffs is already a sensitive matter—that it seems undesirable.

Presumably, one vice-president would continue to preside over the
Senate and to take on such additional duties as the president saw fit to
allot to him. The other vice-president would be assigned as a general
presidential assistant. No doubt there is plenty of work around the
White House and the president would have no difficulty in finding
jobs for any willing hand. But unlike such other high staff assistants
as the director of the budget and chairman of the Council of Eco-

nomic Advisers, vice-presidents cannot be fired. Even if a president had originally chosen a particular person as second vice-president, the chief executive might change his mind after a year or two. If this vice-president was charged in the Constitution or by statute with specific responsibilities, the president would be in the anomalous position of disagreeing with a high official he could not remove. Moreover, it might be costly to "dump" this vice-president at the next national convention.

It has been customary in recent years for presidential candidates to choose their running mates. One would imagine that this custom might carry over to the choice of a second vice-president. Yet it is conceivable that party leaders, who are prepared to concede the choice of the first vice-president, might find a rationale for a greater voice in the selection of any additional vice-president. While Lyndon Johnson was able to remove Robert Kennedy from consideration for the Democratic vice-presidential nomination in 1964, for example, he might have found it more difficult to justify refusing him a consolation prize if there had been more positions to distribute. Johnson—or any president—would thus be faced with the prospect of offending an important party faction or working with a vice-president whom he patently did not want and who possessed sufficient independent strength to make himself troublesome over the next four years.

The difficulties created by having two vice-presidents may be avoided by giving the president the right to choose a new vice-president in case there is a vacancy in that office through the death or disability of either the original president or the vice-president. There is much to commend this proposal. The successor would certainly be acceptable to the president, would belong to his political party, would be likely to continue his policies, and would be immediately available. There is something inherently plausible in leaving the choice of a successor to the person who has been elected by the voters and whose replacement should perhaps be similar in essential respects. We trust presidents with matters of life and death so, the argument goes, why not trust them to pick their possible successors? Indeed, the operation of the national nominating conventions pretty much assures a president the right to choose his first successor—his running mate.

This proposal could be extended even further to provide for the nomination of a vice-president after the president has been elected. Since a vice-president is nominated more for ability to gather votes than for experience or ability to be an effective president, nominating the vice-president after the general election could lead to stronger and more qualified leadership. Of course, since an elected president could not be repudiated by his party, the president would effectively choose the vice-president. Arthur Schlesinger, Jr., has suggested that completely abolishing the office of the vice-president and holding a special election in the event of a vacancy in the presidency, with the secretary of state assuming control in the interim, would solve the problem of presidential succession. While this makes sense and is not worse than many of the alternatives, the fact that people have grown accustomed to vice-presidents speaks to their continuance.

Yet allowing whoever is president to choose a successor is not without its difficulties. Such personal action, without the participation of a customary legitimizing body such as the national convention, might be regarded as an unwarranted exercise of personal power. Even under the Succession Act of 1886, a president would be choosing a cabinet member—subject to senatorial confirmation—who might incidentally be a successor, rather than a second vice-president whose major function would be precisely to be available in case there was a need for a president. Even if a two-thirds majority was required to affirm the nomination of a vice-president after the general election, we would still suffer from the lack of legitimacy stemming from taking the election of a potential president out of the direct hands of the people. In addition, the abuse heaped on Dan Quayle is likely to make the nomination of a young vice-president without years of experience unlikely. It would, therefore, not be necessary to take the vice-president off the ballot.

It is not clear whether having the right to name a successor would help or harm a president. A president might be helped if a vacancy occurred at a time when he wished to establish the new successor as heir apparent in a future presidential nomination and election. Other party people, however, might not approve. Furthermore, a president might be harmed if he wished to retain freedom of maneuver in the choice of a running mate or of a candidate for nomination in a future election. The very fact that he designated a new vice-president during his term of office might make it difficult to disavow that person in the future. President Lyndon Johnson, for example, apparently decided to hold off naming his choice for the vice-presidential nomination in 1964 in order to determine who might be best in the light of future events, such as the identity of the Republican candidates. He would have had trouble doing this if he had been forced to name a successor immediately. Presumably, a president who succeeded another because of death or disability would have to name his successor within two weeks or thirty days after assuming office. Yet it is hard to believe that any president would wish to undertake this difficult assignment when he was desperately trying to guide the nation through a trying period of transition. Further delay, however, would violate the criterion of immediacy.

The attack on the legitimacy of the plan providing presidential choice may be mitigated by a somewhat different plan, which calls for acceptance or rejection of the new president's nomination of a vice-president by Congress. While it might solve the problem of legitimacy, this proposal would not be acceptable to those who feel that the choice of a successor as well as the successor should be confined to the executive branch. They would argue that congressmen have different, narrower constituencies than the president, that the president and congressmen have different perspectives, that Congress may be controlled by the opposite party, and that the separation of powers would be violated by giving Congress an important part to play. A president could hardly afford to have a nominee rejected. A narrow approval might inflict severe wounds and might question the legitimacy of his choice. Hence, the president would have to conduct the widest consultations in order to make certain that the candidate was approved by a substantial, if not overwhelming, majority. In this case the power to reject, to use the traditional formula for senatorial confirmation, might become the power to select. Consequently, a president might be forced to accept someone he really did not want or pay the price of a long and bitter conflict.

A strong case in favor of having Congress act as the legitimizing authority can also be made. If individual representatives have rather narrow constituencies, Congress as a collective body spans the nation. Moreover, the increasing urbanization of the United States gives senators broader constituencies than in the past. A majority of congressmen, however, might belong to a political party other than that of the former president and a new successor. This means that bipartisan compromise would be reflected in the choice of a new vice-president so as to assure reasonable cooperation between the legislative and executive branches of government. The separation of powers, as Richard Neustadt told us, is a form of shared power. Nothing is accomplished by treating the different branches as if they lived in separate worlds, when the daily activities of government require their mutual cooperation. While the president might not wish to take the trouble to find an immediate successor, the chief executive's responsibilities to the nation far outweigh any temporary inconvenience suffered in doing so. A person who cannot deal with small political troubles, it might be argued, does not belong in the White House.

Still another variant of this plan calls for having Congress choose among three to five candidates selected by the president soon after a vacancy arises. If, however, the president indicated a first preference, even informally, the purpose of the plan would be thwarted and he would be faced with the prospect of having his choice publicly rejected. Indeed, there could be no guarantee that Congress would accept any of the president's suggestions or that it would be able to arrive at a decision at all, at least not without extensive hearings and lengthy debates. Aside from the mischief and dissention in Congress that this plan might create, it hardly comports with our ideas of an immediate, simple, and tranquil succession.

In a message to Congress supporting what was to become the existing Succession Act, President Truman declared, "The Speaker of the House of Representatives, who is elected in his own district, is also elected to be the presiding officer of the House by a vote of all representatives of all the people of the country. As a result, I believe that the Speaker is the official in the federal government whose selection, next to that of the president and vice-president, can be most accurately said to stem from the people themselves." The legitimacy of the Speaker becoming president could not be questioned. More than that, a Speaker is bound to be a product par excellence of American political life. Having come up through the ranks over a period of many years, Speakers know what kinds of behavior are acceptable and they are unlikely to be people who would threaten our liberties. Conciliation, respect for others, and the ability to bring people of diverse points of view together for common purposes are their stock in trade. A Speaker is also likely to have a wide-ranging acquaintanceship with other governmental officials and a broad knowledge of the major issues of the day, especially in regard to domestic affairs.

The objections to the Speaker assuming the presidency are numerous. It is said that the Speaker is of lower caliber than other officials such as the secretary of state, that he is likely to be too old, that he could not be sufficiently well informed, that he has a congressional rather than presidential orientation, and that he might belong to a different party from that of the late president or vice-president. Far more evidence than has thus far been supplied, however, would be required to demonstrate that the late Sam Rayburn would necessarily have been a worse president than any of the secretaries of state who served during his long tenure as Speaker, or that Secretary Rusk would have made a more vigorous, determined, and forceful president than Speaker McCormack, or that "Tip" O'Neill would have been worse than Alexander Haig or George Schulz. If a Speaker or potential Speaker does not manifest the toughness, administrative ability, intelligence, and force to run a large body such as the House of Representatives, he is not likely to last, as the deposition of Speaker Wright suggests.

The political skills and the breadth of knowledge a Speaker develops provides excellent training for the presidency. Age or seniority is not the prime factor in determining who becomes or survives as Speaker. The Speaker is chosen in a contest between different factions within his party for ability to lead and serve the membership. In this sense the Speaker becomes experienced in a prime task of the presidency—leading, serving, and resolving conflicts among a broad and rather heterogeneous collection of interests. True, Speakers are usually somewhat older than secretaries of state, though this is by no means an invariant rule. Yet an infirm person could hardly carry on as Speaker, so great are the demands of the position. The long service in government required to reach the position of Speaker may be considered an asset in terms of experience as well as a liability in terms of age. But in the era of DeGaulle, Adenauer, and Reagan, disqualification on grounds of age seems out of place.

It may be that Speakers are more oriented toward a congressional view and to domestic politics than secretaries of state. But excessively parochial concerns can hardly dominate the thoughts and actions of Speakers when they must accommodate, to some degree, a large party in the House as well as the president of the United States. Harry S. Truman, the one recent president who came to the White House almost immediately after long congressional experience, although not from the speakership, had one of the best records in foreign affairs of any president in our time. A Speaker is extraordinarily busy and might not have as much time for intensive study as other officials, but it would be foolish to suggest, as have some writers, that the Speaker would necessarily be blatantly uninformed, or that the formal separation of powers would provide a serious obstacle to sending information to a person from a rival branch of government. Indeed, it could be argued that a Speaker, with whom the president must cooperate and who has many sanctions at his disposal, is in a much better position to demand information than the much less powerful vice-president is today. Could it be that secretaries of state are thought to be generally more distinguished than Speakers because their jobs require them to issue lofty pronouncements, while Speakers, like presidents, are immersed in the muck and mire of partisan politics and domestic strife?

A most serious obstacle in the path of the Speaker is that he might belong to a different political party from the President's and might change the party in the White House, contrary to the expressed wishes of the voters. Nowadays, the system would most likely produce this result if the president was a Republican. Since a majority of the House is Democratic and would elect a Democratic Speaker, a Democratic president would probably be succeeded by a Democratic Speaker, but so too would a Republican president. No doubt a Speaker, realizing this and sensitive to his position, would be loathe to alter radically the personnel or the policy direction of the previous president until the voters had made known their approval in an election. He might choose a type of national coalition government in which members of both parties would be represented in the cabinet. It is also true that the partisan attachments of some secretaries of state have been ambiguous. In fact, the present secretary (James Baker) has no base of support in the Republican party. Nevertheless, a change of party in the presidency should be avoided if possible. The question is whether other plans, which lack this defect, do not contain others of equal or greater importance.

There are a host of proposals that leave the decision of a specific successor up to Congress. One calls for the selection of a new vice-president by a majority vote of a joint session of Congress; a second would have the House of Representatives choose the successor, and a third would have the House choose from among a number of individuals nominated by the Senate. A different stipulation is that the members of one or both houses should confine their selection to a member of the president's party in Congress. All of these plans share a common defect: they usually propose that part or all of Congress meet soon after a vacancy has occurred. Yet it might be too late if both the president and vice-president are unavailable. To be sure, such plans may provide for an interim president, and while not violating the criterion of immediacy, they run counter to the criterion of continuity. What could an interim president do while Congress was in the midst of debates on the identity of the successor? If the congressional debates reveal a lack of consensus, the new president would be handicapped from the start, assuming that terrible events had not occurred in the meantime. Should the election be confined to the House, the authority of the Speaker might be undermined by the choice of another person. Confining the choice to members of the president's party is contrary to all congressional precedent. It might be regarded as lacking the legitimacy of full congressional approval, and it would in no way guarantee that the successor would be a follower, rather than an opponent, of the late president. These proposals combine the disadvantages of locating the choice in Congress, without the advantages of having an official like the Speaker immediately available for the presidency.

We could also hold a special national election if there were more than one year left until the next presidential election. This would create legitimacy but sacrifice immediacy, and would allow the successor to be of a different political party from the former president. Moreover, special elections without any limit to their frequency would be disadvantageous, since any disruption in the continuity of the president's office is bound to be traumatic, and would be even more so if we were to hold three national elections in four years.

It is apparent that none of the succession proposals give certain promise of meeting all of the relevant criteria. There are five, however, that merit discussion in an imperfect world, because they violate the fewest criteria. If one is willing to accept the prospect that in the future, vice-presidents may be of low quality and that they may create continued difficulty for presidents, the nomination and election of two vice-presidents may be acceptable. Selection by the president may be advocated if one believes that the problem of legitimacy will not be serious, that the president will not have to compromise inordinately, that an immediate decision will not prove too taxing, and that the nation can afford to wait for however long it takes. Nomination by the president and confirmation by both houses of Congress may be appropriate so long as the prestige of the president and a possible successor is not damaged and the possible lengthy delays in this procedure do not materialize (or are not likely to be dangerous if they do). If one believes that succession need not be kept in the executive branch, or that a change of party in the White House ought to be permitted, then succession by the Speaker may be desirable.

Although I have argued that the secretary of state would not necessarily turn out to be better than the Speaker or a presidential nominee, there is little reason to assume that he would be worse. The secretary of state would most likely meet all our criteria except "legitimacy." Yet how would we know this would be the case?

We can examine the criteria in another way, by dividing the various proposals into two categories: those that promise to solve the direct problem of presidential succession but may have undesirable side effects, and those that minimize side effects but may be less than adequate in dealing with succession. If one chose to put the greatest weight on handling the succession itself, then the alternative of two vice-presidents would emerge as by far the best choice. If, on the other hand, one takes the position that other values should not be sacrificed just to deal with a succession problem that has never yet materialized, then allowing the president to choose a successor would clearly be superior.

Placing the analysis in this light suggests why the Bayh amendment—named after the chief sponsor, the Democratic Senator from Indiana—received such widespread support and easily became the Twenty-fifth Amendment. It provides that vice-presidential vacancies shall be filled through nomination by the president, subject to a majority vote in both the Senate and the House. This is a "satisficing" proposal. It sacrifices some immediacy and creates some instant difficulties for the president in order to secure legitimacy and to minimize his problems with the vice-president in the future. Not every criterion is perfectly satisfied, but neither is any one criterion blatantly violated. No other proposal is evidently better, and many are clearly worse. Avoiding the worst is not the same as getting the best, but there is something to be said for it in the context of great uncertainty.

The Twenty-fifth Amendment was first used successfully in 1973 when, pursuant to the amendment, President Richard Nixon nominated Gerald Ford to be vice-president, following the resignation of

Vice-President Spiro Agnew. Ford's nomination and confirmation hinged not upon whether he agreed with all of President Nixon's policies, but on whether he exhibited those characteristics that would make him an effective leader, thereby meeting the intent of the amendment. First and foremost, Ford satisfied the criterion that the successor be a "good" man, and his nomination was thus confirmed by both Houses of Congress. Shortly thereafter, President Nixon resigned and Gerald Ford became president and nominated Nelson Rockafeller as vice-president. After his confirmation, the United States, by virtue of our succession laws, had a president and vice-president, neither of whom had been directly elected by the people. While the smooth transition from Nixon to Ford illustrated the effectiveness of our Constitution, it also showed that these "successful" procedures could give rise to a situation that lacked the legitimacy of an ordinary election. The absence of the Twenty-fifth Amendment, however, would have further heightened tensions, since pursuant to our statutory succession law, the Democratic Speaker would have replaced the Republican president. The American people remedied the situation in 1976, however, when we expressed our political preference at the next presidential election and elected Jimmy Carter.

A situation in which there had not been a vice-president to assume the presidency after Nixon resigned, or the possibility of an attack that could kill all cabinet members, many congressmen, and a good part of any institution designated to choose a successor, leads us to consider the desirability of lengthening the line of succession. There are those who say that such an eventuality is too horrible to contemplate, but it would be morally impermissible for government officials to take this view. Their task is to help the living by taking whatever steps they can to promote continuity in government. The most obvious move is to reduce the probability that all top government officials will be incapacitated at one time. The president and vice-president can travel separately whenever possible, and there is certainly no reason why the secretaries of state and defense and other cabinet members should be in an airplane at the same time, as happened when President Kennedy was assassinated. Although the likelihood is not great, no one can guarantee that a huge explosion, taking place at a time such as thepdelivery of the State of the Union message, might not create a vacancy in the presidency with no living successor.

We might meet this problem by designating additional members of

Congress and the executive branch to stand in the line of succession. Further protection might be obtained by including the governors of the fifty states. A permanent order of precedence among governors might be fixed by adopting a wholly arbitrary procedure—taking the states in alphabetical order or in order of their admission to the Union.

The existing succession laws raise questions concerning the three crucial time periods between the election and inauguration of a president-elect. If the president-elect were to die before December 15, when the electoral college voted, the national committee of the president-elect's party would select a new nominee. Since this has never occurred, it has yet to be tested in the courts. If, however, the electoral college had met but the president-elect died before January 6, when Congress counted the votes, the outcome would depend on whether or not to count the votes for the dead candidate. If they were counted, the vice-president-elect would become the president-elect, but if not, the House of Representatives would choose a president-elect.

In the event the president-elect died between the time Congress counted the votes on January 6 and the inauguration on January 20, the vice-president-elect would become the president-elect and would nominate a vice-president after inauguration. Congress should legislate concerning these time periods, in order to provide clear guidelines to be followed in the event of a tragedy.

To raise the question of how a successor to the presidency should be found may imply that some solution is at hand. It is tempting to define problems as things to which there are solutions. Yet there may be problems for which there are no solutions. Let us examine a problem in a related area—presidential disability—for which there appears to be no apparent solution.

Disability

The problem of disabled presidents retaining their offices occurred during the terms of several U.S. Presidents, including Woodrow Wilson, Franklin Roosevelt, and John Kennedy. In each case there was found to be a correlation between the president's ill health and his decision-making ability. Woodrow Wilson's physical and emotional illness was known to have affected his handling of the League of Nations and Versailles. Because of his strokes, fatigue, and depression Wilson was unable to conduct skilled negotiations at Versailles. Instead of helping the country, the president's wife and personal physician covered up the president's illness until he died.

Franklin Roosevelt's run-down condition in 1944 was kept secret from the American people because of the loyalty of the president's physician and cabinet. John Kennedy, unbeknownst to the public, suffered from hepatitis, ulcers, malaria, and Addison's disease, causing him to be weak and to have low blood pressure and anemia. The knowledge that the health of these presidents has, or might have, affected their abilities to discharge effectively the powers and duties of their office, has led to discussions concerning the least intrusive way to deal with this eventuality.

Proposals concerned with presidential disability are designed to deal with four kinds of events:

1. The president is so badly incapacitated that he cannot communicate with the vice-president.
2. The president knows he is disabled and tells the vice-president to take over.
3. The president recovers health and takes back his office.
4. The president really cannot carry out the responsibilities of the office but insists on retaining office.

History has taught us that vice-presidents have been reluctant to take responsibility when a president was out of commission because they feared being accused of usurping power. The opprobrium Secretary of State Haig courted when he appeared to "take over" after Ronald Reagan was shot demonstrates that this is no idle concern. And at least one president failed to ask a vice-president to take over because the chief executive and his friends feared it would be difficult to get his job back.

For a long time, however, the matter did not seem urgent, and the obvious remedy was not adopted because congressmen could not agree on any single proposal. Different factions coalesced around different plans and, as we have seen, it was always possible to show that each plan had some glaring defect. Since Congress would not act, President Eisenhower, aware of public concern over his illnesses, entered into an informal agreement with vice-president Nixon that effectively took care of the first three circumstances outlined above. It was agreed that if the vice-president took over, he succeeded only to the powers and

duties, not to the office itself. The president, realizing he was disabled, could thus call upon his vice-president to take over. Or the
vice-president, after consulting the cabinet, could take over if the
president was unable to make the announcement. In both cases, the
president could take back his job as soon as he felt able to do so
simply by announcing that his disability was over. All presidents have
since adopted similar agreements with their potential successors. The
fourth instance, however, in which key officials disagree about the
president's ability to act as president, remains troublesome.

The Twenty-fifth Amendment provides for the possibility that the
president is unwilling to declare his own disability. If the vice-president and a majority of the cabinet (or other body so designated by
Congress) conclude that the president is unable to discharge the duties
of the office, they inform Congress. Both Houses of Congress, within
twenty-one days, must decide whether the president is disabled. If
Congress, by a two-thirds majority, declares that the president is disabled, the vice-president assumes the duties of the presidency; otherwise the president retains his office.

If a president is declared to be disabled, the possibility that he
might wish to regain office before he is ready must be taken seriously.
He might be mentally deranged or he might fear that the acting president was entrenching himself unduly and thus be motivated to take
back the office prematurely. Who is to umpire disagreements between
the president and vice-president over when the president is ready to
go back to work? The Bayh amendment states that this decision would
be made by the vice-president and a majority of the cabinet, which
would have to be ratified by a two-thirds majority of both houses of
Congress. The solution proposed in the amendment is acceptable because there is only one vice-president but would create insurmount-
able problems if there were two vice-presidents. Would one or both of
the vice-presidents be empowered to initiate proceedings to declare
the president disabled? How would we resolve a situation in which
the vice-presidents disagreed over whether the president was disabled?

On the positive side, the Bayh amendment safeguards the president.
By the time the vice-president (assuming there is only one) and a
majority of the cabinet decide that the president is unable to resume
his office, and two-thirds of both houses agree, there is very little
possibility of a successful plot to deprive the president of his office
without due cause. Moreover, the cooperation of the executive and

legislative branches of government in this proposal would appear to assure the legitimacy of the action, which would be of the utmost importance when such an unusual act—keeping a duly elected president out of office—was taking place. If one suggests that the scales are being weighted in favor of a president's resuming his office, a proper answer is that he should be denied this right only in the most extraordinary circumstances. Yet there are aspects of this proposal that leave me uneasy.

A president who is tired of the trials and tribulations of his office one year after he is elected or reelected could use the amendment to nominate a successor, thereby effectively taking the election and the choice of a president out of the hands of the people for up to three years. It is unlikely, however, that a president would undergo the rigorous campaigning necessary to be elected in order to help someone else ascend to the presidency. What this and other suppositions show is that by taking care of one remote contingency, we may subject ourselves to others.

The amendment could have allowed President Nixon to take advantage of the system and declare himself disabled in order to avoid impeachment proceedings. It might have posed a legal problem, since he could not then have been impeached, but as a practical matter there was sufficient public pressure to deter such action. Indeed, it is on the good sense of public officials and the citizenry that our ultimate safety depends.

One could argue that the evils that a dispute over a president's right to office would bring about would be so great that prevention, rather than cure, must be our hope. An extended trial procedure in Congress would keep the nation in a state of peril; it would also limit the possibility of emergency action, which is perhaps the greatest good to be obtained by formally dealing with the problem of presidential disability. If an obviously disabled president seeks to hold on to office while unable to exercise its duties, Congress might be given the power of impeachment to deal with such sins against the Republic. If impeachment is too severe a remedy, especially since he could no longer hope to resume office, a president who had, in effect, been declared guilty of hiding a disability could serve no useful purpose. A disagreement between the president and vice-president would inevitably be serious, but the suggested arrangement, far from aggravating the difficulty, merely recognizes it and offers a way out.

Another criticism of involving Congress in the matter is that it might alter the separation of powers between the executive and legislative branches. A hostile two-thirds majority of Congress might then get rid of a president without following the arduous impeachment procedures specified in the Constitution. Since the vice-president and a majority of the cabinet would have to initiate the procedure before Congress could act, however, it is improbable that all these people would be able to agree on a course adverse to the president. Indeed, a more cogent objection to the plan may be that it requires such widespread agreement as to make it unlikely that any president, if sufficiently determined, could be prevented from exercising his office. Can we, then, devise any plan that would include sufficient safeguards to be acceptable to a president and that would, at the same time, prevent a determined but disabled president from regaining his office?

This problem became apparent on March 30, 1981, when President Ronald Reagan was shot. There was confusion over who was in charge, which was heightened by Secretary of State Alexander Haig's announcement that he was in control, since Vice-President Bush was away from Washington. President Reagan did not at any time, while under anesthesia or during his stay at the hospital, relinquish control of his office or duties. This situation was successfully resolved due more to the good fortune that there was no crisis during that time than to the system. Had a situation arisen that demanded an immediate decision be made, Vice-President Bush would have been in control, and in his absence the Speaker of the House would have assumed command, pursuant to the Presidential Succession Act of 1947. If Bush had been unavailable during a military emergency, the secretary of defense would have been empowered to take over.

President Reagan perhaps learned from the confusion caused by his first mistake, and formally and successfully invoked the Twenty-fifth Amendment in 1985 when he underwent surgery for colon cancer. In a letter, President Reagan indicated that he did not wish to set a precedent, but since he was undergoing surgery for eight hours, he temporarily transferred presidential authority to Vice-President Bush until he was again able to discharge the duties of the presidency. Pursuant to the amendment, when the surgery was over and Reagan signed the letter stating that he was able to resume his duties as president, he automatically did so. There was not a question regarding presidential authority during Reagan's temporary inability, due to the objective and physical nature of the problem and to Reagan's willingness to offer a solution.

While physical illness is still a significant problem, it is perhaps more easily detectable than mental illness. Before and during the Watergate scandal, there were reports that President Nixon was unstable and irrational, and that he may have been drinking and acting suicidal. There was not, however, any attempt to engage the president in psychiatric treatment. Besides the difficulty of diagnosing psychosis, the stigma attached to treating it creates additional hardships. It may be advantageous, as Dr. John Gambill says, to have a board-certified psychiatrist as one of the president's personal physicians, thereby eliminating the need to go outside for treatment and possibly making the president more willing to seek psychiatric help. But there is probably no good way to tell with borderline mental illness. For who would say whether it was real or feigned, in the president or in the imagination of opponents who believe he would have to be mad to disagree with them. A psychiatric presence in the White House would only reinforce rumors about crazy presidents.

It is difficult to see how any solution can be found for the problem of a president who is prepared to ruin his country in order to retain his office. So long as the president remains adamant, his cabinet and vice-president are unlikely to insist that he give up the powers and duties. Anyone who resisted a president's will in such circumstances would find it rather awkward to continue. Congress would find it difficult to act in the midst of these uncertainties; it would have to institute a lengthy investigation, followed by prolonged and perhaps bitter debate, before it arrived at a decision. If Congress was closely divided near the two-thirds mark, as is possible, the resulting uproar, delay, and chaos would be precisely what we wish to avoid. There would also be the problem of conducting a sound foreign policy in the midst of a debate concerning the president's competency. It may be, therefore, that there is no effective remedy in our system for a president who cannot be trusted to protect the nation or that such remedies would have to be worked out on the spot.[2]

By now the fundamental dilemma has become apparent. The structure of problems like presidential succession and presidential disability is very different from that encountered in making most policy recommendations. Ordinarily, we would expect to cumulate experience and adjust our practices accordingly. If our theory was inadequate or required calculations we could not make, we could try various incremental moves and let these small acts generate consequences that we could study while taking further action. If our policy proved to be successful most of the time we would probably be satisfied. But in the case of presidential succession, the stakes are so high that we require a mechanism that will work every time, especially the first time. We might not recover from an experience that tells us that whatever policy we adopt has proven disastrous. No science that I am aware of can claim total predictability for chains of circumstances that, if not unique, are at least highly irregular.

To end on this note would, however, be too pessimistic. It is true that we cannot be confident that the best alternatives will work out exactly as we would like. But we have perhaps not used all the resources of political theory at our command. Let us now add an aspect of American political behavior that we have neglected. I refer to the existence of political activists whose members manifest a high degree of commitment to democratic processes and an overwhelming determination that free government should continue. Whatever the unforeseen specific events, therefore, we could expect, with a high degree of certainty, that presidents, congressmen, cabinet members, and other members of the political stratum would do everything in their power to prevent catastrophe. Whatever their other differences might be, these men are likely to put preservation of the system before other preferences. If the concept of the "public interest" has any meaning at all, the political stratus would work together to protect their nation against the evils stemming from the absence of a president, disagreement over who is president, or questions surrounding the legitimacy of the person who is president. Should ideological polarization proceed further, however, these assumptions may have to be reconsidered.

Notes

1. This article will not discuss the dangers of transitions, except to note that the disaster of the Bay of Pigs resulted, in part, from a lack of communication and information between the outgoing and incoming administrations.

2. Citizens of the United States do not really know whether their political system contains sufficient safeguards against a president who tries to establish a dictatorship because no president has ever tried to become a dictator. In principle, of course, the political system does contain effective safeguards. We can show that political leaders go through a socialization process in which those who do not accept basic democratic procedures are screened out. There is plenty of evidence to suggest that political activists manifest a high degree of commitment to democratic norms. Presidents do not wish to become dictators because they and their leading associates, including military officers, have internalized the desirability of such rules as free elections. As in so many other cases, we have "solved" this problem by never having had to face it at all. Its very appearance in serious form might be a sign of extreme degeneration of the political system for which no remedy might be appropriate.

15

The Plebiscitary Presidency, or Politics without Intermediaries

The real questions posed by proposals for electoral college reform are not about direct election of the president, which we already have in essence, but about a mass society, without intermediaries like parties, which we do not want. The mediation of the major political parties presently structures choice through competitive two-party elections. These would be replaced under so-called electoral college reform by crowds of candidates making their appeals to people solely through the media.

The consequences of so profound a change in so basic a political structure as the electoral college cannot be limited merely to the presidential election process. I argue, *inter alia*, that it would change the presidency itself and alter parties and party politics. Direct election would change the way the votes for president are counted. That much is obvious. But it would also have other consequences that, perhaps because they are less obvious, are less well-known.

Winners and Losers

No one will openly argue that substituting four national elections— a national primary, a run-off primary, a general election, and, at least as often as not, a runoff general election—for a single one will make work for the media managers and campaign cohorts instead of simplifying choice for citizens. Yet that would be the result of abolishing

Originally published as "The Plebiscitary Presidency: Direct Election as Class Legislation," *Commonsense* 2, no. 1 (Winter 1979): 1–10.

the Electoral College mechanisms for electing presidents. Campaign managers, party consultants, and media advertising executives will be forever grateful. But citizens bereft of party guidance in two of the four national elections and feeling that voting has become a chore, will soon wish for the good old days.

No one says that multiplying the number of political parties and candidates by removing the remaining rationale for a two-party system in presidential politics will confuse voters instead of enlightening them. Yet this would surely be a consequence of direct election.

No one asks citizens whether they want "one man—one vote" even if it means removing the restraints of federal structure on presidents. Yet those restraints would fall if the electoral college system were abandoned. Why, then, is there such substantial support for a plebiscitary presidency?

Polls suggest people favor direct election. Usually, the formula is to ask, "Do you favor majority rule?" Put that way, of course the answer is yes. Would people also favor a unitary rather than a federal government? Would they prefer multiple parties and numerous elections? The answers you get depend on the questions you ask.

The disadvantage of the electoral college rule is that on rare occasions it is possible for a candidate to be elected president while receiving less than a plurality of popular votes. So what? Every mode of election contains weaknesses as well as strengths. If every electoral procedure with negative elements was *ipso facto* rejected, it would be impossible to have elections at all. A better question is, "Compared to what?" That is, how do existing arrangements compare to alternatives, especially to a current proposal to count votes on a straight national basis rather than summoning them up as the electoral college does, state by state on a winner-take-all basis? After all, there would be little interest in electoral methods if they did not distribute power differentially to various interests in society. Who wins and loses under these alternative arrangements is of prime importance.

Who stands to gain from a plebiscitary presidency? People with time do—those with dispensable occupations and communications skills who want more access to political power. On the other hand, people who need intermediaries stand to lose from direct elections. Political participation by the poor or working or middle-class citizens requires intermediary organizations like trade unions or political parties. Left alone, without the customary anchor of party and faced with a bewildering array of candidates, many of them unknown or appearing for the first time, citizens will have little on which to base their choice. Once having chosen, they might have even less on which to hold incumbents responsible when, in the absence of strong party identification, a quite different array of forces and choices is likely to appear every four years.

Those who use politics and government to earn their living would be advantaged compared to others who just need government in order to live their lives. The mediation of the major political parties would be foreclosed. Federal elections, mediated through the states, would be replaced by national plebiscites mediated, if at all, only through the media.

The Two-Party System and Direct Election

The major parties still provide the arena in which the presidential contest is decided, and the contest for the presidency, at least, remains reasonably competitive. Under the electoral college's ground rules, the competition is federal in nature and the winner is the one who wins not just the most votes, as under direct election, but the most votes in the most populous states with the largest number of electoral votes. Thus, the candidates and parties are forced to make broader, less extreme appeals, and politics, as a result, is both more moderate and more stable than it might otherwise be.

Abolition of the electoral college system, by removing the requirement that pluralities be achieved in sufficient states to create national majorities, would negate the main function of a major party—to nominate a candidate who can coalesce regional priorities into national priorities. By removing the main incentive our political parties have to coalesce—the necessity of creating a coalition across diverse states to make a majority—abolition of the electoral college would drive the last nail in the coffin of our party system. So what? Political parties can be organized on many bases—interests, regions, tribes, ideologies, races. The result is likely to be a far more divisive politics than the United States has known since the Civil War.

Another immediate effect of nonfederal elections for presidents would be to increase vastly the number of elections, parties, and candidates confronting voters. This multiplicity is not problematic but inevitable. The only uncertainty is exactly how many there will be at a given time. Thus, there is the rather remote possibility (which has not yet occurred in this century) that under the electoral college procedure, a candidate with a plurality might win a two-party race. This must be weighed against the vastly increased probability, under direct election, that there will be many more candidates, parties, and elections without, however, knowing in advance precisely how many there will be. The adoption of direct election would mean trading away a small and calculable uncertainty for a large and incalculable one.

Under either system, elections themselves are easy to understand. Under the proposal, there must be a runoff, that is, a second election unless at least one candidate (and the vice-presidential candidate on the ticket) receives at least 40 percent of the vote. Evidently, if past rules prevailed, at least one and probably two such candidates (one presidential and one vice-presidential) would exceed 40 percent, deciding the election then and there. But that is just the point: Past rules will not prevail. Additional parties and candidates would be tempted to come in, both to publicize their cause and to better their prospects.

Extremism as a Defense for Moderation

Tiny parties and cause candidates, enticed by the prospects of public financing for their campaigns, would enter so as to use their unparalled opportunity for publicity. Minor-party and celebrity candidates would enter, either hoping they might be the lucky ones, or trying indirectly to influence the outcome. Let us suppose that parties of the radical right and left, together with cause candidates, will get, all together, 10 to 20 percent of the vote. This would leave 80 to 90 percent to be divided by the candidates of today's two major parties. What is worse, these two candidates would probably face competition from several others for the center vote. This would make it far less likely that any candidate would get even 40 percent of the vote, much less as much as 45 percent, half of the nonextreme 90 percent. But surely the losers in the major-parties nominating processes would be tempted to enter either as spoilers or on the chance that lightning might strike, diluting the "winner's" plurality even more. If they were to divide evenly, it would be clear to everyone that the winner was, in effect, a minority president who received less than half the total.

Under these or similar circumstances, bargaining with party extremes would become more difficult because the wings, left or right, could run their own slates, convinced that their votes would not be wasted. (They would be correct.) It would also become more necessary because, in the absence of such bargains carefully, if not gingerly, struck, the "wings" could reduce the mainstream candidate's total below the necessary 40 percent. Plebiscitary elections, therefore, will either lead to more extreme major parties or more numerous minority parties or (more likely) both.

The only real chance of retaining a single presidential election—by evolving a dominant major party—is undesirable. As the minority party (or, more likely, parties) becomes less and less representative, it would be reduced to its hard core, thus making more and more extreme appeals. The real election, as V. 0. Key showed in his classic work on southern politics,[1] would be driven to the primary of the major party where personal appeal provides a poor substitute for party principle.

The Withering Away of the States?

A plebiscitary election, of course, is bound to lead to a plebiscitary primary. Once the states have been eliminated from national elections, it would be anomalous to include them at the nominating stage. A convention of state parties selecting a presidential nominee would give way, predictably, to a nation of the individuals choosing among candidates with no party labels to help the voters differentiate.

The likelihood of a runoff in the primary would be even greater than in the general elections. It is quite probable that many candidates—perhaps as many as ten of them—might obtain enough signatures on nominating petitions to get on the ballot. Imagine a crowd of challengers hustling all over the United States, campaigning in a national primary. It would take enormous amounts of money. Although government financing might be available, this would have to depend on demonstrated ability to raise money in order to discourage frivolous candidates. The preprimary campaign, therefore, would assume enormous importance and be exceedingly expensive. It would also help if each of our hypothetical, but predictable, ten candidates were already well-known. It is not hard to forecast that nobody would win a clear majority in a primary with such a large number of contenders. Since all contenders would be wearing the same party label, it is hard to see how voters could differentiate among candidates except by already knowing one or two of their names in favorable or unfavorable contexts, by identifying or not identifying with their ethnic or racial characteristics, or by some other means of differentiation aside from their policy positions.

Suppose, then, that the primary vote were divided among several candidates and that, as was the case for gubernatorial elections in some southern states before the South became as competitive as it is now, ten or twelve aspirants divided the voters. One possibility is that the party nominee would be the candidate with the highest number of votes. Nineteen percent of the total vote would be impressive under such circumstances. Another possibility would be for the two highest candidates to contest a fifty-state runoff after the first primary and before the general election. That campaign would begin to remind observers (those who can remember that far back) of a marathon jitterbug contest. The party might end up with a good candidate, of course, if there were a candidate with anything left to give.

The Two-Party System and National Primaries

Such national primaries would also weaken the party system. If state experience with primaries is any guide, a prolonged period of victory for one party would result in a movement of interested voters into the primary of the dominant party; it would be largely the diehards who were left. They would nominate candidates who pleased them but who could not win the election because they were unappealing to a majority in the nation. Eventually, the losing party would atrophy, seriously weakening the two-party system and prospects of competition between the parties. The winning party would soon show signs of internal weakness as a consequence of the lack of competition necessary to keep it unified. The institution of a national primary would, in this respect, be especially dangerous.

Every four years, then, the nation would face the likelihood of at least two elections, national in scope (the regular election and the runoff primaries), and the increased probability of more than one regular election. One predictable consequence is confusion. Another is exhaustion. A third is delegitimation as elections succeed each other without notably clarifying issues (candidates too far apart have little to say to one another and are more likely to challenge those like them who seek the same votes), or illuminating candidates (whom the electorate sees only on television and who need no certification by party leaders), or changing policies (since winning the presidency would be disconnected from other elements of political life, such as Congress, whose cooperation is essential).

Not only would the presidency be disconnected from the rest of political life, so would presidential voters. Without the effective mediation of parties, they would have to face alone a confusing array of candidates who conduct themselves as just described.

The Political System

Abolition of the federal electoral base of the presidency must be considered in its relationship to the rest of the political system. Separation of powers and checks and balances, enmesh Presidents in relationships with others—state and local officials, Congressman, interest groups—almost all of whom have a federal base. What is to be gained by requiring Presidents to cooperate with forces from whose electoral connections they have simultaneously been severed?

A plebiscitary presidency is a perilous presidency. Do we want Presidents appealing over the heads of Congress, governors, and anyone else out there, not as an extraordinary matter, but as part of the usual method of operation? Has our experience taught us to love Presidents so well we wish to set them up outside the political structure we depend upon to restrain them? Do we hate them so much we wish to separate them from sources of party support in the states and in Congress, which they will need in hard times?

What should be done? The defects of the electoral college are its anachronistic appearance, its complexity, and the possibility it can produce a minority candidate. Obviously, a simple and more modern method would be desirable. Equally obviously, direct election, as it is called, is worse. One change would be desirable: requiring electors to vote for the candidate to whom they are pledged. This would eliminate skullduggery even as a threat. The disappearance of this remote eventuality would enable us to ask whether we want federal elections or unitary elections. Debate could focus on the consequences of different voting rules for power, politics, and people. Then the question of who benefits from a plebiscitary presidency might receive the attention it deserves.

Note

1. V.O. Key, Jr., *Southern Politics* (New York: Alfred A. Knopf, 1949).

16

The Human Side of Government

If readers approach *Steering the Elephant* as an effort to provide an impartial account of how Republican appointees tried to impose their preferences on administrative agencies, they will be disappointed. The book is avowedly ideological: Liberals and social conservatives need not apply. Competitive individualism and Laissez-faire capitalism, with but few exceptions, are the norm. The hopes and disappointments of its advocates provide the moral and emotional center point.

The substance of *Steering* is best expressed in the deliberate irony of the title; the elephant stands both as an analogy for government—ponderous, overweight, crushing—and as a symbol of the Republican party, divided as usual. Understandably, given the differences within the Republican party, we are never quite sure whether the problem addressed is controlling a balky government or a recalcitrant party. Indeed, it would be fair to say that the appointees discussed in this volume had more difficulty in persuading the Republican administration to steer in the direction they thought had been agreed upon than in getting the bureaucracy to follow a clear command.

Readers who come to *Steering the Elephant* for what it does have to offer will be amply rewarded. It is fascinating. When the remains of our times are exhumed by interplanetary archaeologists, they will find *Steering* to be indispensable source material about how people sharing certain values and trying to legitimate certain social practices viewed their world, tried to act on it, and were in turn reacted upon.

Originally published as the foreword to *Steering the Elephant: How Washington Works,* ed. Robert Rector and Michael Sanera (New York: Universe Books, 1987), xiii–xviii.

The focus is on controlling a presumably hostile bureaucracy. The ambience is one of moving into uncharted islands amid hostile natives. Yet the actors (insiders now like to refer to them as "players") differ markedly in their approach to the natives. Some, expecting hostility, generate it in return, thereby reconfirming their initial hypothesis. Although dark murmurings of bureaucratic sabotage are heard, significant evidence of such behavior is seldom presented. On the contrary, there are numerous examples of bureaucratic cooperation, if not exactly of enthusiasm, at having their agencies chopped and their missions thwarted. Other actors express regret at discovering, perhaps too late, that they could have made friends with many of the natives. Still others, like Jeane Kirkpatrick at the United Nations, attempt to intervene in the personnel process to assure themselves of competent staff, willing to support the new dispensation. They then attempt to improve the conditions of their bureaucrats so as to enable them to serve effectively. No sense in obtaining better staff if they cannot afford to live near enough to where they work. Gradually, after the identification of the "the bureaucracy" with all their troubles wears off, these bright-eyed and bushy-tailed reformers, albeit they usually want to do less rather than more, begin to realize that the disagreement on policies they once thought they were supposed to be carrying out against bureaucratic opposition has causes much closer to home.

They are all for the president, if only they were allowed to carry out what they are sure would be his wishes if he were in their place. Yet they never quite seem to get the authoritative presidential pronouncement, followed by active White House implementation, that would enable them to realize his (as well as their) aspirations. The hoped-for call from on high is just around the corner—they are in fact right about his and their policy congruence—yet it seldom comes into sight. Why is that?

By common consent, Ronald Reagan is a splendid communicator of political ideas. By my own assessment, with increasing but by no means unanimous agreement, he is also a superb political strategist.[1] All the more reason, then, to depend on and welcome his help. Why does it come (read these accounts) so seldom and so late?

A leading characteristic of President Reagan's political style is that he chooses only a few high-priority items in which to invest himself. This self-imposed limitation has served him and the nation well. The sense of frittered effort and disappointed hopes that enveloped the

Carter administration in its own malaise has been avoided. Major objectives have been achieved. The down-side of this accomplishment for the president's appointees, however, is that they are left on their own. It is up to them to bring him the necessary support for what are undoubtedly his own policy preferences, so he can afford to back them. That they were expected to bring support to him, not he to them, it would be fair to say, did not comport with most initial expectations. When the rules of the game are based on an antileadership culture, in which authority does not inhere in position but must be earned anew policy by policy, each relying on somewhat different coalitions, the players are limited by the overall capacity of the system.

There's the rub. The president's appointees are limited by the political system's capacity to support authority. Now, enhancing the authority of American institutions is an objective one might think conservatives would share. But these actors are not social but economic conservatives. They are individualists. They believe in competition, not in collectivism. The Republican party, however, so well exemplified in the person of Ronald Reagan, is a coalition of hierarchical collectivism (namely, defense and abortion) and competitive individualism. The hierarchical, socially conservative wing has to be concerned about shoring up authority to legitimate intervention in social life. Even the individualistic, economically conservative wing requires presidential authority to undo governmental intervention it does not like. Why, then, do they often beat down on the bureaucracy, which is (and must be in a modern society) a major repository of authority?

One might think that a two-track approach to bureaucracy would commend itself: on the one hand, a concerted effort to abolish agencies and programs; on the other, respect for the officials who administer the programs that the representatives of the people in their wisdom have decided to retain.

The conflict—condemnation of the activity versus respect for its administrators—comes out nicely in the discussion of the Small Business Administration. Its head was apparently a splendid administrator. Evidently that is not enough to satisfy those who believe that government should not subsidize industry and certainly not provide selective subsidies. Does that view, which I share, justify the actions of some players in denigrating the civil servants who continue to obey the law, or the director who has greatly improved its operations? I don't think so. Conservatives, who in other areas call for defense of American institutions, cannot inculcate respect for authority by denigrating its most visible manifestations. Similarly, they would not justify any administrator's attempt to thwart presidential policy once the decision to shut down an agency had been made.

Among the many interesting uses to which *Steering* could be put would be to solicit comments from civil servants. Do they see themselves accurately portrayed here? What do they see as their proper role—doing as they are told, suggesting better alternatives for accomplishing the same purposes, rallying opposition to proposed changes (after all, members of Congress are part of government too)? What do bureaucrats think of their power? Not much, I expect. And their situation may well get worse. If liberal Democrats occupy the executive office, they will heap more tasks on the bureaucracy while challenging its authority as inegalitarian. The further the ideological differences between Democratic and Republican elites, moreover, the more difficult it will be for bureaucrats to discover what they are supposed to do or to whom they are supposed to be accountable. None of this matters, of course, except for those who care about respect for American institutions. Perhaps the actors who write about their hard times here would reply that they will love government more when it becomes small enough for them to embrace.

How much, the reader may wonder, in an effort to assess the applicability of advice on *Steering the Elephant*, would liberal activists entering a future government have to learn from these accounts? A great deal, I think. The advice given is often surprisingly neutral, almost antiseptic. Clarity of purpose, knowing what you want, is essential, though it is difficult to imagine how anyone not already gifted with this invaluable trait will be able to acquire it. Modifying what is desirable with what is feasible, not allowing the best to become the enemy of the better, makes sense. The trouble is that the advice is contradictory. If you don't try, you won't know how far you (or your ideas) might have gone. True. Gramm-Rudman-Hollings and tax reform testify to that. But if you go to the well once too often, or fail too blatantly, your future chances may be much diminished. Also true.

The importance of personal energy, a resource presumably available across the ideological spectrum, is once again reaffirmed. Continuing to push, maintaining contacts, and making yourself and your ideas available to others pays off.

It is difficult to accomplish anything if you are worried about failure. It is difficult not to be worried, however, when you suddenly get fired or are savaged at hearings. The rule of American life—what you were before doesn't matter as it would in a class system—has now been rewritten to say that you can be held accountable from birth on. In such a heated context, political appointees are wise to cultivate friends and to seek allies against adversity. People who take the reigning ideologies too seriously, as if adherence to them constituted a protective shield, should know better. For them, as for the bureaucrats they are concerned about, government has become a dangerous place.

William Niskanen's heartfelt advice to political appointees is right on: If they can't support the president who appointed them, they should have the good grace to resign before they bring down with them the institutions on which the proper functioning of government depends. I would add that loyalty can only imperfectly go two ways. It has to be given but it cannot always, perhaps often, be expected to be given back. Keeping your bags packed, while remembering there is life outside of Washington, as Niskanen suggests, is the best advice in the book.

"The Firing of Ed Curran" contains the moral. Upon discovering that the secretary of education had not assumed his position to preside over the liquidation of that empire, contrary to the president's pronouncements, Curran tried to tell the chief executive what everyone in Washington knew. In the process, he discovered something only insiders know, namely, how to address a letter with a special code bringing it to the president's personal attention. Curran couldn't have known that when the president was away, a senior staffer would send that communication to the secretary, who promptly fired his subordinate. Long afterward, upon learning about what happened, the president is reported to have said that maybe the firing was a mistake. The attentive reader will observe, however, that the staffer occupies a still more prominent position, while Curran does not.[2]

In the first chapter of *Steering the Elephant,* M. Stanton Evans proposes a different theory of why conservative appointees have a hard time: The permanent government rejects them. This is why affirmative action is enforced, not because it is the law but because bureaucrats insist. I submit that the difficulty in getting the president to sign an executive order abolishing or modifying it—wasn't Reagan elected?—suggests otherwise. The reason it is necessary for appointees to follow Evans's excellent advice to get involved with the war of information is not that faceless bureaucrats and consultants prevent popular rule, but rather that under the separation of powers and a disinclination to accept authority, elections cannot control most outcomes. The campaigners do not usually specify positions clearly enough. We cannot know which of their positions voters support. And the balance of power is in flux. Hence, the need both for support and for clarification of alternatives is continuous. Appointees get a license to try, not a guarantee that they will catch anything except trouble.

The human element in these stories sets *Steering* apart from the usual literature on the Washington community, the joyful "How I Came and Conquered" school, the proud "How I lost but Didn't Sell Out" genre, and the dispiriting "You Can't Beat City Hall on the Potomac" wail. The editors are to be congratulated on producing a mosaic of hope emerging out of disappointment whose personal stories stay with you long after more desiccated accounts have faded from view.

Notes

1. See my "President Reagan as a Political Strategist," in Kay Lehman Schlozman, ed., *Elections in America* (Boston: Allen & Unwin, 1987), 221–38.
2. After being fired at the Department of Education, Ed Curran served as deputy director of the Peace Corps, and was nominated as head of the National Endowment for the Humanities (NEH). The position at NEH would have been considerably higher than Curran's former position at the Department of Education, but his confirmation was blocked in the Senate. This latter fact points to a second lesson: Aggressive action based on one's convictions is not a sure road to personal advancement in Washington.

17

Making The Process Work: The Procedural Presidency of George Bush

With Kerry Mullins

> *"George Bush continues to puzzle those whose job it is to figure him out."*
> — *The Economist American Survey,*
> April 21, 1990

Where it was easy to observe that President Jimmy Carter was more interested in management than in politics, and President Ronald Reagan was more interested in politics than in administration, it is not so easy to get a fix on President George Bush. What is one to think of a president who, after some thirty-odd years in politics, has few apparent policy preferences? Why, during one of the greatest revolutionary periods in world history, when the American values of democracy and capitalism have received the most remarkable validation by other peoples, has the president of the United States virtually nothing to say except to raise fears of instability? Where is the evidence of what the best vitae in American public life has brought George Bush in terms of applied wisdom to guide his behavior as president? What kind of leadership is it that refers more to world events over which human beings have little control than to the president himself? What is one to make of a leader who regards "the vision thing"—charting a path and then moving people in that direction, as his predecessor had done—as if it were a disease?

Here we attempt to make explicit the values and beliefs that would make sense out of George Bush's presidential style. Using the resources of cultural theory,[1] which relates shared values to the patterns of social relationships they justify, we shall try to recreate the cultural context out of which President George Bush works. Cultural analysis posits several ways of life, each operating from a different set of premises. Given different views of how the world works, different behaviors are rational. Which ones in relation to what objects, we ask, fit George Bush?

Intertwining Hierarchy and Individualism

His is, above all, a cultural context of inclusive hierarchy whose object is to integrate all elements of the American polity (classes, races, regions, interests, even political opponents) into a cohesive whole in which leaders serve followers and, in return, followers, seeing the leaders sacrifice for the whole, grant them the authority that inheres in their positions. This is not the exclusive hierarchy in which those who do not obey the letter of the law are expelled; in George Bush's encompassing hierarchy, there is always room at the inn. Because inclusive hierarchies are so accommodating, however, theirs is not a hierarchy of command but of persuasion, in which authorities have the right to say what ought to be done, but citizens need not comply unless they are persuaded.

George Bush is also partly individualistic. He likes competition and capitalism. Individuals, especially those born to advantage, need the opportunity to prove themselves against their equals. Economies grow best when they allow room for entrepreneurs to innovate so as to better serve their fellow citizens. Yet competition, important as it is, must not be allowed to destabilize the accommodations among groups of diverse Americans that hold this potentially explosive people together. American vitality, Bush believes, is best expressed through individualism. But American unity is best preserved through the sense of a caring collective conveyed by leaders whose main purpose is not, as conservative theorist Michael Oakeshott expressed it, to steer the ship of state in a particular direction but rather to keep it on an even keel while nurturing the gentle arts of civility. In this moderating and civilizing task, Bush believes, none are better qualified than those who have devoted their lives to public service, to becoming part of a government that includes ever-larger sections of the population in an expanding consensus.

Bush's individualist sympathies are particularly evident in the economic realm. Rather than taking a paternalistic attitude toward social welfare issues, he appears to prefer market solutions and freedom of choice. Free-enterprise zones are offered as a remedy for economically distressed areas of the country. He took a strong stance against a large increase in the minimum wage, emphasizing employer choice over worker protection. And despite his strong defense of the family, he has resisted limiting employer discretion by mandating three months leave for workers to take care of family responsibilities. But the most obvious example was his "no new taxes" pledge. By emphasizing the private market as the source of growth, he legitimates individual profit over extension of central government.

As long as he maintained his "no new taxes" pledge, Bush could not perform as a hierarchical leader. Hierarchical governments require extensive tax revenue to demonstrate concern for the less well off and to build impressive displays. Bush cannot use the highway and airport trust funds, which stand idle, because their presence reduces the deficit. He cannot take the lead against homelessness or fight the drug wars. He cannot tell foreign nations to sacrifice (e.g., Japan and/or Korea on diminishing protection of home industry), if he, the president of the United States, does not go first. How can Bush bail out Gorbachev to maintain international stability without the wherewithal to do so? Where individualist Ronald Reagan needed money mainly for defense, so a decline in danger would be met by lowering taxes, Bush, as a hierarchical leader, wishes to do so even more. In addition, a hierarch's devotion to balance is much greater than the individualist who sees opportunity in instability. For all these reasons, we expected Bush to raise revenues. And, following the hierarchical belief in sacrificing for the collective, Bush's higher taxes, insofar as possible, will be placed on consumption.

Governmental intervention in individual and corporate decision making is necessary to the hierarch, abhorrent to the individualist. Bush spent eight years in an administration well known for its dislike of most forms of governmental regulation, playing a central role as head of the task force on deregulation. His actions as president, however, have distressed some strong opponents of regulation.[2] His administration's policies in areas such as the environment, occupational health, and gun control reflect at minimum a shift in emphasis from the strong antiregulation flavor of the Reagan administration.

In his attitude toward AIDS, Bush demonstrates a blend of individual and collective responsibility. His strong preference for traditional family structures would indicate a suspicion of homosexual activity. Yet he also believes that the system must take care of its members, and he appears unwilling to define gay men as external to his hierarchy. He has thus defined nontraditional sexual activity as wrong, as behavior for which the individual must bear some responsibility. But it remains incumbent on society to forgive and to work toward alleviating the damage done. "We don't spurn the accident victim who didn't wear a seat belt. We don't reject the cancer patient who didn't quit smoking cigarettes. We try to love them and care for them and comfort them. We do not fire them. We don't evict them. We don't cancel their insurance."[3] Thus the president has continued but not expanded funding on research to fight the disease.

Elements of individualistic values in Bush's world view certainly exist but have perhaps weakened over the years. On at least two occasions, both during his twenties, he deviated from the traditional path. Against the wishes of his family and older friends, he delayed his entrance to Yale by joining the navy in 1942, becoming the youngest naval aviator. Then, after graduating from Yale, he turned down a safe position in his father's financial firm for a job in the Texas oil fields. In both instances he chose competition and danger over safety and security. Moving to an alien region (although not without family friends supporting him) stands as the most dramatic break from tradition. It is remarkable precisely because it is an unusual event in Bush's life. Having tried and tested himself, his governmental career is largely the story of deference to hierarchical values.

Perhaps it takes one politician to know another. "The Americans," the Leader of the Opposition in Britain, Neil Kinnock, said, "are no longer wedded to the magic of the market place." That notion was reinforced by Dennis Healy, a former deputy leader of the Labour party, who told the BBC that Prime Minister Margaret Thatcher and President Bush did not get on because "Bush . . . represents the sort of upper-class wet she most dislikes in Britain" (In Thatcher terminology, 'wets' are members of her party who cry too much about poor people.) As for a president who believes in the rules of the democratic game, including an honorable place for opposition, he opened his door to all such leaders because "that's the way it ought to be."[4]

Bush was raised to value competition, but competition among equals guided by shared rules. Recognition of one's worth must come from others rather from oneself. Thus a win is only a win when judged as such by the society. And a game fairly played is not to be regretted or resented if lost. A similar mixture of hierarchic and individualistic attributes, with the balance favoring hierarchy, can be seen in his personal style. Most attention has been devoted to characteristics consistent with hierarchy: conciliation, cooperation, and personal warmth. There is, however, a different side of Bush that can emerge under conditions of adversity.

On several occasions, Bush has evidenced a carefully controlled combative streak. He was reported to have described his debate with Geraldine Ferraro by saying he "kicked some ass." His celebrated "debate" with Dan Rather, in which Bush was deliberately combative, was viewed by many as improving his image. Negative campaign tactics led to confusion on the part of political forecasters, who could not decide whether that tone, or Bush's more general tendency toward conciliation, would dominate the administration's relations with Congress.

During the campaign, Bush absorbed continual charges of inability to lead. As president, his foreign policy had been repeatedly attacked as indecisive and reactive. Panama, especially, had been a sore point for several months. Sustained criticism alluding to personal weakness seems to spur Bush to more aggressive behavior. Such assertiveness strikes a shrill note, however, when contrasted with his general preference for coalitions over confrontations. Perhaps he feels the need, or the justification, to strike back only when criticism has exceeded what he considers the boundaries of fair play.

Bush says he had developed a fairly high tolerance for criticism. He prides himself on not letting it get "under his skin." "I've gotten immune to criticism. It used to bother me but now I think all you can do is be what you are, get back to real values and do your best."[5] He almost seems to be saying that he has moved from an individualistic (substantive, bottom line) to a hierarchical (procedural) mode of response. He often refers to his experience with an ulcer as the event that changed his attitude toward handling stressful situations.[6] "That's why I had ulcers 20 years ago, because . . . I kept it all inside, but I've learned now to get out there, do your best, get the best information you can, have confidence in good people. And those fundamental principles are guiding me now."[7] It is possible that his mellow attitude does not come naturally, that it is something he has had to learn at some personal cost. Bush connects not worrying about negative comments with reliance on values. But he does not usually say what these values consist of. He knows, of course, but we surmise they are no less important for being platitudinous—hard work, fair play, faith, friendship. As Bush put it in his inaugural address, "The old ideas are new again because they are not old, they are timeless: duty, sacrifice, commitment, and a patriotism that finds its expression in taking part and pitching in."[8]

Analysis of President Bush's twelve vetoes reveals a striking hierarchical pattern. Three stem from his early anti-abortion stand, one is a technicality, another is opposition to a too-high minimum wage, and the other seven are in defense of presidential prerogatives. Thus Bush vetoed a foreign aid bill because "it interfered with my constitutional authority to conduct" foreign relations. He vetoed a bill that would have made it a crime for governmental officials to use what were termed "indirect means" in support of foreign policy objectives prohibited by law, on the grounds that it would "impermissibly constrict" the president. Other vetoes involved dealing with China and Japan his way and restricting the ability of Congress to make partisan appointments and to regulate railroads outside the executive branch.[9] With this much data and a little political understanding—as Republicans win the presidency and Democrats gain majorities in Congress, each party tends to identify with the branch of government in which it is strongest—these vetoes begin to make sense. At one and the same time, Bush is defending his party and his powers. Moral boundaries (such as abortion) and institutional boundaries (the separation of powers) are joined, as we would expect from a person with hierarchical beliefs.

Insiders versus Outsiders

From a more hierarchical perspective, Bush's response to situations of adversity may be explained by reference to insiders and outsiders. He is willing to tolerate a great deal from those he considers part of the system. As an inclusive hierarch, his tendency is to define people and institutions as part of the system. If they are not, he tries to make them—Russians, Chinese, whoever—part of his extended family. Yet once the invisible line is crossed, the rules are changed and friendly competition becomes serious adversity. Despite Bush's assertion that he never holds grudges, several former allies seem to have had a different experience. Bush's refusal to bury the hatchet with columnist George Will is well known. Conservative activist Paul Weyrich, who was responsible for some of the allegations against John Tower, has found himself excluded form policy circles, as have several other associates.[10]

Moving from outside to insider is also possible. The evolution of Bush's position on the Soviet Union can be seen as one example. He was initially very skeptical of Soviet conversion and much more reluctant than was Reagan, foe of the "evil empire," to trust Gorbachev. In an international context, America was the relevant hierarchy, and the Soviet Union most definitely external. Trusting the Soviet Union meant reordering his concept of who was included and who was excluded in his definition of the system. Redefinition on this scale may account for some of his hesitancy in reacting to changes in both the Soviet Union and Eastern Europe. As William K. Muir suggested to us, Bush's service in the United Nations may have disposed him to see the Soviets as more human.

China, on the other hand, has been a part of Bush's world for a long time. He developed personal bonds and an identification with the people of China during his tenure as chief of the U.S. Liaison Offices in the mid-1970s.[11] His treatment of the Chinese leadership as part of his hierarchy is reflected in his policy toward them in the aftermath of Tiananmen Square. Bush felt strongly enough about his relationship with China to defy Congressional and public opinion. He risked a near defeat on his veto of a popular bill to protect Chinese students. He has continued China's status as a "most favored nation" enjoying the lowest tariffs on imports. Rather than confrontation through formal channels, he chose personal negotiation and moral pressure. These are the tactics appropriate between parties within the same system. Whether China actually fits the status Bush would like it to have is another matter. The fact that China supported United Nations sanctions against Iraq has made Bush's overture seem more desirable than it did on its own.

Bush's definition of insiders and outsiders affects his view of domestic problems, particularly the drug issue. His discussion of drug use contains some of the strongest rhetoric he has used as president. "Perhaps the greatest challenge of our times . . . the continuing struggle to keep drugs out of our high schools . . . a form of pollution, a poisoning of the mind, a corruption of the very soul of young America."[12] Drug use is defined as far beyond anything acceptable to his system. By labeling drug providers, and to a lesser degree, drug users, as enemies, certain policies are suggested. "The tolerance . . . of casual users or the exclusion of one echelon of society for using drugs and then going after another is unacceptable. . . . The day of tolerance for those who break the law in using drugs is over, and should be over.[13] Drug use, for Bush, casts one completely outside of society. No longer can this be mediated by class status or extenuating circumstance. No distinction is made between various kinds of illegal drugs; all are external—and thus a threat—to the system. A useful effect of blurred distinctions is that easier victories (i.e., the destruction of domestic marijuana crops), lend their glory to the much more difficult and tragic battles with crack cocaine.

Bush's emphasis is on interdiction and on punishment of deviants. The military and the police play the largest role in a war against the drug scourge. Although treatment is not excluded from the agenda, its secondary role is an attempt to resocialize deviants back into the system. Given the seriousness of the threat to order, lesser values such as the right to privacy may have to be sacrificed.

Working from a perspective of hierarchical exclusion and inclusion, Bush's puzzling treatment of minorities gains some degree of coherency. From his first involvement in politics, he has emphasized improving the Republican image among blacks and Hispanics. He worked hard as a county chair in Texas to include minorities. As president, he has attempted to demonstrate a sensitivity to issues of minority rights. At the same time, however, his individualist inclinations suggest taking opportunity, not welfare, is the right route to go.

Some say his rhetoric does not always square with his actions. Bush has been criticized for failing to pursue policies aimed at substantial improvement for minorities. According to Congressman Don Edwards (D-Calif.), "In civil rights, Mr. Bush has not been kinder and gentler."[14] Assuming Bush is simply mouthing empty rhetoric for political reasons fails to explain the consistency of his focus on inclusion of blacks and Hispanics. His predecessor felt no need to address the issue at all.

Bush desire for inclusion makes the issue of minority exclusion a serious problem, a contradiction in his coherent system. An individualist will see, perhaps, the need to improve the condition of competition. Bush sees the need to make everyone feel welcome, to be invited in to take part in discussions, to be given the chance to contribute for the good of the whole. To entertain the idea that the system itself might require fundamental change to integrate the historically excluded threatens the stability Bush holds so dear.

Bush's urge is to pull everybody into one cooperative whole. Family, faith, and country are the principles needed for a system of mutual support in an unpredictable world. The crucial position of the traditional family structure in maintaining stability intertwines both moral and institutional values. The family is the most basic hierarchy on which all others depend. "As I look at the fabric of society, and then look at the instability of family relationships, I see a real threat to our future."[15] He believes that "so many of the problems out there are because of this new trend towards single parent families."[16] Any orderly structure has to be complete.

To Bush, "family and faith represent the moral compass of the Nation."[17] His most passionate rhetoric centers around hierarchical concerns. "The underpinning of society . . . comes from the family. And I do not want to see one piece of legislation passed that diminishes the family choice or that weakens the family in any way, whether it's welfare legislation, child care legislation, or whatever legislation."[18]

The strength of his moral values, particularly religious ones, may present problems with the separation of church and state—an issue he claims to have thought about when shot down in the Pacific during World War II.[19] Hard as it is to believe that such thoughts occupied a young soldier expecting capture by the enemy, perhaps it was then that he formed his compromise on the dilemma. By conceptualizing faith as morality instead of religion, the problem evaporates. He avers, "We believe in the separation of church and state, but not in the separation of morality or moral values and state."[20]

Despite the attempt to eliminate the issue, moral/religious questions remain central to some of the most divisive political debates: prayer in schools and abortion. What is particularly interesting is that he has altered his position on both of these issues in recent years. Even his attitude toward the family has undergone a certain shift in emphasis; once a strong supporter of family planning, he now vetoes birth control legislation. By reversing his stand on the Equal Rights Amendment, he throws his support behind a traditional family structure and stronger hierarchial order. As the strength of social conservatism has grown within the Republican party, Bush has moved along with it.

His preferences concerning appropriate child care legislation also support a strong family structure. Rather than emphasizing direct provision, his program is one of tax exemptions. Parental choice is thus protected. Here, the goals of hierarchy mesh with those of individualism—parental authority and freedom from government dictates are both served equally well.

The Hand of Fate

The sense of the value of order and the consequent fear of disorder that come from an inclusive hierarchical conception of the good society, leavened by a sense of the adventure of enterprise, would not, by themselves, cause the aversion to vision that George Bush shares with such preservationist conservatives as Edmund Burke. Bush need not have read them to share their sense of the fragility of institutions, the importance of manners in governing consent, and the desirability of limiting change so as not to rend the social fabric. Yet there is something more to Bush's "follow the events" leadership style.

Bush does not quite believe that society operates in random ways, so there is no way of intervening in it with good effect. Nor, evidently, does he believe that human nature is treacherous, so that no one outside the family can be trusted. These hallmarks of fatalism, whose adherents believe they can do nothing positive to affect their fate, obviously do not apply to a man who has done a great deal to elevate himself to the presidency. Nevertheless, Bush reveals a fatalistic streak, albeit in a much milder manner. He acts as if he sees the world. if not exactly random then at least highly uncertain, with large, perhaps dominant, unpredictable elements. If one believes that each new sets of events is different from any that preceded it, no general theory of public policy will serve. Nor would the holder of such views expect to push events in a predetermined direction. The best one might do is avoid going too fast, latching on to events in order to nudge them slightly in one direction or another. The path of vision is fraught with danger to a hierarch tinged with fatalism, because it unleashes passions that threaten disorder without the hope that any abstract vision can be realized or, lacking sufficient social complexity, that if realized, is likely to be found good.

The policy-political groupies (ourselves included) who are likely to write about presidents think so much in terms of leadership as proposing substantive programs, they are puzzled when they do not find what they expect—Carter's lack of politics, Reagan's lack of administration, Bush's lack of policy. Where Carter thought primarily of effective implementation, and Reagan of new directions (especially because he did not believe they were impossible), Bush sees people of all kinds, shapes, and varieties who must be persuaded to consent.

That sums up the differences and the difficulties we-the-observers have in understanding Bush-the-president. Given good people who are loyal and competent (in that order), as demonstrated by experience and only by experience, and who relate to one another in protective ways, good things can happen, if not always, then sometimes. For if the world is a precarious place, often out of joint, held together barely by the one enduring factor—personal relationships—expecting loses as well as gains is the beginning of wisdom. Pinning hopes on any one action is unwise. A good batting average, tasking advantage of situations in which the previously unknowable becomes manifest, is the best a good leader can do.

We will not, as Bush's staff so often reminds the media, lose sight of his high popularity ratings at the time of writing (Spring 1990), but we are mindful of contingencies. Should (or, rather, we think, when) Bush seeks to reduce the deficit and has then to give up his no-tax pledge, his popularity, especially among Republicans, may plummet. As things stand, Bush has not yet been tested under adversity.

These may be easy times. Bush's approval ratings have generally remained close to 70 percent. This is not unusual for the first year of a presidential administration.[21] What deserves more comment is his continued rate of support, particularly among Democrats, who show increasing approval over his term, making him the only recent president to demonstrate this ability.[22] At the beginning of his second year, Bush showed the highest Gallup Poll approval ratings recorded for a president at that point in the administration, with 80 percent of respondents indicating approval of his performance. This was the second highest ever recorded in this poll for any point in an administration. John F. Kennedy achieved the record at 83 percent following the Bay of Pigs invasion in April 1961,[23] an irony that Bush, with his awareness of how the world makes nonsense of human (perhaps especially, presidential) pretensions, is more mindful of than his critics.

The Presidential Network, or Government by the Friends (and the Friends of the Friends) of George Bush

Avoiding sharp edges and angularities, Bush seeks the smooth integration of disparate parts. People are resources to be molded into networks of advisers, each part contributing to the whole like a well-oiled machine. Bush's approach to those he selects to be around him is characterized by an emphasis on cooperation and a strong desire to maintain close relations.

Consistent with the logic of inclusive hierarchies, Bush wishes to bring those around him under the umbrella of his personal organization. Once there, ties remain and are rarely eroded by time or political distance.

Our portrait of Bush as a networker par excellence resonates well with the image of the eastern patrician milieux in which he was raised. Ties between families often span generations, friendships nurtured in exclusive schools and clubs mature into valuable contacts in adult life. One of Bush's earliest political successes—appointment to the influential Ways and Means Committee as a freshman representative from Texas—was seen as a favor to his father, a former senator. Bush's membership in Yale's secret Skull and Bones Society is perhaps the most widely recognized example of strong bonds forged early in his life, bonds that continue to provide a source of support.[24] His presidential campaigns included top fund-raisers who were high school friends.[25] Several influential members in Bush's administration trace their original connection through family ties. White House counsel C. Boyden Gray, for instance, is the son of a man close to Bush's father, and Treasury Secretary Nicholas F. Brady was a close friend of Jonathan Bush, the president's brother. Friends of Bush's children have also found their place in the Bush White House.[26]

Bush has expanded the practice of making and keeping personal contacts far beyond family and school. Rather than importing a discrete set of advisers from a specific region or period in his life, as did both of his immediate predecessors, Bush tapped associates from nearly every phase of his career. According to Shirley M. Green, a special assistant to the president, he assembled his advisers by "dropp[ing] back to a lot of his former lives," and he "never loses track" of people he's known.[27] He has drawn upon friendships from his early days in Texas (Secretary of State James A. Baker III, Commerce Secretary Robert A. Mosbacher, White House personnel director Chase Unter-meyer, Treasury Secretary Nicholas Brady, among others), associates in the Ford administration from his tenure as director of the CIA (National Security Adviser Brent Scowcroft, Defense Secretary Dick Cheney, U.S. Trade Representative Carla A. Hills), contacts through the Reagan administration (Agriculture Secretary Clayton K. Yeutter, press secretary Marlin Fitzwater), and connections he made working with the United Negro College Fund (Secretary of Health Louis Sulli-van). At least ten people in his sixteen-member cabinet have known him for at least ten years.[28] In his first nine months in office, he placed a higher proportion of friends and supporters (forty-eight out of eighty-seven of his selections had previous personal or political connections) in ambassadorial posts than either Reagan or Carter.

It is not only by rewarding loyal supporters that Bush builds his network. His style of operating revolves around making connections with individuals and pulling them into his coalitions. He has been known as a tireless and committed party operative since chairing the Harris County Republican Committee in the early 1960s. He is given some share of the credit for the current Republican majority among voters under thirty in Texas.[29] The experience served him well in 1973, when, as Republican National Chair, he had the unenviable duty to be in charge of damage control during Nixon's Watergate problems. He "responded to the crisis by traveling around the country almost nonstop to bolster sagging morale"[30] Eddie Mahe, Jr., who worked as RNC political director during Bush's stint as chair, claims that Bush "not just intuitively understands the party, he is the party" and he "thinks in party terms."[31] When he sought the presidency in 1980, his campaign was notable for its organization more than its wide support. In 1981, as vice-president, Bush spoke at thirty-five Republican fund-raisers, earning about $3 million for the national party candidates, and signed letters for state candidates that his staff claimed raised an additional $5 million.

Coalitions are Bush's preferred method of problem resolution. He emphasizes the involvement of all parties, including those who disagree, particularly when encountering difficult issues. His approach to educational reform calls for "all of the players—administrators, school boards, local business leaders, parents, teachers' unions—around the table working together."[32] His policies on the environment, drug use, and the transportation system, all problems defying easy resolution, also call for widespread involvement on all levels. Indeed, they were not "his" policies until they emerged out of this consensus-raising process. Much of this consultation can be attributed to his desire for the widest possible inclusion. But it also serves as a substitute for strong ideological commitment and a vision for how these problems might be solved.

These facts, we argue, are best viewed as emerging from a coherent set of values. The intertwined ethics of loyalty, trust, and personal graciousness surface again and again in Bush's life. Building coalitions and rewarding the faithful are not merely utilitarian matters of trading favors and stacking up political debts, but a reflection of deeply held adherence to spreading ideals of family and friendship into politics. His career consistently demonstrates a belief in politics as a very personal process. Asked to characterize where he has left his mark in life and politics, he replied, "Friendships with people."[33] He lays claim to having "probably more friends than anybody in public life."[34]

His reputation for personal politics spans his career. As the new ambassador to the United Nations in 1971, he was described as "excell[ing] at the game of meeting 300 strangers at one cocktail party" and "greet[ing] each as if he had just met a new brother-in-law."[35] His long-standing habit of writing personal notes has been widely reported. As president, he has made it a point to know all the senators and half the congressmen on a first-name basis, to appear on the Hill for a game of racquetball or a chat in the dining room, to invite members of Congress over for Friday night movies, and to offer personal tours of the White House to members of Congress and their families. Every member of the Congressional Black Caucus was invited to the White House in mid-March, and the dozen who came were treated to a complete White House tour.[36]

In the words of one commentator, "If personal friendships were crucial to a successful foreign policy, George Bush should soon be winning a Nobel Prize."[37] Bush engages in what Gerald Seib calls "a little Dialing for Diplomacy"—he writes and phones various political figures, adversaries as well as allies, seeking advice and cooperation.[38] The pace of his personal diplomacy efforts far exceeds those of his predecessors; Bush participated in 190 phone conversations and 135 meetings with world leaders during his first year in office.[39] Some examples indicate the range of his involvement. After the escalation of Colombian drug violence, Bush called Britain's Prime Minister Thatcher to discuss an international response. The two leaders decided that Britain would coordinate its aid package with American assistance.[40] Bush has had seven meetings with West German Foreign Minister Hans-Dietrich Genscher since the fall of the Berlin Wall, and four with Chancellor Helmut Kohl between November 1989 and April 1990.[41] When confronted with the Lebanese hostage crisis, President Bush called a dozen world leaders, including the Pope.[42] He called five Middle East heads of state, urging them to contact the Shiites and their Iranian sponsors and convince them to spare the life of the second American hostage. He telephoned Mr. Gorbachev concerning an orderly transfer of power in Nicaragua. During the phone conversation, Bush and Gorbachev also discussed German reunification and plans for a summit meeting of the two leaders in Washington in June.[43]

In addition to his constant use of the phone, the president habitually sends notes and cards to world leaders. He sent a handwritten note to Soviet President Mikhail Gorbachev to discuss the Malta Summit.[44] He also personally authorized diplomatic notes to Iranian President Ali Akbar Hashemi Rafsanjani to find a way to free American hostages in the Middle East.[45]

He has worked hard to establish personal relationships with world leaders. Egypt's Hosni Mubarak has become a key ally in Bush's Middle East strategy, their relationship apparently solidified over a Baltimore Orioles baseball game. Inviting Mitterand to the Bush's Maine retreat provided an opportunity to generate a closer relationship with the notoriously frosty French leader.[46] World leaders are frequently treated to such typical Bush entertainment as fishing trips and speedboating. These are casual settings, designed to increase personal understanding.

A preference for personal relationships, however, can sometimes be misleading. When the Iraqi leader, Saddam Hussein, misled Bush's confidants, President Mubarak of Egypt and King Hussein of Jordan, the president was also temporarily misled. Perhaps a severe warning early on would have deterred the invasion of Kuwait. By the same token, the president was able to orchestrate an impressive global response, including China, the Soviet Union, and Egypt against the Iraqi onslaught through established personal relationships.[47]

Bush's personal touch in foreign policy raises some questions concerning his balance between the exclusivity of intimacy and the inclusiveness of cooperation. His preference for direct communication with world leaders exemplifies a cooperative approach to decision making, yet at the same time excludes many in his own policy team from negotiations. He has been sharply criticized for his "abiding penchant for secrecy,"[48] staff members often complaining they were not informed of key decisions.

Bush decisions have frequently come as a surprise to staff members and even close advisors. His staff had so little advance warning on Brent Scowcroft's appointment as national security adviser, they were barely able to notify the nominee in time for him to make it to the announcement.[49] Bush's decision on a raise for federal employees sent staff members scurrying to rewrite a press release composed in anticipation of a slightly different decision.[50] Neither Secretary of Defense Cheney nor Director of the CIA. Webster knew of Bush's plan for the Malta summit until they were made public.[51] Selecting Dan Quayle for the vice-presidential spot was an early example of decisions made without consultation.

We have, on one hand, a portrait of a man emphasizing a consultive style of decision making. Advisors in both the cabinet and within the White House staff were chosen for their loyalty and their competence, and Bush appears to rely on these traits, allowing a freer reign to his cabinet than had his predecessor. Chief of staff John Sununu has not acted as a strong gatekeeper; access to the president is fairly open.[52] Bush also reaches beyond official channels to lower levels in the bureaucracy and to individuals outside the formal decision-making process. Yet sudden, independent decisions repeatedly surface, providing a confusing, if minor, counterpoint to the main theme of consultative decisions.

The explanation may lie in Bush's desire to assert leadership capabilities in the face of public criticisms of weakness. Kicking over the traces in Bush's way of reminding himself, and therefore others, that he has the final voice. The occasional independent decision reflects a commitment to secrecy as necessary for some types of decision, combined with a strong belief in role distinction. As president, his job is to make certain decisions, and he wants to remind people of who is in charge.

A reputation for secrecy contradicts our image of President Bush as open, warm, and inclusive. Yet it emerges from the same set of values and understandings about the world, albeit directed toward another sphere of life. Although a remarkably inclusive one, George Bush is at heart a hierarch. While he may wish to bring people into the system, he maintains strong feelings about their roles once in that system.

> My starting point has been a respect for American institutions—for Congress, for the dedicated civil servants in the executive branch, for State and local governments, for the concept of public service—and a firm belief in the constitutional powers of the Presidency. Each has its role; each can be enlisted in the work at hand. The emphasis is on cooperation, not confrontation as the surest route to progress . . . When I took office, I told the Congress that the American people hadn't sent us to Washington to bicker. They sent us to govern, to work together to solve the urgent problems that confront us."[53]

The view that authority ought to go with position is hierarchical.

Bush straightforwardly defended what he believed to be his prerogative to make foreign policy. "I have an obligation as president to conduct the foreign policy of this country the way I see fit."[54] The trouble is that the American political system of separation of powers contradicts that rule. The implicit assertion that only presidents, and not Congresses, have such powers is contrary to fact.

According to one former Reagan aide, "Bush thinks there are a lot of things people would like to have in the end—but you could never get them done if you had to debate them."[55] Bush used a similar defense when criticized for sending secret envoys to China. "I point back to the original relationship with China, and I don't believe you'd ever have one if there hadn't been some secret diplomacy."[56] Even reading the sentence over a few times, however, reveals no similarity between the situation Nixon and Kissinger found themselves in and Bush's position after the massacre at Tiananmen. When Bush acted, the United States had an ambassador in China.

Those who are in a position to make decisions and formulate foreign policy, Bush believes, must be trusted to do so. The office must be respected. Hence, those who serve them must maintain their confidences. Put another way, friendship implies partiality and mutual trust.

Splitting the Difference

Bush began his presidency with a call to conciliation, and his relations with Congress frequently reflect that commitment. After the divisive vote on protection for Chinese students, he commented, "I will pledge right here to work with the Congress. I love the way their debate ended with both Senator Mitchell and Dole saluting each other for the way in which the matter was discussed. And I think that's a good signal for the political fights that ... that may lie ahead."[57] According to one pundit, "Bush is a brick layer. He's split the difference on practically every issue he's confronted, except taxes and abortion."[58]

Bush's conciliatory style can be seen in his compromise over supplying aid to Nicaragua. The Reagan administration was unsuccessful in maintaining its commitment to the Nicaraguan Contras; in the end, Congress refused to authorize military aid. In an attempt to lessen the bitterness typical of Central American policy, Bush cut a deal with Congress. Nonmilitary aid was approved for the Contras through November, with further aid necessitating a letter of approval from four congressional committees. Despite the loss of prerogative this agreement entailed, the administration cooled down the controversy sufficiently to see the Sandinistas defeated in the elections.

In an effort to facilitate clean air legislation without imposing heavy costs on the economy, the administration once again compromised with the Senate on a complex package of auto pollution controls. The administration agreed to the committee's standards, which were considerably more stringent than those originally proposed by the administration. In return, the implementation of the program was slowed down.[59]

At this point, two features of the political context are so obvious there is some danger they will be neglected. The first is President Bush's partisan disadvantage; he faces overwhelming Democratic majorities in the House of Representatives and a small majority in the Senate. There is little chance, therefore, that a program acceptable to him, let alone to strong conservatives, could pass. His vetoes (as of

May 1990) have been sustained by only a few votes. They have to be chosen carefully lest he lose so often that the threat of veto loses its punch. The second feature is that while Bush is not a dyed-in-the-wool conservative, neither is he a flaming liberal. His conciliation, therefore, begins from moderate premises.

If we think of ideology as coherent and connected policy positions, Bush is not very ideological. But if ideology is about how people ought to live together, about the process of decision making, then he is ideological. Compromise and conciliation are made much easier in the absence of strong ideological policy commitments. At the same time, a preference for negotiation and broadly based coalitions make a rigid policy ideology difficult to sustain. Bush rejects ideological policy labels; he does not "think people are in quest of ideological conformity."[60] Yet he appears to have trouble connecting his disdain for policy ideology to his problem with "the vision thing." From his perspective, shifts are necessary to respond to changing circumstances. He thinks of himself as pragmatic rather than ideological. As a result, a Bush loyalist could say, "I don't know what George stands for. I think of George Bush and get certain impressions—loyalty, hard work. But tell me what he stands for."[61] We shall try.

Belief in inclusive hierarchy is a world view that could properly be called an ideology. It tells adherents about what constitutes better and worse kinds of social relationships. If it appears "pragmatic," that is because its ideology (recall that it is not only hierarchical but also inclusive) calls for bringing within its ambit as many groups as possible, which requires much accommodation, which in turn blurs policy differences.

Indeed, in order to perform the extraordinary feat of enlarging civic inclusiveness while maintaining civic peace, it is necessary to play down policy with which there is found to be disagreement, and to play up process in the hope that agreement on the rules of political life will substitute for agreement about its policies. This process of orientation takes time to produce results. But, as the response to the invasion of Kuwait shows, it does bring results. Part of the president's anger at Saddam Hussein, in our opinion, is due to the Iraqi president's double violation of international trust. Saddam not only invaded Kuwait, he also lied about it to leaders of other nations. That a presumably sophisticated president should be surprised at such a lie is unusual; that it would further international security if not lying to other leaders became the norm is probably true.

The Process Is the Purpose

Much of the answer, it seems, is that George Bush stands for the system, and to Bush, the political and economic system is expressed as process. Perhaps he stated this view most succinctly when he said, "I believe in the integrity of the process. I believe our institutions can still cope."[62] Joining the two, he might have added that coping is possible only when the guardians of the institutions that relate each part to the whole are respected.

The logic of hierarchy implies a set of approaches to the world, and particular expectations about its behavior. Individual differences are valuable when performing the role for which they are best suited, and dangerous when not contributing to the system. Hierarchy assumes the necessity of role differentiation. Individual needs must be subordinated to the needs of the group. Vesting authority in position ensures group cohesion.

It is through rules and processes that variations in individual abilities are channeled toward the maintenance of order—everyone and everything in its place. The system and the processes it requires for the individual parts to mesh with the social whole thus become crucial reference points for the hierarch.

The nature of a system lies in its rules, in its rights and obligations. This concentration on form as substance has been a source of confusion to observers seeking to isolate Bush's central political beliefs. By examining Bush's relationship to process, a more coherent explanation emerges.

Enhancing the process is President Bush's purpose. The need to reaffirm the basic rightness of the system that produced him, the emphasis on widely shared values, and the celebration of progress within a framework of stability can be said to provide the organizing rationale behind Bush's actions. Within this world view, proper execution of duty earns one the right to claim rewards from the system, while deviance upsets the balance. By the same token, those who have been advantaged have a disproportionate responsibility to put something back into the system. Here we see at work the hierarchical norm of the sacrifice of the parts for the whole.

Within a hierarchical world view, the health of the system always takes precedence over the needs of individual parts. Bush is aware of the advantages from which he has benefitted, together with the obligations this implies. References to public service as a sacred duty abound in his rhetoric. He is also aware that many people have not had the same opportunities. "I do feel an awkwardness in terms of having been able to take care of my kids when they were sick or raise them properly. . . . I feel a certain privilege."[63] Along with his position in society, Bush inherited the norm of noblesse oblige, a tradition that justifies inequality largely in terms of returning value to the system. Bush's ideals of duty and obligation are consistent with a belief in the primary importance of the system as a whole. "Those who go to fine private schools . . . have a disproportionate obligation to put something back into the system."[64]

For the individualist, pursuit of self-interest produces well-being through market competition. For the hierarch, self-restraint and denial are necessary to a viable system. His comments on the savings and loan crisis can be read as a more general statement that "nothing is without pain when you come to solve a problem of this magnitude."[65]

Bush has demonstrated this system-protecting attitude consistently through his willingness to obey orders and to accept positions for the good of the system. In the words of journalist R.W. Apple, Jr., "George Bush's entire public career has been built on self-effacement, on loyalty, on his willingness to button his lip, on his readiness to play second or, if need be, seventy-third banana."[66] Much of this perception stems from his behavior as vice-president. Role differentiation and sacrifice for the system are mutually reinforcing values that produce a vice-president with "strong feelings as to what the level of visibility and assertiveness of the Vice President should be."[67] It is also likely, we would add, that had Bush revealed more of his own views, they would not have jibed entirely with those of the far more individualist Ronald Reagan.

A more dramatic example can be found in Bush's decisions to accept positions widely regarded as politically damaging. In 1975 he resigned from his post as chief of the U.S. Liaison Office in China, a job he found greatly rewarding, to head an agency under intense congressional scrutiny and public approbation. The Central Intelligence Agency was then in the midst of a crisis of legitimacy, and Bush was called upon to restore its credibility. It is hard to view this move as motivated by political ambition. As Senator Byrd remarked during the confirmation hearings, "If a person did have political ambitions, this is about the worst place possible to use as a stepping stone."[68]

This was not the first time Bush had sacrificed a job he loved for one likely to prove troublesome. In 1973 he left his post as ambassador to the United Nations to become the chair of the Republican National Committee. His tenure as party head was almost entirely devoted to controlling the damage as the Watergate scandal broke. It was during this period that he made what he describes as the most difficult decision of his career[69]—he had to ask his president to resign. Loyalty to an individual could not be sustained when it threatened the system as a whole.

Bush's sensitivity to unequal advantage emerges in his calls for a "kinder and gentler" public policy. However, it does not function as an indictment of the system, but as a reaffirmation of the need for people in high positions to use their influence to help those worse off.

An incident early in Bush's political career provides an interesting example of equality before the law, treating each person in fair and predictable ways, as a hierarchical value. As a freshman Congress member from a solidly conservative district, Bush upset his constituents in 1968 by voting for an open housing bill. Returning to his district to face their anger, he justified his vote largely by reference to black and Hispanic veterans. It was the service these men had provided to their country that made it morally reprehensible to deny them equal housing. "I reminded them that even as we met black Americans were fighting in Vietnam to protect our freedom and way of life. How did they feel about a black American veteran of Vietnam returning home, only to be denied the freedom that we, as white Americans, enjoyed?"[70] Implicit in this statement is a belief in reciprocity, in reward for duties properly executed in the service of one's country. Bush did not call for open housing as a way to change a racist society. Quite the opposite. His defense of open housing appealed to the very system that denied it. Bush spoke in terms of patriotism, the ultimate defense of the system. He has little trouble acknowledging the need for adjustment in that system, provided that adjustment is seen in terms of promoting larger values and of protecting the system from fundamental attack.

Appeals to patriotism played a central role in Bush's presidential campaign. All candidates for national office pay homage to motherhood and apple-pie issues, but few have so successfully made them the heart of an election. The negative elements of this campaign never seemed to do serious damage to Bush's image as a fatherly figure wanting to include everyone in his family. Rather than seeing this image as the product of manipulation by political experts, it may be more understandable as one emerging from Bush's own deep commitment to the existing system. The vision of America he chose to paint was one of interlocking communities working together to solve problems.[71] His acceptance speech reflected this vision: "For we are a nation of communities, of thousands and tens of thousands of ethnic, religious, social, business, labor union, neighborhood, regional and other organizations, all of them varied, voluntary, and unique."[72] The image is one of organic solidarity, of an almost biological entity, with all its specialized parts functioning smoothly together for the greater good.

We also know from writer Peggy Noonan's scintillating account (she was brought in especially because Bush as a candidate lacked punch) that she had to work hard to get him to articulate his feelings.[73] The fact that no one with her verve has been called on since is evidence that as long as he feels his public persona is working, Bush will not articulate more than he has to.

Bush does have an enduring faith that the process will indeed produce the answer. "I am an idealist about this country, " he states; "I am a total believer that we in the United States can solve any problem we want to solve."[74] More recently he quoted Winston Churchill, saying "Give us the tools, and we will do the job."[75] Perhaps this emphasis on tools helps to explain why science and technology have been favored items in his budget.[76] If the system is fundamentally sound, and its politicians sacrifice part of their views in the national interest, there should be a value-free, logical way to reach this harmonious goal.

Bush's preference for agreed-upon rather than ideological solutions has been noted by political insiders. A Republican source stated that Bush "separates politics from government the way Jimmy Carter did."[77] A former Reagan administration official called Bush "a neutral political functionary" who would "come to a lot of Cabinet Council meetings, listen for a while, raise a few points and say 'why can't we overcome this problem?' . . . He had this sense that there was a disembodied solution out there that involved no political or ideological position."[78]

The observation, we think, is correct, but the inferences drawn from it are not. Bush is searching for a policy that will command

widespread agreement. That is his (though not everyone's) understanding of the politician's art. He understands perfectly well that no
technical formula can create consensus. He seeks, instead, a partisan
agreement so that the technicians can get on with their jobs.

Relations with Congress early in his administration reflect Bush's
faith in the process of government for problem resolution. Rather than
charging into the presidency with a policy agenda, Bush stressed cooperation and a division of duties. He has repeatedly expressed faith
in the congressional process. Responding to public rejection of the
Catastrophic Health Care plan, he said, "We are letting the congressional process hash this out."[79] When questioned about his decision to
keep negotiations with China secret, he responded, "You have the
checks and balances of the Congress. . . . I feel encouraged that the
process worked out this way."[80]

Throwing up a problem to the mercies of the process may be a way
of avoiding responsibility, or it may be an observation born of experience; either way, there is a belief that the pulling and hauling in
Congress may result in a more creative outcome than anyone could
otherwise envisage.

There have been times, however, when the process has not worked.
Failure to make use of the attempted coup in Panama in early October
1989, a less costly way of deposing the Panamanian dictator Manual
Noriega, earned Bush some of his strongest criticism. Much of this
criticism focused precisely on procedure. Bush responded that "in
terms of procedures . . . I don't see any serious disconnects at all. . . .
if we can fine-tune our crisis management systems, so much the better
. . . but the fact that I say that should not indicate that I think there
was something fatally wrong here.[81] The remarkable aspect of Bush's
remark is that he did not defend his decision, only the process out of
which it emerged. It is as if he ought not be expected to succeed, only
to put in place a proper procedure. But is not success the test of
procedure? In the academy, the question has been debated long and
inconclusively.

The internal discord that surfaced during this episode seemed to
bother Bush a great deal. Reacting to a spate of negative comments in
the media, attributed to his own staff, he apparently laid down the law
in no uncertain terms. Aides were instructed to adhere to the administration line. According to reports, he indicated that internal criticism
could be a "firing offense."[82]

Such an uncharacteristically strong response suggests Bush saw a fundamental issue at stake. The ordering of subordinate and superior was threatened by staff dissent. By airing dirty laundry in public, outsiders were invited to intervene in a process best left to those who know best. The system depends on adherence to discrete, defined, and distinct roles populated by people directly or indirectly responsible to the public. It requires building a solid staff of experts, a feat Bush believes he has accomplished in his presidency. In one exchange with reporters, he referred three sequential questions on three separate matters to three administration experts.[83] He believes a structure is only as solid as its foundation, and a president can only be as good as his staff: "My commitment to this Cabinet council structure reflects my conviction that effective decision making depends on the President receiving the best information available from his senior advisors."[84]

Bush's reliance on expert advice means not only listening to trusted advisers, but ensuring that those advisers are indeed experts. He has "never subscribed to the Washington theory that someone who has studied Russian ought to be immediately sent to France."[85] "Amateur" interference threatens the chain of command, thus any blurring of roles, or any attempts to infringe on another's authority, are inherently dangerous.

Desire for personal power, leaders of hierarchies supposedly believe, must be secondary to support for the process as a whole. That is why, upon defending Judge Souter's nomination to the Supreme Court, President Bush was careful to state his belief that

> Judge Souter is committed to interpreting, not making the law. . . . Our country serves as a model for the world at a time of special significance . . . and I believe that we have set a good example of selecting a fair arbiter of the law. . . . I'm not viewing this as some personal Bush imprint on the Court. I've pledged to get —to seek out excellence.[86]

Whether Bush succeeds or not, he is trying to turn Supreme Court nominations away from ideological warfare.

At several points in his career, Bush has deliberately sought to restrict the influence of his own position when he believed it extended beyond its appropriate place. Most obviously, he did not use his previous foreign policy experience to become a key adviser to Reagan on foreign policy issues. In the words of one observer, "He does not want to be portrayed . . . as a potential usurper of the functions of the secretary of state."[87] To venture into the secretary of state's territory would be to invite conflict and promote disharmony.

His comments on two of his earlier positions reflect similar concerns. He served as ambassador to the United Nations and as director of the Central Intelligence Agency. Both positions, he feels, should be below cabinet level. "The CIA director is the President's intelligence officer, he's not a policy maker. The CIA chief should be out getting the best possible intelligence for the President. He ought not to be sitting around in Cabinet meetings talking about interest rates or farm programs."[88] Note that this rationale contains exactly what his critics claim the president lacks on public policy; it is precise, succinct, and informative. It states exactly what ought to be done and why. Bush appears to have little difficulty making clear judgments on proper process.

Conflict with the secretary of state also provides the rationale for reducing the status of the UN ambassador. "[Cabinet level status] creates unnecessary tension with the Secretary of State. . . . Foreign policy is risky enough without having two conflicting voices in the Cabinet, talking to the world in two different ways."[89] "Risky enough" suggests a view of foreign policy as inherently dangerous, sending a signal (to Bush at least): handle with care.

Bush practices what he preaches. Combined with his ethic of loyalty and obligation, the picture of him in his previous positions emerges as "a man who knows his place. Except for a few occasions when events have thrust him into the limelight, he has been as unobtrusive as a dash of cologne in a meat-rendering plant."[90]

The attention such behavior received during his presidential campaign sparked Bush to emphasize his leadership capabilities. He reasoned that when placed within a role requiring leadership, he would exhibit those qualities, just as he had performed the role of subordinate when that was called for. A remaining question, however, is whether his tendency to defer will undermine his efforts at leadership. Put more precisely, the question is whether his sense of the world as chaotic, perhaps notinfluenceable, will enable him to lead.

His reaction to the rejection of John Tower as secretary of defense provides an illustration of Bush's emphasis on procedure (in this instance, his ability to pick good people). The incident has been cited as the point where originally congenial relations with Congress began to sour, largely because of Bush's insistence on using the issue as a referendum on his own credibility.[91] Bush obviously took the issue personally. His strongest objection seemed to revolve around the use of innuendo and unproven accusations, although he has been around long enough to know that it is par for the course. "I don't think it's fair to a man who has been in public life and has served his country with honor, " Bush objected, "to be tried by perception and rumor."[92]

Focus on change, on the how (rather than the what) was also apparent in Bush's reaction to the admission of China to the United Nations. This was the first major issue he dealt with as UN ambassador. The central concern for the United States was to keep a place for Taiwan, a project consistent with Bush's emphasis on rewarding loyal allies. Yet in his statement he also emphasized the need to adhere to precedent and process. "If we are going to start playing with the right of members to sit in this organization as if that right were a chip in some international poker game, we will have started the United Nations itself down a very perilous slope."[92]

The president's attitude toward revision of the tax code also focuses on maintaining the integrity of the system, even when that system is admittedly flawed. "In a world where you were starting over maybe we could design a better tax system, but I don't want to open up the entire tax system at this point."[94] The tax system can well serve us as an example of a complex policy whose every provision contains hidden traps for the unwary.

Emphasis is on change at the margin, never on fundamental change. Bush's approach is guided by the advice he offers: "Don't look for shortcuts and don't try to circumvent the process. Most important of all, follow the rules."[95]

What can such a wispy-wimpy phrase signify? If rules of good conduct are broken, no one is safe. The strong Bush reaction to the invasion of Kuwait is not only a matter of oil, but of establishing an international security regime. Were the Bush presidency known not so much for the end of the Cold War, which, so to speak, fell into its lap, but for the beginning of an international rule of law, old-fashioned virtue may come back into style.

A preference for certainty leads to hesitancy when faced with the unknown. Some of the most frequent criticisms about Bush concern his "wimp" image. He has been forced to defend himself against the charge on numerous occasions. "Democrats on Capitol Hill have been calling me 'timid.' I have other, better words, like 'cautious,' 'diplo-

matic,' 'prudent.' We have a good team, well seasoned. We're unified."[96] Let us translate. Loyalty, unity, and caution are the best guides
to policy.

Bad Bush

George Bush's understated style, his lack of big, new proposals, the
absence of calls to follow him on this or that crusade (except for hard
drugs) had led to a cacophony of criticism. So confused are the critics
that they vacillate between characterizing Bush as a wimp and wondering whether there must not be some method to this mindlessness.

A good collection of presidential characterization comes from columnist Clarence Page's article, "George Bush's Dynamic Inaction."
Not exactly terms of endearment, these descriptors include "political
paralysis," "governmental gridlock," a "paralyzed presidency," and
"White House passivity." President Bush himself is termed not as
Reagan was, a "Teflon President" but a "Revlon President—all cos-
metics."[97]

"Prudent" or "passive," R.W. Apple wonders. Could George Will
be correct in terming George Bush's an "unserious presidency," whose
symbol "should be a wetted finger held up to the breeze"? Representative David McCurdy commented that Bush "makes Jimmy Carter
look like a man of resolve." Is this behavior prudent or merely timid?[98]

A reporter known for her saltiness, Helen Thomas put it on the line
and got one of Bush's best quips:

> Question: President Carter says you've really been slow on the uptake on
> one of the most transforming political events of our times. You have failed
> to show the leadership. You've failed to put the U.S. ahead of the curve on
> these things that are happening. And you are going to the summit without
> any initiatives at all. I mean this is boasted about. Why don't you have
> some new ideas of what to talk. . . .
>
> Answer: Now Helen, that is not a kinder and gentler way to phrase your
> question. We have done plenty. And the fact that some critics are out there
> equating my progress with spending more money doesn't bother me in the
> least. Look at the dynamic changes that are taking place around the world
> . . . well, I'd like to hear some specific suggestions other than triple the
> spending on every initiative. We are working closely with our allies. We
> are trying to facilitate the change. . . . We've got a seasoned team that are
> . . . that's evaluating the change. I will have a wonderful opportunity to

discuss the change with Mr. Gorbachev. But I can't be all concerned when
... when people jump up and say the answer is to spend more money.[99]

Can George Bush, or any president, renounce the role of inspira-
tional leader by saying, "I'm just not an emotional kind of guy"?[100]
Nor do we think this is an accurate self-portrait. Bush may not be
passionate about policy but, as we have seen, he does have strong
convictions about process. This conviction is so strong that the president may actually believe he ought to follow it himself. Bush may not
wish to appeal directly to the citizenry because he views that as rejecting the process by (as the usual phrase goes) "appealing over the
heads of Congress." And he does talk a lot to the media, which he
views as the proper institutional conduit to the public.

Having provided an explication of President Bush's cultural context, it remains to examine his mode of operation in the light of its
substantive validity: How well does George work? How effective has
he been as a policy maker?

The reason we dwell on alleged failings is to offer a comparison
between a procedural and a policy presidency. And to do this we have
to get at potential flaws in a procedural presidency. Fundamental
principles are almost by definition unchanging. Rather than an elabo-
rate, and often contradictory, set of ideological beliefs, reliance on a
handful of procedures makes the world a familiar place. It is these
that can guarantee a level of stability in an uncertain world. As Bush
stated in reference to changes in Eastern Europe, "The enemy is unpredictability, the enemy is instability."[101]

The President as Administrator

Because we have a president who operates "as if policy itself were
a mistake," most likely, as Elliot Abrams put it, "to get in the way
of the flexibility needed to conduct foreign relations,"[102] it is especially important to look at how foreign policy is made. When we do,
we will see a pattern familiar at the State Department, Office of
Management and Budget, Housing and Urban Development, and elsewhere. The pattern is so consistent as to suggest that it reflects beliefs
about the political context in which decisions are made.

We have seen that the Bush administration by and large does not
attempt hands-on government. It is content, instead, to leave political

administration to the departments while attempting to reserve policy for itself. Thus a new presidential level of decision making has been created in full view of the public but with hardly a comment. The National Security Council remains as it was, through smaller, this time part of, rather than challenging, the secretaries of State and Defense. Its small size is a special advantage because it can fit more easily into the tiny size of the State Department's staff, from five to seven top professionals and the secretary. On any given issue, these seven, plus the NSC director, Brent Scowcroft, the NSC staff man, and the president (including the chief of staff, if interested) make whatever decisions are to be made.

The most distinctive feature of this group is that it is a government of friends and friends of friends of George Bush. It is far and away the most personal government the United States has had in modern times. It is loyal to the president and the president is loyal to it. By the same token, President Bush is going to find it difficult to divorce himself from his extended political family's actions. A second feature of this arrangement is that they are team players. All are competent; none are known for deviant thoughts. Therefore, if the unexpected occurs, new policies are hardly likely to arise.

And there's the rub. The kind of people George Bush has assembled, and the people his people have chosen to work for them, are the kind who respond well to their leader's policy initiatives. Secretary Baker, for instance, is a superb deal maker. But who will guide him in what deals to make? And who will provide indispensable guidance to the friends of Bush's friends, if his friends have his friendship but not his guidance? Bush has built an advisory and management apparatus that would respond wonderfully to the policy guidance he believes it would be unwise for him to provide.

It is strange that in this instance alone, the president appears to be departing from the hierarchical way by not using the existing administration process. The surface view may be mistaken, however, in that the president may believe he is actually reinvigorating the administrative process by more clearly separating it from the political level. Where most suggestions for reform either drive political appointees further down into the executive branch or, conversely, raise the civil service higher up the chain of command, the Bush administration does neither. Instead, it reduces the size of the plainly political apparatus while keeping it closer to the White House. This is only one of the many ways in which Bush administration is different from other governments.

A Policy of Personalities

There are advantages to being flexible. The fewer the policies, the fewer the commitments, the less the unwanted baggage to carry around as events render firmer views insupportable. The disadvantage is that hanging loose misses the opportunity to shape events. Of course, if one does not believe that events are shapeable, this is no loss. Yet keeping one's options open is a policy of sorts for the Bush administration, and open options means a policy of relying on a single person, namely, Gorbachev.

When there is policy congruence, as there was between the United States, Britain, Germany, and France when NATO was formed, the strong personal ties between Acheson, Bevan, and Schumann helped solidify the alliance. Without such congruence, however, personal relationships may be more of a snare, ignoring systemic differences, than a help.

The lowest point in modern American foreign policy, or so we think, was President Franklin D. Roosevelt's belief that he could change and cajole Uncle Joe Stalin into decent behavior. As Averill Harriman put it, "Roosevelt lacked understanding of the Bolshevik brand of communism and was certainly over-optimistic about what he could achieve personally."[103] Amidst dire warning from State Department Soviet specialists, and cable after cable from Ambassador Harriman in Moscow asking that FDR insist on reciprocity, he persisted in relying on personal blandishments.

Although George Bush lacks Franklin Roosevelt's magnetic personality and his expansive public persona, as well as his optimism, his style of work bears great similarity to FDR's. Distrustful of theorizing, of making up one's mind before being on the ground but loving political interplay, they both believe in flying by the seat of their pants. As late as 1944, for instance, Roosevelt had no policy toward Germany, whose defeat was by then assured. Pressed on the matter, he replied that policy toward Germany depends on "what we find when we get there, and we are not there yet."[104]

Making policy by reacting to events as they occur has the advantage that hindsight is better than foresight. This "just-in-time" foreign policy system also depends on certain criteria that must be met. First is the ability to make up one's mind quickly. If a seat-of-pants approach is combined with innate caution, touching many bases, and seeking diverse viewpoints, delay is the likely result. Muddling through, if that is what this is, may be satisfactory if the decision maker learns from small incremental moves. But if, like Bush, he is loathe to apply the experience of one place to another, there can be little learning.

There can be learning, however, in regard to Bush—of a different kind, *i.e.,* learning about people. Again, we have to ask what is being learned. Is it about competence or loyalty? "Franklin Roosevelt," Lazallier noted, "often adhered to the political maxim that an ounce of loyalty is worth more than a pound of brains."[105] We cannot say whether a policy or a process approach to foreign affairs is superior. Perhaps reading people is as good as, or even superior to, reading the entrails of events. But if personalities change or prove untrue or cannot make good their commitments, what then?

What Does Bush Learn from Experience?

Let us begin this critique of George Bush's performance as president by attacking the one claim he makes that has so far been unassailed, though, as the reader will see, it is not unassailable. We refer to his claim to gain from experience. On close inspection, it is not easy to see exactly what this experience consists of (aside from knowing who to call for advice) when observed in the coin of action.

One might think experience would advise some such adage as don't promise (at least not in public) what no reasonable person believes you can fulfill. Bush has been taken to task for not putting resources behind promises. But this may be due to conflicting promises vis-à-vis not raising taxes versus higher spending. We refer to promises like that of the "education summit" with the nation's governors in which Bush promised, among other things, that American students would lead the world in scientific performance by the end of this century. No way. That would require motivating large numbers of students to enter science in the first place, to say nothing of greatly improving their performance in mathematics as well as science. One does not have to go far out on a limb to acknowledge that this is not going to happen, and that we know now that it is not going to happen. Drug

Czar William Bennett was slapped down for saying this was nonsense, but he was right.

Emerging from his "drug summit" with the presidents of a number of nations in Latin America, President Bush let loose what can only be called his pique at accompanying reporters. Through proceeding the days and weeks that followed, the president had been accused of withholding information from the American people by sending advisers on secret missions to China. This time Bush was especially angry because he had tried to be open with reporters, so that when asked whether he expected an agreement among Western allies about the unification of Germany, he said he did not. Circumstances changed so quickly that an agreement was forthcoming the next day and, to his chagrin, Bush was accused of misleading the media. The press inferred that Bush had deliberately lied about a possible conference of world leaders, while knowing all the while that such an agreement would be discussed the next day. They believed he was withholding information, while Bush believed he was acting in good faith. He was so outraged at the insinuation that he repeatedly answered "No comment" to questions concerning Germany, China, and his trip to Colombia. He threatened to reduce the media's access (he gives incessant conferences as opposed to former President Reagan's infrequent ones) and refused to answer except in jest. When asked if Colombian President Virgilio Barco had called him the previous night, Bush told reporters that he was aware they knew the phone rang, but he would not comment on the caller's identity.[106] Observers of the national political scene must wonder where Bush has been. Has he not observed reporters trying to get at presidents since LBJ's time? How could he imagine it would be different for him than for all his predecessors? Consider the case of one Gerald Ford.

When Ford was asked what he should have done differently as president in view of his failure to win the next election, he replied that he should have shucked the tamales. Going on one of the obligatory ethnic tours into a Mexican-American neighborhood, he was served a dish that he had never seen before, a tamale. So with the best of intentions, he ate into it, covering and all. This led to a roar of laughter from people who knew that one is supposed to remove (shuck) the covering. Mexican-Americans might have concluded he was not intimately familiar with their customs. But the incident did not end there. It was the beginning of innumerable reports that President Ford was clumsy and uncoordinated and, therefore, might not somehow be the ideal symbol of the nation. In reality, Ford was a superb athlete who would have ranked very high in coordination among all presidents, and even among all people. Nevertheless, he was hounded on this issue, and it hurt him. Now, knowing that, why did President Bush act surprised when he got a bare taste of the same?

One reason the president may have taken offense is that he had indeed gone out of his way to accommodate the media, or so the innumerable conferences and special interviews would indicate. Yet most everyone down there is sophisticated enough to know that if the president is doing this, he thinks it is in his interest to do so, and that he is hard at work trying to manipulate them just as they are doing the same to him. To them it must sound false to be berated for doing what comes naturally.

The danger signal for President Bush is that he could fall into the same trap as Jimmy Carter and, indeed, John Adams and John Quincy Adams before him. They were presidents of a hierarchical disposition who had the misfortune to believe that the political system within which they worked was one in which authority inhered in position. Therefore, all they had to do was figure out the correct policy position and others would fall in line. This does not happen in a separation of powers system combined with a federal structure. The confrontations with the media are not personal but institutional. By their role as critics of established authority, and by their political ideology (far more liberal than conservative), the media are not any president's friends. Academics who vary between exceptionally and extremely thin-skinned are not the ones to cast stones at anyone in this regard. Here, however, the thin skin suggests an inattention to what has been happening over a long period of time. An alternative explanation is that Bush has a well-worked-out strategy for handling the media— subdue them with attention, submerge them in data, make the conscious of their responsibility as semiofficial conveyers of information from the president to the people. Perhaps his tendency to use existing processes is reinforced by his lack of capacity for self-dramatization. President Bush's reliance on reporters to get his message across is more likely due to his belief that his task is to reinvigorate by actually using the ordinary processes of government.

Bush's Policy Toward Lithuania

Much has been made, especially by George Bush, of the dilemma for American foreign policy posed by Lithuania's bid for independence from the Soviet Union. Obviously, Bush and Secretary of State Baker would have preferred to pass this one up. They had no wish to complicate their relationship with the Soviet president by bringing up a new issue that might weaken him at home while they wanted to fry the big fish—joint reduction of strategic missiles (i.e., those that hit us and them), reduction and removal of Soviet ground forces in Europe, and agreement to the unification of Germany, together with retaining its participation in NATO. A tall order, but one that Gorbachev had at one time or another indicated he would support. Together with his active help in toppling hard-line regimes in Eastern Europe, this appeared to make Gorbachev "our man in the U.S.S.R.," one in whose continuance in power we had a large stake. As the usual unidentified White House source put it, "The president knows he has to help Gorbachev—at the right time."[107] Hence, President Bush's penchant for personalistic diplomacy and the requirements of foreign policy appeared uniquely to mesh.

Having for fifty years steadfastly refused to recognize the Soviet conquest of Lithuania, the government of the United States watched its declaration of independence with dismay. Verbal statements of hope for a peaceful resolution could not hide the U.S. abandonment of Lithuania. Thus America had to watch while a tiny country was pushed around by a giant country. The question arose as to whether the United States could benefit by the subjugation of a small people. Facing opposition from Democrats (who might well have done the same thing had they been in power) and from embarrassed Republicans (who would have to explain why they "lost Russia" as Gorbachev was replaced by a far more intransigent successor), the Bush administration wavered between telling the Soviets that relationships would be damaged if harsh action were taken and asking the Lithuanians to be more accommodating. Meanwhile, back in Lithuania, menacing moves by Soviet troops and the oil blockade were taking their toll.

We have gone this far in providing a bare outline of Lithuanian events in order to show that the administration faced a difficult problem, and to suggest that there was an alternative to its policy, for the question—What else could Bush and Baker do?—suggests they followed a course dictated by events, thereby validating Bush's view that "vision" is of no help when the world changes so rapidly.

With a different sense of how the world works and Lithuania's place in it, it would have been possible to craft a different policy toward Lithuania. Suppose the United States government thought of the Union of Soviet Socialist Republics as fragile. On the one hand, the U.S.S.R. has loosened its control over the population; on the other, its command economy is fatally flawed (it is losing GNP) and, although the current leadership has been in power for five years, it has yet to move decisively toward the only known method of economic growth, a capitalist market economy. The Gorbachev administration is in trouble not because it has made economic reforms but because it has not. Consequently, it has acted to raise demands while simultaneously reducing its ability to meet them. The result is an instability dangerous not only to the Gorbachev administration but also to the United States. What are we to do to alleviate the situation?

One possibility is that nothing America can do will be relevant. Another is an accommodating stance in order to keep Gorbachev in power. Such an accommodation means not only allowing Lithuania to swing in the breeze but also not pressing any position that Gorbachev claims would destabilize him. Like the child who controls his parents by threatening to fall apart ("and then you'll be sorry!"), the United States is hostage to claims of instability.

A third possibility is that the United States set as its goal the creation and maintenance of viable, independent states between Western Europe and the Soviet system, believing that these are the best guarantors against future Soviet aggression. Such a view of American interests suggests a complimentary conception of Soviet stability. The less the system tries to hold on to unwilling populations, the more stable will be the core. In regard to Lithuania, moreover, it is no loss to fail to hold on to a territory to which the Soviets never had a legal right. The United States should be encouraging the Soviet Union to divest itself of its empire of unwilling subjects, not hoping they will carry on.

A fourth possibility is that a combination of time, the Gorbachev government's dependence on good relations with leading officials of the United States, and internal developments within the U.S.S.R. (especially support for Lithuania by other Soviet republics wishing greater autonomy from the U.S.S.R.) will lead to a temporary settlement.

Who can say that the Bush administration's wavering (or was it artful dodging?) has not produced good results—no blockade, no disunion yet, and all options open?

Whichever alternative is chosen, even relying on Gorbachev has a theory behind it. The question is always, what kind of theory? Is the "Gorbachev is the best thing we've got going over there"[108] theory robust enough, we wonder, to support the big financial bailout we expect Bush to propose?

Bush's Learning Curve

Near the beginning of his term, George Bush was confronted with what appeared to be a new variant of the hostage crisis. Rumors began circulating that, given the appropriate responses from Washington, the hostages held in Lebanon might soon be released. President Bush was out on a speaking tour. He could presumably have taken a hard-line stance in which the United States held Iran accountable until the Iranians found a way to deliver the hostages. But this would not have commanded widespread support. Or, based on what had been learned from the two previous crises, the president might have ignored these informal overtures in order to avoid the syndrome in which hopes are raised only to be dashed amidst contempt from the captors and their supporters. But Bush did neither. He rushed back, began seeking contacts, issued hopeful statements, only to see once more the mixture of ridicule and disappointment that had greeted his previous efforts. This leaves open the question of what Bush learned during the previous hostage crises.

Policy aficionados gain experience at a distance by imagining that they are part of the decision-making apparatus, asking themselves what they would do under this or that contingency, including the possibility that there is nothing useful to be done. In this and in other episodes, Bush does not appear to have asked or answered such questions. Whatever he learned, it was not about what to do. Had he had a strong idea of what to do, he would have behaved differently and not rushed back to determine what it was he ought to be doing.

The literature on President Bush as director of the CIA or of the Republican National Committee or as ambassador to the UN or to China or as vice-president is remarkably sparse on what he did. He brought in some new people or tried to improve procedures. When things went badly (e.g., right after President Nixon's resignation) he traveled widely to shore up morale; otherwise the trail is cold. In the Reagan administration Bush headed up the effort on deregulation, which did further that particular cause. Conversations with those who served with him are revealing. Bush appeared interested, always making those who worked with him feel they were being listened to attentively. But did he pay attention to what they told him or what he told them? Maybe yes, maybe no. Several participants reported that if the same or similar subject came up soon after, the vice-president would still be attentive and interested, but there did not appear to be any carryover in understanding (perhaps they meant agreement) from the first to the second or even the third time.

Here a comparison with Presidents Carter and Reagan may prove instructive. Jimmy Carter would have remembered everything, but because the details were new and he believed it important to master them, he would likely have asked specific questions, at least in writing, about the circumstances. Ronald Reagan led with his conservative values out front. His "priors" were few but powerful. He wanted deregulation, but he also wanted agreement within his administration. Upon being assured of that agreement, he would say yes without wanting to know the details. Bush had few priors on policy. He might, in a general way, have been in favor of deregulation, but he was also in favor of regulation where warranted, so that he lacked a context in which to put what he was hearing. All of it was a collection of facts that he could master, but facts did not tell him what he ought to favor the next time around. He also tended to believe that each case was different. Because he thought of government as a potential source of good not only in the defense and justice areas (in which Ronald Reagan believed it ought to stay), he was ready to hear arguments on that side, unencumbered by free-market principles.

Early in his term, President Bush stated repeatedly that he would not be stampeded into precipitous foreign policy decisions but would take his time to go at them in a systematic and orderly way. Responding to a question during a press conference concerning the contradiction between his campaign image as closely involved in foreign policy decisions and his need for a six-month policy review prior to action, he justified his actions by repeatedly referring to prudence and the rapidity of change.[109] From Ronald Reagan or Jimmy Carter, who had no formal foreign policy experience and did not pretend to know all there was to know, this might be expected. For George Bush, however, whose career had largely been occupied with foreign policy assignments, we regard this as extraordinary. Of all possible potential presidents, Bush should have been the one most ready to go. Of course, he might not agree with everything the Reagan administration had done, but one would think he would be aware of his disagreements even if he did not, out of loyalty or caution, verbalize them in public. How might this be explained?

If Bush believed that there were regularities in foreign policy that could be learned, presumably he had had an awfully long time to learn them. Only if he thought that each set of events was discrete would he have to learn again what, ostensibly, he already knew. Yet Bush does not appear convinced that knowledge is cumulative. In his confirmation hearings as director of the Central Intelligence Agency, he dodged a question concerning whether the United States has the right to interfere financially and militarily in a dispute in another country, by saying, "I think each case has to be looked at on its own merits."[110] His comments frequently indicate his strong belief in the limits of knowledge and prediction. Referring to the Cheney-Webster disagreements over arms reductions, he stated, "Nobody is smart enough. None of us sitting in this room predicted the changes that have taken place so far, so why would we now be insisting one or the other is correct when we don't know?"[111] Further, "I don't think any of us think we can see with clairvoyance what's going to happen the day after tomorrow."[112]

It is possible that Bush wanted to get his new team committed to whatever policy would emerge. Aside from the secretary of state, however, all his top appointees were experienced people who knew each other, and who knew defense and foreign policy. Nor is there any reason to believe that Bush had preconceived notions.

The foreign policy review came up empty, which was entirely predictable. Experienced people, one might think, would already know that there are good arguments on behalf of many different foreign policies. In order for a study group of subordinates to come up with something valuable, there has to be a sense of direction imparted by the president. Otherwise, the review is likely to regurgitate the standard arguments of the past, leading to no further resolution than had hitherto been achieved. What happened was that as an important NATO meeting approached, the president hurriedly worked out with his advisers some minor adjustments in the American posture that, for the moment, suited the Europeans. Where was the experience there?

Aside from the defense buildup of his first term, the major foreign policy initiative of the Reagan administration occurred at Reykjavik during his second term, when the president sought massive and speedy mutual reductions of nuclear weapons, especially those that could threaten the United States or the Soviet Union. Although it was difficult to argue against the treaty limiting intermediate nuclear forces in Europe, the Reagan initiative was met with a storm of opposition from the usual informed sources. They claimed that the president was ignorant because he did not understand the logic of extended deterrence that committed the United States to make a nuclear response against the main perceived threat, which was a Soviet ground thrust through the friendly forces of Eastern Europe. The commentaries in private were even more scathing, claiming that if a missile were put up the president's backside, he would not know which side was up. Did Bush have an opinion? It is hard to say, but indirectly he must have agreed with the professionals. The evidence is that Bush made a point of not being hurried into nuclear negotiations—dragging his feet, as the Soviets protested—suggesting that these reductions were the last rather than the first things to be done. Only the collapse of communism in Eastern Europe persuaded the president to begin the START negotiations, thus leaving the United States in the uncomfortable position of being part of a kiss-fest with the Soviet Union, yet facing virtually the same nuclear arsenal that existed during the heyday of the cold war, except that now it was incrementally larger.

Just to show that the outcome of the foreign policy study group was not a fluke, the same thing happened for the same reason when Bush convened an interagency study group on antipoverty measures. The group came up with a dozen or so major alternatives, similar, we presume, to those known by most specialists. Lacking presidential guidance, however, the Domestic Policy Council decided that all the recommendations were either too expensive or too controversial. The comment made by a staff member on what had emerged—"Keep playing with the same toys. But let's paint them a little shinier"[113]—does not reflect well on the administration's policy apparatus. It also shows that Bush has not succeeded any more than his predecessors in stopping staff from shooting off their mouths. The episode does show that Bush is different in that his three predecessors (Reagan, Carter, and Nixon) announced their welfare programs within a few months of taking office.

Experience, for George Bush, appears to consist of believing what everybody else believes until it is contradicted by events. Not a bad rule, though not a rule a DeGaulle or a Nixon or anyone who had ideas of his own on foreign policy would adopt. Since events change rapidly (especially since the beginning of the Bush administration) the president often finds himself climbing down a hill on which he started to climb up. The number of policy reversals is much greater than commonly recognized.

If our interpretation of President Bush's behavior has merit, it should explain his flip-flop on taxes. Although we expected Bush to go on his antitax pledge, we were surprised by the offhand manner in which he did so. This indicates how little we had learned about his style of leadership, which we were trying to teach by writing this essay. Bush wants to work through the system. We heard him on the radio saying that the budget process must be made to work. By going directly to the people, Bush may have felt he would be doing what previous presidents have been criticized for, namely, going over the heads of Congress. Here, however, he did not follow his usual practice of viewing the media as the proper institutional channel for reaching the people.

No doubt Bush preferred to wait until a bipartisan deal had been made so that he could endorse the outcome as a validation of the system. As a strategic move, however, announcing his turnaround before a deal was set put the president at a disadvantage. He lost all he had to lose. This put pressure on him to agree even if the agreement was undesirable. No doubt he was told the Democrats would not move until he made his announcement. But presidents do not have to believe everything they are told.

To understand, however, is not necessarily to agree. We think Bush did not sufficiently consider the fury of the opposition presidents often face. Perhaps the brutality of the attacks on him via his son, Neil Bush, for his involvement in the savings and loan debacle, will cause the president to think again. In any event, we expect President Bush to be subject to increasing attack not only for changing his position but for immorality. "Read my lips—I lied," as the *New York Post* had it, is only a foretaste.[114] Or "I told the truth [about tax increases], and I paid the price," Michael Dukakis declared. "Mr. Bush did not tell the truth, and now we must all pay the price."[115] The president has to hope that Governor Clinton of Arkansas was wrong when he commented, "Now he's saying 'unread my lips.'. . . This has contributed, along with the saving-and-loan crisis, to eroding confidence in government. The American people liked President Bush and trusted him, and now that he's changing his tune he's hurting all politicians."[116] The meaning of being part of an antileadership political system is that others are out to get whoever is in authority.

It is easy to lose track of the numerous times President Bush has changed his mind on public policy and/or the reasons for it. In explaining himself, Bush reveals his conception of a world always in flux. Sometimes he manages wry humor:

> Question: Mr. President, you said when you originally picked your Cabinet that you didn't want to pick anybody from the House or Senate because you didn't want to deplete the ranks of Republicans in Congress. Now you've picked Mr. Cheney. What happened to that rule?
>
> Answer: That is the exception that proves the rule.
>
> Question: You said that Senator Tower was the best qualified for this job. Where does Congressman Cheney stand in this priority assessment?
>
> Answer: I said that on December whatever it was. And now we're in March whatever it is, and as of today, Dick Cheney is the best and the proper choice.[117]

Planned Parenthood is another case in point, for George Bush has a family connection to that issue. In a foreword to a book on population control, he related how his father, Prescott Bush, had possibly lost his bid for reelection when columnist Drew Pearson revealed that the senator supported Planned Parenthood. As for the younger Bush, this is what he said way back then:

> As we amended and updated the Social Security Act in 1967 I was impressed by the sensible approach of Alan Guttmacher, the obstetrician who served as president of Planned Parenthood. It was ridiculous, he told the committee, to blame mothers on welfare for having too many children when the clinics and hospitals they used were absolutely prohibited from saying a word about birth control. So we took the lead in Congress in providing money and urging—in fact, even requiring—that in the United States family planning services be available for every woman, not just the private patient with her own gynecologist.[118]

As the headline put it in the first month of Bush's presidency, however, "Bush Backs Away from Birth-Control Program." The congressman who worked with Bush to pass the Family Planning Service Act, James Scheuer (D-N.Y.) commented that "it's bizarre that twenty years later he's acting the way he is."[119]

Often Bush changes without necessarily being aware he is doing so, perhaps, again, because he thinks general rules cannot cover specific circumstances. Here follows a typical colloquy, this time on Panama.

> Question: You . . . said only a month ago that you didn't think it would be prudent to launch a large-scale military operation. What changed your mind, and particularly why did you opt for the maximum use of force in this situation?
>
> Answer: I think what changed my mind was . . . the death of the marine, the brutalizing, really obscene torture of the navy lieutenant, and the threat of sexual abuse and the terror inflicted on that navy lieutenant's wife, the declaration of war by Noriega, the fact that our people down there felt that they didn't know where this was going and they weren't sure what all that meant and whether that meant we could guarantee the safety of Americans there.
>
> And so I made a decision to move and to move with enough force—this was the recommendation of the Pentagon—to be sure that we minimized the loss of life on both sides and that we took out the PDF, which we did, took it out promptly. And so I would like to think that what I said some time ago still stands.[120]

The president does exactly the opposite of what he previously said was wise, yet he does not see that. What were these momentous events? A killing and a beating and a threat, all vile but not exactly what one would call the stuff of war. And the larger context—How important was Panama compared to the collapse of communism in Eastern Europe or other momentous events that might arise? Did the president want to give the Soviet Union or some other country the excuse to intervene at will? Could Noriega not have the fallen of his own ineptitude or been brought down anytime the situation got much worse?—was left out. Perhaps the Panama invasion was an effort to restore an image of vigor after the fumbling response to the earlier failed coup attempt against Noriega.

If there is to be a policy of cultivating good relations with foreign officials, giving them the benefit of the doubt in difficult situations, it should also be acceptable to crack down when the rules of reciprocity have broken down. Bush may have come to believe that the former Panamanian strong man was one such lesson. And Bush may view Iraq's dictator, Saddam Hussein, as another. That, coupled with the industrialized world's dependence on Persian Gulf oil, may explain the Bush administration's massive deployment of armed forces to Saudi Arabia.

Bush's ability to mobilize international, including United Nations, support has done him credit. If however, (whatever the provocation), American forces attack, this support may well decline. But if American forces sweat it out for months in the desert, while the embargo against Iraq fails to have its intended effect and many more people are held hostage, public opinion in the United States may turn against the president. Will Bush's be the third administration to be discombobulated by hostages?

If we internalize George Bush's preference for proper procedure as the best means for maintaining moral order, we can generate a different hypothesis. Coming so soon after the decline of the cold war, the Iraqi conquest of Kuwait tests the possibility of an international security regime, one that would do better than the League of Nations. For the grand purpose of establishing an international rule of law, a little discomfort may be worthwhile.

Reprise

There is both praise and criticism of George Bush in the media. What has been missing so far is understanding. Nor is this surprising. Bush is different. In order to understand him, one must think of events in people, not policy, terms. Thus it may be, as often suggested, that Bush said so little to the American people about the collapse of communism because he was brought up not to brag. Perhaps, alternatively, the president, as an upholder of order, worried that it was easier to tear down than to build up. Perhaps he thought it wrong to appear to go over, rather than through, Congress. As Michael Duffy noted in *Time,* Bush "would prefer that his face not appear on the nightly news."[121]

Vacillation

The president's policy objectives in the Persian Gulf, his desire to set up a process to punish violations of appropriate norms of international behavior, is at odds with his desire to gain the largest possible coalition of nations. In order to get and keep this support, he has to satisfy these new allies that the United States is doing everything it can to avoid military action. And this inevitably leads to vacillation. Of the three main conditions he laid down for Iraq, therefore, the Bush administration temporarily went back on two (Iraq was told it could reinstate its old grievances about access to the sea and oil fields on its borders with Kuwait, and that a big push would be on to "solve" the Palestinian problem, undoubtedly by pressuring Israel to make concessions). Soon enough, however, the administration began to understand that a future security regime would not be worth much if this episode showed that crime did pay. So the president reiterated the earlier three demands including, of course, Iraqi withdrawal from Kuwait, and suggested new conditions, like reparations and war-crimes trials for the Iraqi leadership, to make it worthwhile for Iraq to make concessions now. There was consistency of a kind; when looking at security policy, one line is followed and, when looking at allies, another.

Suppose a group from Congress comes to the president in the morning and says that it can achieve his target of a $500 billion deficit reduction over five years without raising income taxes. He may doubt this but as a procedural president he will tell them to go and do it if they can. Supposing another group of legislators come in the afternoon and tell the president that if he gives a little on a higher income tax they can make a deficit reduction package work. He probably doesn't like that as well but because his desire for agreement on the package is stronger than his desire to keep taxes down, he will tell them to try and do it. Consistency to Bush means supporting an action that would make the domestic policy process work by reducing the deficit substantially and that would show other nations that the United States can get its own financial house in order. But "consistent" is hardly the word most Americans would apply to Bush's shifting policy positions.

We have a president in George Bush who knows what he wants—to make process of mutual accommodation work at every level, from the family to the family of nations—but not how to explain what he wants. He is "ill at ease in any bout with self-analysis."[122] Nor is he sure he ought to explain. Processes, he feels, belong to those who operate them. What is owed the public is good outcomes, though not every time. Hence the difficulty others have in understanding him and his difficulty (sometimes) in explaining to others his concerns. For they are as different as policy and process.

In regard to policy, Bush expects differences. In regard to process, however, he expects support. Previously, we have suggested that Bush responds combatively to public criticism. If he figures out how to use conflict creatively, that is fine; if this sensitivity suggests that he is less secure and comfortable in a leadership role than he appears, that is not so good. If he is suited only for easy times, when he can get everyone to like him by spreading consensus, the hard blows that undoubtedly lie in wait for him—those that are due to life and afflict any president, as well as those that come from the antileadership elements among political elites—might make him defensive. Is the hint of irritation that creeps into his press conferences understandable in view of the sometimes idiotic and often hostile questions he is asked, or is it something else again?

George Bush may find the international arena more accommodating than the domestic. At home, ideological differences between Democratic and Republican activists continue to widen, the Democrats becoming more egalitarian and the Republicans more individualistic and more hierarchical.[123] Congressional differences on the deficit, for instance, parallel these ideological splits. In the midst of growing dissensus among the politically active comes George Bush, a believer in integrative hierarchy, not quite what the social conservatives in his party had in mind. The usual fate of those who interecede in fierce family quarrels is to get beaten by the opposing forces. Bush believes he can form a middle American way based on agreement on process and procedure. To do that, however, he must do by demonstration what he cannot explain in theory. Now that America has a president who believes in its procedures, it does not know what to do with him, and he does not know how to tell his fellow citizens that by helping make the process work, they help themselves as well as him.

Notes

1. Michael Thompson, Richard Ellis, and Aaron Wildavsky, *Cultural Theory* (Boulder, Colo.: Westview Press, 1990).
2. Albert Karr and Michel McQueen, "Adjusting Course," *Wall Street Journal,* (November 17, 1989).

3. Bush, quoted in Phillip J. Hilts, "Bush, in First Address on AIDS, Backs a Bill to Protect Its Victims," *New York Times,* March 30, 1990.
4. *The Independent* (London), April 18, 1990.
5. Quoted in Maureen Dowd, "Aides Fret, but Bush Has to 'Be Me'," *New York Times,* August 8, 1988.
6. George Bush, *Looking Forward* (New York: Doubleday, 1987).
7. Bush, press conference, November 8, 1989.
8. Bush, inaugural address, February 9, 1989.
9. *Albuquerque Journal,* July 15, 1990.
10. Michel McQueen, "When Bush Fishes for Advice or Information, He Casts His Net into a Wide Sea of Contacts," *Wall Street Journal* December 8, 1989.
11. Bush, *Looking Forward.*
12. Bush, remarks at the Boy Scout National Jamboree in Bowling Green, Virginia, August 7, 1989.
13. Bush, press conference, August 15, 1989.
14. Maralee Schwartz, "Liberal ADA Gives President Failing Marks," *Washington Post,* January 18, 1990.
15. Bush, remarks at a luncheon hosted by the Forum Club, March 16, 1989.
16. Bush, remarks at a White House briefing for the State Legislators' Working Group, March 20, 1989.
17. Bush, address before a joint session of Congress, February 9, 1989.
18. Bush, remarks at a White House briefing for the American Legislature Exchange Council, April 28, 1989.
19. Bush, *Looking Forward.*
20. Bush, remarks at a breakfast meeting with religious leaders, May 4, 1989.
21. Rhodes Cook, "Approval of Bush Is High, but Ratings Are Slippery,' *Congressional Quarterly* (November 1989): 3097.
22. The American Enterprise Public Opinion Report, March/April 1990, 98–99.
23. Graham Hueber, "Bush Rates Second Highest in Poll's History," *San Francisco Chronicle,* January 1, 1990.
24. Bush, *Looking Forward.*
25. Cynthia Ward, "A Conversation, with George Bush About the Election," *Conservative Digest* (August 1988): 7.
26. Burt Solomon, "A Tangle of Old Relationships ... Binds Cabinet, White House Aides," *National Journal,* September 30, 1989, 2418–19.
27. Ibid.
28. Burt Solomon, "When the Bush Cabinet Convenes ... It's a Gathering of Presidential Pals," *National Journal,* July 1, 1989, 1704. Compare with Hugh Heclo's *A Government of Strangers* (Brookings Institution, 1977)

for evidence of the lack of personal relationships in earlier administrations.

29. Burt Solomon, "Bush's Zeal for Partisan Duties ..." *National Journal,* October 28, 1989, 2650.
30. John W. Mashek, "Bush's Theme: Time for an Insider in the White House," *U.S. News & World Report,* October 22, 1979.
31. Solomon, "Bush's Zeal," 2650.
32. Bush, remarks at a White House briefing for members of the American Business Conference, April 4, 1989.
33. Quoted in Carole Horner, "George Bush," *Philadelphia Inquirer,* February 28, 1988.
34. Quoted in Maureen Dowd, "Aides Fret, but Bush Has to 'Be Me'," *New York Times,* August 8, 1988.
35. Nadine Brozan, "George Bush, New Ambassador" to the U.N. Eases into His Post Genially," *New York Times,* March 4, 1971.
36. Fred Barnes, "Playing Ball," *New Republic,* April 9, 1990, 9.
37. David Gergen, "Bush's Very Own Ford Foundation," *Washington Post,* April 2, 1987.
38. Gerald F. Seib, "Personal Touch," *Wall Street Journal,* November 30, 1989.
39. David Hoffman and Don Oberdorfer, "Bush Makes Personal Contact Hallmark of His Diplomacy," *Washington Post,* April 13, 1990.
40. Seib, "Personal Touch."
41. Hoffman and Oberdorfer, "Bush Makes Personal Contact."
42. Burt Solomon, "Bush Talks and Listens and Meets During Lebanese Hostage Crisis," *National Journal,* August 12, 1989, 2052.
43. Robert Pear, "Bush Seeks Soviet Help in Nicaragua Transition," *New York Times,* March 1, 1990.
44. Seib, "Personal Touch."
45. Michael Duffy, "Mr. Consensus," *Time,* August 21, 1989, 16.
46. Seib, "Personal Touch."
47. Michael McQueen, "Bush Is Handling Crisis Through Personal Ties with Foreign Leaders and Advice of Close Aides," *Wall Street Journal,* August 8, 1990.
48. David Hoffman, "Zip My Lips: Bush's Secret Conduct of U.S. Policy" *Washington Post,* January 7, 1990.
49. Gerald F. Seib, "Capital Insider." *Wall Street Journal,* December 14, 1988.
50. Michael Duffy, "Mr. Consensus."
51. Maureen Dowd, "Basking in Power's Glow: Bush's Year as President," *New York Times,* December 31, 1989.

52. James P. Pfiffner, "Establishing the Bush Presidency," *Public Administration Review* (January/February 1990): 66.
53. Bush, remarks at the Associated Press business luncheon, April 28, 1989.
54. Quoted in Hoffman, "Zip My Lips."
55. Ibid.
56. Bush, press conference, January 25, 1990.
57. Ibid.
58. Fred Barnes, "Mr. Popularity," *New Republic,* January 8 and 15, 1990.
59. Michael Weisskopf, "Senate, White House Negotiators Compromise on Auto Pollution Controls," *Washington Post,* March 1, 1990.
60. Quoted in Elizabeth Drew, *Portrait of an Election* (New York: Simon & Schuster, 1981, 101.
61. Quoted in Francis X. Clines, "George Bush–Loyalty to the Cause," *New York Times,* October 7, 1984.
62. Drew, *Portrait of an Election,* 90.
63. Bush, press conference, January 27, 1989.
64. Quoted in James M. Perry, "To George Bush, Seeking Presidency Seems Almost a Duty," *Wall Street Journal,* July 6, 1979.
65. Bush, question and answer session with reporters, February 6, 1989.
66. R.W. Apple, Jr., "A Self-effacing Nominee," *New York Times,* August 18, 1988.
67. Bush, quoted in Dick Kirschten, "George Bush—Keeping His Profile Low So He Can Keep His Influence High," *National Journal,* June 20, 1981, 1096.
68. Confirmation hearing of George Bush to be director of Central Intelligence Agency, before the Committee on Armed Services, United States Senate, Ninety-fourth Congress, December 15 and 16, 1975.
69. Bush, *Looking Forward.*
70. Bush, *Looking Forward.*
71. Peggy Noonan, *What I Saw at the Revolution: A Political Life in the Reagan era* (New York: Random House, 1990).
72. Bush, speech at the Republican National Convention, August 18, 1988.
73. Noonan, *What I Saw.*
74. American Enterprise Institute, "A Conversation with George Bush about the Election, October 19, 1979.
75. Bush, address before a joint session of Congress, February 9, 1989. The occasion was the anniversary of Winston Churchill's radio address in 1941 in which he used the phrase.
76. William Booth, "Science and Technology Fare Well in Bush's Budget," *Washington Post,* February 2, 1990.
77. Jack W. Germond and Jules Witcover, "Why Do Conservatives Hate Bush?" *The Washingtonian,* April 1982.

78. Randall Rothenberg, "In Search of George Bush," *New York Times*, March 6, 1988.
79. Bush, press conference, October 14, 1989.
80. Bush, "Excerpts from the President's News Conference on China and Other Matters," *New York Times*, January 26, 1990.
81. Bush, press conference, October 13, 1989.
82. Anne Devroy, "Bush to Aides: Stop Second-Guessing" *Washington Post*, October 11, 1989.
83. Bush, remarks and a question-and-answer session at a luncheon with regional press, March 31, 1989. The questions referred to drug policy (William Bennett), the Savannah River Plant (Energy Secretary Watkins), and the Chicago mayor's race (Lee Atwater).
84. Bush, statement on the roles of the economic and domestic policy councils, February 8, 1989.
85. American Enterprise Institute, "A Conversation with George Bush."
86. "Comments by President On His Choice of Justice," *New York Times*, July 24, 1990, A8.
87. Kirschten, "George Bush—Keeping His Profile Low."
88. Quoted in Ward, "A Conversation with George Bush," 11.
89. Bush, *Looking Forward*, 250–51.
90. Germond and Witcover, "Why Do Conservatives Hate Bush?"
91. Pfiffner, "Establishing the Bush Presidency," 69.
92. Bush, remarks at a luncheon hosted by the Forum Club, March 16, 1989.
93. George Bush, "United Nations Votes to Seat People's Republic of China and Expel Representatives of Republic of China" *Department of State Bulletin*, November 15, 1971, 550.
94. Bush, interview with *Wall Street Journal*, February 2, 1990.
95. Bush, *Looking Forward*.
96. Quoted in R.W. Apple, Jr., "Possibility of a Reunited Germany Is No Cause for Alarm, Bush Says," *New York Times*, October 25, 1989.
97. Clarence Page, George Bush's Dynamic Inaction," *Chicago Tribune*, October 22, 1989.
98. R.W. Apple, Jr., "Prudent Meets Timid," *New York Times National*, October 15, 1989.
99. Bush, press conference, November 8, 1989.
100. Walter S. Mossberg and Robert S. Greenberger, "Policy Void. Upheaval in Europe Tests Bush's Capacity for Leadership of West," *Wall Street Journal*, November 14, 1989.
101. Bush, "Excerpts from the News Conference Held by Bush and Kohl," *New York Times*, February 26, 1990.
102. Elliot Abrams, "Bush's Unrealpolitik," *New York Times*, April 30, 1990.

103. G.R. Urban, ed., *Stalinism, Its Import on Russia and the World,* (Cambridge, Harvard University Press, 1986), 39.

104. Colin S.J. Campbell, "Presidential Leadership Under Reagan and Bush," in Gillian Peele, Chris Bailey, and Bruce Cain, eds., *Developments in American Politics* (London: Macmillan, 1990), 338.

105. James Herbert Lazalier, "Surrogate Diplomacy: Franklin D. Roosevelt's Personal Envoys 1941–1945" (Ph.D. diss. University of Oklahoma, Norman, Okla., 1973), 250. From Amos Perlmutter, "FDR's War Policy 1941–45," 103, manuscript.

106. David Hoffman, "Bush to News Media: Mums Going to Be the Word," *Washington Post,* February 16, 1990.

107. "Bush Paves Way for Billions in Aid to Soviet Union," *Albuquerque Journal,* July 14, 1990.

108. *New Republic,* April 23, 1990, attributed to Bush or NSC director, Brent Scowcroft.

109. Bush, press conference, March 7, 1989.

110. Confirmation hearing.

111. "The Bush Message," *Washington Post,* March 18, 1990.

112. Jack W. Germond and Jules Witcover, "Bush Seems Out of Touch with World Affairs," *National Journal,* February 17, 1990, 409.

113. Robert Pear, "Anti-Poverty Proposals Rejected," *San Francisco Chronicle,* July 6, 1990.

114. Quoted in George Will's column, *Oakland Tribune,* July 1, 1990.

115. *New York Times,* June 27, 1990.

116. *Wall Street Journal,* July 30, 1990.

117. Bush, press conference, March 10, 1989.

118. George Bush, Foreword to *World Population Crisis* (New York: Praeger, 1975).

119. Kenneth H. Bacon, "Bush Backs Away from Birth-Control Program ..." *Wall Street Journal,* February 2, 1990.

120. Bush, press conference, December 22, 1989.

121. Michael Duffy, *Time,* March 12, 1990, 67.

122. Ibid.

123. This literature is summarized in Nelson W. Polsby and Aaron Wildavsky, *Presidential Elections,* 7th ed. (New York: Charles Scribner's Sons, 1988), 127–42.

Index